BRITISH INTERPARTY CONFERENCES

A STUDY OF THE PROCEDURE OF CONCILIATION IN BRITISH POLITICS, 1867–1921

JOHN D. FAIR

CLARENDON PRESS · OXFORD

1980

© John D. Fair 1980

Published in the United States
by Oxford University Press, New York

ISBN 0-19-822601-2

British Library Cataloguing in Publication Data

Fair, John D
  British interparty conferences.
  1. Political parties—Great Britain—History
  2. Great Britain—Politics and government
  —1837–1901
  3. Great Britain—Politics and government
  —1901–1936
  320.9′41′081   JN1120   79-41045
  ISBN 0-19-822601-2

Printed in Great Britain by
Butler & Tanner Ltd, Frome and London

To
William Baskerville Hamilton

Acknowledgements

This study is based largely on manuscript collections and I am indebted to numerous individuals who have assisted me in gaining access to these records. I gratefully acknowledge the permission of Her Majesty the Queen to use documents under the Crown copyright in the Royal Archives and photographic copies of *Cabinet Minutes* in the Public Record Office of original letters also preserved in the Royal Archives. Sir Robin Mackworth-Young and Miss Jane Langton were of assistance in my use of these papers and the latter provided continued counsel as the study progressed. Much of my research was done in the British Library and to the trustees of that institution I am thankful for the use of its facilities. I am grateful also to Mr E. G. W. Bill of the Lambeth Palace Library for allowing me to examine the Tait and Davidson papers and for permitting me to make photographic copies of the latter. I appreciate the assistance of the archival staff at Hughenden Manor in giving me access to the Disraeli papers. To the librarians of the university libraries at Oxford, Cambridge, Birmingham, Edinburgh, and Liverpool I express my gratitude for their kind and efficient service. The manuscripts of J. L. Garvin were used with the permission and assistance of the curators of the Humanities Research Center, The University of Texas at Austin. I also acknowledge the assistance of the archivists at the Public Record Office, the House of Lords Record Office, the Plunkett Foundation for Cooperative Studies, the Wiltshire County Record Office, and the West Sussex County Record Office. The manuscripts deposited in the National Libraries of Scotland, Ireland, and the Public Record Office of Northern Ireland were very useful in this study and I am indebted to those who allowed me to see them. I am also grateful to Mr A. J. P. Taylor for his personal assistance in the use of several collections and for allowing me to participate in periodic seminars at the former Beaverbrook Library. For his many letters of introduction and his kind assistance in acquainting me with the research facilities of London I am indebted to Mr A. T. Milne, formerly of the Institute of Historical Research.

I gratefully acknowledge the permission of the following persons to use passages in this study for which they hold the copyright: Julian Amery, M.P., the Earl of Balfour, Sir Walter Barrie, Mrs Mary Bennett, the Earl of Birkenhead, the Hon. Mark Bonham Carter, Earl Cairns, the Earl of Carnarvon, Winston S. Churchill, M.P., the Duke of Devonshire, Sir John Dilke, H. C. Le Neve Foster, Sir William Gladstone, Lord Gorell, A. R. B. Haldane, C.B.E., the Earl of Iddesleigh, the Marquess of Lansdowne, Viscount Long of Wraxall, the Marquess of Lothian, the Earl of Midleton, Captain Peter S. Montgomery, D.L., the Earl of Morley, Mark Oliver, Viscount Rothermere, the Marquess of Salisbury, Viscount Scarsdale, Laurence P. Scott, the Earl of Selborne, Lord Southborough, and A. J. P. Taylor. I wish to thank the editors of *Albion*, the *English Historical Review*, the *Journal of British Studies*, the *Journal of Ecclesiastical History*, and the *Journal of Modern History* for permission to reprint the substance of articles which first appeared in these journals. For their assistance in preparing this manuscript for publication I am grateful to Professors Donald Bogie and Guinevera Nance of Auburn University at Montgomery, and to my wife Sarah I owe a special note of gratitude.

Montgomery, Alabama   John D. Fair

Contents

Abbreviations

Add. MS	Additional Manuscript, British Library
Cab. Mins.	Cabinet Minutes, Public Record Office
Confidential Report	Sir Horace Plunkett, *The Irish Convention, Confidential Report to His Majesty the King by the Chairman* (1918)
Parl. Debs.	*Parliamentary Debates*
Parl. Paps.	*Parliamentary Papers*
RA	Royal Archives, Windsor

Introduction

A realistic survey of the British Constitution to-day must
begin and end with parties and discuss them at length in
the middle.

SIR IVOR JENNINGS[1]

From the emergence of modern constitutionalism in the late
seventeenth century to the surge of democracy two hundred
years later Great Britain experienced a degree of stability which
was the envy and ideal of many European countries in the
throes of political and social upheaval. To some extent this feli-
citous condition may be attributed to the harmonious working
relationship established between the three great estates of the
realm—King, Lords, and Commons—based as they were on
the maintenance of a flexible hierarchy of élitist social
structures. But the permanent effectiveness of this system
depended more on the development of responsible government
within its structure. This dynamic element permitted further
constitutional alterations by its ability to accommodate new
ideas and changes in the governing class through existing institutions of Parliament. Nowhere is this distinction between the
'dignified' and 'efficient' parts of the British government so ably
articulated as in Walter Bagehot's classic study of *The English
Constitution*. Clearly the most important aspect in this operation
was the Cabinet, which he perceived as a 'hyphen' or 'buckle',
which attaches the executive and legislative parts of the government.[2] Yet during the half century after Bagehot wrote this system was challenged by the widespread admission of the democratic ideal and the concomitant themes of nationalism and
socialism. This fostered a further transfer of power whereby the
Cabinet itself was subjected to the influence and often control
of extra-parliamentary bodies. It appeared then that Britain
might no longer be able to incorporate societal changes so effectively through existing institutions or sustain the political
stability which had become such an essential part of British
heritage.

This threat was manifested by the rise of modern political parties in the late nineteenth century. It coincided with a generational change in the political life of the nation whereby a new breed of political figures emerged to supplant those which were prominent at mid-century. Furthermore the kaleidoscope of parties from that period was replaced by a two-party system structured roughly on ideological lines and endowed with energy and purpose by the mass electorate emergent from the second reform bill. These developments have not been unnoticed by scholars of that era. The most seminal work descriptive of the rise of parties in Britain was written around the turn of the century by Moisei Ostrogorskii, entitled *Democracy and the Organization of Political Parties*. This is essentially an analysis of the use of party machines to organize and control the new democratic electorate.[3] During this same period there appeared two other social scientific studies which reflected and supported many of Ostrogorskii's ideas. One was a statistical study by A. Lawrence Lowell, President of Harvard University, who monitored the rise of modern political parties in Britain by taking a sampling of party votes in the House of Commons for much of the nineteenth century.[4] The other was a more general sociological study by Robert Michels of the oligarchical tendencies implicit in modern democracies.[5] The combined effect of these pioneering studies was to provide conclusive evidence and explanation for the growth and polarization of mass political parties in Britain during the late nineteenth century. Later studies have served mainly as commentaries on this phenomenon, rightly interpreting relationships in terms of conflict rather than co-operation. The most brilliant of these efforts was George Dangerfield's *Strange Death of Liberal England* which has set the pace for historical investigation on the subject since its appearance in the mid-thirties.[6] Subsequent studies have tended to become increasingly esoteric by examining specific movements, events, or persons within the context of party— to such an extent that the degree of contoversy and conflict during this period has been established beyond any reasonable doubt. Similarly there has been a proliferation of studies on all facets of party history, organization, policy-making, and relations with the electorate. In a 1977 survey of the British Politics Group, an Anglo-American professional association, the significantly greater number of projects in progress dealt with some aspect of the party system. Traditional topics, such as the monarchy or the House of Lords, were totally absent from this listing.[7] The emphasis of current investigation is clearly on the dynamic processes rather than the ancient structures of the British constitution.

What most authors have failed to appreciate is that partisanship and conflict, though most logical and apparent, were not the only manifestations of the operation of the party system. The successful conduct of any two-party competition requires that each contestant recognize and respect the existence, rights, and privileges of the other party within that system. Otherwise a monistic form of government, more restrictive of personal freedoms and less tolerant of alternative points of view, might prevail. The British polity has traditionally adhered to a pluralistic approach, thereby leading to a greater receptiveness of the principles of tolerance and compromise, and cultivating a degree of enrichment and sagacity not often found in the governments of other western countries. Additionally the exchange of alternative viewpoints provided an indefinable quality of life and spontaneity in the conduct of public business. Occasionally this mutual recognition of a spirit of competition was threatened by the actual domination of one combatant over the other. In the early period of British history equilibrium was usually restored by the reassertion of strong central authority. In the modern era, however, the monarchy is no longer in a position with power to counteract extremism and factionalism for the sake of the national interest. This void was to a great extent filled by the emergence of the interparty conference which, with the countenance of the Sovereign, acted as a balancing mechanism to encourage the interchange of opinion and thereby ensure the operation of the dual-party concept. This critical nexus was established not so much by the dictates of reason, but as perceived to be necessary to restore stability to the ship of state. It was an undeliberate and in some cases a fortuitous response to immoderation, and violated the canons of logic and self-interest normally thought to be implicit in political behaviour.

The earliest precedent for employing the conference method to resolve parliamentary disputes occurred in 1373 during the

reign of Edward III.[8] As a survey of governmental procedure
Erskine May's *Law, Privileges, Proceedings, and Usage of Parliament*
recognizes the development of so-called conferences and free
conferences whereby messages were exchanged between representatives of the two houses over matters in current dispute.

When the time appointed for a conference has arrived, business is
suspended in both houses, the names of the managers are called over, and
they leave their places, and repair to the conference chamber. The Commons,
who come first to the conference, enter the room uncovered, and remain
standing the whole time within the bar, at the table. The Lords have their
hats on till they come just within the bar of the place of conference, when
they take them off and walk uncovered to their seats; they then seat themselves, and remain sitting and covered during the conference. The lord (usually the lord privy seal) who receives or delivers the paper of resolutions or
reasons stands up uncovered, while the paper is being transferred from one
manager to the other: But while reading it he sits covered. When the conference is over, the Lords rise from their seats, take off their hats, and walk
uncovered from the place of conference. The Lords who speak at a free conference, do so standing and uncovered.[9]

As mass political parties began to form after 1867 it became
apparent that such formalities were not only irrelevant to the
modern state of the constitution, but completely ill-equipped
to reckon with the serious ideological and emotional issues at
stake. The only possible response which might accommodate
the shift towards a democratic society was a direct appeal to
the party system—hence the interparty conference. What follows is, in the first instance, a study of the multifarious
expedients employed by British politicians to alleviate political
stress, and latterly, a determination of the extent to which interparty conferences constituted an attempt to systematize relations between the political parties and to assist in the operation
of the party system. It is within this latter context alone that
there is any justification in studying interparty conferences.

The focus of this investigation was determined to a great
extent by the seismic disturbances of the Irish question which
periodically raised the temper of British politics. Indeed the
threats posed by Irish nationalism to British feelings of security
and national well-being were omnipresent throughout this
period. In spite of the salutary result of the Irish land acts fears
persisted that any expropriation of land in favour of the Irish
peasantry would violate the sacred right of property in that

country and portend a social revolution in England. More to
the point were the apprehensions expressed by English Unionists over home rule. A. V. Dicey in *England's Case Against Home
Rule* described it as a 'half-way house to Separation' which
would constitute a substantial loss in population and capital,
and be interpreted throughout the world as a sign of declining
strength and spirit in Great Britain.[10] Above all, any application of home rule in Ireland would set a dangerous precedent
for other parts of the empire, such as Egypt and India, where
other, more incipient, forms of nationalism were emerging. The
Irish question therefore was as great a manifestation of English
as of Irish nationalism. This is also essentially the conclusion
of L. P. Curtis in his study of *Anglo-Saxons and Celts* where he
ascribes opposition to home rule and a negative response to Ireland in general to English ethnocentrism and consequent anti-
Irish prejudice.[11] Furthermore any scholarly understanding of
Irish home rule can only be achieved by appreciating its
emotional capacity for either satisfying or frustrating some of
the most powerful human drives. For this reason it proved to
be a subject which the rational mechanism of interparty consultation was unable to solve.

Finally conferences between political parties must be set
against the background of changes in the nature of the British
constitution. This involves what Samuel Beer recognizes as the
concept of legitimacy which lay behind the functions of modern
institutions of government.[12] In the latter half of the nineteenth
century the hereditary bases of the monarchy and the House
of Lords were brought into question by an increasingly democratic society. Even the traditional paramountcy of the House
of Commons was threatened as sovereign power gravitated to
an ever greater extent to the Government, which was controlled by one or more of the great parties of state. Successful
management of the newly expanded electorate required a rigid
adherence to the precept of majority rule to satisfy its needs.
Recognition of this principle led not so much to the demand
for a written constitution as to the utilization of the more
expedient method of legislative enactment. A. J. Balfour, at the
outset of the constitutional crisis of 1910, pointed out the
dangers attendant upon this procedure. In most countries, he
recognized, 'there is a broad distinction drawn between the pro-

cedure required to alter the framework of Government, and that required to pass ordinary legislation. In the United Kingdom alone is it possible to destroy immemorial institutions by a procedure identical with that adopted in the case of the simplest public measure.'[13] Ultimately the monarchy and the Lords retained their legitimacy by being rendered powerless, but other less distinctive features of Britain's constitutional order, especially Ireland, remained vulnerable to precipitate change by the party holding a majority in the House of Commons. Interparty conferences sought, though not always successfully, to involve the Opposition in the decision-making process and thereby create some semblance of national consensus for any projected changes in the constitution.

The earliest of these modern conciliatory gatherings occurred in 1869 when Gladstone's bill to disestablish the Irish church became stalled in the House of Lords. It being recognized that it was impossible to settle this sensitive issue by any kind of parliamentary process, a resort had to be made to the party leaders, who were at the source of the conflict. With the encouragement of Queen Victoria and the Archbishop of Canterbury, leaders from the Government and the Opposition were able to adjust a judicious compromise. Although this event was more of an incident than the establishment of any set process, it did serve as a prototype for the resolution of later conflicts between political parties. Significantly the issue at stake pertained to Ireland. On this occasion, however, there was never any question over the major principle of disestablishment; only the details of disendowment were involved. As a disagreement between the houses it could have been referred to a more formal conference, but for the fact that the acceptance of a more representative government in 1867 had placed the responsibility for power squarely in the hands of the party leaders. On the occasion of the passage of the Reform Bill of 1884 the controversy raged not over whether the bill should be passed or even amended, since the principle of a more democratic electorate had already been conceded, but on whether a redistribution bill should immediately accompany it. Again the leaders of the contending parties averted a collision between the houses of Parliament by consenting to negotiate their differences. Here the conflict was characterized more by a test of wills, and it raised for the first time the question of how far leaders might stray from their party's position in an effort to reach a consensus. Clearly an element of luck was involved in these two initial successes for the cause of conciliation, but they did furnish valuable procedural precedents which were not overlooked by practitioners of power in the succeeding century.

In the twenty years following the passage of the Third Reform Bill, during which British government was dominated by a succession of Conservative regimes, there was little attempt to disturb the existing order and consequently no major domestic crises. This period also witnessed the continued growth, consolidation, and polarization of political parties through the caucus, which sought to involve and manipulate the new mass electorate. Within Parliament these changes were reflected by an increased obedience of M.P.s to the party leadership through the exploitation of party whips, and a greater control by the Government over the business and time of the House of Commons. During those brief interludes when the Liberal Party was in power, Gladstone introduced the emotion-charged Irish home rule issue into British politics. Ideologically this served to widen the gulf between the parties by providing a contentious issue on which to focus their struggle. Structurally it further divided the two houses by making the Conservative Party more inclined to rely on the tremendous majority it had gained in the House of Lords as a result of the flight of the Whigs from the Liberal Party. Yet the long period of Conservative control at the end of the nineteenth century, by moderating progress towards effective democratic and social change, brought into ever more bold relief the demands of an expanded electorate for more immediate actions. This set the stage for a massive conflict whenever the Liberals reassumed power.

The overwhelming Liberal majority gained in the general election of 1906, and the over-confidence which accompanied it, inaugurated a period of extreme political stress—a situation for which the interparty conference was frequently suggested as a remedy. This prolonged controversy began with the House of Lords' destructive amending of the Government's education bill in 1906. The ensuing struggle, however, was waged less over the educational or religious provisions of the bill than the right of the hereditary upper house to resist a measure enacted by a popularly elected legislature. The failure of the party leaders to resolve the education issue through a conference, in spite of the encouragement of the King and the Archbishop of Canterbury, opened the way for a more embittered conflict between the Lords and Commons. With its continued disregard for the prerogatives of the lower chamber the House of Lords was finally called to judgement following its rejection of Lloyd George's 1909 budget. The relationship between the houses of Parliament was the subject of a prolonged interparty conference in the summer of 1910. These discussions broke down ostensibly over the inability of the conferees to separate constitutional subjects from other forms of legislation, but in the end the Conservatives were unwilling to relinquish their party's vested privileges in the House of Lords, especially with the noisome Irish issue looming on the horizon. Nor were the Liberals overly eager for a settlement. It was far more convenient for the Liberals, with Irish and Labour support, to limit unilaterally the veto power of the House of Lords than to carry out a wholesale reform of that chamber in league with the Opposition. But this expedient, secured by the passage of the Parliament Act of 1911, increased party strife by eliciting an irreconcilable opposition from the Unionist Party to the inevitable passage of home rule. The parliamentary and popular divisions instigated by Gladstone over Ireland in the previous century had by now deepened amongst the English and Irish peoples to the point where a civil war became a distinct possibility. In 1913 and 1914 the King played a major role in bringing the party leaders together in a negotiation setting, but the conference at Buckingham Palace in July 1914, the climax of these conciliation efforts, failed to reach an accord.

The outbreak of international war in 1914 postponed any possibility of an immediate solution to the Irish question. But Ireland's extremists capitalized on England's preoccupation with the continent by imparting to Irish nationalism a new and more virulent temper in the Easter rebellion of 1916. Confronted with the necessity of pacifying Ireland in the midst of the war, Asquith deputed Lloyd George to secure a home rule agreement between the northern and southern Irish leaders. Owing chiefly to Conservative intransigence in the Cabinet and in southern Ireland neither a conference nor a settlement ever materialized. But the reverberations of this failure contributed to a train of crises and criticisms over the conduct of the war which brought the Asquith Government to its knees by the end of the year. The accession of Lloyd George to the premiership was brought about in December 1916 by a conference held at Buckingham Palace for the purpose of determining a satisfactory method for choosing the country's next leader. Coincidentally this served to end the decade of Liberal ascendancy which began with the election of 1906 and elevated the Conservatives to a position of responsibility.

The ensuing period of war and reconstruction may be characterized as the Lloyd George era, dominated as it was by the leading pre-war radical in association with the country's leading Conservatives. This combination embarked upon a programme of national reorganization not formerly thought possible between two such disparate agents of power. One of the most pressing issues confronting them was the need to extend the franchise to soldiers and sailors on active duty. But any admission of additional male suffrage would arouse latent demands for women's suffrage and a host of other electoral proposals which had been conspicuous before the war. A *modus vivendi* was found in a conference, not in the usual sense of party leaders, but of a larger group of representatives from all the parties in Parliament under the chairmanship of the Speaker of the House of Commons. This body, by untangling the intricacies of electoral reform, furnished the basis for the Reform Bill of 1918, the twentieth-century counterpart to the great reform measures of the previous century. The unexpected success of the Speaker's conference provided inspiration for the utilization of similar means to solve some of Britain's other outstanding problems, including Ireland. The Irish convention was the most spectacular and disappointing of these endeavours. Summoned in 1917 and representing Irishmen of many points of view, the convention was an attempt in part by the British Government to wash its hands of the Irish enigma and enable the Irish to settle what were thought to be their own differences. This too failed because of continued Unionist opposition to any home rule settlement which included Ulster. Besides, the organizational problems of getting such a host of individuals to agree on such a controversial issue proved insuperable. Equally unsuccessful was the conference which met in 1917 and 1918 under the chairmanship of James Bryce to consider a reform of the second chamber. Although the conference report made some useful suggestions which were widely discussed, the coalition Government made no attempt to translate them into legislation. Somehow the new party relationships formed during the war removed the urgency of enacting a constitutional change which would formally bury the political power of the aristocracy.

The most ambitious of the medley of conferences in this era was the Speaker's conference on devolution. The purpose of this gathering was twofold: to placate Ireland by ensuring that it enjoyed a reasonable degree of autonomy through federalism, and to relieve the legislative burdens of the imperial Parliament by delegating a portion of its responsibilities to provincial legislatures. Owing to the Government's resumption of control over the Irish question and an irreconcilable split in the conference over devolution, it succeeded in neither design. More compelling was a settlement of the internecine conflict which had arisen in Ireland during the war. Unionist opposition had circumscribed all attempts towards an Irish settlement for over three decades. Now the Conservative-dominated Government of Lloyd George had the responsibility of coping with the militant forces of Irish nationalism. When a policy of military occupation proved ineffective the Unionists slowly came to a realization that a negotiated peace, including provisions for commonwealth status for southern Ireland and partition for Ulster, was the only answer. While holding his more extreme Conservatives in check Lloyd George, through the Anglo-Irish conference of 1921, manœuvred the Irish leaders into an acceptance of this position. This agreement constituted the deouement of interparty co-operation in this period, but it so strained those bonds that the parties were riven apart for the next decade.

The Anglo-Irish Treaty of 1921 marked the end of an era. By this time the expansion of the electorate was virtually complete, the House of Lords no longer held pretensions to real political power, and the Irish home rule tumour was at last surgically extracted from the British political body. In handling these matters the device most frequently adopted, for a variety of reasons, was some form of interparty negotiation. It was most successful in settling those issues where there was already some prior disposition for agreement and where the party leaders were able to compromise the ideals of their respective parties. It was least successful where expectations were too high or where negative predispositions were rigidly set. The most that can be said for interparty negotiation in those instances is that it was a means of conciliation which helped to avert violence by causing delay and an opportunity for the innocuous release of party tensions. Such a conditioned response to political and constitutional problems evolved and adapted to changing circumstances during the fifty-year period when the foundations for a democratic society were established in Great Britain. The late nineteenth century saw the appearance of the basic outlines for this approach, as party leaders, with the support of the monarch, discovered an advantageous means to settle their problems outside the bounds of Parliament. These precedents were later cited when the Liberals assumed control after 1906 and conferences were strategically invoked, again often at the instance of an influential outside figure, to lessen the strain of party politics. Eventually, as a sense of co-operation began to prevail with the formation of a coalition Government, the concept of interparty consultation became more representative and regularized to the point that it was applied almost indiscriminately to any problem which might endanger that joint undertaking. That interparty conferences constituted a threat to party government was often suspected, but in retrospect it would appear that they served to neutralize the self-interest often implicit in that system for the sake of promoting national unity.

It must be reiterated at the outset that the interparty conference has never been formally recognized and that its outward features are as imprecise as the constitutional system from which it emerged and as diverse as the many controversies to which it was applied. As an unpremeditated response to political exigencies it has confounded and eluded scholars who are likely to describe it as an unrelated series of singular incidents. Likewise the researcher is handicapped by a paucity of sources relating to these informal and often secretive gatherings.[14] In its broadest outlines, however, the conference might be considered an attempt to apply conciliation in any form towards the resolution of a great controversial issue or crisis. Therefore it might include not only small private meetings of distinguished party leaders, but talks between larger groups of representative politicians. It might even encompass those intimate conversations between the party leaders behind the Speaker's chair to determine the course of House business or the ongoing co-operation entailed by the existence of a coalition Government. These latter instances, however, are beyond the purview of this study, as they can be interpreted largely as states of being. Conciliation, on the other hand, implies some sense of action or becoming which is the very condition which makes the concept of conferences so indefinite and elusive. Nevertheless it did evince certain recognizable features of continuity and growth for several generations in the late nineteenth and early twentieth centuries when Britain was experiencing an unusual degree of political partisanship and stress. British interparty conferences served as an occasional antidote to factious behaviour and were an attempt to restore or preserve a sense of equilibrium in British politics between controversy and consensus, which is essential to the stability of any modern society.

Procedural Precedents

I

The Disestablishment of the Irish Church in 1869

From Gladstone's first government of 1868–74 there starts the regular rhythm of the Lords' activity in the modern period: a vigilant and destructive opposition to the programmes of all Liberal Governments, alternating with complete acquiescence and submission whenever the Conservative Party was in power.

A. L. ROWSE[1]

The Reform Bill of 1867 inaugurated a new era in the political history of Great Britain. By substantially enlarging the size of the electorate in the boroughs and thereby permitting the establishment of greater party organization along the lines of the caucus, this act brought to a close that period of the mid-nineteenth century when the parties were in a state of relative flux. This was manifested in Parliament by an accretion of party spirit around the personages of W. E. Gladstone, the Liberal leader, and Benjamin Disraeli, who headed the Conservative Party, and a growing disparity between the popularly elected House of Commons and the hereditarily based House of Lords. In 1868 and 1869 these bodies converged in a struggle over the disestablishment of the Irish church. By toppling Disraeli from the premiership and acquiring a clear mandate from the electorate for a change in the status of the Irish church Gladstone was able to make an irrefutable case for disestablishment. When Gladstone placed his bill before Parliament opposition developed in the first instance, as expected, from churchmen and Tories in the House of Lords who feared passage of disestablishment would admit a host of further changes in the constitution. Through the efforts of Archbishop Tait, however, and other moderates the upper house wisely passed the principle of the bill. But opposition to the measure was based not so much on upholding the principle of establishment in Ireland, which was indefensible, but on a disagreement with the substance, or the details by which the Irish church was to be disendowed. During the committee stage the House of Lords precipitated a crisis by so amending the bill as to maintain the financial security of the Irish church. For the purpose of arranging a compromise on the disendowment clauses of the bill a conference of party leaders was eventually arranged, which set a precedent for the treatment of such matters. To this end the mediation efforts of Queen Victoria and others had been directed. But any settlement of the crisis depended in the final analysis not so much on the mere existence of an interparty conference, but on the extent to which Conservative opposition had developed and the ease with which party divisions could be bridged.

The struggle began on 16 March 1868, when Gladstone declared to the House of Commons that the Church of Ireland must relinquish its attachment to the state. A week later he introduced three resolutions for the disestablishment and disendowment of the Irish church and for the sacrifice of the royal prerogative over church temporalities.[2] It may be assumed that Gladstone, as a high church Anglican, had no particular prejudice against the ecclesiastical establishment, and that he did not wish deliberately to provoke a quarrel between the Lords and Commons. Gladstone's action stemmed mainly from his conviction of the much-belated need to do what was morally right in Ireland. The existence of an established church in Ireland which contained less than one-eighth of the Irish population, was one of the most glaring examples of inequity in the country.[3] Always a man of great humanity, though not without an eye to political advantage, Gladstone also saw in 1868 the need to extract Ireland from the malicious grasp of Fenianism which had swept the country the previous year. He wrote to Granville in April 1868, ' "I must own that for years past I have been watching the sky with a strong sense of the obligation to act with the first streak of dawn." He now believed the full sun was up,' his biographer concluded, 'and he was right.'[4] Undoubtedly too the Liberals adopted the Irish church issue as a strategem to counteract the advantage won by the Conservatives in the recent manœuvres over the Second Reform Bill. Gladstone's action would clearly identify the Liberals with a large segment of the new electorate receptive to the idea of further constitutional reform.

The immediate reaction to Gladstone's resolutions from those who stood in defence of the establishment was one of alarm. Disraeli, who had inherited the premiership only a month earlier from the ailing Lord Derby, was labouring under the handicap of leading a Conservative Government in a House of Commons where the Liberals maintained a majority exceeding seventy. The existence of the Government therefore depended on a continued unity within Conservative ranks and disunity amongst Liberals which had so recently formed the basis for the passage of Disraeli's reform bill. For Disraeli, who must have realized that this state of affairs could not continue much longer, the Irish question provided a major test of his leadership. With the suspicion that Gladstone had raised the religious issue merely 'to give a colour to the character, and a form to the action, of the newly enfranchised constituencies', it was understandably difficult for him to see in Gladstone's action any motive beyond that of political gain.[5]

In royal circles the mood was no less apprehensive as to the outcome of the resolutions, but for a different reason. Lieutenant-General the Hon. Charles Grey, the Queen's private secretary, refused to believe that Gladstone would use the religious issue 'as a means of Party warfare'. But he did recognize the dangerous and divisive character of Gladstone's proposals and counselled moderation on the Government. 'The old Orange feeling is by no means dead in Ireland,' he assured the Queen, 'and the moment their ascendancy is threatened the Protestants of the North become worse Rebels—and more dangerous because of their superior intelligence and station in life—than the ignorant Catholic Peasantry in the South. ... It will be a miserable thing for Ireland, and for the empire, if Your Majesty's Gov. becomes again, as in the days of George III and the Regency, the Govt. of an intolerant Party.'[6] The Queen also recognized that Gladstone's declaration was likely to aggravate sectarian strife in Ireland and she admonished Disraeli to steer a careful course.[7] But all parties recognized that if the resolutions passed, no ultimate solution could be reached without an appeal to the hustings.

On 30 April Gladstone's first resolution passed by a majority of sixty-five and a week later the second and third were carried without a division. In addition Gladstone managed to secure the passage of a suspensory bill through the House of Commons which would prevent the Crown from creating fresh vested interests or from filling offices which might fall vacant before Parliament reached a decision on the fate of the Irish church. Under normal circumstances such a series of defeats would have been sufficient to precipitate the resignation of the Government or a dissolution. But an immediate appeal to the country was not possible until the new electoral registers initiated by the recent reform bill were ready. In the meantime the actions of the House of Lords served to draw attention to the Irish church as an election issue. When the supensory bill arrived in the upper house on 25 June it was subjected to a three-day debate, then rejected by a majority of ninety-five. Lord Grey, an independent Whig, explained the Lords' opposition to the bill 'not as being determined to resist a complete change of system with regard to the Church of Ireland, but on the ground of its being a crude, partial and mischievous proposal, calculated not to promote but to impede a fair settlement of the question'.[8] Later on 11 October after the summer recess the Lords rejected Gladstone's proposals to disestablish the Irish church by a similar margin. The House of Lords clearly represented the major stumbling-block, even in the face of a reconstituted House of Commons, to any legislation which would alter the Irish church. By mid-November the new electoral registers were completed and the Queen was able to dissolve Parliament. The ensuing elections returned a Liberal Government under Gladstone with a majority of 112 seats.

With electoral support Gladstone now entered on his disestablishment programme when Parliament reassembled at the beginning of the year. For this purpose he had prepared two papers—one on the general policy and effect of the measure and another describing the principal clauses of the bill.[9] The latter proposed to sever the tie between the Irish church and the state as of 1 January 1871. Irish bishops were to lose their seats in the House of Lords, ecclesiastical courts were to be abolished, and the constitutional connection between the English and Irish churches established by the Act of Union was to be dissolved. But the most important clauses in the bill dealt with the proposed disendowment. One of the foremost grievances of nineteenth-century Irish Catholics was the disproportionate wealth of the Irish church compared with that of the native church and people of Ireland. Under the provisions of the bill no clergyman would be hurt directly by its operation, but corporately the Irish church would lose nearly half of its sixteen million pounds of property. It would retain all of its church buildings, burial grounds, and schools, and it could sell the rent charges which it possessed in lieu of tithes back to the landowners. But it would have to buy all ecclesiastical residences it wished to keep, and, most important, it lost all other private endowments given before 1660. The residue left to the state after disendowment was to be used mainly to relieve suffering in Ireland, in particular for hospitals, asylums, and other institutions, but not for any religious purpose.[10]

The Queen, who was shown these articles, had initially been opposed to Gladstone's attempt to destroy the Irish church. Now that this seemed inevitable, her main determination was to oversee this dismemberment with as little disruption as possible. Her criticisms centred on the proposed removal of the royal patronage in the Irish church which she thought would result in confusion and dislocation. 'Why could not the Episcopal Church have been left in Ireland,' she queried, 'deprived also of whatever property cannot be shown to belong to it, without dispute in its character as a Protestant body, as part of the English Church?'[11] Gladstone assured the Queen that disestablishment would not preclude the exercise of the royal prerogative, only forbid its compulsory exercise. Any dislocation caused by the suspension, he believed, would be prevented by voluntary action on the part of the bishops, the clergy, and the laity to ensure the smooth running of the church. Additionally Gladstone told the Queen that the Irish church would retain the great bulk of lands which had been conferred upon it prior to the Reformation and it would continue to maintain strong ties with the church of England.[12] Satisfied that Gladstone was pursuing a responsible course, the Queen offered her services 'to help in smoothing matters over and to speak to any one, of the opposition'. Lord Granville, Gladstone's Foreign Secretary and leader in the House of Lords, suggested to the Queen that Dr William Magee, the Bishop of Peterborough, who had knowledge and connections with the Irish church, would be the logical person to contact.[13] This indicated a willingness by the Government to respect the opinions of the Conservative churchmen in the upper house by subjecting its proposal for permanent change in the established church to the scrutiny of one of the leading representatives of the Anglican point of view.

On 11 February the Bishop of Peterborough arrived at Osborne and was immediately shown the heads of the Government's proposed measure as well as the correspondence exchanged between the Queen and the Government. In his discussions with the Queen and General Grey the Bishop indicated that the Irish church would be willing to accept the principles of disestablishment and disendowment as inevitable. But under the terms which this settlement was proffered the church had no choice but to fight. It would surely insist on the retention of all post-Reformation endowments. Among other objectionable features the Bishop was violently opposed to the provisions of the suspensory clauses of the bill, which he interpreted as intended simply to deprive the church of thousands of pounds of income. He insisted that the assurances of Gladstone would not suffice because 'no clergyman could be appointed to the temporary charge of such a Living, without giving up any other Living he might hold, and thus losing life interest in the latter'. With the conditions of disestablishment and disendowment (provided the latter applied only to pre-Reformation endowments) the Bishop was in basic agreement, but the details of the measure were 'utterly objectionable'. The subject of negotiations also arose. The bishop thought that any compromise of the provisions of the measure might be carried out most successfully by the English bishops rather than by the Irish clergy. Grey concluded from his conversation with the bishop that it would be unfortunate if the Government were hastily to introduce its measure and thereby commit itself to details from which it could only with difficulty recede. To avert this possibility Grey thought negotiations might be entrusted to the Archbishop of Canterbury before the Government had committed itself to the introduction of its bill.[14]

The Queen was immediately taken by the suggestion of negotiations between the English bishops and the Government to ameliorate the clauses of the proposed bill. She told Gladstone that 'the country would feel that any negociation conducted under the direction of the Archbishop of Canterbury would be perfectly safe.' From the concessions the Bishop of Peterborough had expressed his readiness to make, the Queen was sanguine that the Government would be able to redeem entirely its pledges to the country.[15] Gladstone replied that he had been rebuffed in his attempts to accomplish this during the previous two months, but in the sixteen days remaining before the introduction of the bill he was willing to receive communications from the Archbishop and his brethren for a settlement. He absolutely refused, however, to allow any postponement of the bill's introduction for negotiations as this would be injurious to the confidence of his House of Commons majority.[16] The Queen nevertheless felt sufficiently assured of his conciliatory disposition to communicate with the Archbishop of Canterbury, Archibald Tait. She insisted that Gladstone seemed 'to be really moderate in his views, and anxious, so far as he can properly and consistently do so, to meet the objections of those who would maintain the Irish Church.' Gladstone allegedly had assured the Queen of his readiness, 'indeed his anxiety', to communicate his views freely with the Archbishop and she expressed her hope that the Archbishop would meet him in the same spirit. Acting under this command disguised as a plea the Archbishop arranged a meeting with the Prime Minister.[17]

Their subsequent interview passed satisfactorily enough, but under somewhat unrealistic conditions and without resolving the issue under contention. Tait was pleased to learn that the Government would not press for any abrupt break in the legal or historical connections between the English and Irish communions. He was relieved also to discover that the suspensory clauses of the bill would provide for the filling up of all offices which might become vacant, disallowing only the creation of fresh pecuniary life-interests. Their main point of dispute arose over Gladstone's refusal to retain for the church all of its post-Reformation grants and bequests, a point which remained outstanding to the final stages of the controversy.[18] Although the interests of the church were at stake, control over the safeguarding of those interests lay not so much with the Archbishop as with the secular leadership of the Conservative Party in Parliament. The discussion between Tait and Gladstone had been friendly throughout and served as a useful preliminary to further talks, but the focus of negotiations obviously had to be redirected so as to coincide with the realities of political power.

On 1 March Gladstone in a three-and-a-half-hour speech unfolded his proposition for disestablishment and disendowment to the House of Commons. The former was to take place on 1 January 1871, while the latter would proceed at the actual moment of the passing of the act. As for the extent of disendowment, Gladstone surprised his listeners by fixing 1660 instead of the Reformation as the dividing year prior to which the church would lose its private endowments.[19] In the intervening days before the bill's second reading the Archbishop and Disraeli hastily mapped out a strategy for ridding the bill of its most objectionable features. Disraeli was confident that dissension in the Liberal Party would cause a reassessment of the Government's attitude regarding the Irish church and perhaps force a repeat of the circumstances which defeated Lord Russell's Reform Bill. He had little faith in the ability of the Liberal Party to hold together in times of stress or crisis and with this clung to the hope that some portion of the establishment might be saved.[20] What Disraeli failed to reckon with was the fact that the recent elections had altered the temper of the House of Commons. Even after his party's defeat on the second reading by 118 Disraeli still underestimated the threat to the Irish church and the popular spirit behind it. On 24 March he complacently told the Archbishop that the Government's victory was 'expected' and that 'it was a mechanical majority. The new House has fulfilled its pledge, and the same force cannot be counted on by the Government on matters of comparative detail.' What was important now was the conduct of the House of Lords, which he thought should be 'brave, firm, unfaltering', but there should be little or no appearance of 'party purpose and organization'.[21] To these ends Disraeli parleyed with the leading members of his party. With Lord Cairns, Lord Stanley, Gathorne-Hardy, and others Disraeli prepared a series of amendments to mitigate and to delay the worst effects of disestablishment and disendowment in the upper house and in the remaining committee stage in the House of Commons.[22] To the dismay of the Conservative leadership each of its amendments moved in the committee stage was rejected by an immense majority.

The failure of Disraeli's strategy in the lower house had a sobering effect on opinion in the House of Lords, whose lone responsibility it would be to decide the fate or character of the Irish church bill. Conservative peers and bishops met on Saturday 8 May, at Lambeth Palace, to decide further what course the party should pursue in the upper house. A division of opinion was manifest. Lord Derby, who felt strongly that disendowment was a violation of the sacred right of property, refused to attend the meeting for fear that it might compromise his opinions.[23] Lords Harrowby and Redesdale, who were present, likewise felt no hesitation in recommending the rejection of the bill on its second reading. Others, however, believed a second reading was imperative to avoid a constitutional crisis and were inclined to wait for the committe stage of the bill to make necessary changes. This was the opinion of Lords Salisbury and Cairns, whose views carried considerable weight.[24] The Archbishop informed Disraeli that 'the general sentiment was, that it wd not be wise to divide on the second reading in the Lords, if a division could be avoided, and that the true feeling was to insist on very extensive amendments'.[25] But the outcome of the second reading depended largely on a meeting of Conservative peers to be held on 5 June at the Duke of Marlborough's house. The Queen, fearful of the consequences of this meeting, dispatched A. P. Stanley, Dean of Westminster, to contact the Archbishop of Canterbury. He found the Archbishop apprehensive too that the more extreme councils of the party, in spite of Cairns's and his own wishes, would prevail. If the second reading was rejected Tait feared the Irish question would mushroom into the 'graver and more absorbing question of the conflict between the Lords and Commons'.[26] Tait was receptive therefore to a proposal by the Queen that he should communicate with Gladstone in one last attempt to negotiate. He subsequently explained to Gladstone his conviction that the wisest course for the House of Lords would be to give the Irish church bill a second reading and then 'to endeavour materially to alter it in Committee'. This had the greatest possibility of securing for the church an optimum endowment. After the meeting of the Duke of Marlborough's he feared that this would scarcely be possible.[27] These suggestions, however, were not welcomed by Gladstone. He was certain that any material alterations in the form of amendments would be regarded as tantamount to rejection by the House of Commons. Gladstone thereafter made no pretence of trying to keep open the lines of communication with the Opposition.[28]

With this rebuff the Conservative peers meeting at the Duke of Marlborough's assumed an even more radical posture by deciding to oppose the second reading. Lord Derby, as expected, spoke strongly for rejection of the bill. But on this occasion he was supported unexpectedly by Lord Cairns, who as Conservative leader in the upper house, held the balance of power in his party.[29] Lord Salisbury, therefore, was left alone to lead those of moderate persuasion. C. J. Ellicott, Bishop of Gloucester and Bristol, reported to the Archbishop that Lord Stanhope, who supported Salisbury, 'did not make much impression—made a bad hit saying we ought not to *refuse* negociations'. The meeting expressed its opposition to the bill by agreeing to support Lord Harrowby, who would subsequently move a rejection of the second reading. Although extremism apparently won the day, the Bishop of Gloucester was able to report that 'the hue of the meeting was distinctly *blue* not orange. It was a party and Conservative rally.'[30] The Queen, who was alarmed by the impossibilist attitude of the Tories, implored Lord Derby that the House of Lords should not oppose the second reading, but wait till the committee stage to make its amendments.[31] In reply Lord Derby reiterated his reasons for opposition to the bill. But he believed that a majority in the upper house might still support the second reading in the hope that some substantial amendments would be made in the committee stage. This probability would be greatly increased, he admitted, if 'assurances were given by your Majesty's Ministers that such amendments would be favourably, or even fairly considered'. But Derby had little reason to anticipate such a conciliatory gesture. Every amendment which his party had proposed in the lower house to mitigate the severity of the bill had been 'summarily, and even contemptuously rejected by Mr. Gladstone, and the majority which blindly follows him'. Even the Government organs in the press, he said, 'have not hesitated to say that any amendment of importance would be tantamount to a rejection of the Bill, and to menace the House of Lords with the most serious consequences to which they venture to assume your Majesty's consent.' Derby abhorred this supercilious attitude expressed by the Liberals. Speaking for himself, as well as for Cairns, he expressed his regret that they could not recede from the position which they had taken publicly in spite of the Queen's wishes to the contrary.[32]

Failing to reconcile the Tories, the Queen turned her efforts on the Government, hoping to elicit an assurance from Gladstone that the House of Commons would respectfully consider any amendments made in the upper chamber. She sent to Gladstone a copy of a recent letter from Tait in which the Archbishop insisted that the outcome of the second reading was very much in the hands of the Government. 'If a conciliatory speech introduces the measure', wrote Tait, 'intimating a readiness on the part of the Ministry to consider any amendments made by the House of Lords ... a large body would stand aside, and the second reading might very probably be carried.'[33] The Queen, hoping also that Lord Granville would make such a declaration, dispatched Lord de Grey to urge Granville to 'do *all* he *can* to enable the moderate Conservatives to prevail'.[34] Granville ultimately acceded to these wishes by announcing on the first day of the second reading that

determined as we are earnestly to adhere to the principle and to the main provisions of the Bill—we are not only ready to gratefully welcome any alteration in the details which appeared to us likely to have a beneficial effect, but we should think it an absolute duty to carefully consider every alteration that may be proposed by your Lordships. More than that I cannot say, and more or less I ought not to say.[35]

This accomplished, the only incident which threatened the second reading occurred on 17 June when John Bright, President of the Board of Trade, addressed an open letter in *The Times* to his constituents. A defeat of the Government's Irish church bill by the Lords, he maintained, would stimulate discussion on some more serious matters which had lain dormant for many years. He advised the peers to align themselves with contemporary opinions and necessities. 'In harmony with the nation, they may go on for a long time; but, throwing themselves athwart its course, they may meet with accidents not

pleasant for them to think of.'[36] Quite unashamed of these in-
flammatory remarks, which were intended to evoke popular
pressure on the Lords, Bright defended them to Granville
merely as 'freedom of communication' with his constituents.[37]
Granville, however, when pressed by Cairns for an explanation
of his colleague's action, repudiated any intention by Bright
to convey threats to the upper house. What he meant to convey,
according to Granville, were reactions to views either stated
or implied in the speeches of the members of the House of Lords,
and that if he inadvertently caused distress he regretted having
done so. More importantly Granville denied that the government was involved in the issue of the letter.[38] On the following
evening the House divided and the bill was carried by a
majority of thirty-three.

This submission delayed, but did not solve the ultimate question of substantive changes in the Irish church bill. Grey feared
that the passage of the second reading, while it put the House
of Lords in better stead with the country, would 'only make
the fight on amendments to be proposed more fierce'.[39] In order
to make the Lords' amendments more palatable to the House
of Commons Gladstone and Granville devised a strategy of persuasion. Both recognized Cairns as the 'principal agent' of the
Conservative Lords. But the foremost advocate of conciliation
was Salisbury, who was presumably in close touch with
Cairns.[40] Granville therefore proposed to Salisbury that they
might negotiate with one another in order to avoid a road block
in the settlement of the Irish church question. Such a private
meeting of leaders might also help keep this grave issue from
becoming a matter of public controversy. Salisbury subsequently met with the two Liberals in the Prime Minister's room
after the adjournment of the House of Lords on 22 June. Their
exchange of views was very congenial, but there is no evidence
that Salisbury committed himself to any more than an
assurance that he would exert his influence to minimize the differences between the Lords and the Government. Furthermore
there were no signs as yet that either Cairns or Disraeli were
amenable to the idea of extensive compromise or negotiation.
With the belief that no further communications would be of
any advantage the leaders awaited the next steps which would
be taken by the House of Lords.[41]

For seven long nights in early July the Lords added amendments to the Irish church bill. Their demands went far beyond anything that the Government was willing to concede. These included a provision by the Archbishop of Canterbury to push back the date for the reckoning of post-Reformation endowments to 1560, thus allowing for the retention of the Ulster glebe lands granted by James I. An amendment by Cairns sought to push the operational date of the bill back to 1872. Another, moved by Peterborough, increased the annuities to be paid to the existing clergy by reducing the deductions to be made from them. But the most important provision was Lord Carnarvon's clause which sought to restore to the Anglican church some four million pounds which had been retracted by the bill in its original state. Granville was certain that the Commons would reject these amendments. He told Salisbury that he was sure neither the change in the operational date nor Carnarvon's clause would pass the Commons and enquired what might be done as a solution.[42] Salisbury indicated that both he and Carnarvon would work to reverse the operational date from 1872 to 1871, but they could not give up Carnarvon's clause. Salisbury expected '1,200,000£ from it, that money is the thing that he wants, that we [the Government] are in a fool's paradise about the Clergy commuting, or the laity subscribing', Granville reported to Gladstone. Salisbury also regretfully believed that there was little chance of passing an Irish church bill in the present session.[43]

This placed the monarchy in the potentially awkward position of mediator. Although Gladstone recognized that the crisis had not yet reached a climax, he foresaw the possibility of a situation paralleling that of 1832 in which it might be necessary to call on the Queen's 'great and just influence, and mediating power'. He therefore requested that the Queen delay her annual mid-summer sojourn to Osborne and venture no greater distance than Windsor between the 15th and the 19th or 20th of July.[44] In the meantime, the Very Revd Gerald Wellesley, Dean of Windsor, whom the Queen had consulted over the bill, advised her not to do anything until such time as the Government might propose it. 'Your Majesty will not be able to hasten matters to a conclusion in any other way.[45] Wellesley also warned Gladstone that in any future communication with the

Queen he should avoid referring to any time when he might have to request the Queen to do anything she does not wish to do. But he assured Gladstone that the Queen was willing to see anyone the Government might propose or listen to any proposal which might expedite a settlement when the critical time arrived. On 10 July the Queen dined with Granville and arranged for him to see the Dean, whom he found to be 'sensible, calm and moderate as possible'. Granville told Wellesley that 'the great thing to impress upon the Queen was not to commit herself, not to encourage the opposition, or threaten her Ministry'. Wellesley told Granville that he intended 'to advise her to adhere to generalities, to counsel moderation to both sides, to admit their respective difficulties, but to remind the Archbishop of the dangers of delay, and to appeal to you to make all possible concessions'. But the Dean admitted that the Queen cared more about her arrangements being disturbed than about the intricacies of the Irish church question.[46]

As the Lords approached the end of their amending period Conservative opinion seemed to harden and to insist upon its amendments. Disraeli thought the Lords should 'now observe the utmost reticence and give no inclinations of yielding further or entering on negotiations'.[47] On 12 July the amended bill was read a third time and sent back to the House of Commons. Among the principal changes proposed by the Lords were (1) concurrent endowment, authorizing the use of some portion of the surplus to provide residences for Roman Catholic priests and Presbyterian ministers, as well as for the clergy of the disestablished church; (2) better terms of commutation for beneficed clergy and assistant curates; (3) a lump sum of £500,000 to be given to the church in lieu of Gladstone's suggestion that the church retain all post-1660 private endowments; (4) Lord Cairns's amendment leaving the disposal of surplus funds to the future wisdom of Parliament; (5) and that the date of disestablishment should be postponed from 1 January to 1 May 1871. The effect of these alterations for the Government was to reduce disendowment to a mere shadow of that provided in the original bill. To Gladstone the prospect of 'a Church possessed of nearly all the ecclesiastical property of the country, yet wholly exempted from State control' seemed utterly ridiculous. 'This proceeding seems hardly consistent with good faith, as between the Legislature and the country', he told the Queen. 'It cannot be accepted by the House of Commons.'[48] Gladstone was most vociferous in his criticism of concurrent endowment which Conservatives and Liberals alike had denounced in the recent election. He insisted that the Lords could 'no more discern the minute particulars of our transactions than a man in a balloon can see all that is passing on the earth below. Had the House of Lords gone through the experience of such an election as the last it would be absolutely impossible for them, as honourable politicians, to have consented to the clause which they have put into this Bill.' Secondly he objected to the Lords' attempt to appropriate the surplus from the Irish church. The bill originally had made no provision for the application of this surplus, and Gladstone objected to the Lords' infringement on what he regarded to be the Government's prerogative.[49] By the end of its period of consideration of the Lords' amendments on 16 July the Commons had rejected all but several of their alterations.

But at this point both sides seemed more disposed to conciliate. Meeting in the forenoon of 17 July the Cabinet decided that differences between the houses regarding the disposal of revenue and other points should not stand in the way of a settlement. Gladstone explained to the Queen that 'the Government was prepared to make further pecuniary concessions if the Lords would not press their amendments'.[50] The amount of this concession, Gladstone later told the Dean, would be some £170,000 or £180,000 and if this was applied to encourage commutation it would be of much greater value to the church than the same amount given in any other way.[51] In the meantime leading Conservatives had met at the Duke of Cambridge's and decided on concessions. Cairns, Stanhope, Salisbury, Carnarvon, and Lord Grey decided that the Lords should not insist on concurrent endowment, but should insist on Cairns's amendment regarding disposal of the surplus. 'We agreed (Grey dissenting)', Cairns reported to Disraeli, 'to insist on all the main amendments except the date (1 May)—the Bp of Peterboro's—and the concurrent endowment. The commutation amendmt to be insisted on either in specie, or with modifications.'[52] During the next two days Disraeli prepared a memorandum from these proposals which Lord Bessborough placed in Lord Granville's hands. Disraeli represented these terms as those which he had with much difficulty induced Lord Cairns to approve. The decisive issue had now settled on the amount of pecuniary concessions to be allotted to the church. The Lords' amendments originally had assigned nearly £2,800,000 in money to the church, besides some £1,100,000 as its share of the concurrent endowment. The Commons conceded only £780,000 and rejected concurrent endowment. Disraeli's new demands lowered the Lords' request to £1,750,000 and conceded concurrent endowment. Even this was unacceptable to Granville and Gladstone because another quarter of a million was all the Commons could be expected to concede.[53] Thus three-quarters of a million pounds was the gulf which separated the two parties, an amount which would appear to be negotiable.

As a sort of committee on the Irish church question members of the Government met on the afternoon of 19 July. They agreed that Disraeli's overture had to be rejected, though without closing the door on further negotiations. Granville then transmitted the following message to the Conservative leaders:

The Govt have already (in their own judgement) now strained every point in favour of the Church as far as the merits are concerned. All that remains is to say to the majority of the H. of Commons *such and such a sum* is not worth the quarrel and the postponement. This sum must be moderate. The sum asked is according to estimate of the Govt between £900,000 and a million. No such sum nor any sum approaching it, could be asked of the majority.[54]

In the interval the Archbishop, at the insistence of the Dean, had seen Cairns, but his terms were higher than Disraeli's. The absolute maximum for the Government, Gladstone confidentially informed the Archbishop at a meeting in Downing Street, was £300,000.[55] On 20 July when the bill once again returned to the House of Lords all hope of a settlement nearly disappeared. After a party meeting at the Duke of Marlborough's house in the afternoon the Conservative lords proceeded to exclude from the preamble of the bill that clause inserted by the Commons which had precluded any measure of concurrent endowment. This amendment, not to mention those which were to follow, contained matter which the House of Commons would never accept. Granville thereupon moved the adjournment of the house in order to take counsel with his colleagues. Granville was left with little hope that a compromise was possible and that the only recourse for the Government would be another appeal to the country. Upon encountering Cairns in the house Granville asked, 'I presume you have nothing to say to me?' 'No,' was Cairns's reply.[56]

At eleven o'clock the following morning the Cabinet met to decide what course to take on the Lords' action. Gladstone's inclination was to allow the Lords to carry out their destruction, after which there would be an appeal to the country. Most of the Cabinet, however, favoured a moderate course which would allow the House of Commons to consider the Lords' amendments yet another time. A compromise was reached by the decision to proceed as far as the end of the amendments concerning the endowment.[57] Then at six o'clock Granville was surprised by a visit from Cairns, whose anxiety for a settlement had increased. Granville told Cairns that if he could prevent the Lords from insisting on certain principal amendments he did not think an agreement was impossible on the other clauses. But Cairns restricted their discussion by saying that the surplus was the only point on which he could negotiate. Under these conditions Granville broke off their conversation, saying 'with so capital a difficulty in the background, he must feel it was no use our showing our cards'.[58] In spite of this momentary setback the parties were actually proceeding quickly towards a settlement. What was needed now was another opportunity for a conference to channel the goodwill already expressed on both sides into an agreement over details.

The events of 22 July were crucial to a settlement of the crisis. Cairns had in the meantime learned, though not from Granville, of the Government's decision to continue with its bill in the lower house. This indicated to Cairns that the Cabinet was still receptive to a compromise and prompted him to contact Granville for yet another round of negotiations.[59] They subsequently met at the Colonial Office where Cairns proposed a clause which would give double compensation to incumbents and their curates, and one which would provide 5 per cent of the endowment in addition to the 7 per cent offered by the Government for the livings of the clergy. In line with Salisbury's amendment he also proposed a clause which would give to incumbents their houses, gardens, and glebes at ten years' purchase. Granville, however, disagreed with the double compensation idea and argued strongly how untenable the third proposal would be, particularly after the recent debates on concurrent endowment. Granville also questioned whether Cairns, the Archbishop, and himself could carry any terms they might agree upon. 'Yes, certainly,' replied Cairns.[60] Afterwards Granville saw Gladstone, who noted that although the Ulster glebes were gone, the new terms were 'not very greatly improved'.[61]

Granville then met Cairns a second time in the latter's room in the House of Lords. As a preliminary to their discussion on the other amendments Granville asked Cairns how he proposed to deal with the preamble. Cairns said he intended 'to leave it as amended by the Lords'. Granville then proposed words by which the preamble was to be reduced to a simple legislative declaration that the property of the Irish church should be applied in such a manner as Parliament should subsequently direct. Cairns was at first taken aback, but admitted that he had no objections to this procedure. Granville objected totally to Lord Salisbury's clause regarding glebe houses. Cairns was uncompromising at first, chiefly on Salisbury's account, but later gave way. They also agreed on the commutation clause, on the condition that the 7 and 5 per cent were lumped together. Complaining of the difficulty of his position and the risk he was running within his party, Cairns asked if he could consult Salisbury and the Archbishop before they proceeded any further. After consulting with their colleagues Granville and Cairns met a third time, at four o'clock at the Colonial Office, with the Irish Attorney-General also present. There seemed little likelihood that they could reach a compromise on the curates question, but by 4.30 Cairns again gave way by accepting five years rather than one. Granville thereupon shook Cairns's hand which he noted was 'trembling with nervousness'.[62] Granville was able to telegraph to the Queen that he had 'had three interviews with Lord Cairns—everything is settled'.[63]

In the evening Lord Cairns made a full statement concerning his deliberations with Granville and the crisis which had passed. 'Nothing could be more culpable', he explained, 'on the part of either side of the House than to encourage or promote controversy on the details of a measure of this kind, where the materials for the solution of the controversy were at hand. It was in that view and with those sentiments that any communication which has occurred in conference between the noble Earl and myself was conducted.'[64] Herein lies the main reason for the success of the first interparty conference. Before entering into negotiations the leaders had agreed in spirit to compromise on the disendowment clauses of the bill. Through the services of Grey and Wellesley, the Queen had exerted her influence in favour of a settlement, but she never mastered the details sufficiently to be of great material assistance. Likewise the Archbishop of Canterbury, in spite of his prejudice on the side of the established church, also encouraged the cause of peace. 'No Archbishop is . . . very handy in Political communications,' the Dean of Windsor noted, 'but it is very lucky that the Church had at this moment one as sensible and as little prejudiced as D. Tait.'[65] That the Archbishop and his followers did not assume an intransigent posture towards Gladstone's attempt to sever a wing from the ecclesiastical establishment undoubtedly eased the struggle. But the Archbishop, no more than the Queen, could be termed a decisive agent in the passage of the Irish church bill.

The most important factor which led to a settlement was the absence of any concerted opposition by the Conservative leadership in Parliament. Had Disraeli been able to rally his party and the country behind a 'no Popery' crusade or to use the electorate to his advantage, as Gladstone had done in the 1868 election, it is unlikely that the Irish church would have been dismantled so smoothly. Disraeli's dilatory leadership thrust the full responsibility for opposition on the House of Lords, which was not prepared to challenge the Government on an issue which had been decided so conclusively by the electorate. In a more positive sense a settlement also resulted from an innovation in parliamentary procedure. Instead of a prolonged party conflict between the houses of Parliament over the Irish church question, a novel means of conciliation was found to channel differences between the parties into an agreement. The three informal meetings between Granville and Cairns, and to a lesser extent the other communications between party leaders, constituted the embryonic stages of a practice which would allow heads of parties to compromise their principles and thereby expedite governmental business without arousing the opposition of their massive followings. The concept of interparty negotiations was emerging as a useful method for removing legislative disorders and for promoting a greater sense of harmony between political parties.

Although a major crisis had been averted and the Irish church bill secured passage in 1869, the fundamental question of the relationship between the Lords and the Commons remained unsettled. To offset the growing disparity between the houses caused by an overweight of Conservative peers, the Government in August recommended the creation of a large number of Liberal peers. In a statement accompanying this request Granville described the Government's position in the upper house to the Queen as 'almost intolerable. The majority were wise enough at the last moment to pass the Irish Church bill, supported as it was by the Commons and the Country, but it is absolute in all ordinary matters of Legislation, on which the credit and utility of a Govt. so much depend. It does not scruple to exercise that power, a course ultimately sure to create great dissatisfaction.'[66] But the Queen was not favourably disposed to follow the recent ecclesiastical changes with a restructuring of the composition of the House of Lords. Further discussions and correspondence with the Sovereign on this subject proved fruitless, with the result that the structural imbalance between the houses of Parliament combined with the continued growth of party spirit remained a major factor in the precipitation of future constitutional crises.

II

Reform and Redistribution in 1884

Steersman, be not precipitate in thine act
Of steering, for the river here, my friend,
Parts in two channels, moving to one end—
This goes straight forward to the cataract:
That streams about the bend.
But tho' the cataract seems the nearer way,
Whate'er the crowd on either bank may say,
Take thou 'the bend', 'twill save thee many a day'.

ALFRED LORD TENNYSON[1]

The controversy over the Irish church bill was an indication of the possible effect which the recent extension of the suffrage to a considerable portion of the unpropertied classes might have on British institutions. Indeed the Reform Bill of 1867 was not long in effect until political opportunists sought ways to manipulate this potential power to the advantage of their particular party or point of view in Parliament. One of the first persons to utilize this approach was Joseph Chamberlain, who organized the Birmingham caucus in support of Gladstone's effort in 1868 to disestablish the Irish church. Conservatives, too, quickly grasped the importance of party organization through their concept of 'popular Toryism' which swept Disraeli back to power in 1874. Then in the general election of 1880 Gladstone discovered the power of impassioned oratory on the masses in his Midlothian campaign. By the mid-1880s both parties understood the effect of extra-parliamentary organization on the balance of power at Westminster. However much Conservatives initially or inherently opposed the further extension of the franchise, they could no longer afford to do so once the door was opened—or only at the risk of relinquishing ministerial office to the radicals. Disraeli recognized this when he 'dished the Whigs' in 1867, as did Lord Randolph Churchill, and even Lord Salisbury who had earlier bolted his party on this issue. Successive reforms of the House of Commons, therefore, acted as a catalyst for the rise of Britain's modern party system and set the stage for a political struggle. In 1884, however, the parties quarrelled not so much over whether there should be a further expansion of the electorate, but over which party should benefit most from this democratic innovation.

In his unfinished autobiography Arthur James Balfour first raised the question of the cause for the constitutional crisis of 1884. Both parties, he contended, were prepared to accept measures of reform and redistribution and both realized the inexpediency of holding an election on the basis of the one without the other. 'Where, then, lay the difficulty?' he asked. 'Simply, it would seem, in finding a method of doing a very simple thing which majorities on both sides of both Houses were quite prepared to do or see done—indifferent fuel, one would think, wherewith to feed the flames of a great political conflagration.'[2] As Balfour discerned, it was not the details of reform or redistribution which were at stake. It was a spirit of mutual distrust and unwillingness of either party to yield the slightest possible electoral advantage which caused the Conservative House of Lords to decline to pass the Government's franchise bill and the Cabinet to refuse to consider redistribution during the 1884 session. The most authoritative of the plethora of scholarly studies which have appeared in connection with this political struggle is *The Politics of Reform, 1884* by Andrew Jones.[3] Attempts have also been made to assess the role of the Queen as a mediating and conciliatory influence throughout the crisis.[4] Finally attention has been focused on the details of redistribution as an independent factor in the passage of the franchise bill.[5] What all of these studies imply, but never actually lead to, is the calling of an interparty conference. The legislative occlusion in 1884 was eventually overcome by recalling and elaborating of the 1869 precedent for dealing with such matters. The very act of summoning a conference of party leaders on the details of redistribution was the means by which the procedural question, which had constitutional implications, was resolved. Only by an appreciation of these circumstances and a knowledge of the deliberations which eventually took place can the extent of conciliatory activity be fully understood.

The crisis opened on 7 July 1884, when Lord Cairns, on behalf of the Opposition, moved an amendment in the upper house to restrict the progress of the franchise bill until an adequate measure of redistribution was framed. Led by Lord Salisbury, Conservative Party leader, and his chief lieutenant, the Duke of Richmond and Gordon, the Tory peers on the following day succeeded in stopping the reform bill by a vote of 205 to 146.[6] It was feared that Gladstone would attempt to dissolve Parliament under the new franchise without a corresponding redistribution measure which might benefit the Conservatives. As Richmond pointed out, the Conservative Party had no desire to reject the franchise bill, but they considered it absolutely necessary to have 'some substantial guarantee that the Franchise Bill should not come into operation till a Redistribution Bill has been proposed'.[7] In the strictest confidence Lord Granville, the Foreign Secretary, attempted to satisfy these demands. He told Cairns and Richmond that if both houses by resolution would guarantee the passage of the franchise bill the Government would 'introduce and use every effort to pass in the ensuing Session a Bill for the Redistribution of Seats in the three Kingdoms'.[8] For his own part Cairns was willing to regard Granville's proposal as an adequate assurance of redistribution.[9] But this was not enough for those Conservatives who demanded action in the present session rather than promises of what might follow later.[10] Salisbury was fearful that in six months Gladstone might no longer be premier and new men could hardly be bound by the present Government. What was lacking in these exchanges was a spirit of good faith, which stifled all hope of an agreement until the final stages of the crisis.

During the next four months the Queen attempted to facilitate an accommodation between the parties. To a much greater extent than in 1869 she realized the necessity for her active mediation to prevent a collision between the houses of Parliament. Acting through Sir Henry Ponsonby, her private secretary, she commanded Lord Rowton, the late Lord Beaconsfield's private secretary, to converse with Lord Salisbury. The Conservative leader, however, saw no possibility of an agreement unless a redistribution of seats was enacted simultaneously with the franchise bill.[11] Ponsonby also talked to the Duke of Richmond and to leading members of the Government, but to no avail. Under these circumstances the only way that Gladstone could proceed with his Government's legislative programme was to ask the Queen to call an autumn session. Although she much preferred a recourse to a dissolution, she consented.[12] But should the Lords again act in a hostile manner against the Government's bill in the autumn session a constitutional struggle over the powers of the upper house would most likely follow.

This dangerous possibility kindled strong emotions on both sides. On 10 July Sir Stafford Northcote, Conservative leader in the lower house, told Salisbury that there was a great desire at the Carlton Club for a joint meeting of peers and commoners 'to cheer each other up, and to give a fillip to the speakers at Public Meetings' before the autumn session. Gladstone's action, he maintained, 'alters our position, and renders compromise impossible'.[13] Lord Salisbury, too, seemed ill-equipped with the gifts of pliancy and conciliation to come to terms with the Government. Leadership required a sixth sense of caution to safeguard party interests.[14] The Liberals were gradually coming to believe the House of Lords' opposition to the franchise bill was evidence of the hostility of the Conservative Party to reform. Illustrating the radical viewpoint, John Morley believed that the Tories were 'as little friendly to a lowered franchise in the counties as they had been in the case of towns before Mr. Disraeli educated them. But this was a secret dangerous to let out, for the enfranchised workers in the towns would never understand why workers in the village should not have a vote.'[15] Such statements worked mischief among the party rank and file and contributed to the waning of confidence between the party leaders. The *Manchester Guardian* predicted that the rejection of the franchise by the House of Lords would 'provoke the bitterest struggle between privilege and democracy that has been seen by this generation'.[16]

To counter these destructive propensities the Queen supported the conciliation efforts of moderates on both sides. On 12 July Lord Wemyss, a moderate Tory, announced his intention to introduce a motion the following week for the Lords to consider the fanchise bill immediately, on the understanding that a redistribution bill should be considered during the autumn session. He was actively supported by Lord Rosebery in the Liberal camp and Lord Randolph Churchill in his own ranks. The Queen also encouraged these efforts by offering her intervention as a means to reaching an accord. But on neither side were the attitudes towards Wemyss's proposal heartening. Northcote remarked to Cairns that 'the move is a disagreeable one, and may place us in a difficult position'.[17] Gladstone's reaction to the proposal, which was presented to him by Rosebery, was not hostile but was hardly encouraging for a compromise.[18] The only quarter which actively endorsed the scheme, aside from its authors, was the Queen working through her private secretary. Finally at a party meeting held on 15 July at the Carlton Club, Salisbury, after 'profoundly considering her Majesty's representations', advised his followers to reject Lord Wemyss's resolution.[19] This course was strongly supported by Northcote and a vast majority of the members, and the measure was formally defeated two days later in the upper house by 182 to 132.

Failing in this approach the Queen turned to the Duke of Argyll, Gladstone's former Lord Privy Seal, for assistance. 'I told you the other day', she wrote him on 17 July, 'that I had no one to help me, or to turn to, in my anxiety to prevent such an unnecessary *breach* between the two Houses.'[20] At the Queen's insistence Argyll spoke to the leaders of both parties. He found Gladstone not indisposed to concession 'if some device could be arrived at which would not demand from him certain things which he regards as inadmissible'. Lord Salisbury was not at home when Argyll called, so he talked with Lady Salisbury. She assured him that the Opposition 'did *not* wish to force a Dissolution, provided they had some security as to the kind of Redistribution that is to come. All depends on *that*—' he concluded, 'whether any means can be found of giving the Conservatives *some* confidence in a FAIR scheme of Redistribution.'[21] But in spite of his keen desire to bring about a settlement, Argyll was no longer a power in the Liberal Party and exerted even less influence on his Conservative colleagues in the upper house.

As the summer recess drew near the Queen's most intense efforts were devoted to combating the activities of Liberal Party militants. 'Sir C. Dilke has already begun to attack Peers,' she protested to Gladstone on 11 July. 'You told me in the winter that he and Mr Chamberlain must be told to be prudent in their language out of Parliament for the future. If you wish for future conciliation, threats and abuse of the House of Lords must not proceed from members of the Government.'[22] More than anything else, it was the speeches of Joseph Chamberlain, the President of the Board of Trade, which upset the Queen. Chamberlain believed that 'the House of Lords would yield only to fear and that unless the agitation was very powerfully supported they would undoubtedly carry out the intention which had already been expressed on their behalf and reject the Bill a second time'.[23] This sort of language provoked strong reprimands from the Queen to her ministers.[24] But in attempting to redress the constitutional imbalance between the two houses the Queen seemed insensitive to violent remarks by important Conservatives. She apparently regarded the possible reduction of the powers of the House of Lords and its consequent effect on the monarchy as a far greater danger to the country than the failure of her contemptible Liberal Government to carry out its measure of parliamentary reform. Gladstone, hard pressed to reconcile the demands of an angry Queen with the actions of his more irresponsible colleagues, finally on 13 August drafted a discreetly worded memorandum to Her Majesty. In this exposition Gladstone demonstrated his ability to understand the position of the Opposition and showed remarkable tact in dealing with the very delicate House of Lords issue. The Queen moreover was much impressed by what he had said, and acted at once to press the Liberal point of view on some of the leading figures of the other party.[25] On the advice of Granville and Ponsonby she decided to invite Richmond, as a country neighbour, to Balmoral in order to disclose Gladstone's thoughts to him.[26] 'That seems to be the only door open to her intervention,' wrote Edward Hamilton, Gladstone's aide.[27]

In the course of several audiences with the Queen at Balmoral the Duke of Richmond agreed to assist her in any way possible. He refused, however, to bind Salisbury, Northcote, or any other leader in his party. 'I never saw H.M. better,' he reported to Cairns, 'and she treated me much more as if I were her friend than her subject.'[28] Cairns was more resolute in his support of the Queen's efforts to win Salisbury to conciliation. The dispute, he maintained, if not settled by a compromise, might disturb England's balanced constitution through the defeat and humiliation of one of its component parts.[29] Richmond, though still not happy in his role of assistant mediator, concurred with Cairns's remarks and soon arranged an interview to discuss matters with Salisbury. 'I wish H.M. had not drawn me into the discussion,' he told Cairns, 'but when she appealed to me and said she had no one with whom she could now consult I felt bound to assist her as well as I could.'[30] But the Queen never had a programme of her own outlined for her assistants. Throughout the crisis her efforts were directed at bolstering the compromise proposals formulated by others.

Encouraging signs now seemed to be appearing from an important section of the Liberal Party. Apparently on his own volition Lord Cowper, a Gladstonian Whig, published a letter in *The Times* on 18 August calling on the Government to present a redistribution bill in the autumn.[31] Although Gladstone regarded the proposal as 'capable of doing mischief', Lord Hartington, the Secretary of War, thought the Lords might come into such an arrangement. He believed they only wished to see the Government's redistribution bill.[32] Throughout September the principal Whigs in Gladstone's Government—Hartington, Granville, and Selborne—encouraged the cause of conciliation within party ranks. Even Dilke, though neither a Whig nor a friend of the Lords, appeared to have accepted the proposition of an introduction of a redistribution bill. In July he had begun preparation of a redistribution scheme and with the nominal assistance of a Cabinet committee had completed by mid-September a measure suitable for presentation to Parliament.[33] By this time 'compromises and bridges', in the words of Salisbury's biographer, 'soon began to be popular themes for discussion on the ministerial side'.[34] An opportunity for a possible settlement with the Conservatives developed sooner than expected when on 1 October Lord Salisbury delivered a lengthy speech to local Conservative associations in St Andrews Hall in Glasgow. Though his remarks about the Liberal Party were not complimentary, he proposed, in essence, the same plan for settlement as Cowper had recommended in August.[35] Picking up this line on 4 October Hartington made a bold move in a speech to Lancashire Liberals at Rawtenstall. He rejected Salisbury's insistence on an actual introduction of a redistribution bill in the autumn, but he thought the Conservatives should be satisfied merely to see such a measure. Then relying 'upon the good faith of Ministers and upon the good sense of Parliament' they would pass the franchise bill with the confidence that redistribution would eventually follow.[36] This concession fell short of the security envisaged by the Conservatives.

As the attitude of the Whigs mellowed, their radical counterparts, feeling that things were being carried too far, moved to check the advance. 'How disgusting,' Morley wrote to Chamberlain, 'this readiness on the part of our men to talk about compromise. Thank God, Salisbury is infatuated enough not to listen.'[37] Even Gladstone, the fulcrum on which the delicate balance of Liberal factions was sustained, sided with the radicals at a Cabinet meeting several days after Hartington's speech. Chamberlain did not even attend the meeting but had sent his resignation with Dilke in the event that the Cabinet should accept a compromise in Hartington's sense. Gladstone later apologized to Chamberlain for Hartington's use of the word, compromise, and assured him that such a word had never passed his own lips.[38] This renewal of party passion coincided with an unfortunate riot at a Birmingham demonstration in mid-October. The Queen deplored such incidents. 'I do wish that there was some patriotism', she exclaimed, 'instead of "Party", "Party", in all this painful agitation. ... Party will ruin the country.'[39]

Meanwhile deliberations were taking place at Gordon Castle between Salisbury, Richmond, and Cairns. The major part of the discussion dealt with the course to be followed by the upper house when Parliament assembled in the autumn. They decided that Hartington's remarks, though conciliatory and encouraging, could not be accepted in their present form; only by passing both bills simultaneously were the Conservatives to be satisfied. Lord Salisbury believed that the majority of the Conservative peers earnestly wanted to settle the difficulty and 'if we had to deal with Lord H. alone I believe we shd. obtain it'.[40] Upon hearing this the Queen immediately besought Hartington to confer with Salisbury, whom she insisted was in no way opposed to some compromise being arranged.[41] Unfortunately Hartington felt that the Cabinet was not disposed to introduce a redistribution bill under any circumstances and that any fresh overtures for a compromise must come from the Opposition.[42] By this time too the violent demonstrations were beginning to have their effect and Salisbury had drawn even further back. He told the Queen that he wished he could see his way to a proposition that would satisfy the Government 'but the speeches of Mr. Chamberlain, Sir W. Harcourt, and Lord Hartington himself (since Rawtenstall) seem to place the controversy on a ground from which issue is difficult'.[43] By the opening of the autumn session, in spite of almost continuous mediation by the Queen, all approaches to a peaceful settlement seemed to be blocked.

The idea of an interparty conference as a solution was first formally proposed not by the Queen, but by a Conservative peer on 21 October in a speech at Hackney. Lord Carnarvon said he could not see why a scheme of redistribution could not be devised free of party bias by three or four men of 'fair and impartial temper' enjoying the confidence of the leaders of both parties.[44] Gladstone at once saw merit in this suggestion and began to press it on some of his Whig supporters whom he knew would encourage the idea.[45] The Conservatives were understandably reluctant to accept any such proposal because it would imply tacit acceptance of the franchise bill. But anxious not to appear unreceptive to any reasonable overture, Northcote insisted that the Government specify whether a conference on redistribution also meant considering it with the franchise. He wrote, 'I suppose it is meant that, if the two parties had agreed upon the general principles of a Redistribution bill, there would not be much difficulty in treating the two questions of Franchise and Distribution together and so obviating a recurrence of the deadlock which we encountered last Session. It is manifestly important before proceeding any further to ascertain whether this is what is meant.'[46] Although Carnarvon never clarified his proposal, it nevertheless had the effect of diverting some attention from the procedural issue as more influential figures began to endorse the idea of a conference. On 29 October Hartington met with Sir Michael Hicks Beach, formerly Disraeli's Colonial Secretary, at the War Office. In their discussion of the details of redistribution Hicks Beach outlined a scheme which was much more radical than anything Hartington had expected. But with respect to the operation of the bills Hicks Beach said that he did not think the Lords would pass the franchise bill without some suspensory provision or accept a redistribution scheme without some security of its becoming law.[47] In subsequent meetings Hartington tried unsuccessfully to draw his Conservative adversary into committing his party more deeply to a discussion of the redistribution issue.[48]

The Queen had by this time seized upon the idea of a conference and began to press it upon the leaders of both parties. At the suggestion of the Duke of Richmond, on 31 October she wrote letters to Gladstone, Salisbury, and Northcote urging them to hold an interparty conference. 'The object of such a meeting would be the exchange of views as to the assurances to be given of the character of the Redistribution Bill.'[49] Both parties reacted to the Queen's invitation as a command, signifying their willingness to confer with each other. Lord Salisbury expressed 'great pleasure to consult with anyone, with whom your Majesty wishes him to consult' providing everything said was regarded as 'strictly private and confidential'.[50] Gladstone's reply was also positive, but he hoped that the Hartington–Beach talks would be productive before resorting to a meeting of the chiefs.[51] When they were not, Gladstone told the Queen that he was ready for direct communication with the Opposition.[52] What neither the Queen nor anyone who favoured such a course fully understood was that, given the existing state of confidence between the parties, no settlement of the details of redistribution was possible until the more basic question of procedure was resolved.

This was apparent during the fruitless machinations which preceded a formal confrontation of the party leaders. On 13 November Walter Northcote, acting through Algernon West, Gladstone's ex-private secretary, secured a clandestine meeting between Gladstone and his father, Sir Stafford Northcote. To appease the Prime Minister's fear of a daylight encounter, the meeting was scheduled for 11 p.m. at West's house after his dinner guests had departed.[53] On this occasion Gladstone appeared to concede nearly everything the Conservatives demanded. He intimated that a redistribution scheme could be produced at once and 'he did not know why, if there was a prospect of agreement, the Seats bill should not be introduced even before the

2d. R. of the F. bill in the other house'. But Gladstone made it clear that his major concern was the passage of the franchise bill without delay. There was some talk on the details of a redistribution bill, but there were no great differences between the leaders in regard to grouping, single-member districts, or even the university vote. Gladstone also placed in Northcote's hands a paper asking him what assurances he required about the character of a redistribution bill to ensure the passing of the franchise bill without delay or difficulty.[54] On the following day Northcote reported the results of his conference to Salisbury. But the introduction of the Government's redistribution scheme was not sufficient security for Salisbury. In answer to Gladstone's query he bluntly stated that the House of Lords would not part with control of the franchise bill until it had the redistribution bill before it.[55] This abrupt reply brought the negotiations which had looked so promising to a sudden halt.

The Cabinet, however, was still eager to secure the passage of its franchise bill and, when informed of the Opposition's discouraging answer, decided to pursue a settlement by means of a ministerial statement to Parliament. This would suggest an interparty conference and reaffirm the Government's readiness to meet any reasonable demand in regard to redistribution so long as the franchise bill was passed immediately.[56] But Gladstone no longer believed that the initiative for a settlement was in his hands. 'It is for Richmond and Cairns to move', he believed, 'if they wish to change the position: not for us, after S and N have told us in so many words that they *will not pass F Bill till the Lords have got the Seats Bill.*'[57] At this time neither the Queen nor her secondaries, who were in Scotland, were aware of all that had been passing between the Government and the Opposition. On learning, however, that Richmond and Cairns were going south she sent Ponsonby to meet them at Perth station. In a letter which Ponsonby conveyed to them the Queen expressed her great anxiety that they should 'use all their influence with Ld Salisbury and Sir Stafford Northcote to prevent a dangerous crisis. ... We must find some means to settle this question.'[58] On reaching London on 16 November Richmond and Cairns were met by a telegram which the Queen had sent them through Charles Peel, Richmond's nephew and secretary to the Privy Council. Having heard about Gladstone's proposed statement to Parliament the Queen wired that she had reason to believe a conciliatory declaration would be delivered by the Government and she was most anxious that it should be received in a friendly spirit.[59] At dinner that evening Richmond and Cairns assured Peel that they would do everything in their power to secure an amicable settlement.[60]

The chief obstacle to fulfilling the Queen's wishes, as Richmond and Cairns realized, was Lord Salisbury. Although his position was maligned by many, it appears, from all available evidence, that he would not commit his party until he had every reason to trust the Government's intentions regarding redistribution. On the morning of 17 November a few peers gathered at Salisbury's house on Arlington Street and it was here that Richmond and Cairns pursued a strong line for conciliation. Their plea was not successful. They did receive their leader's permission, however, to talk with Granville, who scarcely needed to be convinced of the benefits to accrue from a conference.[61] Richmond nevertheless went through the motions of outlining the Queen's proposal to Granville. He also advised him not to fear because Cairns's clear judicial mind, and his entire agreement with Richmond, would 'make him useful' to the Liberals. Both Gladstone and Granville were pleased with this overture and were encouraged to believe that their statement in Parliament would be favourably received by the Opposition.[62]

The break finally came in the evening of the 17th, but hardly in the way that the Liberals had been led to expect. The *Parliamentary Debates* tell the story of how Gladstone and Granville, in addresses to their respective houses, held out the lure of a conference on redistribution as a means of getting an assurance for the passing of the franchise bill. 'Our object', Granville declared, 'is to secure the passage of the Franchise Bill without delay. ... we could enter into no understanding or take any steps as to the immediate introduction or prosecution of a Redistribution Bill, or as to anything connected with it, unless we have a sufficient assurance that we should thus secure our principal object.' If such an assurance were provided the Government would be ready to submit the main provisions of a redistribution bill to 'immediate friendly communication before its introduction, and to make every reasonable effort for the purpose of accommodation'. To clarify this statement Salisbury asked whether the passing of the franchise bill during the autumn session was a 'condition precedent' to a conference on the redistribution bill. Granville assured him that it was.[63] On leaving the house Salisbury felt convinced that his party could not accept the Government's terms. When he talked to his nephew A. J. Balfour, however, he learned that the drift of Gladstone's speech in the lower house was quite different.[64] Gladstone's message was more conciliatory and contained three added particulars: (1) as an alternative to a conference the Government was prepared 'to present a [Redistribution] Bill at once to the House' conceived along lines already favourably received by Northcote; (2) that the Government would be willing to prosecute such a measure with all possible speed, 'even to the point of moving the second reading [in the Commons] simultaneously with the passing of the Franchise Bill into Committee in the House of Lords'; (3) and finally that the Government was willing to make the passage of the seats bill 'a vital question' to the point of staking the existence of his Government on the passage of the redistribution bill through *both* houses, even though he had no control over the Tory majority in the Lords.[65]

In order to ascertain the extent of Gladstone's willingness to conciliate, Salisbury addressed to him the same question that he had previously asked Granville in the House of Lords. Dispatching Balfour with the message Salisbury again asked whether the pledge to pass the reform bill '*is* or *is not* to precede an agreement with regard to the provisions of the Redistribution Bill'.[66] Acting through R. B. Brett, Hartington's private secretary, Balfour returned with a message from Gladstone in Hartington's handwriting just as a small meeting of peers at the Carlton Club was about to reject the Government's proposals. Gladstone answered: 'We should receive a request for consultation in a spirit of trust, and assuming that the intention was to come to an agreement should not ask for the "adequate assurance" beforehand'.[67] Gladstone's concession gave Salisbury and the peers the satisfaction they needed and changed the tenor of the discussion immediately. Brett told Hartington that 'Mr. Gladstone's words, which you wrote down, made all the difference'.[68] For his own part Salisbury recognized that

Gladstone's note changed the meaning of Granville's speech and made an agreement 'more possible'. But even in accepting the proposition of an interparty conference he was anxious to guard his party's position. 'If we take this course', he told Northcote, 'I should keep the Franchise Bill in our house till we had agreed upon the Redistribution. If we agree we shall be sufficiently protected by the *de die in diem* pledge—and the vital question pledges and the F. bill might pass'.[69] At a meeting at the Carlton Club on the morning of 18 November Conservative Party members unanimously approved Salisbury's recommendation to accept Gladstone's proposition.[70] In the afternoon on the second reading of the franchise bill in the upper house Salisbury made a final statement of his understanding with the Government in order to make the matter perfectly clear. Reviewing the events of the previous twenty-four hours, including a full transcript of his exchanges with the Government, he referred to his communication from Hartington as a statement of which the importance is 'impossible to exaggerate'. He assured the house that the 'spirit of trust' proffered by the Government would be 'entirely reciprocated on our side, and that we enter into these communications with the sincere and earnest desire of finding a common ground between the two Parties, and we have no *arrière pensée*—no reserve feeling of any kind—which would hinder that desire from being brought to a fortunate issue'. From this point there was little difficulty in committing the Conservative Party to a conference.[71]

The acceptance by both parties of an interparty conference on redistribution marked the end of the constitutional crisis. That the ensuing conference proceeded without a hitch is the strongest evidence possible of this. Convinced that the Government would act decisively on the matter Salisbury took the opportunity to learn as much as possible about the details of redistribution. For sheer knowledge of the technicalities of this subject Dilke was without rival. On 18 November Salisbury first approached Dilke at the Local Government Board where he asked him a great number of questions in preparation for the next day's conference. Dilke was surprised to learn that Salisbury was not opposed to the creation of single-member electoral districts and was therefore much in line with his own views.[72] At the first meeting of the conference on 19 November at 10

Downing Street Salisbury and Northcote pressed Gladstone and Granville on the question of Government responsibility for prosecution of the seats bill. Gladstone's assurances that every effort would be employed to expedite the provisions of the redistribution bill when completed were entirely satisfactory to the Conservatives. It was also agreed that their conversations should be absolutely secret, subject only to communication by the Conservatives to certain members of the late Lord Beaconsfield's ministry. The main points of redistribution were then discussed and a full statement of the proposed heads of a bill, prepared by Dilke, was read by Gladstone and placed in the hands of Salisbury and Northcote for their perusal.[73] Reaction to these novel proceedings was undeniably positive, though Gladstone, in his report to the Queen, indicated that there would 'very probably be on both sides a resolute disposition to expedite them, were it only because any serious prolongation of them would be likely to provoke public uneasiness'.[74]

At the second session of the conference, on 22 November Hartington and Dilke were added to the Liberal side, excluding Granville, who was preoccupied with the Egyptian crisis and knew relatively little about the particulars of redistribution. Dilke, with his great mastery of the subject, guided the deliberations. Salisbury, his 'pupil', took complete charge on the Conservative side, leaving Northcote sitting on the sofa 'like a chicken protected by the wings of the mother hen'.[75] Salisbury surprised Dilke and the others by advocating single-member districts, or '1s', nearly everywhere including the traditionally Tory county strongholds. Dilke wrote to Chamberlain:

We got on very well. He [Salisbury] has not yet consulted his front bench, (but he doesn't mean to 'take' their advice). We meet again Wedy at 4 when he will have done so. ... He said we had been overgenerous to some English agric! counties, wh. is true!!! He seems anxious that we shd. pass our Bill. He asked that the Metropolis shd. be in 4's with the (1) *one* vote only! The worst form of United vote. we objected. I then sent him with a *few* more 1s. He went for 1's everywhere in counties to wh. we agreed. He then tried 1s in big boro's to wh we objected. He will decide as to his 1's upon Wedy, but he means to yield. Mr. G. and I wd do far better without Harty who is not a good diplomatist.[76]

By the middle of the afternoon with the help of a few cups of tea the conference had gone through the whole business of redistribution. Chamberlain afterwards admitted he could not 'make head or tail of Salisbury. He appears to be swallowing every word he has ever written or spoken about Redist.'[77] The explanation for Salisbury's stance lay in the fact that he felt Conservatives could compete on a one-to-one basis with Liberal candidates under the conditions of a mass electorate, and should not have to rely on such devices as the minority vote and grouping of districts to gain seats in more populous areas. So great was the Queen's approval, however, at the conciliatory spirit displayed on both sides in the conference that Hamilton thought this might be an opportune time to revitalize the relationship between the Queen and Gladstone by bestowing the Garter upon the latter. 'Fancy "Sir William Gladstone!"'[78]

During a respite from the interparty talks during the next four days there was some discontent expressed amongst backbenchers on both sides concerning the secret and exclusive nature of the conference. Similarly John Bright, one of Gladstone's oldest and most respected colleagues, feared a possible compromise of Liberal ideals. To this Gladstone replied with a definite assurance that in the conference 'Liberal principles, such as we should conceive and term them, are in no danger'.[79] In the interim Salisbury also resumed his private communications with Dilke. He suggested to the latter the possibility of grouping a number of small boroughs, such as Chesterfield, Crewe, and Macclesfield, into single constituencies exceeding the 15,000 mark. The effect of this alteration would be to reduce the number of disfranchised boroughs and to keep the otherwise Conservative counties free of urban invaders. 'I was aghast at this suggestion', exclaimed Dilke, 'because it was a very difficult thing, in a Parliamentary sense, to create a few such groups in England; and if the thing was carried far and not confined to a few cases only it would entirely have destroyed the whole of the work we had done, because all the counties would have had their numbers altered.'[80] Although there was some uneasiness on the Conservative side over what they regarded as a stiffening attitude, by the time the conference resumed its regular sittings Salisbury had given up the grouping idea altogether.

The third meeting of the party leaders occurred on 26 November. Here the boundary commission drawn up by Salisbury and Dilke was formally approved and it was agreed that the principle of single-member districts should be applied universally to the counties; but borough representation posed a problem. Gladstone proposed either to create 184 single-member seats while retaining 100 for double-member constituencies, or setting up a two-thirds to one-third basis of division. The Tories, however, preferred single-member districts everywhere except the city of London, in return for which they were prepared to assure passage of the franchise bill, give up their insistence on a decrease of Irish representatives from 103 to 100, and relinquish all vestiges of minority vote and grouping. Dilke and Gladstone were prepared to meet them on this proposal, but Hartington feared an 'extinction of the Whigs by an omnipresent caucus for candidates' selection' under this system.[81] On 27 November Gladstone disclosed Salisbury's proposal to the Cabinet. Dilke was its warmest advocate and in a bid for Chamberlain's support told him privately that an extra seat might be made available for Birmingham at the expense of Scotland. Still the Cabinet was not unanimously in favour of the scheme; Lord Richard Grosvenor, the chief whip, and H. C. E. Childers, the Chancellor of the Exchequer, being the most outspoken dissentients. But the trio of Gladstone, Dilke, and Chamberlain had the enormous advantage of being the only ones who fully understood the subject, so that the others were unable to resist except in the form known as 'swearing at large'. With the Cabinet's approval Dilke was dispatched to inform Salisbury that an agreement was possible along the lines he had proposed.[82]

At three o'clock on the 27th the conference of party leaders met again at Downing Street to adjust a final agreement. Chamberlain, to safeguard radical interests, placed himself in another room while Dilke somewhat comically shuttled back and forth between him and the conference to keep the radical chief informed of the transactions.[83] Altogether agreement was reached on eight basic points which Gladstone submitted in a memorandum to Salisbury: (1) An increase in Scottish representation by an enlargement of the House of Commons, pending its approval; failing this, a reduction in Irish representation; (2) Minorities not to be directly represented; (3) Boundaries to be settled by a commission; (4) Grouping abandoned in principle; (5) Boroughs and groups below 15,000 to be merged into county divisions; (6) No diminution in the number of county members; (7) All counties and boroughs to be single-member districts except London and those boroughs between 50,000 and 150,000; (8) The franchise bill to pass forthwith.[84] With the belief that all major points of controversy were hereby settled Gladstone sent his congratulations to the Queen for her part in the arrangement and acknowledged Salisbury and Northcote 'for the manner in which they have conducted these difficult communications'.[85]

These salutations, however, proved to be premature as Salisbury was still not satisfied with the security of his party's position. University representation, a traditional bastion of conservatism, would be abolished under the new redistribution scheme, but curiously Salisbury did not object until after the conference had adjourned. Then he wrote in forceful terms to Gladstone: 'What was said this evening about Universities came upon me like a knock-down blow. I did not like to say anything until I had consulted the original document you gave me. ... I am afraid I must ask for another meeting tomorrow— for this matter is vital.'[86] Not wishing to reconvene the conference on this issue Gladstone empowered Dilke to assure Salisbury that the Government was willing to retain the nine university seats and that Gladstone would personally bind himself to this proposition.[87] These assurances were quite satisfactory to Salisbury and the university seats matter was settled almost as quickly as it had arisen. But Salisbury recognized the possibility that other similar questions might arise which had been overlooked in their original agreement and which the Government might choose to settle in a unilateral manner. Therefore he insisted that no changes deemed vital, as the universities question had been, should be admitted without consent of the Opposition. When Dilke visited him at his home in Arlington Street in the afternoon of 28 November Salisbury gave him a proposal to this effect which was subsequently revised by the Liberals and inserted after the seventh point in Gladstone's original memorandum summarizing their agreement. Only now some difficulty arose in the wording of instructions to the boundary commissioners and before everything was settled Dilke had made four trips both ways to satisfy the leaders.[88] Finally a redistribution bill based on the consent of party leaders on both sides was ready for presentation to Parliament. This was embodied in two memoranda which subsequently became known as the 'Arlington Street Compact'. In conclusion Salisbury wrote to Gladstone, 'I have—on Northcote's behalf and my own—to thank you most sincerely for the courtesy and conciliation with which you have conducted our abnormal Conferences.'[89]

In the aftermath of the conference the entire Reform Bill package was treated as a body of agreed legislation and therefore immune to the kind of organized party opposition encountered by most ordinary legislation. Although Childers resigned from the Cabinet over the issue and there was some irritation over the secretive nature of the conference, neither side experienced any real difficulty in selling the agreement to its respective followers. 'I suppose some of our men will ask generally what amount of liberty they are to have in discussing the Bill,' Northcote apprehended. 'I shall say that we are in honour debarred from any vexatious or dilatory opposition; and that, so far as the leaders are concerned, we shall support the bill as it stands, and use our best influence to induce our friends to do so.'[90] The Conservatives, however, never secured their object of a redistribution bill to accompany the franchise bill in the 1884 session. While the latter was signed by the Queen on 6 December 1884, redistribution (though it was read a second time in the Commons on 4 December) did not become law until June of the following year. What the Conservatives received was something much greater—a reason to trust Gladstone's Government to secure passage of a redistribution bill before the next general election. Gladstone's concession to Salisbury on 17 November for a non-conditional discussion of redistribution was tantamount to an assurance of its ultimate safe passage. Though the notion of party responsibility remained an uppermost consideration for both sides, the amicable deliberations of the subsequent interparty conference did nothing to dispel this confidence.

What transpired between the party leaders in 1884 over the passage of parliamentary reform and redistribution reinforced the method adopted in 1869 to pass the Irish church bill. Again a conference technique was employed to bridge the communications gulf between the parties and thereby alleviate a political

controversy which had constitutional significance. Owing to
the continued growth of democratic ideas in British society an
extension of the suffrage to rural constituencies had to be made
as a complement to the 1867 bill which enfranchised urban
dwellers. But the memory of the circumstances surrounding the
passage of that earlier measure, in which the Conservatives had
jockeyed for support amongst the working classes, no doubt
created an atmosphere of mutual distrust. The Liberals hoped
for an unilateral extension of the franchise which might accrue
to their benefit, while the Conservatives were determined that
no such substantive change would be allowed without their
sanction. By the same token neither party could afford to delay
indefinitely the inexorable advance to universal manhood suffrage simply for the sake of preventing the other party from
getting credit for it. Some medium of understanding and co-
operation was needed to promote a bilateral agreement. An
interparty conference performed this function and in so doing
brought about a resolution of the controversy.

By this time too certain recurrent features of interparty
negotiation were becoming apparent. Aside from the obviously
unusual and slightly illicit nature of these secret gatherings
between leaders of opposing parties, the chief interest attached
to them lay in their extra-parliamentary character. Clearly on
these occasions the degree of controversy between the houses had
reached a point where the only recourse was a direct appeal
to the real source of power within the British parliamentary
system—the political parties. Significantly, the most important
communications were carried out during the period before the
meeting of a conference as the leaders carefully tested the propensity of the other side for compromise. Such processes were
often imperceptible behind the rhetoric and rivalry which
necessarily formed the essence of normal party relations, and
leaders were always keenly aware of the need first to satisfy
party sentiment. Often the only visible agent of unity and co-
operation was the monarch, who played a critical, though
hardly decisive, role by exercising her dignified powers toward
the establishment of a spirit of conciliation. By the time an
actual meeting of party leaders took place the all important
predispositions for compromise were set with the avowed intentions of both sides to reach a legislative accommodation. The

physical act of sitting together to adjust the details of disendowment and redistribution respectively merely confirmed
the previous spiritual consensus. But it was of the utmost importance that these early examples of interparty conciliation were
successful. Otherwise it is unlikely that they would have been
cited as useful precedents or that similar methods would have
been so persistently applied in subsequent stages of party controversy in the twentieth century.

A Decade of Liberal Ascendancy

III

The Education Bill Crisis
of 1906

No constitutional change ... has ever lasted, which has
been accepted with enthusiasm by *one* party. The reason
is that permanence can never be secured by one party
'triumphing' over the other, even though it be a large
majority which 'triumphs'.

F. S. OLIVER[1]

One of the most ironic features in the operation of the British
political system has been the fact that the party most responsible
for the enactment of a substantial measure of electoral reform
has usually not been returned to power in the ensuing period.
On nearly every occasion political opportunists seeking electoral advantage from a grateful electorate have been disappointed. Such was the case after the passage of the Third
Reform Bill. During the next two decades the British government was dominated by a succession of Conservative regimes
under Lord Salisbury and his nephew, A. J. Balfour. Although
consideration was given on several occasions to reforming the
House of Lords as a means of relieving democratic pressure for
its abolition, the Conservatives made no serious attempts to alter
the composition or powers of the upper house.[2] Only during
those brief occasions when the Liberal Party was in office were
any real efforts made to amend the constitution. These were
manifested most fully by Gladstone's two attempts to legislate
home rule for Ireland and Lord Rosebery's intention to resolve
the House of Lords problem. In connection with the latter the
radical Henry Labouchere on one occasion even carried a
motion in a sparse house to abolish the upper chamber. The
Queen deplored all such attempts to tamper with the constitution, insisting that the House of Lords is '*part* and *parcel* of the
much vaunted and *admired British Constitution* and CANNOT be
abolished'.[3] With only a tenuous majority in the House of Commons, a handful of Liberal peers, and the certain opposition

of the Queen, Rosebery abandoned his programme, expressing the belief that any reform of the House of Lords 'must be accomplished by a Tory Govt.'.[4] But if the Liberals lacked the power, the Conservatives lacked the necessary desire to institute any sweeping changes.

The neglect of any structural reform in the political system for over two decades set the stage for a momentous constitutional struggle when the Liberals returned to power in January 1906 in the most one-sided electoral victory in the nation's history. The Lords' ensuing obstruction of Liberal legislation, either by extensive amendment or outright veto, cast into bold relief the imbalance between the houses of Parliament. The major issue was not so much the legality, but the constitutionality of the Lords' action. Did the hereditarily based upper chamber possess the right to stifle the efforts of a popularly elected assembly? More precisely what had to be determined was the extent to which the present functioning of Britain's constitutional order was incongruous with the demands of mass society. The test case for this issue was the disagreement between the houses of Parliament and political parties over the education bill of 1906. With the encouragement of the Archbishop of Canterbury and King Edward VII the party leaders attempted to avert a collision between the houses by calling an interparty conference. Unfortunately the conciliation factors which fostered a settlement in the nineteenth-century conferences were never sufficiently present. The gulf separating the upper chamber, which had become increasingly aristocratic in temper since 1886, from the 1906 House of Commons, which had a distinctly democratic hue, was not so easily bridged. The leaders were unable to converge on some middle ground in their discussions on what role religion should play in state education. Underlying these efforts was the idealistic notion that a legislative settlement could be fashioned which might satisfy the antithetical desires of both political parties and recent attitudinal changes in society. Their failure and the consequent loss of the Government's bill launched a period of almost continuous stress which lasted until the outbreak of international war in 1914.

Following its overwhelming victory in 1906 the Liberal Government under Henry Campbell-Bannerman proceeded to carry out some of the pledges it had made in the election campaign. This commitment resulted in the introduction of measures on such subjects as plural voting, trade disputes, and licensing. But the bill on which the Government pinned its greatest hope was the education bill, by which it hoped to reverse the effect of the Education Act passed by the late Conservative Government in 1902. That act had encouraged the principle of denominational teaching by providing for the support of voluntary (church) schools from local rates.[5] The crux of the controversy in 1906 was that the Government was attempting to minimize religious instruction in those schools which had recently been brought under the aegis of the state. Nonconformists, who made up a great part of the Liberal majority, demanded that teachers should be appointed only by the local education authority, that sectarian tests for teachers should be abolished, and that teachers should not be required to teach even undenominational religion in state-supported schools. The only remnant of ecclesiastical influence would be the allowance of denominational instruction by special teachers two days a week in transferred (formerly church) schools. Further than this the Nonconformists, and therefore the Liberal Government, were unwilling to go. On 9 April 1906, Augustine Birrell, President of the Board of Education, introduced in the House of Commons a bill modelled on these lines.[6] From the outset it was the subject of most acute controversy between the parties. As Birrell recalled, 'I have freely consorted all my life with Catholics, Roman and Anglican, with ardent Evangelical English churchmen, with Nonconformists of every shade, with Modernists, Agnostics and Atheists, but never have I drawn my breath in so irreligious and ignorant an atmosphere as that of the House of Commons when debating religion.'[7] The huge Liberal majority, however, bolstered by over two hundred Nonconformists, easily pushed the education bill through the House of Commons without having to rely on assistance from the Irish Nationalist section.

But the Conservatives had no intention of yielding full control of the country's affairs to the party in power. As Balfour had stated in an election address in Nottingham, it was of paramount importance 'that the great Unionist party shall still control, whether in power or whether in opposition, the destinies

of this great Empire'.[8] Balfour envisaged the House of Lords
as a 'theatre of compromise' where issues which the Unionists
lost in the House of Commons would undergo 'serious modifications'. Their object, he told Lord Lansdowne, Tory leader in
the upper house, was that the party in the two houses should
'not work as two separate armies, but shall co-operate in a common plan of campaign. This is all important,' he said. 'There
has certainly never been a period in our history in which the
House of Lords will be called upon to play a part at once so
important, so delicate, and so difficult.'[9] By 4 August the House
of Lords had passed the education bill through its first and
second readings without a division. But Lansdowne warned
that 'we do desire it to be clearly understood that in giving a
Second Reading to the Bill we do not abate one jot or tittle
of our right to deal with it as we think proper at a future stage'.[10]
The Conservatives clearly believed that the recent Liberal victory did not imply a mandate for overturning the country's laws
or any drastic change in the operation of the British government. Some method had to be derived to lessen party strife and
possibly bring about a reconciliation between the parties over
the education bill.

Chief spokesman for the church's point of view, but also in
the awkward position of mediator to the impending conflict,
was Randall Davidson, Archbishop of Canterbury. Davidson
demanded that religious instruction should be made available
in all schools for those who desire it and that the church should
have some voice in the appointment of teachers. Every teacher,
he argued, should be permitted to offer distinctive religious instruction to his students. Throughout the spring of 1906 the
Archbishop had repeatedly made remonstrances to the Government to alter its bill, but in vain. He expressed his willingness
to Francis Knollys, the King's private secretary, to work with
the Government towards 'an amicable and reasonable and permanent solution, and I have no desire (if it can possibly be
helped) to identify myself with the sort of uncompromising
Tory opposition which will be loud when Parliament meets
again'. Still he could not accept provisions which would be 'disastrous to our children both religiously and educationally'. It
seemed particularly unfair to Davidson that the state should
forbid teachers from giving special religious instruction for

which the church was prepared to pay.[11] When the Archbishop returned from holiday in Italy in September he arranged a meeting with the Prime Minister at Belmont Castle in Scotland to discuss the education bill. He found Campbell-Bannerman 'perfectly ready to listen to reasonable amendment', but ill-prepared to discuss details. A related question which deeply concerned Davidson was a ruling in August by the Court of Appeal which cut at the heart of the Education Act of 1902. It held that the West Riding County Council was justified in refusing to pay teachers in denominational schools for religious instruction and in deducting from their salaries an amount proportionate to the time spent on such teaching. Although this judgement coincided with their own beliefs and policy, Cabinet members were undecided on whether to use the decision as a lever on the Opposition to secure passage of their bill, or to await final judgement by the law lords before proceeding with the education bill. According to Davidson the Prime Minister 'was in favour of appealing'.[12] Still it seemed as if the Government would proceed with its bill when Parliament met again in the fall.

The constitutional aspect of this question was first raised in the public utterances of some of His Majesty's ministers, particularly those of the President of the Board of Trade, David Lloyd George. Anticipating rough handling of the education bill by the House of Lords, Lloyd George spoke throughout the autumn in favour of restricting its powers. On 4 October at Llanelly he said:

> The Education Bill would have an easy walk through, perhaps when the Lords were sleeping or partridge shooting, or was it grouse, or foxhunting—he was not quite sure about those things (loud laughter).
> Most of those Bills had yet to go to the House of Lords. What would happen to them? They were on the eve of the first conflict with that house, and he did not believe that the last was far off (hear, hear). Did the Lords mean to treat those Bills as they threatened to treat them? According to the *Daily Telegraph*, which seemed to represent all that was left of the Tory Party (laughter), the Lords would destroy the Education Bill or, if it did pass, what would happen would be worse than passive resistance—an organised system against paying rates, a revolution, in fact. That was very dangerous talk for a Party possessed of so many unjust privileges. The Bishop of Manchester had been talking recently. What was the new Manchester school? The Bishop had said that, when the Education Bill came to the Lords, he would propose that they should omit, not amend, Clause I, Clause II., Clause III, Clause

IV., V., VI., VII., IX., X (renewed laughter), and reconstruct the rest (more laughter). The Bishop said that he was not killing the Bill, but reconstructing it (laughter). Fancy, after hanging, drawing and quartering a man, saying: 'I didn't mean to kill him, but to reconstitute him' (renewed laughter).[13]

This sort of language elicited an angry response from high quarters. The King reacted in much the same way to the utterances of Lloyd George as his mother had done to those of Joseph Chamberlain and other radicals in her day. Through Lord Tweedmouth, the First Lord of the Admiralty, who was visiting Balmoral, the King expressed his displeasure to the Prime Minister.[14] But unhappy as he was with the conduct of his ministers the King, unlike his mother, did not persist in his efforts to subdue the violent tone of his ministers' speeches.

The Archbishop, however, was more active in his efforts to reduce conflict and reach an accord. Following his conversation with the Prime Minister in late September Davidson carried out numerous conferences with leaders on both sides. These efforts culminated in a further meeting with Campbell-Bannerman on 28 October, who was joined on this occasion by Birrell and Lord Crewe, the Government leader in the House of Lords.[15] Davidson spoke for over half an hour on his objections to the Government's bill and the necessity for amending it in the upper chamber. The Government insisted, however, that it was absolutely necessary to resist the Lords' amendments '*at present*'. Birrell remarked: 'The time for giving way is not yet. It will come later, and certainly it wd not be my wish to resist everything *then*. But we must for the present, resist substantial amendments, and thus keep our friends quiet.' Not many details were discussed, but it was agreed that the question of teachers giving denominational teaching in council schools presented the greatest obstacle for settlement, and neither side foresaw an acceptable solution. The Archbishop disliked what he called the 'anti-church feeling' behind the Government's bill, although Birrell unconvincingly assured him that this was a misinterpretation of the Government's attitude.[16] As discussion proceeded on the education bill in the House of Lords the chances for a settlement diminished still further. Conservative lords on the one hand and bishops on the other produced two separate sets of amendments, which together amounted to a wrecking of the original bill. Against this formidable combina-

tion the Liberal minority was defenceless; and with Lord Loreburn, the Lord Chancellor, ill, and Lord Ripon, Lord Privy
Seal, in an uncertain state of health, the whole brunt of defending the Liberal position fell on Lord Crewe. The Cabinet could
do nothing but await the final steps of the bill in the upper house
before acting. But it was evident to Campbell-Bannerman that
the Government 'cannot expect, or indeed invite, the House
of Commons to accept any of the fundamental alterations if they
are persisted in'.[17]

From this point until the calling of a conference of party
leaders in mid-December the movements of the Archbishop are
essential to understanding the progress and ultimate failure of
interparty negotiations. On 16 November Davidson arranged
a meeting with John Morley, who was Secretary of State for
India, to discuss the details of the controversy. Much to Davidson's surprise Morley agreed with all of his criticisms on the
conduct of the education bill through Parliament, including the
unsatisfactory response of the Government representatives in
the upper house to the proposals of the Conservative lords. 'You
agree then', said Davidson, 'that we are now speaking in the
House of Lords to nobody that matters at all as regards the
ultimate solution.' Morley also allegedly admitted that a
'great central phalanx' in the House of Commons had been
actuated by a real hostility to the Church of England beyond
any educational considerations. Morley was quite moved by
the whole situation, according to Davidson, 'groping round as
it seemed to me almost helplessly for some way out of the
impasse'. They then compiled a list of moderates on whom they
might rely to work for a compromise. Haldane, Grey, Asquith,
Bryce, Devonshire, and St Aldwyn were among those named,
but none was judged to possess both great influence and great
understanding of the issue. In closing Morley referred to the
precedent of the Irish church bill of 1869. That crisis, he maintained, had been settled by the Archbishop, but that was 'a
comparatively simple thing then because the arrangement
turned upon questions of money which can always be arranged.
This does not: it turns upon questions of religious principle,
which are the most difficult of all things to deal with.'[18]

These discussions led to a further meeting between the Archbishop and the Prime Minister at Windsor Castle on Saturday

17 November, under the auspices of the King. Both leaders found His Majesty much interested in the situation, but not very knowledgeable about the details. The King was much distressed with Campbell-Bannerman, whose attitude he described to Davidson as 'profoundly unsatisfactory. I have never seen him like this. He will hear no reason, but simply denounces the Lords as having destroyed the Bill, wh. was MOST conciliatory and kind to the church—"too kind" he maintains. In short he evidently means War', continued the King, 'and won't be persuaded in any way. When I spoke of the good of talking it over with you he said, "I am quite willing to talk, but no good can come of it so long as the Lords behave like this etc." '[19] It appeared that the hopeless atmosphere created by the Prime Minister's obstinacy in his conversation with the King had doomed the Windsor Castle talks to failure. Then on the following day Campbell-Bannerman requested an interview with Davidson. They talked for an hour and a half after church service, the former defending his party's original bill and the latter defending the Lords' amendments. They met again in the evening without coming any closer to agreement. As they discussed various conciliatory schemes Campbell-Bannerman kept saying: 'It is an impasse; I see no way out.' Then the Prime Minister suddenly altered his tone and said, 'I think we must have a conference of some sort. There ought to be private communications of a formal kind before the Report stage in the Lords.'[20] This brought the two leaders no closer to an agreement, but it fostered the hope that a discussion in a more formal conference setting might encourage understanding between the houses. The King was relieved and others at the palace were inclined to think that a settlement was in the making. Lord Esher, an aide to the King, took a more realistic view. He recalled that 'The Queen settled the Irish Church controversy with great skill. It was an easier task, I admit, for the point was narrowed down. Here the differences are scattered through a long Bill. Also there is no Mr. Gladstone to negotiate with.'[21] The weekend discussions concluded with dinner on Sunday evening, but everyone tactfully avoided the education question, fearing any comment which might disturb the delicate spirit of conciliation.

During the next few days the Archbishop attempted to bring

the party leaders together, but inauspiciously neither side would accept the responsibility for assuming the initiative. Then after an almost continuous strain of meetings and church duties the Archbishop was temporarily immobilized with gastric influenza. His work, however, was carried on by Morley, who counselled moderation on the Cabinet. He suggested that they should follow the precedent of 1869 and that the Prime Minister should consider any proposals made to him by the Archbishop or the Opposition before asking the House of Commons to consider the Lords' amendments. Although this course was generally accepted by the Cabinet, the Prime Minister in his letter to the King did not even allude to the fact that the education question had been discussed. When Edward discovered what had occurred from other sources he was dismayed that the Prime Minister had taken no action.[22] On 25 November the King, on the advice of Morley, wrote the following missive in his own hand to Campbell-Bannerman recommending a compromise on the Lords' amendments:

> The King would, therefore, ask Sir Henry to consider whether it would not be highly desirable that Sir Henry should discuss the matter with the Archbishop of Canterbury in the hope that some *modus vivendi* on the line of mutual concessions could be found to avoid the threatened collision between the two houses.
>
> For the King thinks it would be deplorable, from a constitutional and every point of view, were such a conflict to occur.
>
> The King proposes to send a copy of this letter to the Archbishop and would wish also to call Sir Henry's attention to pages 7 to 43 in the 2nd volume of *Archbishop Tait's Life*, when a contest was on the eve of taking place between the Houses on the Irish Church question 1869.[23]

That evening the Prime Minister came to Lambeth Palace for a discussion with Davidson, author of the *Life of Tait*, who was still in bed. Unfortunately neither leader had anything to add to what was already said at Windsor and Campbell-Bannerman had cooled on the idea of a conference, which he thought was not possible at least until after the report stage and probably not until after the third reading or later. The whole interview was a disappointing climax to all conciliation efforts thus far undertaken and had come about only to please the King.[24]

Meanwhile Conservative attitudes also hardened towards

the possibility of a conference. Three meetings attended by the thirteen most prominent men in the Unionist Party took place at Lansdowne House to decide which amendments should be pressed at the report stage. Lord Thring, an aged Liberal who had served as parliamentary counsel, attended the first meeting on the 23rd to acquaint the Opposition with what amendments the Government would be likely to find permissible.[25] On 26 November at the second meeting the moderates, led by the Duke of Devonshire, were able to get some of the more extreme amendments eliminated and they generally dominated the proceedings.[26] But that evening a small group of Conservatives from the lower house—Balfour, Walter Long, Austen Chamberlain, Alfred Lyttelton, Aretas Akers-Douglas, William Anson, and Sir Alexander Acland Hood—held a meeting in Balfour's room at the House of Commons. They expressed strong disapproval of the compromising attitudes of Devonshire and the Archbishop and urged their leader not to give way on the Lords' amendments.[27] At the final Lansdowne House meeting on the 27th Balfour relied on this support to prevent any further alteration in the character of amendments along lines which the Liberal Party might accept.[28] Such intransigence only inspired renewed threats by Liberal ministers from the public platform. Lloyd George, speaking at Oxford, claimed that the Lords were 'destroying the British Constitution'. In the next election, he warned, a much larger measure than the education bill would come up for consideration, if the Lords persisted in their present course. 'It will come on an issue of whether this country is to be governed by King and peers or by the King and his people.'[29] The King was enraged at Lloyd George for using his name in a statement which was critical of the upper house. Knollys explained to Campbell-Bannerman that 'in King Edward's view the monarchy and the House of Lords seem to be equally bound up with the hereditary principle, and a threat to the hereditary Chamber inevitably touched the throne'.[30] To satisfy the King an apology was subsequently extracted from Lloyd George.

By early December, in spite of the threats of Lloyd George, the Cabinet had reluctantly decided to pursue a course of cautious compromise which might save the bill and avert a crisis. Campbell-Bannerman told the King that Birrell would make a general statement in Parliament indicating the changes which the Lords had effected in the bill and what concessions the Government might be willing to consider in its position. 'These indications however cannot be made at all unless we have reason to believe that they would be accepted as the price of the rejection of all the other amendments which cannot be accepted by the Government.' In order to set the stage for these vague concessions the Cabinet had decided to reject the Lords' amendments *en bloc* rather than consider them *seriatim*. Although novel, the Speaker agreed that this procedure would not be out of order. The Lords would then be invited to restore the bill to some semblance of its original state.[31] Though inclined to be slightly conciliatory, these concessions were so conditional and weighted as to place the Government in a distinctly advantageous bargaining position, and therefore unlikely to elicit a favourable response from the Opposition. The success of any subsequent conference was absolutely dependent on the absence of any prior conditions or restraint of trust.

Such maxims were recognized by the King, who told Campbell-Bannerman that he could 'not quite see where the spirit of concession "comes in" in the proposals of the Cabinet' and feared that the chances of a compromise were 'not very bright'. He doubted whether the Lords would interpret the rejection of their amendments as a conciliatory gesture and he failed to understand how the Opposition could be expected to react favourably to the Government's concession 'unless the Cabinet put themselves into communication with Lord Lansdowne and Mr. Balfour previous to Mr. Birrell's speech'.[32] To facilitate a better understanding of the Government's intended course the King showed the Prime Minister's letter to Devonshire, who discussed the Government's proposed course of action with Balfour and Salisbury.[33] More importantly Crewe had been in communication with Lansdowne and arrangements were made to include Asquith in their preliminary talks on 10 December.[34] At this meeting the Liberals explained to Lansdowne that their decision to reject all of the Lords' amendments 'was not intended as a flouting of the House of Lords or a rude rejection of its proposals as unworthy of consideration but as the simplest mode of securing such position as might lead to compromise and settlement'. They also indicated the points on which con-

cessions would be considered, but no details were discussed.[35]
There was still considerable uncertainty surrounding the
Government's intentions and its expressions of goodwill. Campbell-Bannerman explained to the King his reluctance to reveal
more fully the details of his Government's concessions as
'caution lest they "give away" themselves and their friends in
vain'.[36] Obviously the Government's reticence and its reluctance to compromise its near absolute control over legislative
initiative, normally the prerogative of the party in power,
revealed a fundamental lack of good faith between the parties.

Whether an interparty conference would be held now
depended on the substance and tone of Birrell's actual speech
in the evening of 10 December and the reaction of the major
Conservatives. Birrell, however, said nothing to reassure the
confidence of the Tory lords that the Government had any intention of conciliating. He held the Lords in contempt for trans-
forming the Government's original bill into 'a miserable,
mangled, tortured, twisted *tertium quid* ... something which no
man will father'.[37] The immediate reaction of the Archbishop
was 'a keen feeling of depression'. He objected to the Prime
Minister that although Birrell foreshadowed the possible acceptance by the Government of certain amendments, 'the
general tone of his utterance was ... of a sort to make it extra-
ordinarily difficult for the House of Lords to propose them.
There is throughout the speech, whether intentionally or not,
a sort of demand that the House of Lords shall come almost
apologetically or "hat in hand" to ask the Government to listen
to its proposals, and that it shall begin by practically withdrawing what it has now suggested, and substitute something quite
different in its place.' Davidson contended that Birrell got
somewhat carried away by the cheers of those who sought to
humiliate the House of Lords. He appealed to the Prime
Minister, in his forthcoming pronouncement, to follow a conciliatory line 'by the tone and manner, as well as by the matter,
towards the House of Lords'.[38] Campbell-Bannerman's speech
on the evening of 11 December did reveal a much more conciliatory spirit than Birrell's diatribe.[39] This placed the Conservative Lords in the uneasy circumstance of not knowing
which speech reflected the true attitude of the Liberal Party.
Consequently at subsequent meetings of the Opposition leaders

there was still much dissatisfaction and great confusion over the Government's decision to reject all of the Lords' amendments. 'Our real difficulty', remarked Lord St Aldwyn, 'lies in the fact that the leader of the party does not want a peaceable solution.'[40] This was hardly the proper spirit to ensure the success of an interparty conference.

In the meantime the Cabinet on 12 December reached a firmer decision on the points on which it would be prepared to allow amendment. Concession, it was agreed, would be most possible on those clauses which dealt with special facility schools and the position of the teacher in transferred schools. In regard to the former, the Cabinet was willing to allow the substitution of three-fourths for four-fifths as the number of parents requesting denominational teaching, which it was hoped would satisfy the Roman Catholics. In the transferred schools in urban areas the teachers might be allowed to give special religious instruction for a specified period (five years was cited) as an experiment. This provision was intended to meet the grievances of the Anglican church. Campbell-Bannerman explained to the King that these views could not be stated publicly 'because they could only be recommended to the Party as the price of saving the Bill, and settling the controversy at least for a time; and we must first know this would be their effect.'[41] With this view in mind Crewe, Asquith, and Birrell were dispatched to confer with leading members of the Opposition. In these preliminary discussions the Government members showed respect for the Lords' position and their concessions were well received by Lansdowne, Balfour, and the Archbishop.[42] What remained now was to decide on a suitable procedure to summon a formal conference of party leaders. These arrangements were made by Crewe and Lansdowne, who decided that the former should formally move consideration of the Commons' message rejecting the Lords' amendments after which Lansdowne would make a statement complaining of this action. Crewe would then explain the Commons' action, and if this was satisfactory adjournment would be moved. After this Lansdowne thought private consultation would be possible. Neither leader, however, was overly sanguine of the acceptability of these plans for the House of Lords majority or of the eventual outcome of a conference. 'So the matter stands thus at present,' Crewe informed Devonshire, 'leaving the door open, but not very wide open, I'm afraid.'[43]

On 17 December, when the House of Lords met to consider the Commons' disagreement with the Lords' amendments, both Lansdowne and Crewe spoke in a moderate tone. As arranged the latter outlined the concessions the Government was prepared to make, the most important of which was its willingness to allow assistant teachers, who were so willing, to give denominational teaching in urban schools. The Government was also prepared to lower the proportion of parents needed for setting up special facility (denominational teaching) schools from their original figure of four-fifths and agreed to recommend that a parents' committee should have only a 'consultative voice' in the appointment of the teacher. 'I believe', Crewe concluded, 'that if we do give cool consideration now to the whole matter in the light of what I have been able to tell your Lordships, it is by no means impossible that we may be able to arrive at some successful conclusion without any real sacrifice of principle on either side.' This conciliatory statement apparently satisfied Lansdowne and others who did not attempt to block adjournment of the debate.[44] What then passed between Lansdowne and Crewe was never recorded, but it resulted in the long-awaited conference of party leaders.

This body held its first meeting at 11 a.m. on 18 December at Crewe House. It was represented by Crewe, Birrell, and Asquith on the Liberal side and Balfour, Lansdowne, and Lord Cawdor from the Conservative Party. At the suggestion of the King, the Archbishop was added. As the leaders went over the various clauses of the bill the profound differences which separated the parties quickly surfaced. The teachers question emerged as the issue most critical to a settlement for both sides. The Conservatives demanded that head teachers, as well as assistants, should be allowed to give denominational instruction in all schools, with or without the assent of the local authority. These conditions were totally unacceptable to the Liberal leaders and to the Cabinet. 'Such a scheme', Campbell-Bannerman told the King, 'would imply the continuance of all the present denominational schools, with the addition of a seat being paid for them. The purpose for which the Bill was introduced was the exact reverse of this, and therefore the Cabinet

cannot hope to save the Bill.'[45] Later when the Conservative
leaders met, Balfour read them a memorandum which was critical of the Government's refusal to admit any more than minimal church influence in the schools. Not surprisingly those
present empowered their delegates to stand firm on the all-im-
portant teachers question.[46] This tendency by both sides to consult closely with their respective followings only served to promote negative dispositions and dogmatic attitudes injurious to
the prospects of a settlement.

When the party leaders resumed their conference on the evening of the 18th, discussion on the teachers' question prevailed
over all else. In a negotiation process compromise on relatively
minor issues sometimes can set a conciliatory tone or momentum for the breakdown of major obstacles. The reverse process,
as instanced here, is less likely. The discrepancy of views on
the teachers question was simply too great to be overcome without some initial conditioning for a compromise. Conservatives
reiterated their demand for 'full freedom for all teachers in all
schools. We were told plainly', said Lansdowne,

> that this demand was wholly inadmissible, and that all we could expect was
> that no teacher should be permitted to give religious instruction except with
> the consent of the local education authority; that, with or without such
> permission, no head teacher could be allowed to give such instruction; and
> that even assistant teachers could not in any circumstances be allowed to teach
> in schools except those with 250 pupils. ...
> Lord Crewe and his colleagues almost went so far as to discourage discus-
> sion on other points, admitting that the difficulty as to the teachers lay in
> limine, and that unless it could be overcome it was useless to approach other
> questions. They indicated plainly that, at this as well as on other points, they
> had advanced as far as they dared, and that they were, to use Lord Crewe's
> words, already on the edge of a precipice in consequence of the concessions
> which had been made.[47]

Very few concessions, in fact, had been made on either side,
though at one point Birrell had hinted that the Liberals might
be willing to allow the head teacher to give religious instruction.
But this was conceded only on the condition that the local authority give him permission to teach and that the Conservatives
sacrifice the remainder of their demands.[48] As the meeting
broke up there was a general feeling that the negotiations had
failed. Final decision, however, was delayed until Balfour could
consult his colleagues once more.[49]

In an attempt to save the conference Davidson asked Crewe to call at Lambeth Palace the following morning. He asked Crewe whether it was vital for the Government that the local education authority be supreme everywhere and have the power to refuse any teacher the privilege of giving denominational teaching. In his affirmative reply Crewe stated that the Cabinet would never look at any proposal which fell short of that. Davidson then pointed out several areas where he thought a compromise might be possible, but Crewe replied that the line taken by Balfour and his colleagues the night before 'had been really so stiff as to almost repel advances towards compromise and peace'. Crewe agreed, however, that this was not the point and that 'the real question was whether or no the gulf was unbridgeable, and he clearly indicated that he thought it was'.[50] The Archbishop reported this discouraging news to the Conservative leaders who had gathered at Lansdowne House, and to the King. He explained to Knollys that the final rupture had taken place over the question of using the teachers to give denominational teaching in special facility schools. 'I may be prejudiced,' Davidson admitted, 'but I thought that on that point it was honestly impossible for the Unionist leaders to give way, and I fully hoped that the Govt. would make some material concession. But they thought it impossible to do so, frankly avowing that it was the opinion of the Nonconformist extremists which rendered it impracticable for them.'[51] All agreed that no further negotiation was possible.

The failure of the education bill conference of 1906 instigated a constitutional struggle which neither party seemed reluctant to pursue. In the evening of 19 December a complete deadlock was reached when Lansdowne moved in the upper house that 'this house do insist on its amendments to the Education Bill'.[52] When the House of Commons met the following day the Government decided not to proceed any further with its bill. But the Prime Minister declared that 'the resources of the British Constitution are not wholly exhausted, the resources of the House of Commons are not exhausted, and I say with conviction that a way must be found, a way will be found, by which the will of the people expressed through their elected representatives in this House will be made to prevail'.[53] In simple political terms the conference failed because the forces of moderation were insufficient to stem the rising tide of party sentiment, but there were other factors. Archbishop Davidson, who possessed strong views about the church's place in education, was not a good mediator. In spite of his professions of neutrality and his great knowledge of the 1869 crisis the Archbishop was unalterably prejudiced towards the Conservative cause, which served the interests of the established church. Whether the King, who would have been the ideal figure to inspire national co-operation, could have saved the situation if he had acted with greater resolution cannot be determined. From a more humanistic perspective the conference failed because neither party had any confidence that it would succeed. By limiting their discussion to the stubborn teachers question the leaders had recklessly steered the conference on a disastrous course. As Crewe said, 'from the moment the negotiations began I had not the faintest expectation that they would meet with any success'.[54] Lansdowne too later admitted privately that he 'would have sacrificed a good deal in order to secure a settlement but I do not think it was really within reach'.[55] This attitude, which was manifested by both sides throughout the conference proceedings, was a premonition of further disagreements.

The unusual circumstance of twenty years of Conservative domination of the Government followed by a stunning Liberal victory at the polls upset the balance of power between the parties and threatened to destroy the sense of propriety which had governed political relationships during most of the nineteenth century. More than any other event the education bill controversy of 1906 inaugurated that prolonged period of constitutional stress which prevailed in British politics for nearly a decade. So long as the Liberals were so clearly ascendant they were far more likely to follow the will of the democratic electorate and organization which had placed them in power rather than seek the co-operation of the opposing party which was based on a system of privilege and vested interest. Under these circumstances no amount of special pleading or conciliatory gestures was sufficient to bend the rigid attitudes which were established on both sides. This constitutes arguably an instance where party orthodoxy triumphed over the national interest. Nevertheless the education bill crisis did contribute to the development of the concept of interparty negotiation by axiomatically pointing out its limitations. Despite the application of conciliatory techniques gleaned from the previous century, including mediation by the monarch and the Archbishop of Canterbury, it was shown that no two political crises are exactly the same, and that the resurrection of precedents from another era was no substitute for spontaneous action. In any case merely going through the motions of conciliation would not necessarily result in a settlement. Under optimum conditions an interparty conference could serve as a valuable parliamentary adjunct to facilitate and channel national aspirations through the legislative process. Under the conditions which predominated in 1906, however, no amount of special machinery or elaborate procedures could compensate for the absence of any desire for an agreement. It was the human propensity for compromise, when present in a sufficient degree, and nothing inherent in the method, which allowed British interparty conferences to operate successfully.

IV

The Constitutional Conference
of 1910

PART ONE

When Pack meets with Pack in the Jungle, and neither
will go from the trail,
Lie down till the leaders have spoken—it may be fair
words will prevail.

RUDYARD KIPLING[1]

The failure of the education bill could have provoked a Liberal
attack on the established church in England; instead it took
the form of a frontal assault on Conservative obstruction in the
House of Lords. According to Balfour's biographer, 'from the
moment when the Peers refused to pass the Education Bill of
1906 as it stood, till the final trial of wills over the Budget of
1909, the coming collision was the dominating fact towards
which everything was tending'.[2] Still the illusion persisted that
the eminent good sense of English politicians, and their willingness to confer and conciliate, would somehow extricate the
nation from the impending crisis.[3] To this end numerous
expedients were proposed, modelled roughly on the emerging
conference method. The most important of these constructs was
a Cabinet committee scheme in 1907 to set up a joint session
of members from both houses to settle disagreements. To Campbell-Bannerman this suggested a return to 'the old plan of
formal Conferences between the two Houses' used in the previous century. This would be a mob, not a conference, he
believed, and any real deliberation or discussion would be impossible.[4] The Tories, on the other hand, were more inclined
to favour House of Lords reform. Although comprehensive
reform of the upper chamber was regarded as the only ultimate
solution on both sides, it was widely believed that no Liberal
Government would tolerate a corresponding increase in the
powers of the second chamber, even with a sacrifice of the hereditary principle. The Liberal-dominated House of Commons

demanded control of, not parity with, the upper house. Moreover, there was good reason to doubt the Conservatives' sincerity concerning House of Lords reform. When given the opportunity to secure this innovation during their long period of dominance in the late nineteenth century they had failed to take appropriate action. Additionally neither party welcomed the prospect of drastically and methodically restructuring institutions of government—there was something un-English about it.

Meanwhile a third alternative gained increased acceptance in Liberal ranks after 1906 as the House of Lords continued to mutilate Liberal legislation. Though abhorred by Conservatives, the Liberals were prepared to employ their majority to enact a suspensory veto which could conceivably limit the period which the Lords could delay legislation to as little as six months.[5] The acceptance of this final step by the Liberal Government in 1910 was induced by the introduction of a new element into the mounting crisis—the Irish issue. The Lords' rejection of Lloyd George's 1909 budget necessitated a general election in early 1910 in which the Government was returned with no overall majority. This forced the Liberals to rely on the assistance of the Irish Nationalists, who demanded as the price of their support the immediate curtailment of the powers of the House of Lords in order to obtain home rule for Ireland. Had the Liberals been able to retain some semblance of the 1906 majority they would have possessed sufficient electoral support to enact the budget and possibly some relevant social measures. Suddenly the Irish problem, which had lain dormant for several decades, was elevated to a new significance as a critical underlying feature of the House of Lords question. Surely in the absence of such an affiliation the Liberals would have been much more willing to conciliate. The imminent clash between the Lords and Commons was delayed, but not halted, by the death of King Edward VII in May 1910. While the nation waited in suspense for five months an interparty conference applied every conceivable remedy to relieve the constitutional deadlock—but to no avail. This outcome reinforced the lesson from 1906 that a conference can resolve details, but not the principle, of an important political issue. Unable to reach a settlement outside Parliament, the Liberals, reinforced by their Nationalist allies and by a commitment from the new monarch, executed a drastic alteration in the constitution and prepared the way for another.

On 2 December 1909, two days after the Lords' rejection of the budget, H. H. Asquith, who had succeeded Campbell-Bannerman in 1908, declared the action of the House of Lords to be 'a breach of the Constitution and an usurpation of the rights of the Commons'.[6] At the general election which followed in January the Liberal Party returned to power, but only by two seats. Critical to the Government's intention of securing passage of the budget bill of 1909 was the support of forty Labourites (who normally voted for Liberal measures), seventy-one Irish Nationalists, and twelve other home rulers of a more independent stature. But Irish support was contingent mainly on the provision of assurances by the government for a delimitation of the Lords' veto which might ensure and expedite the passage of home rule. This was made clear by T. P. O'Connor, Irish Nationalist M.P. from Liverpool, who told Lloyd George, the Chancellor of the Exchequer, after a canvass of his colleagues, that 'they must *oppose* the Budget unless it be preceded by the announcement of a measure limiting the legislative and financial Veto of the Lords and headed by the statement that there is a guarantee that the bill will be passed into law within the present year'.[7] John Redmond, the Irish party leader, later publicly confirmed these threats.[8] The Cabinet therefore was placed in the odious position of subservience to Irish interests simply to stay in office. However eager it might be to co-operate with its erstwhile allies, the Government could not jeopardize its credibility with the English public by appearing to formulate policy merely to satisfy the demands of the Irish minority. It was for this reason that the Liberals followed a course of equivocation and procrastination during the early months of 1910. Asquith was unwilling to commit his party to any further assurances than that a veto bill should accompany the budget through Parliament, but that 'no guarantees' should be requested from the King for their safe passage.[9]

Such a stance admitted the possibility that the Irish might vote against the budget, particularly since there were several items in it which were contrary to their economic interests. To avert this gloomy prospect King Edward VII appealed to

Balfour, still leader of the Opposition, to allow the budget to pass for the sake of the country.[10] Balfour was not unsympathetic to the plight of the Liberals, but he replied characteristically that saving the country from the embarrassment entailed by a Government defeat would be 'too high a price to pay'. After all, the budget had been 'attacked in the country by every Unionist candidate, and every Unionist member who has been returned is pledged to oppose it. In circumstances like these it would be vain to ask the Unionist party on tactical grounds to vote black where they had before voted white.'[11] Conversely his feeling, expressed in a later conversation with J. L. Garvin, editor of the *Observer*, towards the idea of allying with the Irish was even more hostile—it would be tantamount to 'eating dirt'.[12] There was therefore much speculation with regard to how the Government would act with regard to the King, the budget, and the Irish. The only stock answer that Asquith was able to provide to such queries was to 'wait and see'.[13]

Neither the Government nor the Irish party showed as much temerity in their approaching showdown as their public pronouncements might suggest. Private discussions were taking place between the two groups over the precise terms by which the budget might be allowed to pass. From early February to mid-March Redmond and his chief lieutenant, John Dillon, adhered steadfastly to a position of 'no veto, no budget'.[14] Yet the Government could not honourably or actively pursue the question of guarantees until the elected representatives of the British people were given an opportunity of passing judgement upon a veto bill. When this proved unacceptable to the Redmondites an attempt was made to negotiate around the question of guarantees by dealing with the more pliable nationalist group under William O'Brien. It was hoped that by eliminating some of the more objectionable features of the budget to the Irish, namely a whiskey tax increase and a 20 per cent tax upon the unearned increment of land, that a breach might be made in the solid body of opposition within the official party. But these communications which were carried out by the Master of Elibank, the Liberal chief whip, were to no avail as he was compelled by 'dire necessity' to keep his eye on 'the big battalions'.[15] Indeed the substance of the budget was not the paramount issue, and it could hardly have displaced guarantees as a vital consideration to the Irish. In this light the Cabinet decision on 13 April against any modification of the budget, despite Asquith's claim that 'to purchase the Irish vote by such a concession would be a discreditable transaction', had no significance.[16] An act of far greater importance, later affirmed publicly by Asquith, was the Cabinet's stipulation that if the Lords rejected or otherwise interfered with the progress of the projected veto resolutions the Government would recognize its 'duty immediately to tender advice to the Crown as to the necessary steps to be taken to ensure that that policy shall be given statutory effect in this Parliament'.[17] Although this commitment fell short of Redmond's demand for immediate guarantees from the Crown, it did provide reasonable assurance that the Government intended to act in good faith with regard to home rule. This in turn paved the way for passage of the budget.

Much controversy has centred on the nature of the 'bargain' reached between the Government and the Irish Nationalists. Conservatives especially were convinced that a conspiracy had been perpetrated which was 'notorious and manifest'.[18] This theory was further developed by Tim Healy, an O'Brienite, who claimed that 'Redmond foolishly offered to accept the Budget if a Bill to restrain the House of Lords Veto was passed, and the Chancellor gladly took that *quid pro quo*'.[19] That such a bargain was ever transacted, either orally or in writing, has never been proved. Equally unfounded is the notion that there existed an ideological concord between the parties on the left which induced a united response on the subjects of the veto and home rule.[20] All evidence, to the contrary, indicates that there was a far greater sense of disagreement than accord between the two parties and that the Liberals were determined to maintain their self-respect by pursuing as responsible and independent course as possible.[21] This intent, however, was curtailed by the more urgent need for votes. Ultimately the Government, in consequence of its narrow majority, and aware of the terms of Irish support, naturally took a strong line against the House of Lords. The inability of historians to give credence to such obvious motives may be attributed in part to a confusion over Asquith's equivocal conduct in the early months of 1910. Even Elibank, who was privy to the decision-making process, was unable to explain why the Government agonized for so long before reaching an understanding with the Irish. 'Why in Heaven's name they could not have come to this decision two months earlier and saved all this pother, I for one cannot understand.'[22] What actually occurred in this period was a change in the moral leadership of the Liberal Party from Asquith to Lloyd George, at least so far as the Irish question was concerned. Not only had the latter been the Government's principal negotiator with the Irish, but as Elibank points out, it was Lloyd George's threat to 'leave the Cabinet and join the Irish' which finally prompted the Cabinet on 13 April to reach an immediate decision on the subject of guarantees.[23] From that point until the end of the crisis Lloyd George actively defended the Government's commitment to Ireland, though he and his colleagues were constantly subjected to the temptation to defect.

The immediate result of the formation of the Liberal–Irish entente was passage of the budget and the Government's veto resolutions in the lower house. The latter proposed to abolish the Lords' veto on money bills, to restrict it to three consecutive sessions on ordinary legislation, and to limit the duration of Parliament to five years, with Crown support if necessary. To counter these severe measures the Conservative Party sponsored a solution which would rejuvenate rather than destroy the powers of the upper house. The idea of reforming the House of Lords, which had originated in the previous century, had been actively championed for over two decades by Lord Rosebery and for a while in 1888 was even under serious consideration by Salisbury's Government. In 1908 Rosebery, then politically neutral, chaired a select committee which drafted a series of reform recommendations which eventually formed the basis for a number of proposals to solve the 1910 crisis.[24] The most important of these efforts was instigated by Francis Hopwood, permanent Under-Secretary of State for Colonies, who enlisted the support of J. A. Sandars, Balfour's private secretary, and J. L. Garvin. The 'Hopwood plan' envisaged a strong and efficient second chamber and the elimination of the peerage as the sole principle governing seating in the upper house.[25] Eventually Balfour and Lansdowne agreed, though differing over the basis for composition, to support Lords' reform and carried a series of resolutions to this effect in the upper chamber in mid-March. But the Liberals had already passed the point at which they might accept such a compromise solution. The proposals for upper chamber reform therefore never amounted to more than a flanking movement to attract moderate Liberals in the Cabinet and to assist the King in his conversations with Asquith. Indeed the real concern of the Conservatives was that the Government might be pressing the King for a large creation of peers to secure passage of the budget and eventually a bill embodying the Government's three April resolutions. Communications between the King and his ministers, however, never reached this stage. Asquith, knowing the subject caused the King much distress, had assured him privately that his Government would not tender such advice unless absolutely necessary, and most likely not until after a second general election.[26]

On 7 May the nation was shocked by news of the death of the King.[27] The full weight of the impending crisis now fell on the shoulders of his son, George V. As Duke of York in 1894 he had been informed of his rights and responsibilities through reading Bagehot's study of the English constitution, and from the experiences of his father and grandmother he had been able to observe the mediation powers of the monarch.[28] In a brief prepared for him shortly before his father's death by the Master of Elibank, the King was encouraged to use these powers if it became necessary. Royal mediation, he argued, might possibly avert a constitutional crisis while maintaining the neutrality and prestige of the Crown.[29] But for the monarch to assume such a course of action so early in his reign was only inviting miscalculation and criticism. There was much sympathy from the public and politicians alike for the new monarch and a strong feeling that he should not be forced to cope immediately with the complexities of party warfare. 'His Majesty's intervention could not remain a secret', Lansdowne explained, 'and if it were to take place, and to be unsuccessful, the result would to my mind be most unfortunate. I should not like to see him begin his reign with an abortive attempt, particularly at a moment when political feeling is as bitter as I am afraid it still is.'[30] A period of party truce was therefore in order, not only out of respect for the dead King, but to provide an opportunity for the new reign to succeed.

The suggestion of an interparty conference to provide a hiatus from political strife and possibly settle the nation's constitutional problems was first raised in Conservative circles shortly before the King's death. In a speech at Reading on 5 May Lord Curzon, prominent Unionist and former Viceroy of India, called for a conference between the five wisest men from each party to be convened by some disinterested person, such as the Speaker of the House of Commons. This 'all-England eleven' would 'adjourn their Parliamentary business for six months, go into session with closed doors and produce a draft of a new Constitution for this country' and thereby resolve forever disagreements between the two houses.[31] This was the first instance of a proposal to use the Speakership in a mediatory capacity, a practice which became increasingly prevalent in later conferences. J. L. Garvin, as his biographer notes, became the leading advocate in the press for a conference after the death of the King. Aware of the precedents of 1869 and 1884 he touched the heart of the nation in the 8 May edition of the *Observer*: 'If King Edward upon his deathbed could have sent a last message to his people, he would have asked us to lay party passion aside, to sign a truce of God over his grave, to seek ... some fair means of making a common effort for our common country.'[32] Although Garvin's role in bringing about a conference has been overstated, his editorials did much to establish a public mood for compromise. A series of letters to *The Times* by a correspondent named 'Pacificus' also helped to shape public opinion. The author was F. S. Oliver, a businessman, publicist, and a close friend of many leading Conservatives.[33] On 23 May 'Pacificus' appealed to the politicians to follow 'the way adopted at Philadelphia in 1787, when the Constitution of the US was hammered into shape; the way adopted only last year in South Africa—the way of common sense and sobriety in deadly earnest about an object of vital importance—a conference with closed doors'.[34] Obviously Oliver envisaged the more ambitious undertaking of a constitutional convention, an extension of the conference concept, which might not only diminish party spirit but bring about a reconstruction of the whole instrument of government. On another occasion he outlined in detail the conditions under which a conference would be successful—'it must be small; its meetings must be held with closed doors; it must

be an affair between principals; and above all, it must be free'.[35]
It is difficult to assess the effect of these letters, but public
opinion was overwhelmingly in favour of interparty negotiations.

Still there was considerable reluctance on both sides to a conference and it appeared for a while that the Government would
proceed with its veto resolutions and that the Opposition would
insist on its reform resolutions. A breakthrough finally occurred
on 29 May when Lloyd George, following a lead by Crewe,
committed the radical wing of the Cabinet to a policy of conciliation. He believed that 'some way should be found for meeting a solid grievance under which Liberals admittedly suffer,
rather than enter upon the acute stage of a controversy of which
the issue may be long protracted with much injury to national
interests. I cannot doubt that there is a chance, or even a probability, that a few months of reflection will bring in their train
a readiness to try if some settlement cannot be effected.'[36] Acting on these guidelines the Prime Minister, after consulting a
number of his colleagues, prepared a paper entitled 'The Constitutional Question: Its Origin and Development' which he
submitted to the King. It contained a summary of the Liberal
position and pointed the way to a settlement 'by all reasonable
men in all parties' by advocating a reconstitution of the House
of Lords and the establishment of machinery to handle disputes
which might arise between the two houses.[37] There remained
the difficulty of the Irish, who had no great sympathy for the
monarchy and no desire for compromise. To placate their allies
leading Liberals sought to reassure them of the Government's
honourable intentions in conferring with the Opposition. On
6 June O'Connor reported to his colleagues that Birrell
'attaches no importance to the conference', which would 'not
be more than an exchange of views between Asquith and
Balfour and perhaps one or two others. It will be informal, and
above all it will not be *binding*.' Similar sentiments were
expressed by Winston Churchill, the Home Secretary, and Lloyd
George. Redmond, though far from satisfied, reluctantly
accepted this state of affairs.[38]

Finally at a Cabinet meeting on 6 June the forces working
for conciliation converged. With the exception of one or two
minor members, noted Herbert Samuel, the Postmaster-

General, 'the Cabinet were ... much in favour of trying to arrange a settlement. ... Hence the Conference—a risky, but in the circumstances a necessary experiment.'[39] No Irishman was represented on this body, but clearly home rule, owing to the Government's tacit agreement with the Irish over the budget, was the major issue underlying that of the House of Lords. Lloyd George, a native Welshman, was present as a potential guardian of Celtic interests and was accompanied by Birrell, the popular Chief Secretary for Ireland. Although Asquith and Crewe were included as leaders in the Commons and Lords respectively, Lloyd George, as the Government's chief link with the Irish, was recognized as the leading spirit among the Liberals and, according to Asquith, 'the man who above all others carries his life in his hand'.[40] His counterpart on the Conservative side was Balfour who, despite his generally philosophic attitude towards life and politics, harboured a deep 'distaste for Nationalism and for Irishmen'.[41] This prejudice would no doubt be reinforced by Lord Lansdowne who, as Unionist leader in the House of Lords and absentee landlord of a vast acreage in southern Ireland, would naturally follow a strong line in opposition to any course inimical to British interests in that country.[42] Additionally there was Austen Chamberlain, whose principal interest was tariff reform, and Lord Cawdor, who had little initiative and rarely spoke in public, but was believed to possess sound judgement and would probably carry much weight with the party rank and file. The critical question surrounding these talks was how far the Government would stray from its understanding with the Irish to accept some alternative plan to its veto policy.

The first meeting of the constitutional conference occurred on Friday 17 June, in the Prime Minister's room in the House of Commons. At the suggestion of Balfour it was subsequently decided to divide legislation into financial, ordinary, and constitutional categories.[43] Ironically the financial question, which had formed the subject of acute political controversy the previous year, proved to be the least contentious matter. Discussion therefore converged on constitutional legislation which most immediately touched matters in current dispute. The Conservatives argued that subjects such as home rule, disestablishment, the royal succession and prerogative, relations between the two houses, and the franchise, which were directly related to the operation of governmental machinery, should be eligible for special legislative safeguards. The Government representatives, however, wished to recognize no such distinction and interpreted any categorization of exceptional measures as yet another attempt to obstruct Liberal legislation, stifle substantive change, and further detract from the powers of the House of Commons. But the vital point behind the Liberal opposition was revealed by Birrell towards the close of the second session when he recognized that by such a distinction 'we should be excepting all the questions around which the battle raged. What was left? How could the Irish and Radicals be expected to agree? No one', Chamberlain noted, 'took up this observation.' Finally Lloyd George asked, 'are we not beginning at the wrong end? We are discussing the exceptions before discussing the rule.' It was then agreed that treatment of ordinary legislation would make up the agenda for the next meeting. But the critical issue of constitutional legislation, which included home rule, had been raised and would continue to menace the conference until the end.[44]

On 27 June Asquith suggested, with the concurrence of Lloyd George, that 'if a satisfactory procedure could be devised for ordinary legislation, special safeguards for "organic" legislation might prove to be unnecessary'. It was by this means, to circumvent the difficult question of home rule, that discussion was brought to bear on alternative methods of resolving differences between the houses. While opinion was hopelessly divided on the feasibility of employing a referendum, the delegates did agree that some system of informal conferences, similar to that which they were presently conducting, should be part of any new machinery. Attention was then focused in succeeding sessions on joint sittings, or the Ripon plan, as a means of reaching a settlement in the event that such gatherings were unable to reach an accord.[45] Following a disagreement between the houses the disputed measure would be reintroduced in the following parliamentary session and settled by a joint vote of the entire House of Commons and a Lords' delegation of one hundred, of which twenty would be Government peers and the remaining eighty would be chosen at large from the House of Lords. The advantages of such a scheme were that it would permit a greater degree of compromise and cross voting than in the normal parliamentary procedure, and that minority opinion could be expressed without jeopardizing the existence of the Government. The Liberal members of the conference were much enamoured of the idea, and appeared eager to settle immediately along these lines.[46]

The Conservatives demurred, however, evidently foreseeing the likelihood that the composition of the House of Lords 'would again become a critical question on the first occasion on which in a Joint Session a bill was rejected or amended by Lords' votes'.[47] This raised the logical alternative of reforming the upper chamber, the highly academic ruse traditionally used by Conservatives to counter popular criticism of the House of Lords. The adoption of any such policy at this time, as Asquith ascertained at the tenth conference meeting, would relegate any settlement of the House of Lords question 'to a remote and very contingent future'.[48] While it might serve a Conservative interest in distracting the Liberals from their more immediate legislative aims, there was no obvious compensatory advantage which might accrue to the Government from it. Yet the Liberals were not able to reject outright such an innovation which implied some degree of democratic reform. Therefore when Lansdowne placed it on record that his party was in favour of House of Lords reform, Asquith felt compelled to state that the Government was 'pledged to it up to the eyes'. Unfortunately Lloyd George, acting as the sole guardian of his party's interests, proved stalwart in his opposition to this dictum and continued to express his dissent on every occasion when this proposal was considered.[49] Although House of Lords reform might be ideologically satisfying and afford the only ultimate solution, it would certainly not satisfy the Irish or provide any immediate answer to their present difficulty.

Discussion in the meantime had drifted to a consideration of joint sittings, recently outlined in a memorandum by Asquith. This suggested a slight revision of the Ripon plan whereby legislation on which no common basis for agreement could be reached by either the houses of Parliament or conferences of party leaders over two sessions would be subjected to a joint session made up of a plenum of the House of Commons and a delegation from the Lords which he hypothetically labelled as 'x'. Differences arose over who should determine whether the measure introduced in the second session was 'substantially the same' as that initially introduced. Eventually an arrangement was borrowed from the Australian constitution whereby the Speaker of the House of Commons would decide what constituted 'the same bill' unless both houses should concur on substantial amendments.[50] The most critical aspect of the joint sitting proposal, however, was the uncertain evaluation of 'x'. Under the Ripon plan the Conservative peers would have had a majority of forty-four in the Lords' delegation, but under the arrangements being considered no one was sure how much Conservative weightage should be allowed or in what way it should be determined. Thus no further progress seemed possible as neither party seemed willing as yet to come to close quarters on this controversial point.

On 26 July the conference returned to constitutional legislation where a similar impasse had developed. Balfour immediately recognized home rule as a 'crucial instance' in any test of constitutional questions. Lloyd George, however, proposed a 'narrow definition' of such legislation, confined to bills affecting only the monarchy, the House of Lords, and relations between the two houses. The Conservatives wished to expand this listing to include other subjects, such as home rule and disestablishment, but Lloyd George protested against any special treatment being given to home rule which might further obstruct its passage.[51] Once more the conferees proved incapable of coming to grips with substantive issues and the discussion reverted to financial legislation where there was no fundamental disagreement. The conference was able to reach a tacit agreement on the definition of 'tacking', which was defined as legislation containing provisions not strictly germane to financial objects, or designed to effect important social or political changes under the guise of finance. Additionally it was agreed, following testimony from Elibank on the method used in committee apportionment in the House of Commons, that a joint tribunal should be formed to interpret their definition of tacking made up of two members from the Government and five from the Opposition in the House of Lords and the reverse proportion in the House of Commons.[52]

At the final sitting of the conference prior to the parliamentary recess Lloyd George presented a memorandum summarizing the extent of their agreement on money bills. It also contained an amended definition of constitutional questions which did not include home rule and made no mention of reforming the House of Lords. Such matters of substance, heretofore judiciously avoided or ignored in order to reach a consensus on less serious subjects, now confronted the conference directly and evoked the strongest possible emotional response from both sides. After some desultory discussion on the evaluation of 'x' Balfour precipitated an argument by asking the Prime Minister whether he intended to make any statement concerning their proceedings in the house. But Lloyd George took control by advocating a 'fairly definite' public pronouncement and appeared to insist that his memorandum should form the basis for it. The Conservatives of course repudiated this demand and as the discussion became more heated it seemed to Chamberlain that Lloyd George and Birrell were 'heading straight for a break-up of the Conference'. Thereupon he passed a note to Balfour recognizing the Liberal terms as an ultimatum—'give up Home Rule or we break off— ... If is so:' Balfour replied, 'It is clear to me that Asquith and L. G. are on different sides.' A little later Chamberlain further acknowledged the Government terms to be that questions like home rule, disestablishment, and the franchise could receive no special safeguards and that treatment of legislation must precede any consideration of House of Lords reform. 'Of course we can't agree,' Balfour responded. 'But I am not sure that Asquith does not want to go on!' Presently Balfour asked the Prime Minister whether exclusion of House of Lords reform was a *sine qua non* to any possible conference settlement. 'Asquith hastily replied—"Oh no, no certainly not." The tension suddenly ceased. Lloyd George stopped fighting,' and Asquith drew up a bland statement which he read to the House of Commons the following day.[53]

The chief interest surrounding this exchange is that even at this stage, when for an hour or so the situation was critical, neither side was willing still to admit that home rule was the crux of their disagreement. On nearly every occasion when questions relating to this subject arose House of Lords reform was invoked by Conservatives as an effective camouflage. Obviously Balfour and to a great extent Lansdowne manifested their party's aversion to home rule by their persistent advocacy of upper chamber reform. Lloyd George, in spite of his early support of home rule for Wales, was never more than a passive sympathizer of the Irish cause.[54] Indeed by 1910, though this was not fully appreciated by the Irish, his interest in Celtic nationalism had waned, and his real commitment was to social and land reform for Britain. Nevertheless support of Irish home rule was a critical means to this desired end—a kind of pragmatic detour which Lloyd George never seemed reluctant to take. Asquith, more interestingly, reflects the uncertainty of the English Liberal conscience stemming from the sacrifice of his party's more immediate interests to those of a minority group. This explains not only the Prime Minister's reluctance to place the Government at the service of the Irish in their spring negotiations, but his advocacy in the conference of joint sittings in preference to the old Campbell-Bannerman plan of curbing the Lords' veto power. The first stage of conference interchanges can be understood only as a wilful act of sublimation by both parties to avoid direct confrontation over the only issue on which no rational agreement was possible.

PART TWO

> There is nothing in all this. The new relations between the
> two parties will be beaten out by the usual conflict
> between parties, and will take shape as our Institutions
> always do, as a modification of existing Institutions.
> No written Constitution is conceivable for our people.
>   LORD ESHER[55]

During the intervening months numerous broad formulas were proposed for a national settlement, the most important of which was a plan for coalition Government devised by Lloyd George at Criccieth in early August. In retrospect it appears motivated more by the deadlock which had emerged at the final session of the conference than by any spirit of co-operation revealed by that body. The ulterior purpose behind his coalition proposal, however, was not so much to facilitate the passage of home rule as to evade it. Lloyd George's foremost legislative interest at this time was his national insurance scheme. Indeed the longest section of his twelve-part memorandum, as noted by a historian of his social programme, 'was devoted to an attack on the industrial insurance industry and its resistance to his attempt to provide widows' and orphans' pensions'.[56] Notwithstanding his obdurate defence of party interests in the conference, Lloyd George realized that the parliamentary stalemate incurred by party conflict jeopardized his social reform programme. 'I cannot help thinking', he wrote, 'that the time has arrived for a truce, for bringing the resources of the two Parties into joint stock in order to liquidate arrears which, if much longer neglected may end in national impoverishment, if not insolvency.' For Ireland he proposed the federal solution of 'home rule all round'. While this idea was not inconsistent with his party's commitment to the Nationalists, it had the potential advantage of removing the Irish question from the centre of party politics.[57] Since Lloyd George kept no record of his negotiations it is difficult to trace the path of his memorandum. His confidant C. F. G. Masterman and Churchill seem to have been among the first to be apprised of his plan.[58] But it was F. E. Smith, Churchill's close friend, who informed Bonar Law, future Unionist head, and probably put Lloyd George in touch with Balfour.[59]

The parliamentary deadlock and the novel means being used to resolve it inspired other proposals along national lines. One was fostered by F. S. Oliver, who composed his views on domestic and imperial co-operation in a lucid memorandum which he sent to Balfour and Chamberlain. He described the conference as 'the natural safety valve of popular government in the circumstances in which popular government now finds itself. If you are ever going to make an attempt at Imperial Union this is the only possible method. ... It will be a political disaster of the first magnitude if the breakdown of the Conference should destroy so hopeful an institution in its infancy.' Oliver also foresaw the spectre of a great national crisis developing over Ireland. As a preventive measure he suggested an Irish convention similar to that body later chaired by Horace Plunkett whereby politicians would be motivated by a common purpose and desire of reaching a national settlement. Federalism, Oliver thought, was the plan which would most likely resolve the nation's ills.[60] In spite of his idealism, Oliver did more than any other publicist to encourage recognition of the conference and to formulate some systematic idea of its operation.

Many of Oliver's views were shared by a ginger group within the Conservative Party known as the Round Table movement which was associated with the South African settlement and more recently with ideas of tariff reform and imperial federation. For this body Lloyd George's proposal for federal home rule for the United Kingdom possessed a natural fascination, not only for its potential to settle the Irish question, but for its value in acquainting the public with the federal idea 'under the shadow of Home Rule'.[61] Furthermore according to one of its leaders, Philip Kerr (later Lord Lothian), the Round Table group was in touch with some of Redmond's patrons in America and Ireland and seeking to undermine his party's vital connection with the Liberals. They were being urged to transfer their financial support to O'Brien's independent nationalists, who were more sympathetic towards the federal concept, a ploy not unlike that attempted by the Liberals in the spring to break the parliamentary deadlock. The *ultimate* purpose of these machinations, however, was to transfer 'the Irish vote—agrarian and property—to the Conservative side', an act which might be ideologically irresponsible, but was not regarded as impossible. Notification of these confidential designs to the party leadership was made not through Balfour, who was regarded as 'hopelessly impervious to new ideas for practical action', but through Chamberlain, who was regarded as more pliable owing to his family's association with tariff reform.[62]

As the time approached for reconvening Parliament prospects did not appear very bright for any idealistic plan of reconstruction. On 10 September Lansdowne, who was 'not sanguine of the success of the conference', told Balfour that he was particularly distressed over its inability to arrive at a suitable definition of constitutional questions. But he thought the ultimate break would come on the issue of second chamber reform, which the Government, under the influence of Lloyd George, had absolutely refused to consider seriously.[63] Balfour preferred that if a rupture was inevitable he would 'rather have it on Home Rule;—among other reasons because we are all agreed about Home Rule, but by no means agreed about the best mode of effecting a reform of the House of Lords'.[64] Lansdowne responded that 'a rupture over Home Rule would suit our book well enough', but he thought their case would be greatly strengthened before the electorate if it could be shown that 'our opponents had shirked the question of H. of Lords Reform'.[65] Further evidence that the Conservatives were using this issue as a charm to divert Liberal attention from Ireland was revealed by Lord Salisbury, who had been asked to formulate for his party some proposals, possibly involving concessions, with regard to House of Lords reform. He suggested the inclusion of nominated or elective elements in the Lords as possible ways of achieving a tactical advantage. This would embarrass the Liberals on the issue of democratic reform and give the Conservatives a 'good cry' when the conference broke down. But Salisbury reminded Lansdowne that, '*We are fighting not for our hereditary privileges, but for the Union, and we are prepared to make even the greatest sacrifices.*'[66] Whether this frank revelation of the Conservative conscience had any effect on Lansdowne's stance in the conference cannot be ascertained, but it does constitute an emphatic recognition by a scion of one of the oldest and most distinguished families in the realm of the real issues at stake.

When the conference returned from summer recess on 11 October it resumed discussion on the memorandum Lloyd George had circulated at the last meeting which contained amended versions of his definition of financial and constitutional legislation. With regard to the former the Liberals conceded jurisdiction to the House of Lords over measures involving what was called 'equitable tacking' as interpreted by a joint committee presided over by the Speaker of the House of Commons.[67] Lloyd George and Crewe observed that such a proviso would ' "impair the financial position of the Commons", which their Party especially expected them to maintain'. But they made no attempt to block the proposal. In retrospect it might appear that the Liberals were deliberately giving way in order to justify any later opposition to concessions on more substantive matters. Nevertheless Chamberlain somewhat surprisedly observed that 'there did not appear to be serious difference of opinion as to the object to be aimed at'.[68] Such was not the case in their consideration of constitutional legislation. Here the parties diverged essentially along two lines—the number of reserved subjects and the method for dealing with deadlocks on such matters. The Conservatives preferred referendum rather than a general election or joint sittings (as had been tentatively agreed upon for ordinary legislation) for settling constitutional conflicts. This was obviously another red herring for the Liberals, who were not about to be drawn from any party advantage they possessed by a democratic lure which the Conservatives had no intention of pursuing seriously.

But their reception of referendum would depend, at least in part, on what subjects were reserved for its use. While the Liberals wished to include only matters affecting the monarchy, the Protestant succession, and any act embodying the results of the present conference in their list of constitutional questions, Balfour indicated that the subject on which his party 'felt most strongly was Home Rule', which he apprehended to include any measure of devolution. Other subjects, such as women's suffrage and redistribution, which the Conservatives also regarded as constitutional, the Liberals labelled routine parliamentary business. Any such broad interpretation, Asquith maintained, would render useless any new machinery for settling deadlocks on ordinary legislation as it could not be applied to any of 'the everyday matters of sharp party controversy'. Balfour recognized that the definition of constitutional questions (and how they should be acted on), and what was called 'the evaluation of x' (the determination of the number of peers in joint sittings), were the two greatest outstanding questions and he wondered whether it was worth their while to continue their difficult task if there was no chance of reaching an accord.[69] At the next day's sitting the Conservative four, who had met privately in the interim, decided to insist on home rule and parliamentary reform in all its branches as the 'natural frontier' for reserved subjects. It was their desire that a referendum should be invoked following a deadlock on these issues after two sessions. Although the Liberals countered with joint sittings to resolve constitutional deadlocks, they regarded the Conservative propositions as inimical to their interests and the conference adjourned for a fortnight.[70] Sensing the seriousness of the situation Asquith afterwards told Lord Haldane, the War Secretary, that the conference 'held what may be its last meeting but one to-day. We have been nearing Niagara for a day or two, and now we have reached it.'[71]

Meanwhile numerous visions of a national settlement persisted and the younger Conservatives who were enamoured of the concept of federalism continued to bombard their leaders and the press with letters and memoranda. Garvin waged a campaign in its favour in the *Observer* and Oliver resumed his 'Pacificus' correspondence in *The Times*. It was no doubt with the object of attracting this section that Lloyd George revised his coalition plan to the effect that any measure for Irish self-government 'might form a nucleus for the federation of the Empire at some future date'.[72] Such grandiose schemes, however, were not so appealing to the Conservative leaders as a way of detouring some of the more practical issues confronting them in the conference. On Garvin's activities Lansdowne wrote: 'It is easy to write eloquently of the situation which confronts us; it alarms me as much as it alarms him, but neither he nor "Pacificus" have really shown us the way out.'[73] But Balfour, who measured his followers' opinion on the subject, sensed beneath the surface a deep unwillingness to concede home rule. He told Chamberlain that 'it would be far easier to promise our support to the Government if they were prepared to defy the Irish and their own extremists than to offer to form a Coalition'.[74] Additionally Balfour harboured deep personal reservations concerning any national settlement in which some form of home rule was implicit. He revealed to Garvin his aversion to any such means of resolving their present deadlock and his opinion that federalism under such conditions would be a retrograde step, contrary to the universal trend towards unification 'as exhibited in the United States of America, Canada, Australia, and the Cape'.[75] Likewise Balfour declined Lloyd George's offer for a coalition. Following consultation with former chief whip Aretas Akers-Douglas and a deep consideration of the consequences of his action, Balfour declared that 'I cannot become another Robert Peel to my party'.[76] But it was not just, as Kenneth Young's biography avers, on 'the hard rock of the Party system that he stuck'.[77] Although Peel had obviously twice committed the 'unforgivable sin' of betraying his party, Balfour's sense of allegory went far deeper into his subconscious. After carefully probing for the motives behind his decision in 1910 with his official biographer eighteen years later Balfour concluded, almost as a revelation, that, ' "Ireland must have been the point—otherwise the remark I made about Peel would not apply." '78 It was also therefore in the murky bogs of Ireland that he stuck.

When the conference resumed its sittings on 1 November the leaders concurred that, aside from the definition of 'x', they seemed to be in substantial agreement on the treatment of ordinary and financial legislation. In a general way it was also agreed that constitutional questions should be subject to some further safeguards. That would 'put the fat in the fire', reckoned Lloyd George. The Conservatives would 'cry out Home Rule at once'. Recognizing home rule as the crux of their problems Lloyd George suggested three alternatives for dealing with it. The first was that a home rule bill should be presented to Parliament before a dissolution as ordinary legislation. This would elicit a specific reaction from the electorate at the ensuing election, much like a referendum. The second possibility was designed to take effect when a home rule bill passed by the Commons was rejected by the Lords. After a lapse of one or two years the bill would be introduced in a joint session for a decision. Presumably this would allow time for by-elections, or possibly a general election, to shed additional light on the question. The third alternative, which Lloyd George mentioned 'somewhat shyly and hurriedly "would be to see whether we could not agree upon Home Rule itself or some alternative to it" '. Upon consideration of these proposals Balfour thought the mere presentation of a bill as suggested in the first alternative would be of little value because it was the discussion in Parliament which educated public opinion. Asquith then suggested that they should say 'presented to and *passed through* the H. of C.', which the Conservatives recognized as 'a real concession'. Some discussion followed in which Asquith seemed to say that he thought this proposal could be made applicable to all organic legislation.79 Afterwards Chamberlain told his wife that 'the Govt. are longing to come to terms with us, if they can, without breaking with the Irish charmer altogether'.80

On the following day Balfour expressed approval of the Government's suggestion that their first alternative should receive 'general application'. As Chamberlain predicted, the Liberals drew back at once, saying that they had not contemplated adopting this method as a permanent procedure for all constitutional issues, but only in dealing with their present difficulty over home rule. Lloyd George further narrowed the field of discussion by proposing that the safeguard applied to home rule should continue in force until the bill had been '*once* submitted to the Commons and the Country'. After that it would on all occasions be treated as ordinary legislation. This provoked a renewal of the controversy over what subjects should be reserved and how they should ultimately be decided. In the latter context referendum was discussed extensively, but the Liberals manifestly refused any such mechanism. 'After all,' Asquith explained, 'you must think of those with whom you had to work and the Irish would never accept it.' Indeed their entire field of compromise was severely restricted by this inestimable outside factor. This was apparent when Balfour reiterated that his party considered only two subjects to fall within the purview of constitutional legislation—reform bills and home rule in any form. Asquith recognized that 'the real difficulty was Home Rule' as neither side would allow the conference to break up on 'One Man One Vote'.[81] 'Neither side can get over the Home Rule fence,' Chamberlain later told his wife, 'or (to speak more exactly) the Govt. cannot quarrel outright with the Irish. They are more afraid of them than their own followers.'[82] For both parties agreement was contingent on the other side relinquishing any decisive or permanent advantage on the Irish issue.

On 3 November discussion immediately converged on the topic of home rule, with the Conservatives demanding safeguards with or without the referendum alternative. 'Why should not the Govt. agree to this?' argued Balfour. 'We understood of course that they had to consider the Irish, but if the Irish were ready to accept this condition for the next fight, which was the one on which all their hopes and attention were concentrated—would they mind its being applied also to any future fight?' This proposition obviously carried a strong appeal to the more moderate Liberals as Birrell concurred with Asquith and Crewe on the apparent reasonableness of Balfour's overture. Birrell believed that '"the Irish as men of business would concentrate on x," i.e. the number of the Lords in the Joint Session. If they had a good x, they would be satisfied; if not, the reverse.' Lloyd George, however, differed vehemently with his colleagues and told Birrell that he had always objected to this proposal and absolutely refused to assent to it. This abrupt pronouncement had the effect of drawing the Liberals back to their old positions. Asquith thereupon repeated his party's objection to any distinction between organic and other forms of legislation, and the conference adjourned until the following day.[83]

This unreasonable stance enforced on the Liberal negotiators was reflected in a subsequent exchange of letters between Asquith and Balfour after the twentieth conference session. The Prime Minister insisted that his party was prepared to deal specially with home rule along the lines of Lloyd George's ultimatum, but in light of the concessions his side had already made on financial legislation he felt that no agreement was possible unless the machinery they were creating for ordinary legislation was made applicable to all bills.[84] This Balfour rightly regarded as a retrogression from the previous position the Liberals had assumed on reserved subjects.[85] Asquith responded that they had provisionally consented to special safeguards for such subjects as the Crown, the Protestant succession, and any agreement reached by their present conference. 'But the proposal now under consideration would include in the same category all Reform Bills, big or small, (including the abolition of plural voting), all forms of Home Rule from pure Parnellism to the most modest schemes of devolution, and indeed practically all measures of *political*, as distinguished from social or economic change. It is here where the shoe pinches so acutely that the party Govt. would in our judgement reject it as a misfit.'[86] The main point of this correspondence is that it reconfirmed the deadlock which had been reached in the conference over home rule. Realizing that no further departure was possible beyond those bounds circumscribed by Lloyd George, Asquith interpreted the Conservative position in a non-conciliatory manner. His belief that the Conservatives desired to safeguard nearly all measures of political change was an inaccurate appraisal of their intentions. Though this does not vindicate Balfour for not clarifying his party's position so as to close the loophole from which Asquith might honourably retreat, it does establish that Asquith had the best opening to break and Balfour allowed him to do so.

Yet Balfour harboured an afterthought. In an attempt to save the conference, or at least delay what appeared to be the inevitable outcome, he requested permission to report the situation to his parliamentary colleagues before definitely bringing the negotiations to a close. For this purpose he asked the Government on 4 November to give him some indication of the number they had in mind for 'x', realizing that 'it was not the main point between us or the one on which we had reached an *impasse*—but our colleagues would naturally ask us what sort of number the Govt. contemplated'. Asquith replied that according to the Ripon formula they were able to calculate a twenty-eight to seventy-two ratio, for a new majority of forty-four Unionists, in the House of Lords delegation in a joint sitting. In their discussion of these figures Asquith seemed to waver a bit, but he was kept solid by Lloyd George, who 'regarded 44 as a maximum'.[87] Once again the Liberals under the influence of their watchful Chancellor of the Exchequer resisted any concession, though seemingly minor, which might derogate from their moral commitment to home rule.

While the conference adjourned for the next six days Balfour attempted to deal with Lloyd George on an individual basis. No doubt recalling that his side had come closest to penetrating the Liberal phalanx when Birrell and Crewe had opined that the Irish might be satisfied 'if they had a good x', Balfour planned to negotiate a suitable 'x' with Lloyd George, whom he recognized as the major obstacle to agreement. This would enable the Conservatives effectively to block constitutional changes even when introduced under the rubric of ordinary legislation. No record of their discussion was kept, but a subsequent letter from F. E. Smith to Balfour reveals that the latter was willing to strike up a bargain 'agreeing to everything else', including presumably a one-time safeguard for home rule, for a Conservative majority of at least sixty in the House of Lords delegation in the joint session. Smith indicated that

... (a) 45 is definitely inadmissible but (b) 60 though difficult is possible. I know that a counter ultimatum agreeing to everything else (if again this is possible) but insisting upon 60 instead of 45 will receive powerful support both in the Cabinet and the Conference. I think that (accepting the above hypothesis) a bold counter ultimatum putting this forward would succeed.

I am not sure we can get this. I am positive we cannot get more and if we cannot carry our party on the basis of 60, let us break up and revert to fighting conditions.[88]

But Lloyd George proved stalwart in his opposition to this scheme from the outset. He later told Charles Masterman that he had refused to consent to a Conservative majority of more than forty, but added that 'I might have taken 60'. Lloyd George believed that Balfour would have accepted fifty, but evidently this number was not discussed. Masterman concluded that 'neither side in the Conference could face their own party without having previously weighted the agreement in their own favour, and neither party could yield this to the other side'.[89]

These observations were confirmed when the conference members consulted with their respective colleagues on the outside. On 8 November the Unionist four conferred with their principal followers at Lansdowne House. Responding to a summary of the conclusions of the conference prepared by Balfour, Sir Robert Finlay, former Attorney-General, complained that a Unionist majority of only forty-five in a Lords' joint sitting was 'purely illusory'. He also disliked the home rule provision 'that only one attempt should be safeguarded by a General Election' which would 'leave it open to any Government to get H. R. passed on subsequent occasions without consulting the people, for such subsequent Bills would be treated as ordinary legislation'. Others objected to the general lack of safeguards on constitutional subjects. The consensus seemed to be in favour of discontinuing the negotiations.[90] On the following day when these subjects were discussed by the Cabinet, Churchill passed a note on the back of an envelope to Lloyd George, 'I am going to suggest 60.' Lloyd George returned on the same paper, 'Anything over 40 I resign.'[91] With this staunch rebuttal any hope of a compromise ended and the interparty conference was quickly brought to a close. In due course Asquith was able to extract assurances, contingent on his party's victory in the next general election, that the King would create a sufficient number of peers to pass a Parliament Bill based on its earlier veto resolutions.[92] Meanwhile the House of Lords was given an opportunity to discuss this measure and to place its own plan—the Rosebery reform proposals—before the country. When the electorate returned substantially the same verdict as earlier in the year the dependence of the Liberals on their Irish and Labour allies was confirmed. With this support and the recent assurances from the King the Government was able to secure passage of the Parliament Bill, which restricted substantially the Lords' veto power, in the spring of 1911.

The most obvious effect of the constitutional conference of 1910 on this outcome was to delay a settlement of the House of Lords question for nearly six months after the death of King Edward. The conference, however, must be regarded as more than a delaying device because during the course of their twenty-two sittings the members of this colloquy wrestled with every form of constitutional change which confronted the nation. If it is treated as more than an intellectual exercise then it must be concluded that the conference was attempting, in the words of Asquith's biographers, 'nothing less than to convert the immemorial unwritten into a written constitution'.[93] In the course of these proceedings the concept of the interparty conference received an unprecedented recognition from the public, the politicians, and the press. This stemmed partially from the longevity of the sittings and the fact that they dealt with the leading controversial issues of the day. Additionally, in spite of their failure to agree on more substantial matters, the conference members did display confidence in this method by adopting a system of informal conferences and joint sessions in those areas in which they reached a tentative agreement. But more than any other way a coherent notion of the procedure of conciliation was formulated by the pen of F. S. Oliver. Significantly his inspiration was drawn not so much from earlier domestic precedents as from Britain's experience in imperial consultation in which his own ideas had played an important role.[94] As a result Oliver interpreted the 1910 gathering largely in terms of a constitutional convention which was an extension of earlier conference usages. Such a distinction was not misapplied as the constitutional conference dealt in a comprehensive fashion with issues which affected the very life and structure of the British constitution. Coincidentally it served to show the interrelatedness of various conciliatory techniques and anticipated the application of similar methods to future crises.

V

The Irish Crisis of 1913–1914

The nation is divided into parties, but the Crown is of no party.
Its apparent separation from business is that which removes
it both from enmities and from desecration, which preserves
its mystery, which enables it to combine the affection of conflicting parties—to be a visible symbol of unity to those still
so imperfectly educated as to need a symbol.

WALTER BAGEHOT[1]

The passage of the Parliament Act of 1911 shifted the centre
of parliamentary activity from the House of Lords to Ireland.
The ensuing political crisis which converged on Ulster was
merely a phase of a continuing and larger British constitutional
struggle. The Act of Union was as sacred an article of Conservative faith as the integrity of the powers of the House of Lords
and was entitled to special protection. Since Gladstone first
raised the possibility of Irish political separation in 1886 and
again in 1893 home rule aroused the strongest passions in both
political parties. The recent Liberal Government, however,
had gone much further than the 'grand old man' by effectively
destroying the veto power of the upper house. Now with the
union of Ireland threatened by the Liberal alliance with Irish
nationalism, good Unionists on both islands decided that un-
lawful resistance was the only way to thwart the will of the
House of Commons. Speaking at Blenheim shortly after the introduction of the home rule bill in 1912, Andrew Bonar Law,
the Conservative Party leader, declared that his party would
not be restrained by the bonds that influenced it in a normal
political struggle. In fact he could imagine 'no length of resistance to which Ulster will go' in which he would 'not be ready
to support them'.[2] In 1913 F. E. Smith, later Lord Birkenhead,
made a frank revelation of Unionist motives to Sir Edward Carson, the Ulster Unionist leader: 'We should always remember
that we are now for the first time given a chance of resisting
the Parliament Act in operation. That Act was revolutionary,

perhaps we have our one and only chance of destroying it by
counter-revolutionary means.'[3] Thus Conservatives were intent
upon resisting home rule not simply for its own sake, but as
a means of redressing the constitutional imbalance created by
their recent defeat in the upper house.

This breach between the parties before the war was lessened
somewhat by the application of conciliatory techniques developed during the nineteenth century in which the monarchy
had often played an important role. As previously related,
Queen Victoria mediated such problems as Irish disestablishment and parliamentary reform by encouraging conferences of
party leaders. Later these methods were revived to deal with
other legislative crises, but the task of conciliation was rendered
more difficult by the intensification of party spirit after 1906.
For this reason King Edward and others were unable to compose party differences over the education bill of that year, which
had constitutional overtones. Nor was the constitutional conference, educed by his death in 1910, able to heal party enmities. But the monarchy played a critical, though passive, role
by acting as a justification for the suspension of party strife. The
political struggle finally reached its highwater mark in 1914
over Ireland. King George V, who was drawn to the centre
of the controversy over the possible use of his veto prerogative,
used his influence instead to encourage a reconciliation between
the parties. The mediation of this imbroglio, which was presaged by disagreements over Ireland in 1910 when the King
was relegated to observer status, required that he exert to the
utmost his powers of persuasion and conciliation.[4] The Irish
crisis also provided the most severe test yet for the conference
method, not so much as a means to resolve the home rule controversy, but seemingly to forestall the possibility of a civil war.

The King first became aware of the necessity for his intervention when he visited Liverpool in the summer of 1913. He
sensed among its large Irish population a feeling of frustration
and concern over the militant activities of Protestants in Ulster.
On 24 July the King disclosed his feelings to Augustine Birrell,
the Irish Secretary. His concern for Ireland, though genuine,
was increased by the fact that the home rule bill made his position as sovereign most difficult. Birrell realized that His Majesty
'was being pressed to entertain the idea ... of forcing a *dissolu-*

tion next year' which would bring the issue before the people.[5]
The Opposition was, in fact, demanding this, and more. At the
King's request Lord Lansdowne and Bonar Law had composed
their views in a memorandum. The Conservatives advised a
dissolution as the most logical course of royal intervention, but
suggested that the veto might be used as a last resort to prevent
violence in Ulster.[6] It is doubtful whether King George ever
seriously considered adopting either of these alternatives. But
if he was unwilling to lead the monarchy on a disastrous course
outlined by the Conservatives, it is equally certain that he
would not allow the Government to follow a policy of drift in
Ireland and carry the monarch with it. On board his yacht,
the *Britannia*, in early August, the King carefully reviewed his
position and decided to ask the Prime Minister for his views
on the situation. King George feared that vigorous action by
himself on behalf of either side would place the monarchy in
a very embarrassing position and subject it to the vituperation
of the conflicting party presses. Under these circumstances the
King viewed his own role in the polity as no mere symbol of
authority or as a passive extension of ministerial responsibility.
'In this period', he told Asquith, 'I shall have a right to expect
the greatest confidence and support from my Ministers, and,
above all from my Prime Minister.' The best arrangement, he
reasoned, would be to allow Ulster to contract out of home rule
for ten years, after which a referendum would be held. Otherwise they should try to reach a settlement on the larger issue
of devolution by calling a conference of all parties. 'Would it
not be better', he queried, 'to try to settle measures involving
great changes in the Constitution, such as Home Rule all round,
Reform of the House of Lords etc., not on Party lines, but by
agreement?'[7]

Instead of inspiring Asquith to action, the King's letter
touched off a debate over the constitutional powers of the
monarchy. In early September Asquith prepared two papers,
dealing with the constitutional position of the Sovereign and
the Irish question. In the first the Prime Minister pointed out
that the Crown had not exercised its veto power for over two
hundred years and that in the last resort the monarch must act
upon the advice of his ministers. Asquith admitted that the
Sovereign may have lost some of his personal power and auth-

ority, 'but the Crown had been thereby removed from the storms and vicissitudes of party politics'. Asquith added that the King undoubtedly had the power of changing his advisers, although they still possessed the confidence of the House of Commons. But this had been done only once during the last 130 years 'by one of the least wise of British monarchs'. If the King were to intervene in this way, he would be dragged into the arena of politics and 'it is no exaggeration to say that the Crown would become the football of contending factions'.[8] As for the Irish difficulty, the Prime Minister recognized the danger of organized violence in Ulster, but he he did not think it would lead to civil war. Besides, a reversal of the Government's policy would only increase the likelihood of armed uprisings among the Catholics in southern Ireland. Fearful of jeopardizing his Government before its mission was accomplished, Asquith completely discounted the possibility of a general election. Nor was a conference as suggested by the King a way out. It seemed unlikely to him that either Carson or Redmond would accept an invitation from any quarter 'to come into a room, and sit round a table for the purpose of talking in the air' about devolution or any other topic.[9] Asquith's arguments aroused strong feelings in the King. In his lengthy reply (which is quoted in full by Nicolson), the King cited appropriate passages of Erskine May and Bagehot to uphold his authority and he argued lucidly against every point made by the Prime Minister.[10]

The King's notions of his role as mediator to the crisis in Ireland were also clarified in a conversation with Lord Crewe, still Liberal leader in the upper house, where His Majesty repudiated the imprudent demand that he use his veto power or dissolve Parliament before the next session. But Crewe reported that the King

is not consoled by the doctrine that he had nothing to do but to sit still and take his Ministers' advice, because he feels that in such a situation either his father or his grandmother would have been able to use influence which would have prevented a collision. He is therefore haunted, not by the dread of having to assent to the Bill (or at least not by this in the main). But by the feeling that if he does not take off his coat and work for a settlement of some kind, and there is serious loss of life after the Bill passes he will not only be held responsible by the opposition partisans, but will actually be so to some extent.[11]

The urgent need to settle the Ulster problem and the traditions of royal intervention involving the advocacy of interparty negotiation strongly influenced the King's conduct over the next year; and the simple logic of impartial mediation undoubtedly had a strong appeal to the orderly mind of the sailor King.

Throughout the autumn the King held numerous conversations at Balmoral where he urged conciliation on the leaders of both parties.[12] In mid-September Bonar Law found the King much impressed with a letter that Lord Loreburn, the former Lord Chancellor, had recently published in *The Times*. This was a formal appeal for a conference of party leaders held in the strictest confidence and without prejudice. Loreburn had noted that in Gladstone's time the extension of the franchise was arranged by mutual consent with Queen Victoria's encouragement, the Irish agrarian question was settled satisfactorily by conferences between Irishmen during Balfour's administration, and an effort was made to apply the same formula in 1910 to the House of Lords question without success. He thought British politicians must either make their party system more elastic by 'the more fruitful method of legislation by consent' or else abandon it altogether.[13] Bonar Law assured the King that if the Government invited them to take part in a free conference or an informal meeting to discuss whether a conference was possible, his party would be willing to participate in it. The King's constitutional position was also discussed at length, which revealed a somewhat exalted Conservative view of the powers of the monarchy. Bonar Law intimated that if the King was not satisfied with his ministers' advice, he had the right to summon other ministers who would advise him differently. Acting on their advice, he would be able to dissolve Parliament so as to ascertain the will of the people. Should the position of the Crown become untenable the King told Bonar Law that he intended to write his ministers a formal letter, which he would reserve the right to make public if he dismissed them. This would justify his action and point out the necessity of a general election. Bonar Law thought such a letter, if carefully worded and written with a view to the effect it might have on public opinion, might well terminate the crisis.[14]

In the meantime Winston Churchill, who had also talked to

the King, used the leisure atmosphere at the castle to facilitate a possible negotiation between party leaders. On 17 September Churchill reported to Asquith that he had been playing golf with Bonar Law. The latter, he insisted, was in favour of a conference, not only to discuss the exclusion of Ulster, but also to consider the possibility of establishing a federal system in the United Kingdom and even such topics as second chamber reform.[15] The next logical step was for the Prime Minister to open *pourparlers* with the Opposition, but Asquith was reluctant to summon a meeting of leaders to discuss the possible exclusion of Ulster without Irish support and representation.[16] Similarly F. E. Smith, whose position in the Unionist Party was in many ways analogous to that of Churchill in the Government, took a primary role in the negotiations. At the army manœuvres, which were held 24–5 September in Northampton, he carried on lengthy conversations with the King and Churchill. The King returned from the exercises full of his talk with Smith and had Lord Stamfordham, his private secretary, write to Bonar Law. It was Smith's opinion that Carson would favour any arrangement that would exclude Ulster from home rule. Although Churchill warned that royal intervention was a 'dangerous card to play', Stamfordham assured Bonar Law that the King 'is ready to help in any way possible to arrive at a satisfactory solution: but he would not propose an informal meeting as a preliminary to a conference, unless he felt assured of a successful result of his action'.[17] Several days later, however, Stamfordham informed Bonar Law that the Government would not call a conference because it would look as if they were doing it out of fear of armed rebellion in Ulster. He therefore suggested that the proposal for a conference should come from the Conservative side.[18] The Unionist leaders, particularly Lansdowne, resented these messages. 'H.M. and Stamfordham have been completely misled by F. E.'s indiscretions,' he asserted. 'Nothing would induce me to go into conference upon such terms.'[19] Bonar Law was no less offended by Smith's activities, but he realized it would be unfortunate if a conference did not take place simply because of the reluctance of the leaders on either side to make the first move. This difficulty could be surmounted most easily, he thought, if the King would invite the leaders to confer, as in that case neither party could refuse.[20]

On 6 October, on the heels of the vast procession of politicians who had visited the King, Asquith arrived at Balmoral. After three days of conversations with the King, the Prime Minister was still not convinced that a conference would serve any useful purpose. It would prove to be either 'a tea party or a bear garden'. Asquith did, however, promise the King that he would arrange a private conversation with the Conservative chief to determine whether any basis for a fuller conference existed.[21] On 14 October Asquith met Bonar Law at the home of Sir Max Aitken (later Lord Beaverbrook) at Cherkley Court near Leatherhead. After an initial disagreement over who had originally suggested their meeting, both leaders pointed out the difficulties in their respective positions which prevented them from giving way.[22] Asquith's position no doubt was circumscribed by a caveat from Redmond in a speech on the 12th that 'Irish Nationalists can never be assenting parties to the mutilation of the Irish nation; Ireland is a unit. The two-nation theory is to us an abomination and a blasphemy.'[23] Bonar Law considered the solution to be a general election, the verdict of which the Unionists (though not Carson) were willing to accept. Asquith did not agree, and stated that a general election was inevitable in any case before the bill was brought into operation. Bonar Law then outlined the lengths to which the Unionist Party was willing to go to force a general election. This surprised Asquith and reminded him of the Opposition leader's notorious Blenheim speech. Bonar Law pointed out that he 'had carefully read what had been said on the subject in 1886 and 1893' by Lord Salisbury and other Conservative leaders and what he had said at Blenheim was substantially the same. As to a possible compromise, Bonar Law expressed the opinion that home rule should be given to Ireland, with the exclusion of Ulster. By this, he admitted, he was prepared 'to throw the Unionist minority in the S and W to the wolves'. The crucial question of defining Ulster, on which negotiations ultimately broke down, was not discussed. For the present they decided to leave the controversial boundary of Ulster as 'x'.[24]

During the next fortnight the King and his private secretary pressed the leaders to exercise moderation in their public statements and to continue their meetings. On 29 October Asquith and Bonar Law met again at Aitken's and went over much the

same ground as in their previous talk. This time, however, differences of opinion finally emerged over the geographical
definition of Ulster. Bonar Law was sure that Carson would
settle for nothing less than the whole province, while Asquith
not unreasonably argued that it would be impossible to include
Donegal, Monaghan, and Cavan with their huge Catholic
majorities; and he was doubtful whether it would be wise to
include Tyrone and Fermanagh where the proportion of Catholics to Protestants was about six to five. In any case Asquith
pointed out that nothing further could be accomplished until
he discussed the matter with his Cabinet and the Nationalist
leaders.[25] On 17 November Asquith told Redmond that he had
discussed the alternative of excluding Ulster for a period of
years with Bonar Law. According to Redmond, Asquith had
given 'no countenance whatever to this idea'. He also informed
Redmond of an ingenious proposal, which Lloyd George had
submitted to the Cabinet the previous Wednesday, whereby
Ulster would be exempted from home rule for five or six years
and then automatically included. 'This ... would make immediate rebellion premature and ridiculous, and would give the
Tories the chance of 1 or 2 elections before the automatic inclusion became effective.' Neither this proposal nor any other
plan for the exclusion of Ulster was acceptable to Redmond
or Dillon. Redmond replied that he could accept such a plan
only as a last resort; for the present, he could offer Ulster no
more than administrative autonomy and additional powers in
the Irish Parliament. In conclusion Asquith gave the distinct
impression that he was not prepared to make any proposals
until the end of the year, and definitely not without consulting
first with the Irish.[26]

During the next several weeks, while Churchill intrigued and
Asquith sat on the Irish issue, no further steps were taken to
implement the exclusion of Ulster. The King, however, was
disturbed by the tone of some recent speeches. He again coaxed
Asquith to continue his negotiations with Bonar Law, which
were resumed on 10 December.[27] Here neither leader was very
sanguine of a settlement. Bonar Law regarded Lloyd George's
scheme of exclusion followed by automatic inclusion as a 'hopeless solution'. Redmond's idea of complete autonomy within
home rule was simply out of the question. What the Conserva-

tives demanded was absolute exclusion of Ulster. Bonar Law felt that the Prime Minister had 'no hope whatever of making such an arrangement'.[28] With the Bonar Law talks at a standstill, Asquith approached Carson on 16 December, who suggested some form of exclusion that would eventually lead to a general scheme of devolution.[29] Asquith apparently thought he could persuade Carson to settle for something less than total exclusion as long as he acted on these guidelines. His subsequent plan envisaged the creation of home rule for Ulster within home rule for Ireland, to be followed by a general scheme of devolution.[30] By exclusion, Carson testily responded, 'I meant that Ulster shd. remain as at present under the Imperial Parlmt. and that a Dublin Parliament should have no Legislative powers within the excluded area. ... I do not think I can say anything more specific.'[31] This abrupt answer to Asquith's carefully prepared scheme indicated a serious lack of understanding between the parties and a certain exasperation over the lack of any progress towards a settlement. By mid-January of 1914 when Asquith visited the continent, the negotiations had ground to a complete halt.

The only solution at this point seemed to rest in the resolve of the King to bring peace to his troubled country. He revealed his determination to Stamfordham to persuade the politicians to reach an agreement and to do everything in his power to prevent civil war in Ireland. He candidly confessed that he was worried. 'But I am not discouraged, and, with your kind help, common sense, good judgement and advice, I think I shall come out on top; at least I mean to try to!'[32] For the next few months the King and his private secretary continued to urge the party leaders to resume their negotiations, but to no avail. On 26 January Bonar Law told Stamfordham that he saw little value in continuing their talks, since his interviews with Asquith and those with Carson revealed that the Prime Minister would take no step without the approval of his Nationalist allies.[33] When Asquith visited Windsor on 5 February, the King again urged him to hold a general election. Asquith replied, however, that an appeal to the people would solve nothing and that the responsibility in any case rested not with the King, but with his ministers. Still the King felt he could not allow bloodshed among his subjects without doing his utmost to avert it. He declared his willingness to see the Prime Minister at any time and to send for anyone to induce an agreement by consent.[34] Later in the month Stamfordham, by the King's desire, visited Carson at his home. Carson complained that the Government was blowing hot and cold on the subject of exclusion and expressed doubt whether Ulster would remain quiet much longer. What the Conservative leaders desired was a decisive stand instead of the dilatory course the Government was pursuing.[35]

Finally, as a result of negotiations carried out by Birrell and Lloyd George in early March, Redmond agreed to a plan whereby Ulster would be given the right to exclude itself by plebiscite for a period of years.[36] The King urged the Opposition to consider the Government's new proposals thoroughly. 'Please understand', he told Bonar Law, 'that the last thing I wish to do, is to interfere with your policy. You know my one object is to secure a peaceful solution.'[37] Asquith's offer to exclude Ulster for a six-year period, however, was not welcomed by the Conservatives in the House of Commons. Bonar Law and Carson demanded that exclusion be absolute and without a time limit. 'We do not want', the latter insisted, 'a sentence of death with a stay of execution for six years.'[38] Redmond could go no further. On 19 March the King and his Prime Minister reviewed the dismal prospects of the future. Asquith asserted that 'it was only out of great consideration for the King that he had gone on trying these weary months to effect a settlement'. Throughout, the King had, he considered, behaved in 'exactly the manner a Constitutional Sovereign should act'.[39] Still the parties were hardly any closer to a solution than they had been eight months earlier.

On 6 April the home rule bill passed its second reading in the House of Commons for the third and final time. By this time the air was full of compromise proposals from moderates in all quarters.[40] The King and Stamfordham continued to work for a resumption of interparty talks. In response to their wishes Asquith promised that he would communicate with Bonar Law and Carson once more.[41] When he did not act by the first of May the King obtained the consent of James W. Lowther, the Speaker of the House of Commons, to preside over a conference between the two parties.[42] These arrangements were unnecessary, however, as the Cabinet instructed Asquith to renew his conversations with the Opposition, which pleased the King.[43] In their meeting on 5 May Bonar Law and Carson told the Prime Minister that he had three choices before him: to coerce Ulster, to exclude Ulster, or to hold a general election. The first alternative was impossible for the Unionists; Asquith refused to admit the possibility of the third. On the subject of excluding Ulster they decided to delay the issue by an amending bill which would be introduced and placed on the statute book simultaneously with the original bill. This action would have the effect of excluding Ulster from the operation of the bill until a final settlement could be adjusted.[44] On 12 May the Prime Minister announced in the House of Commons that his Government would follow this procedure. The King welcomed the intention of the leaders to agree on the terms of the bill and presumed 'that they may now realize that they are dealing not with a mere party question, but with one of National and Constitutional importance'.[45]

Although these plans removed the urgency of dealing with the crisis in Ulster, they did not obviate the necessity of reaching a compromise on exclusion. By the early summer unofficial mediation attempts were being executed by Harold Harmsworth, the newspaper magnate recently created Lord Rothermere. With the assistance of Lord Murray of Elibank, former Liberal whip, Rothermere parleyed individually with leaders from both parties. He assured Bonar Law that 'Lord M and myself are doing nothing but attending to this matter. We shall not leave a stone unturned.'[46] The substance of these consultations dealt with the area which was to be excluded from home rule. While the Nationalists desired a simple county option method, Carson and Bonar Law insisted on a rather unusual area consisting of 'Antrim, Down, Derry, Tyrone, North and Mid-Armagh, and North Fermanagh, and Derry City', where a plebiscite would determine not only whether Ulster would enter a home rule parliament, but when it would do so. For Redmond these demands were simply impossible.[47] Nevertheless by mid-July plans were set in motion for an actual meeting between party leaders. With great reluctance Bonar Law consented to meet Asquith and his colleagues in a formal conference—provided it was summoned by the King.[48] It was thereupon decided that the King, at the behest of the Prime

Minister, should invite the leaders of the British and Irish parties to confer at Buckingham Palace under the chairmanship of the Speaker.[49]

Asquith's announcement of the arrangements for an inter-party conference, however, was not generally greeted with favour in the House of Commons. Lest it appear that one side was weakening in its position, both Redmond and Bonar Law made it clear that they were attending the conference only because it was a 'command' of the King.[50] It was also evident that these statements served to counteract any possible charges that the action of the party leaders constituted an excessive usurpation of authority. In the House of Lords one Liberal peer, Lord Courtney of Penwith, expressed the fear that the conference would be regarded by the rest of the world as 'a supersession of Parliament'. Lord Crewe reminded his colleague of a similar application of this method in 1910 and assured him that there was no possibility that the authority of Parliament was in danger.[51] *The Times*, in comparing present conciliation efforts with the conference of party leaders in 1884, recalled the happy solution it had reached.[52] The *Manchester Guardian*, edited by C. P. Scott, cited similar precedents and regarded 'the convening of a conference by the King of the leaders of parties' as 'a quite new precedent in the political history of England'.[53] No one, however, with the possible exception of the King, expressed more than cautious optimism that the conference would be able to resolve the differences between the parties over Ireland.

On 21 July, just after the changing of the guard, the Buckingham Palace conference met for the first time. With Asquith, Lloyd George, Redmond, and Dillon on one side, and Bonar Law, Lansdowne, Carson, and Captain James Craig on the other, the King made an opening statement. 'My intervention at this moment may be regarded as a new departure,' he explained. 'But the exceptional circumstances under which you are brought together justify my action.' He urged the leaders to be earnest and conciliatory.[54] Much of the meeting, however, was consumed by a dispute over what they should discuss. The Unionists wanted to start with the time limit for the exclusion of Ulster; Redmond insisted that they could not discuss that issue unless the question of area was settled. Bonar Law and

Carson eventually gave way, but only on the condition that anything said by them was based on the assumption that the time limit was abandoned. This unpromising beginning was followed by a complete disagreement over the area to be excluded. Redmond pressed for the adoption of a county option plan which would bring those areas with a majority of Catholics under home rule. In a memorandum which he read to the conference Redmond argued that 'the only principle which appeared defensible, was that, so far as practicable, those districts should be *ex*cluded in which the popularity was predominantly Unionist and those districts should be *in*cluded in which the population was predominantly Nationalist'. But even this arrangement, he calculated, would not be equitable to his party.

If the counties of Antrim, Down, Derry and Armagh and the borough of Belfast were excluded by the operation of county option, then 293,483 Catholics would be excluded from the operation of the Home Rule Bill, and these some of the most passionate Nationalists in Ireland; whereas in Cavan, Donegal, Fermanagh, Monaghan, Tyrone and Derry Borough, which presumably, would be included on voting, only 179,113 Protestants would be included within the jurisdiction of the Irish Parliament.[55]

Carson, however, insisted on the whole province of Ulster, adding as a bait that the more Catholics excluded, the more likely it would ultimately opt for inclusion under a Dublin Parliament. According to Bonar Law's account, Redmond and Dillon admitted that if they were 'free agents' this is the plan they would accept. Yet both agreed that neither of them could accept such a scheme and still have a party behind them. Further discussion therefore of excluding Ulster totally was hopeless.[56]

The King's opening statement, which was published with the approval of the conference the following day, provoked an uproar in the press. The radical *Daily News & Leader* called the conference 'a Royal coup d'état' and compared King George's attitude with that of the Czar of Russia to his Duma.[57] The *Morning Post*, the chief Conservative mouthpiece, defended the King by stating that it was the Government who had advised him to call a conference and to deliver a speech. This procedure was followed allegedly because the House of Commons was 'bankrupt' in statesmanship. 'The Army counts, the House of

Lords counts, the King counts; but the House of Commons is treated with contempt by the Government which pretended to make it supreme.'[58] E. H. Mair, C. P. Scott's man at Westminster, told his chief that 'the crucial thing now is the enormous innovation implied in the King's speech. If it is going to be admitted without protest or question that what he said was on his own responsibility and that ministers are not responsible for it then I am afraid every text book on English constitutional history will have to be rewritten.' Mair feared the King's intervention had set a dangerous precedent. The Sovereign might try to form a king's party as George III did or act apart from his Government and make pronouncements on his own as the German emperor was accustomed to doing.[59] Evidence, in fact, reveals that the King had composed the speech himself and later submitted it to Asquith, who then showed it to the Cabinet.[60] Whether this act violated constitutional procedure is debatable; what is certain is that the King convened the Buckingham Palace conference with a full awareness of constitutional propriety and with the belief that a conference was the only possible method of securing peace for Ireland.

On 22 July at the second session of the conference the King's speech furnished the initial topic for discussion. With the view of sparing the King from any unpleasant involvement in party politics, the leaders agreed to arrange a question in the House of Commons whereby Asquith could take full responsibility for the King's action. Inasmuch as total exclusion was utterly objectionable to Redmond and county option was equally anathema to Carson the remainder of the meeting was consumed by a discussion of possibly dividing Ulster. Division on the basis of poor law unions was discussed at first, but it was agreed that 'any such scheme would involve a system of what might be called swapping districts in different parts of Ulster, which was universally agreed to be an impossible thing'. Carson then stated that 'so far as Tyrone was concerned, he was unable even if his judgement led him in that direction, to agree to the INclusion of any part of the county in the jurisdiction of the Home Rule Parliament. Mr. Redmond made a similar declaration with reference to the EXclusion of any part of Tyrone.' When the same situation arose with regard to county Fermanagh, Carson substituted an alternative proposal whereby a six-county block consisting of Antrim, Down, Armagh, Derry, Tyrone and Fermanagh would be excluded as a single unit. Redmond, however, stated that 'he could not seriously consider this proposal, any more than the proposal for the total EXclusion of Ulster'. It was quite apparent that a total deadlock had been reached and the question arose whether there was any valid reason for continuing the conference.[61]

When the conference met again on 23 July there was considerable map study and examination of population figures. Again Carson's suggestion for the total exclusion of Ulster or even the six so-called 'Plantation counties' received no encouragement from the Nationalists. Then Asquith suggested the exclusion of an unwieldy, though fairly homogeneous, area consisting of the four north-eastern counties with the exception of south Armagh. To these would be added the Protestant strongholds of south Tyrone and north Fermanagh. So unfavourable were both groups of Irishmen to this illogical proposal that it was not seriously considered. Neither party, it appeared, was willing to allow any disputed districts, most specifically Tyrone, to fall under the jurisdiction of its opponent. The Prime Minister then suggested 'with great diffidence' that

If an agreement could be come to on everything else except Tyrone, that some impartial authority might be selected who would undertake the task of fairly dividing Tyrone.

Sir Edward Carson and Mr. Redmond both pointed out that the problem had not been narrowed down to the question of Tyrone, by any means; that it would be quite untrue to say that, if the Conference failed, it would be due solely to the question of Tyrone; and that, even if this were so, the suggestion was an impracticable one, without first coming to agreement as the principle upon which such an impartial person as was mentioned was to act; and that this seemed fatal, even without the difficulty of obtaining the service of such an impartial person.[62]

In an effort to save the conference, the Speaker suggested that Tyrone should go into the excluded area for the present, with the right to vote for or against exclusion in one or two years. For Carson acceptance of this proposal would have been tantamount to deserting those covenanters in the three Nationalist counties he had promised not to abandon. For Redmond it would admit the possibility, *inter alia*, of discrimination by the Unionist employers who dominated the area against hiring Catholic workers. By now it was obvious that neither side was hopeful of a settlement. Nothing remained except to decide the nature of the report to be released; yet even on this seemingly insignificant point the conference could not agree. Redmond believed that any disclosure that the conference had broken down over the exclusion of Ulster implied that he had agreed to this principle, an admission he did not wish to make public.[63]

The following day the conference members drew up a general statement of their discussions which the Prime Minister read later to the House of Commons. At the conclusion of the sittings the King conducted a private interview with each participant. Although the conference had broken down, the King was delighted that Redmond and Carson had met one another in such an amiable and conciliatory manner. He still clung to the hope that some arrangement might be found to prevent bloodshed in Ireland. For Redmond it was the first audience he had ever had with the King.[64] As the Speaker and others waited in the adjoining room, they noticed in *The Times* the news of Austria's ultimatum to Serbia. This situation was regarded as very serious, and began to divert the attention of the nation from Ireland to the continent. As Churchill later commented: 'The parish of Fermanagh and Tyrone faded back into the mists and squalls of Ireland, and a strange light began immediately, but by perceptible gradations, to fall and grow upon the map of Europe.'[65]

By the time war intervened the King had been working for over a year to bring peace to Ireland. The most that can be said for the interparty negotiations, which he did so much to bring about, is that they helped avert violence in Ireland by causing delay and provided a safety-valve for the release of party tensions. Aside from this, the Buckingham Palace conference and the extensive mediation efforts which preceded it must be regarded as an unmitigated failure. Regardless of the good intentions of the King, his efforts were doomed because he was acting alone and was unable to generate the necessary goodwill and trust which is basic to the success of any conference. The interparty negotiations of 1913 and 1914 were carried out merely as a gesture to please the King and moderate public opinion. They showed, perhaps better than any previous gatherings, that the mere formality of calling party leaders together will not automatically produce an agreement. The lack of spontaneity and the absence of desire in either party to settle the Irish question, except on its own terms, effectively negated the King's efforts. That he failed to extort a settlement cannot, therefore, be attributed to want of trying. King George utilized all his known resources to preserve the integrity of the British constitution and to enhance the monarchy as a symbol of national unity. But the roots of intransigence in Ulster and the Unionist Party were too deeply embedded in British politics to permit a settlement by resort to the momentary scrutiny of a few conferences.

What was needed perhaps in 1914 was not a conference in the traditional sense, as the concept had developed in the late nineteenth century, but a coalition government which could formulate a compromise on a broader and more continuous basis. Indeed it was this form of conciliation to which the sovereign resorted in 1916 and 1931 to deal with the exigencies of war and depression; and it was ultimately by means of a coalition in 1921 that a settlement was reached on the Irish question. But by the outbreak of the First World War this form of government had not been used in Britain for nearly half a century and the concept had fallen into a state of relative obscurity. Even had the King suggested the idea of a coalition to the party leaders there is little likelihood that it would have been accepted as a method which would eventually solve the Irish problem. Furthermore the King was powerless to implement such a change without the authorization of the people through their elected representatives. Even his limited intervention in calling the Buckingham Palace conference aroused radical accusations that he was exceeding his authority as a constitutional monarch. What was required on the part of British politicians by the summer of 1914 was a greater realization that the Irish question was no longer simply the latest stage of a continuing British constitutional struggle. It had escalated into a national crisis which required extraordinary solutions.

VI

The Irish Negotiations of 1916

The only way to deal with Ireland is for some one to open
a sluice and submerge her.

DAVID LLOYD GEORGE[1]

The outbreak of world war in 1914 instituted a national emergency in Britain which gradually ameliorated the relations
between the political parties. In the two years following the collapse of the Buckingham Palace conference English and, for the
most part, Irish politicians set aside their previous differences
and united in a common effort to win the war. Party loyalties
loosened with the formation of the Asquith coalition in May
of 1915, and Conservative resentment stemming from the Parliament Act and the provisional passage of home rule seemed
to fall into abeyance. In the course of this interregnum from
the normal operation of party government an effort was made
on both sides to effect a spirit of conciliation for the sake of
national unity. In August 1915, following passage of the
National Registration Act, another conference was held at
Buckingham Palace between national leaders to determine
whether and under what conditions compulsory military service should be introduced. Although this gathering was not significant enough to deserve separate attention here, it constituted one of many signs of national co-operation to forestall
possible dissension.[2] Even Ireland, which had been on the brink
of civil war only a short time earlier, now appeared to be lan-
guishing into an uneasy calm. At least this was the situation
until April of 1916. On Easter Monday, the 24th, a handful
of Irishmen representing what was then only a minority point
of view made a courageous but ill-fated assault on British authority in Ireland. Owing to the serious consequences any further
unrest might have on the war effort and opinion in America,
and to the necessity for a better government in Ireland, another
attempt had to be made at a home rule settlement.

For this purpose Lloyd George was selected by the Cabinet as mediator. But his task was a formidable one. It required not merely a reformulation of proposals along the lines discussed by Nationalists and Ulstermen before the war, but an appreciation of the fact that political power in Ireland was gradually shifting to the more extremist elements on both sides which had arisen in the wake of the rebellion. Contrary to the generally centripetal tendencies prevailing in British politics, opinion in Ireland was gravitating away from the provisional terms under which home rule was proffered and towards a position of total independence.[3] It was absolutely imperative that Lloyd George capitalize on the spirit of co-operation generated by the war by calling a conference of party leaders before those forces militating against a home rule settlement had an opportunity to materialize fully. A coalition *cum* conference combination might prove to be the most successful formula in bringing about a settlement. Whether these devices could counter the propensities towards extremism and violence depended the future of Ireland, the credibility of the Government, and possibly even Britain's success in the war.

The initial basis for an accord in Ireland was laid just after the rebellion when John Redmond and Sir Edward Carson joined together in the House of Commons on 27 April in denouncing the recent rebellion.[4] During the next several weeks Carson in particular showed an unusual degree of willingness to co-operate with his Nationalist counterpart in suppressing the disloyal elements in the south, which constituted a threat to both parties. The declarations of the two leaders revealing this common purpose suggested that they might be willing to reach a settlement on the home rule question and thereby blot out the ambitious Sinn Fein Party altogether. This was the idea of Colonel Winston Churchill, who suddenly appeared in the house on 9 May during a debate on whether to include Ireland in the Government's military service bill. He stated that the future of Ireland rested in the hands of Redmond and Carson. 'Together, there is hardly any difficulty which they cannot surmount. . . . I believe this is a time when metals are molten and could easily be cast into new shapes and new moulds. The tragic episodes of Dublin have at any rate shown Nationalists and Orangemen that they have opponents whom they can recognise as opponents at home in common, as well as the foes whom they have recognised since the War began as enemies abroad.'[5] Interviews carried out concurrently by C. P. Scott reinforced this judgement by indicating that Irish statesmen were in greater harmony than at any time since the beginning of the war. Neither Carson nor Redmond seemed averse to an early settlement, though both felt that it would be necessary for the Government to impose terms on the opposing parties.[6] There was little doubt that either leader would be able to commit his respective colleagues to terms on which the two sides might agree. This would furnish a sound basis for a possible resumption of the Buckingham Palace talks.

The resignation of Augustine Birrell as Irish Chief Secretary after the Easter rebellion had thrust the burden of formulating a new Irish policy on the Prime Minister. After setting up a commission to inquire into the causes of the rebellion under Lord Hardinge of Penshurst, Asquith decided to visit Ireland to examine first-hand the conditions in that country. From 12 to 19 May he travelled around Ireland holding consultations with government officials, soldiers, employers, prominent citizens, and even prisoners. In Belfast considerable concern was expressed by the Lord Mayor and numerous Carsonites over the possibility of an invasion from the south. The great majority of them, he noted, 'were clearly of the opinion that the only way of escape was by prompt settlement of the whole problem'. Likewise Nationalists, such as the Roman Catholic Bishop of Cork, seemed to be inclining in the same direction. Asquith concluded that the Nationalists, with the exception of the O'Brienites, would be willing to settle for 'the total exclusion (for the time at any rate) of Ulster. It appears to me to be the immediate duty of the Government to do everything in their power to force a general settlement.' This information was submitted to the Cabinet in a tripartite memorandum at a meeting on 21 May. To allay any misgivings of the Conservatives it included the stipulation that 'the Home Rule Act, however amended, cannot come into operation until the end of the war' and that in the meantime there should be a single minister responsible for overseeing Irish administration.[7] To this end he asked Lloyd George to accept the post of Chief Secretary. After considering this proposal for a brief period Lloyd George declined, but consented, with the approval of the Cabinet, to inquire whether there was any possibility of an agreement between Nationalists and Ulstermen and upon what terms an amending bill to the Government of Ireland Act might be secured.[8]

The Prime Minister's announcement on 25 May of the Government's new Irish policy was enthusiastically welcomed by the House of Commons and the press. *The Times* greeted Lloyd George's appointment as 'the opening of a new chapter in Irish politics'.[9] As Minister of Munitions his performance, at least in popular estimation, was the most outstanding of any Cabinet minister. In this sense Asquith was using his best 'trouble shooter' to cope with Britain's foremost constitutional problem. To the extent that Asquith's choice was politically motivated Lloyd George undoubtedly constituted, by virtue of his success at the munitions office, the most formidable threat to Asquith's leadership. The Irish charge would remove Lloyd George from the centre of the British political arena and possibly ensnare him in the insoluble difficulties of home rule. In Ireland Lloyd George inspired neither the trust nor the enmity of either party. As a Welsh nationalist early in his career and as the engineer of the Liberal–Irish *entente* which paved the way for the third home rule bill Lloyd George was an acceptable choice to the Irish Nationalists as negotiator. For the Unionists his enthusiastic participation in the war effort had somewhat blunted the memory of his pre-war democratic radicalism. Moreover his advocacy of conscription had pleased the Tories, but his insistence that it should not be introduced in Ireland kept him in line with Nationalist views. In the days following his appointment Lloyd George received many encouraging letters expressing hope that he would be able to settle the Irish question. These included a note from Walter Long, Chairman of the Local Government Board, who assured him that his 'knowledge and experience of Ireland, now extending over more than 50 years, and my influence with my friends will be entirely at your service if you think they will be of use to you at any time'.[10] At this point there seemed to be no indication of hostility from any quarter to the negotiations and Lloyd George tackled his new responsibilities with enthusiasm.

From the beginning, however, Lloyd George made the fatal mistake of assuming that there were only two Irish parties of any consequence and that the Irish question could be settled essentially along pre-war lines. Evidence to the contrary was immediately forthcoming from two important bodies of opinion in the south which had been aroused by the rebellion. On 26 May a meeting of Unionist peers and commoners from the three southern provinces, even without any knowledge of the propositions Lloyd George was preparing, expressed grave misgivings over the opening of the home rule controversy during the war.[11] In a subsequent interview with their leader, Lord Midleton, Lloyd George insisted that home rule, with the exclusion of Ulster and special safeguards for the minority in the south, was 'the price the Irish Unionists must pay to the Empire for the war'. An Irish settlement was absolutely necessary as opinion in America had taken an anti-British turn since the suppression of the rebellion. But the Unionist leader remained unconvinced of the desirability of any such settlement. What his party regarded as the foremost necessity was the complete restoration of law and order in Ireland. Any opening of negotiations at this time would surely be regarded as giving way to the violent element in the south.[12] But a negative view toward Lloyd George's mission was also beginning to emerge in the Nationalist ranks. Martial law, the execution of rebel leaders, and many lesser forms of repression had so alienated Nationalist opinion that it was doubtful whether the Irish leadership would be allowed to sanction any agreement which allowed the Crown forces under Sir John Maxwell to remain in Ireland to harass the population. Every day during question time in the house Nationalist M.P.s such as Laurence Ginnell, Tim Healy, and William O'Brien bombarded the Government with critical inquiries concerning the treatment of prisoners, the arrest of innocent persons, and related matters. Even Dillon told C. P. Scott that he was 'deeply impressed by the seriousness of the situation in Ireland. The executions had transformed the Sinn Fein leaders from fools and mischief-makers, almost universally condemned, into martyrs for Ireland. Redmond had been far too complaisant and had largely lost his influence in Ireland.' What was needed, Dillon insisted, was 'some big measure of appeasement' which would go far beyond the settlement envisaged by

Lloyd George to satisfy Nationalist sentiment in the south. When confronted with these views by Scott, Lloyd George curtly retorted, 'Well, he can wreck the negotiation if he chooses; but it is their last chance.'[13]

In the face of such obvious resistance Lloyd George's decision to continue with his negotiations is explicable only in light of what had been the previous power structure and lines of negotiation in Ireland. In 1914, though it was not public knowledge, the feelings of the southern Unionists and the Ulster Nationalists had been disregarded by the major parties at the Buckingham Palace conference. Their disagreement had arisen largely over the delineation of the boundary of Ulster. Now much to his surprise and great relief, very soon after assuming his task as mediator Lloyd George obtained the consent of Redmond to a clean-cut exclusion of six Ulster counties. His only conditions were that the Irish representation at Westminster remain unimpaired and that the agreement be carried out at once. Upon consulting Carson, Lloyd George found him agreeable to these terms and equally 'prepared to deal upon the basis of the immediate delivery of the goods—and so the deal proceeded'.[14] Redmond's willingness obviously stemmed from the necessity of obtaining some tangible form of home rule, however incomplete, before his party was outflanked by the independence-minded Sinn Fein Party.

Carson's motives, however, were less obvious. According to a third-hand account of Carson's decision written by his Ulster colleague, Hugh de Fellenberg Montgomery, Carson was told, presumably by Lloyd George, that 'the Cabinet were quite unanimous in considering it necessary to give Redmond Home Rule at once'. Grey had insisted that it was necessary to woo America and other neutrals, and Bonar Law considered it necessary to satisfy Botha and other home rule enthusiasts in the empire.

With all the Unionist Press except the 'Morning Post' in full cry for a settlement and the bulk of the Unionist Members as well as all the other parties in the House being on the same track and unwilling to listen to Irish or Ulster Unionists, the situation was so unpromising that we were strongly advised to agree to the suggested terms, as the party which refused to agree to Lloyd George's arrangement will be the party that will stink in the nostrils of the patriotic British public.[15]

Undoubtedly the swiftness by which Lloyd George confronted Carson with these persuasions, before any Conservative reaction had a chance to organize behind him, explains in part why Carson accepted essentially the same terms which Midleton had refused. But the decisive factor, as Carson's biographer points out, was that Lloyd George gave him what he wanted. This included the proposal for a clean-cut exclusion of the six counties and an assertion by Lloyd George in his covering letter that it would be permanent. 'We must make it clear that at the end of the provisional period Ulster does not, whether she wills it or not, merge in the rest of Ireland.' Significantly this statement was never included in the proposals, though Carson was led to believe that this was the personal position of Lloyd George. To this understanding Carson added his insistence that the six counties would not be included in home rule 'unless at some future time the Imperial Parliament pass an Act for that purpose'.[16] Thus Carson was led to believe that he had been taken into Lloyd George's confidence and that the exclusion of Ulster would be permanent, while Redmond naturally adhered strictly to the letter of Lloyd George's proposals which stated that the home rule settlement was intended to apply only for the duration of the war or until such a time when Parliament or an imperial conference could make permanent provision for the government of Ireland. Furthermore Lloyd George gave his 'most emphatic assurance' to the Nationalists that he 'placed his life upon the table, and would stand or fall by the agreement come to'. This, he maintained, was also the attitude of the Prime Minister.[17] Obviously any clarification of these discrepancies was out of the question as the Ulsterite and Nationalist positions were essentially irreconcilable, even under the conditions of unity inspired by the war effort. Only an immediate settlement, before Lloyd George's deception could be discovered and any outside opposition could materialize, had any chance of success.

The initial breach in the apparent solid body of support which Lloyd George had built in the two major Irish parties stemmed from the ability of the southern Unionists to attract the concern of British Conservatives for their plight. In view of the unsatisfactory verbal assurances given to them by Lloyd George, the southern Unionists not unnaturally felt abandoned by their brothers in the north. On the same day as his discussion with Midleton, Lloyd George received a caveat from Long that 'there has always been a cleavage between the Unionists in the South and the Ulster people, the former holding strongly that they have not been sufficiently represented or protected by the Ulster people and their agitation'. He believed that this schism was accentuated by Lloyd George's proposals and he suggested that nothing in the way of a settlement should be indicated without the full knowledge and understanding of the southern Unionists.[18] In the next several days Long's apprehensions were fulfilled. George F. Stewart, deputy chairman of the Irish Unionist Association, told Long that after thinking over Lloyd George's terms carefully and discussing them with his colleague, Lord Barrymore, he was convinced of their unworkability. Furthermore he flatly denied an assertion made by Lloyd George to Long that the proposals had been favourably received by the Unionists.[19] Lord Lansdowne, when informed of Lloyd George's proposals by Long, also found them to be 'profoundly alarming'. In spite of the fact that the home rule bill was on the statute book he pointed out that 'at no moment has a satisfactory or even tolerable settlement of the Home Rule question really been within reach. It was not within reach when the war broke out, nor am I able to conceive, even assuming the utmost good-will on all sides, that such a settlement, however much we may insist on its provisional character, will prove to be within immediate reach at the present time.'[20] In the light of the hostile disposition which was forming amongst some of the Conservative leaders it is not surprising that the southern Unionists felt free to pursue a course which would secure the greatest possible protection for their own interests. On 2 June Midleton's group passed resolutions approving the continuation of martial law in Ireland for a considerable period, but declining Lloyd George's proposals as 'unworkable' and likely to be misunderstood as a justification of the recent revolt.[21]

Lloyd George reacted to these rebuffs by appealing to his source of strength. He wrote to Carson that 'Midleton seems to be working hard to prevent a settlement. He is working up his friends to bring all the pressure in their power to bear upon the Unionist members of the Cabinet. Every prominent Unionist in the South of Ireland is urged to write letters to Long and

Bonar Law and Lansdowne, and I have no doubt Chamberlain. Long sends these letters on to me, and in the innocence of his heart he thinks it is all a spontaneous outburst of indignation.' Lloyd George attributed these ravings not to the business community, but the southern landlords. Then as a further indication of his own concern for the Unionists in the south Lloyd George suggested to Carson that the Government nominees to the Irish parliament should sit in the first chamber instead of having a separate chamber during the provisional period. 'We might then arrange that in the Lower Chamber there should be twenty or thirty, or even more, leading representatives of the minority and that in the Executive or Cabinet there should be at least two Protestant Unionists.' Although this arrangement might be subject to later alterations, Lloyd George felt that 'the presence of a powerful minority in the Lower Chamber would give the Protestant Unionists the greater confidence at this period'.[22] But the southern Unionists were no longer interested in trifling concessions to entice them into home rule, and Carson, particularly after his persuasion of the Ulster Unionist Council in early June to accept the exclusion of six Ulster counties, no longer possessed their confidence.[23] What chiefly concerned the southern minority was their own safety and security. Redmond's party had been weakening steadily and it was felt that an immediate conferral of home rule, on any terms, would only encourage the Sinn Fein and possibly precipitate another rebellion.[24]

But any strengthening of the Government's military policy as recommended by the southern Unionists was regarded by the Nationalists as inimical to their own cause. T. P. O'Connor, Lloyd George's chief Nationalist informant in Ireland, reported that the military situation was very bad. Maxwell's arrests and executions, particularly that of Sheehy Skeffington, who was shot without a trial by a subordinate military officer, were forcing more adherents to the Sinn Fein cause. 'Unless he [Maxwell] is withdrawn and military rule in Ireland is brought to an end,' O'Connor insisted, 'I feel very despondent as to our being able to push the settlement through.'[25] The coercive policy exercised by Maxwell's forces was also having an adverse effect on Joseph Devlin's party in Ulster. Although the northern Nationalists had given their tacit approval to Lloyd George's terms, the prospect of excluding the six counties attracted no enthusiasm except from the businessmen in Belfast. 'You have let Hell loose in Ireland,' Dillon told Lloyd George. 'And I do not see how the Country is to be governed.'[26] The brutal fact which now began to confront Lloyd George was that, unless home rule were granted immediately, it was only a matter of time until the Nationalist Party would lose the confidence of the Irish people to the extremist elements who were demanding a total separation from Britain. Under these conditions no negotiations would be possible.

By the middle of June the revolt within the Conservative Party had gained full momentum. Long, Lansdowne, and Bonar Law were being inundated with letters, some anonymous and abusive, from Unionists voicing opposition to the Irish scheme.[27] This furore was precipitated by the publication in *The Times* on 12 June of the official report of the Nationalist Party meeting held two days earlier in Dublin. In his address to the meeting Redmond attributed the initiation of the Irish negotiations to a breakdown of 'Castle Government' and ascribed their purpose to be 'to settle the Irish question immediately on a basis of agreement'. Additionally he referred to Lloyd George's scheme as 'a proposal which we may fairly regard as the proposal of the Government'.[28] Walter Long in a memorandum which he circulated to his Unionist colleagues strongly repudiated these assumptions. 'It was never suggested, and I never realized that we were asked to agree to the final acceptance of any proposals without consulting English Unionists, or for that matter English Home Rulers, and obtaining their views upon the proposals, and I should never have assented to any statement involving the declaration that the Government of the Union had broken down.'[29] These remarks did their destruction as two more Unionist Cabinet members, Lord Selborne and Lord Robert Cecil, joined the ranks of those resisting any kind of a settlement. Long also wrote to Lloyd George expressing his conviction that this was no time to embark on any political experiments in Ireland. He described the situation there as very different from what he had originally believed it to be, 'far graver and more serious', and that it would be impossible for him to assent to any settlement which provided for the adoption of home rule.[30]

This surely must have come as very discouraging news to Lloyd George after several weeks of intense interviewing and negotiating. In his reply to Long he pointed out what a risky and thankless task he had undertaken and criticized Long for not expressing his views earlier. 'Now things have gone so far that they cannot be put right except by my resignation, and in face of your letter I have written to the P.M. withdrawing from the negotiations and from the Government. The task is a difficult one—without loyal support it is impossible.'[31] But Long was not so easily diverted from his wrecking course. He complained that he had never been informed of the terms of Lloyd George's proposals in the early stages of the negotiations and even afterwards he had only a rough idea of the terms from what little was revealed to the Cabinet. He also called Lloyd George's bluff on resigning. 'No charge of unfairness or disloyalty lies at my door and I cannot believe that you seriously intend to base your resignation upon this excuse.'[32] Lloyd George did in fact pen a letter of resignation to the Prime Minister, but it was never sent.[33] Instead he doggedly pressed on with his bid for support from the Nationalists and Ulster Unionists. On the same day he defiantly explained to Asquith that 'if the Nationalists and Carson with his Ulster Unionists support the settlement Selborne and Cecil will rail in vain'.[34] To Dillon he expressed confidence that he would be able to overwhelm the many opponents who confronted him, including the southern Unionists, whom he described as 'moving heaven and the other place to thwart settlement'.[35]

In spite of the combined opposition of the southern Unionists and a stalwart group of British Conservatives, the chances for a settlement still remained good as long as Redmond and Carson retained their faith in Lloyd George and his terms. This was contingent on the continued belief that the proposals carried the approval of the Cabinet and that both leaders retained their initial assumptions regarding the nature of Ulster's exclusion. On 10 June Montgomery remarked almost incredulously to his southern friend, George de Willis, that 'the reasons behind the curtain which have induced Walter Long and Bonar Law, Lord L. and A. Chamberlain to agree to this apparently mad step must have been of extraordinary force'.[36] Nevertheless at a meeting of the Ulster Unionist Council on

12 June it was resolved that Carson should continue his negotiations with Lloyd George on the basis of the exclusion of the six counties, thus forsaking the covenanters who resided in the counties of Cavan, Monaghan, and Donegal. On the same day, however, Redmond stated for the first time in public his belief that the exclusion of the six Ulster counties was to be only a temporary arrangement. This admission aroused the suspicions of the Ulster Unionists that Lloyd George had not been fully candid with the Irish parties in explaining the circumstances surrounding his appointment or in the conditions for a settlement. On 14 June Carson intimated to Bonar Law that he had 'heard some rumour to-day that the Cabinet have known nothing about the negotiations or the terms; but that I do not credit, as I do not suppose I should have been asked to go to Ireland and carry out a most distasteful mission in such circumstances, more especially as the papers have given daily accounts of the negotiations which were going on'.[37] Suspicions heightened amongst the Nationalists too who feared that unless the Government's position regarding the terms of Ulster's exclusion was clarified there would be a further deterioration of their position in the country. According to W. H. Owen, Lloyd George's 'Irish scout', Dillon had made it clear that 'failing a definite pronouncement to the effect that the proposed scheme of settlement is a purely temporary expedient he does not think that the proposals will even be considered by the Nationalists'.[38] An opportunity for the clarification of Lloyd George's intentions presented itself on 14 June when the Prime Minister spoke at Ladybank on the progress of the war. But Asquith's remarks on Ireland contained no specific references to Ulster and were couched only in a general statement that the entire settlement in Ireland was to be 'provisional' in character until the end of the war.[39]

This statement, which was simply a reiteration of the final point in Lloyd George's proposals, settled nothing. While it appeared to ease the position of the Nationalist leaders somewhat, it excited accusations from Unionists that Lloyd George had committed the Government to proposals which admitted the defeat of constitutional government in Ireland and would bring the home rule act into operation during the war. It aroused additional odium by its implication that Ulster's exclusion was only temporary and like the rest of the settlement would come under review at the end of the war. Selborne, who now assumed the leading position amongst the Unionist dissenters, deplored the fact that Lloyd George had led Carson and Redmond to believe that the Government had agreed upon the scheme which was placed before them. 'Not only have I never agreed to any such proposal, but I have never had it made to me, nor have I ever heard it discussed,' he told Asquith on the 16th. 'Unless, therefore, the statement that the Cabinet have agreed to Lloyd George's scheme for bringing the Government of Ireland Act into early operation can be publicly repudiated, I have no alternative but to ask you to accept my resignation.'[40] Selborne and Long also poured forth their indignation to Carson, who was now in the most awkward position of having secured the assent of his party to a policy which had never been approved by the Cabinet and which now appeared inconsistent with his original understanding of it. For the moment Carson expressed no opinion. But his colleague Montgomery expressed his belief that 'Carson will go no further if Lloyd George has yielded to Redmond to the extent of agreeing that the Amending Act shall be a mere Emergency Provisional Measure. Carson was very emphatic on the importance of the exclusion of Ulster being on the Statute Book as well as the Home Rule Act when the Imperial Conference met.'[41]

In an effort to resurrect the truth regarding Lloyd George's appointment, and thereby end the growing dissension within the Unionist Party, Lord Curzon and Cecil on 17 June held an interview with the Prime Minister. Asquith insisted that there was no disagreement between them over the facts—Lloyd George's charge was merely to inquire whether any agreement between Nationalists and Ulstermen was possible. He agreed that the proposals recently submitted to them by the Minister of Munitions had not been accepted by the Cabinet and that he would talk with Lloyd George about any possible deviations from this understanding.[42] This checked the negotiations at a crucial stage. Had Lloyd George secured the Cabinet's approval before any outside opposition had had a chance to mount against his proposals he would merely have had to deal with the major Irish parties. Now the only way to secure the implementation of his scheme was to contend with a handful of hostile Unionists in the Cabinet who were willing to support the cause of the minority in southern Ireland. Against the possibility of a Unionist mutiny and a split in the Cabinet Lloyd George had gambled on the assumption that the Unionists would not block any proposals which had the assent of both Nationalists and Ulstermen, over 90 per cent of the Irish population. 'If the Irish Parliamentary Party and the Ulster Convention accept the proposals', he confided to Dillon on the 17th, 'the Unionist members of the Cabinet will be in the position of fighting not merely the Nationalist leaders but Carson and the Ulster members; and as Bonar Law . . . told me that would be an impossible position for them.'[43] Lloyd George simply refused to believe that the Unionists would abandon the position of their allies in the north for the sake of the tiny, though influential, minority in the south.

The controversy stirred by the revelation of Lloyd George's proposals produced a split in both Nationalist and Unionist ranks. Redmond's control had been severely shaken not only by the continuing state of unrest in the south, but by the hostility of the priests and the newspaper press. In Ulster only the dominating factor of Devlin's personal leadership kept the anti-negotiation forces in a relatively quiescent state. Their chief spokesmen were a Londonderry priest named Father McHugh and William Murphy of the *Irish Independent*. Logically Asquith's mild implication in his Ladybank speech that the exclusion of Ulster was to be only provisional should have closed the ranks of the Unionists. But Carson doggedly stood behind the commitment he had made to Lloyd George. Ulstermen continued to believe, in spite of Asquith's speech, that the exclusion of their province would be permanent because 'no attempt shall ever be made to coerce the six counties to come within the Home Rule Parliament'.[44] This was the argument which had such an unsettling effect on the Unionists in the south, who depended on the total abstention of all the Unionists in Ireland for their survival. Consequently a schism developed in the Cabinet between those Conservatives supporting home rule and exclusion, and those believing in an unimpaired continuation of the union. Lady Carson believed that 'the Unionists in the Cabinet are now trying to throw over Edward and Ulster and say they never knew there were to be negotiations which

is a lie'.[45] Unfortunately Lloyd George never fully appreciated
the strength of the forces in the Conservative Party willing to
oppose Carson. He confidently reported to Asquith that Bonar
Law, though 'frightened and timid', was 'willing to stand by
Carson. Carson says he must stand by the agreement. He
[Bonar Law] was very angry with Long who has actually been
telling his Ulster people to throw Carson over.'[46] Balfour, Bonar
Law, and F. E. Smith stood behind Carson, while Lansdowne,
Long, and Selborne aligned themselves with the southern Unionists. The question confronting both factions was whether they
would allow their differences to destroy the integrity of their
party.

During the next week Lloyd George's terms came under close
scrutiny from both sides and there were attempts to heal the
breach in the Tory ranks. At a meeting of leading Conservatives
at Curzon's house on 20 June it was agreed that there were
three conditions necessary for any settlement in Ireland—sufficient protection for the southern Unionists, guarantees that
home rule would not endanger the war effort, and that the
exclusion of Ulster should be permanent. But their real problem
was Carson's acceptance of Lloyd George's terms, which no one
was sure guaranteed these essentials.[47] On the following day,
before a meeting of the Cabinet, Carson was confronted with
these doubts. But he remained unyielding in his determination
to stand by the settlement, which perpetuated the Conservative
split. As Chamberlain later reported to his wife, 'there is no
satisfactory way out. Carson is vehement for settlement, says
he will not be responsible for Ulster if we break off and that
the rest of Ireland will be "hell".'[48] Lansdowne for his part was
willing to wait till the next Cabinet meeting on the following
Tuesday to decide what action he would take. Selborne, however, refused to wait. He told Asquith that his resignation would
be announced in the Monday morning papers and explained
the following day in the House of Lords.[49] Long was tottering
on the brink.

All of this intraparty turmoil reached a climax at the Cabinet
meeting which was finally held on 27 June in two lengthy sessions. Lansdowne and Long, as expected, came out strongly
against Lloyd George's proposals on the grounds that they
would justify the recent rebellion and that they did not have the

sanction of all groups in Ireland. Crewe and Grey, speaking for the Liberals, spoke equally strongly in favour of the terms. Cecil did not disapprove of the proposals, but thought the creation of an Irish executive should be delayed until the end of the war. Bonar Law's views were more conciliatory. While admitting the possible dangers attendant upon home rule, he saw no alternative to acceptance of the proposals. Their defeat might well drive the Redmondites and Sinn Feiners together into one hostile camp. Provided safeguards were assured to the southern Unionists, he would recommend acceptance of the terms to his party. When Curzon raised doubts about the security of Ireland, Sir John Maxwell was called in to give evidence, and assured the Cabinet that the military situation was well in hand. Then Balfour, whose opinion was respected by both sides, made perhaps the most effective pronouncement of the day. Disassociating himself entirely from the position taken by Lansdowne and Long, he denied that the proposed arrangement could properly be regarded as a 'concession to rebellion'. On the contrary he characterized it as a 'Unionist triumph', the exclusion of the six Ulster counties being the maximum demand of the Unionist delegates at the Buckingham Palace conference in 1914. He also pointed out the absurdity of the contention that the enactment of home rule would impede the war effort. Maxwell had just given evidence that one division could check and repress any further uprising and a settlement in Ireland was badly needed to woo American sympathy to the British cause. He placed himself squarely behind the policy of Carson and Bonar Law. At this point Lloyd George, in an effort to appease the dissidents and to reinforce the strong position established for him by Balfour, suggested that a small Cabinet committee be set up to suggest further military and naval safeguards in Ireland for the duration of the war. Although Long was still recalcitrant, Curzon, Chamberlain, and Lansdowne fell in with this suggestion and a committee consisting of Lloyd George, Cecil, Asquith, and George Cave, the Solicitor-General, was formed. Thus, for the moment at least, the resignation of any further Cabinet personnel was averted.[50]

The winning of any further adherents to the side of conciliation now hinged on the position of Lord Lansdowne. Without his support the refractory movement in the Cabinet would collapse. Chamberlain, convinced that Lloyd George's proposals could be made workable now that they had been exposed to the scrutiny of the Cabinet committee, engaged in a subtle campaign to gain Lansdowne's acceptance. In a careful letter he explained to Lansdowne that Cecil and Cave had drawn up a clause to accompany Lloyd George's terms whereby the Irish executive would remain in the hands of the imperial government for the duration of the war. This, he suggested, was 'a real advance and a great safeguard' and that the Unionists could achieve this as the price of Lansdowne's remaining in the Cabinet and only he had this power.[51] Chamberlain assured Asquith that 'the number of dissentients will largely depend upon Lansdowne's choice whilst for the Lords he is a "pivotal person". I beg you to make no mistake as to his great influence. He is the Hartington of today.' He believed that Lansdowne could be saved if two conditions were met—the acceptance of the Cecil–Cave amending clause and the strongest possible appeal to his patriotism and public spirit.[52] When the Cabinet met again on 5 July Lansdowne was under considerable pressure to concur with the latest additions to the proposals which Redmond, Carson, and most of the Cabinet had already accepted. What weighed on him most heavily was the effect his resignation would have on the integrity of his party and the credibility of the Government. If Lansdowne and others resigned the result would almost certainly be the collapse of the coalition followed by a period of recrimination and political chaos, and very possibly a general election. There was the additional factor that the Ulster and southern Nationalists at recent party meetings had overwhelmingly voted acceptance of Lloyd George's terms. Any abrupt move by Lansdowne in the opposite direction might expose him to the damaging charge that he was deliberately trying to wreck the negotiations. It is not surprising therefore that Lansdowne, though heartily disliking and distrusting the proposed settlement, decided that this was not the moment to resign. Long again reluctantly followed his lead and a draft bill was set into motion.[53]

On 10 July Asquith laid before the House of Commons the general lines on which the Government's bill to amend the Home Rule Act was being drawn. These included a provision for the exclusive authority of the imperial Government over all matters related to the war and a clause providing for the definite exclusion of the six counties of Ulster. Though scarcely noticed by the Nationalists, Asquith's further assurance that the union of Ulster with the rest of Ireland could not take place without passage of a separate bill seemed to satisfy Carson that no attempt would be made to coerce Ulster to enter a Dublin parliament.[54] But Lansdowne's chief concern was the security of the southern provinces, for which Asquith's announcement provided scant guarantee. The Hardinge commission, which had been meeting during the previous month, had just published a scathing indictment of the Government's pusillanimous and negligent policy which led up to the Easter rebellion. In commenting on the relevance of this report in the House of Lords on 11 July Lansdowne believed that the bill based on Lloyd George's proposals would require considerable time for preparation and passage through Parliament. In the meantime it would be necessary to enforce strict measures to maintain security in Ireland, he explained. These would include the retention of a sufficient garrison, the strengthening of the Defence of the Realm Act, and the enforcement of the old Crimes Act by resident magistrates in Ireland.[55] The prospect of such restrictions aroused the immediate indignation of the Nationalists, who regarded Lansdowne's remarks as a deliberate attempt to destroy any negotiated settlement. The Nationalists were also concerned about Lansdowne's assertion that the amending bill under preparation would make certain structural alterations in the Home Rule Act which would be permanent. This touched the vital question of the ultimate status of the six excluded Ulster counties.[56] O'Connor reported to Lloyd George that 'things have been made almost desperate by Lansdowne's Speech. Redmond will ask Asquith at question time if the speech represents the policy of the Government. If the answer be "yes", I think the whole thing is broken up.'[57]

Asquith made no such pronouncement, but Lansdowne did so in a statement published on 14 July in *The Times*. In regard to Ulster's proposed exclusion Lansdowne merely paraphrased the Prime Minister's declaration of 10 July that 'the union of the six counties with the rest of Ireland "could only be brought about with, and can never be brought about without, the free will and assent of the excluded area"'. His statements on law and order in Ireland, he insisted, were also representative of Government opinion and made after consultation with the Prime Minister and some of his colleagues.[58] But the key to Lansdowne's success in wrecking the accord was the organization by this time of a large body of Unionist opinion hostile to the negotiations. This opposition materialized in the formation of an Imperial Unionist Association by mid-July which was made up of nearly two hundred peers and commoners who wished to block the home rule settlement.[59] At a meeting of the Cabinet on 19 July Lansdowne consequently was able to use this evidence of backbench support as a lever to persuade his Unionist Cabinet colleagues to accept two further amendments. One allowed for the permanent exclusion of Ulster and the other provided for a reduction of Irish representation in the House of Commons. Ostensibly these amendments were carried out to provide additional safeguards for Ulster, but their ultimate purpose, and effect, was to make any settlement impossible. Redmond had already publicly rejected any proposal compromising the temporary nature of Ulster's exclusion, but the latest amendments appeared to be a deliberate attempt to emasculate the Irish Nationalist Party at Westminster and thereby ensure the permanent exclusion of Ulster. Redmond warned the Government on 24 July that 'if they introduce a bill on the lines communicated to me my Friends and I will oppose it at every stage'. He refused even to consider an assurance by Lloyd George that the Irish would have full representation in the determination of any permanent settlement in Ireland.[60] Lloyd George had already been forced to retreat from so many of the points he had made in his original proposals that he no longer inspired any trust among the Nationalists. And unable to recede from the demands of the Cabinet Unionists, Lloyd George was forced to abandon his negotiations.

In the remaining months of 1916 no serious attempt was made to pick up the threads of agreement reached between the Nationalists and the Ulster Unionists. What had appeared to be a golden opportunity to settle the Irish question had degenerated into a deadlock enforced by the more extremist elements on both sides. The essential ingredient to Lloyd George's strategy was Conservative support. He later lamented to C. P. Scott that 'if the terms had at once been embodied in an agreed Bill the Unionists could not have gone back on it'.[61] But Lloyd George did not obtain the consent of the Cabinet before submitting his proposals to the Irish parties and allowed a dangerous ambiguity to arise over the nature of Ulster's exclusion. It was in these neglected areas that the anti-negotiation forces were given an opportunity to take root and grow. What is obvious is that Lloyd George overestimated the power of Carson in the Unionist Party and underestimated forces in the Cabinet willing to oppose the Ulster chief. Having secured the assent of Redmond and Carson to his proposals Lloyd George mistakenly believed that he had succeeded. But the Unionist demand for clarification of Ulster's permanent status could not be resisted and the Unionist minority in the south had to be protected. As a result Lansdowne, the leader of the dissidents, was able to attack Lloyd George at his strongest point, Carson's acceptance of the proposals, and thereby smash the negotiations.

The real loser in this fiasco was neither Lloyd George nor the Unionist Party, but the Asquithian Government, which was widely blamed for its inept handling of the negotiations. In a sense Lloyd George's unsuccessful attempt to settle the Irish question may be interpreted as a continuation of the 1914 conference, albeit under the altered circumstances of war. Although they never developed fully, the Irish negotiations of 1916 contained many of the elements of extra-parliamentary interaction which characterized an interparty conference, with the obvious exception of an actual physical confrontation between party leaders.[62] The propositions made by Lloyd George were also unique inasmuch as their underlying purpose was to preserve and capitalize on the spirit of wartime co-operation, whereas previous interparty negotiations had been conducted for the purpose of alleviating party stress or facilitating a legislative accord. Yet the feeling of mutual trust was too precarious and basic disagreement over Ireland was far too great to allow Lloyd George to deal candidly with both parties. Instead, perhaps because of his negative experience in two earlier conferences where the Irish issue was paramount, Lloyd George followed a policy of secrecy and subterfuge hoping thereby to delude the Irish party leaders into an agreement. Not only was he capable of employing such a stratagem, but it seemed to be the only possible way of overcoming the fundamental predispositions held on both sides against a compromise. Unlike the way in which he ultimately resolved the Irish issue in 1921, or even disposed of Asquith later in the year, the political wizardry of Lloyd George was not so apparent on this occasion. If the Buckingham Palace conference had failed because of excessive formality and forthrightness, the 1916 negotiations were aborted by the communications gap created by Lloyd George where discrepancies were allowed to emerge and grow before a settlement could be reached. The failure of the negotiations created further opportunities for the growth of the Sinn Fein Party in Ireland and brought calumny on the Government. This was a step then to the formation of the Lloyd George coalition where the Unionists eventually assumed a dominant role in the settlement of the Irish question.

VII

The Political Crisis of 1916

The combination may be successful. A Coalition has
before this been successful. But Coalitions though successful have always found this, that their triumph has been
brief. This too I know, that England does not love Coalitions.

BENJAMIN DISRAELI[1]

The collapse of H. H. Asquith's coalition Government in
December of 1916, presaged by the failure of the Irish negotiations earlier in the year, was the most serious political crisis
which confronted Britain during the war. Behind it lay a reser-
voir of discontent in the Conservative Party over the conduct
of the war, and the latent desire of its leaders to control the
policy of any new administration. Initially the leading prota-
gonist for change was Sir Edward Carson, who had resigned
office in October 1915 over the Cabinet's alleged betrayal of
Serbia, to lead the opposition forces in the House of Commons.
This defection was followed in 1916 by the slow conversion of
Bonar Law, the Conservative Party leader, to a mutinous position. At the time of the formation of the coalition in 1915 Bonar
Law had said that 'if the party to which I belong had lost confidence in me I should not for a moment dream of continuing to
be a member of the Government'.[2] By the end of 1916 a waning
confidence in the Government's prosecution of the war was acting as a stimulus on the Conservative leader to adopt an anti-
coalition stance. But the leading exponent of change was Lloyd
George, who had progressively increased his influence over
affairs since Asquith began his tenure as Prime Minister in
1908. Lloyd George's insubordination in late 1916 arose largely
from his success at the Ministry of Munitions and his promotion
to War Secretary following the death of Lord Kitchener earlier
in the year. In both positions he appeared to be the most
dynamic figure in what was otherwise a faltering and lack-lustre
Government.[3] This then was the dilemma. Any reconstruction

of the Government, which might entail greater efficiency in the war effort and possibly an Irish settlement, would be impossible under the existing leadership. No changes could be enacted, however, which might disturb the prosecution of the war, subvert the Government's credibility in Ireland or America, or induce a general election.

The immediate task which confronted those who were dissatisfied and wished to control the conduct of the war was to remove Asquith from power. This was the critical issue on which the negotiations of December 1916 centred. Lloyd George's failure in the recent Irish negotiations instilled in him an appreciation of the importance of admitting greater responsibility to Cabinet Conservatives to equate with their veto power. However much leading Conservatives desired a more efficient prosecution of the war, they were suspicious of Lloyd George and extremely reluctant to sanction any alteration in the power structure which might jeopardize their present positions or create a situation which they might not be able to control. A method had to be devised to break the bond of Conservative support behind Asquith and to create a greater sense of confidence in the possibility of Lloyd George's taking over the premiership. According to Lord Beaverbrook in his *Politicians and the War*, the most authoritative account of the crisis, this was accomplished by the execution of a conspiracy which he engineered in the upper echelons of the government and the press. He also insinuated that Asquith was lulled into a sense of false confidence and eventual resignation by a combination of his own insensitivity to political realities and the deception of Lord Curzon, the Lord Privy Seal. What Beaverbrook neglected to point out is that the majority of leading Tories were pursuing a course of duplicity and opportunism whereby they would support whatever regime allowed them to exert the greatest influence. Effectively excluded from a considerable share of power in the formation of the first coalition in 1915, they had nevertheless gained a voice in the conduct of the war without recourse to a general election. Now they were cautiously seeking an opportunity to advance their ministerial standing without jeopardizing unduly their current positions. The combined effect of Beaverbrook's conspiracy and the desire for control within the Unionist hierarchy was to undermine the authority of Asquith and lead to the formation of the Lloyd George coalition. This transfer of power was carried out by an interparty conference, which was summoned to determine a method for choosing a Prime Minister without resorting to the divisiveness of a general election. By raising the Conservative Party to a position where it was able to control the destinies of the war and the empire, the Buckingham Palace conference of 1916 unconsciously removed the basis for constitutional stress which had existed before the war.

Lord Beaverbrook has recorded in explicit fashion how he formulated with Carson, Bonar Law, and Lloyd George a plan which would effectively remove Asquith from any direct supervision of the war effort. In replacement of the present unsystematic war committee arrangement this group envisaged a compact war council of three ministers without portfolio which would meet under the joint leadership of Asquith as *ex officio* president and Lloyd George as chairman.[4] The major ambiguity surrounding the proposal when Lloyd George submitted it as an ultimatum to Asquith on 1 December was who should exercise effective control over the conduct of the war. While Asquith in his response did not object in principle to the new arrangement of a war council, he insisted that 'the Prime Minister must be its chairman. He cannot be relegated to the position of arbiter in the background or a referee in the Cabinet.'[5] This reply hastened Lloyd George to the unhappy conclusion that his only logical alternative was resignation. On the following day he actually penned a letter to Asquith stating that it was his duty 'to leave the Government in order to inform the people of the real condition of affairs'.[6] That Lloyd George never sent this letter was undoubtedly due to his apprehension that his resignation would be accepted and that in the ensuing Cabinet reshuffle he might be left in isolation. He had to be more assured of his indispensability and of the likelihood of Conservative support in the perpetration of any treasonous act. It was for this reason that he delegated the responsibility for the next move to Bonar Law. He dispatched Asquith's letter to the Conservative leader and beseeched him: 'The life of the country depends on resolute action by you now.'[7]

Bonar Law responded by summoning a meeting of Conservative ministers on Sunday 3 December, at his home in Kensington. As the result of a newspaper campaign directed against the Government in the *Daily Express* and the *Daily Chronicle* at the instigation of Beaverbrook (then Max Aitken) and in *The Times* by its proprietor Lord Northcliffe, Conservative opinion had hardened considerably. Furthermore the Sunday edition of *Reynolds* newspaper made Lloyd George susceptible to charges of 'trafficking with the press', since his friend, Sir Henry Dalziel, was its proprietor.[8] It was in this atmosphere of intrigue that the Conservative leaders agreed on the need for a show-down between the two Liberal heads. They resolved that the Government could not continue as it was, and that 'the publicity given to the intention of Mr. Lloyd George' made it now impossible to reconstruct it from within. They urged the Prime Minister in a letter to tender his Government's resignation to the King. If he would not, they authorised Bonar Law to tender their own resignations.[9] The purpose of this resolution, Curzon explained to Lansdowne, was to confront Lloyd George for the first time with the responsibility of forming and maintaining a Government. In so doing he would 'cease to be a merely destructive and disloyal force. He will make terms with the Prime Minister and with all the rest of us. He will soon find out what is the attitude of the Irishmen, the Labour men, and so on. His Government will be dictated to him by others, not shaped by himself.' Curzon thought the Tory ministers would have preferred a reconstruction under the present Prime Minister, but they knew that it would be impossible to win the war with Asquith as chairman either of the Cabinet or the war council.[10] Chamberlain agreed that the ultimate purpose of their communiqué was to put Lloyd George to the test, but 'it was not for us to say which of the rival Liberals would secure the greatest amount of support in the Liberal Party and the Parties which habitually worked with it'.[11] Contrary to Beaverbrook's assertion that the ambiguous Conservative resolution was meant as a display of support for Asquith which he misconstrued as confidence in Lloyd George, it can only be interpreted as a challenge to Lloyd George.

It is not surprising therefore that Asquith was uncertain of his position. The Conservative resolution, though it could not be construed as evidence of support for Lloyd George, as Beaverbrook imagined, could provide a pernicious opening for the ambitious War Secretary and his ideas of reconstruction. Before resigning it was absolutely necessary that Asquith ascertain the precise attitude of the Tory leaders regarding the continuation of his tenure as Prime Minister. Unfortunately Asquith learned nothing from his interview with Bonar Law later in the day that would allow him to pursue with confidence such a radical course as resignation. Beaverbrook devoted much attention to vindicating Bonar Law from the charge of misleading the Prime Minister in order to assist Lloyd George.[12] Such verbiage was undoubtedly deemed necessary to explain Asquith's subsequent conduct, which did not coincide with Beaverbrook's interpretation of the Conservative resolution. The explanation of Beaverbrook's biographer is even further afield. Taylor explains Bonar Law's reticence in his discussion with Asquith as an attempt to hide Beaverbrook's complicity in the press campaign and to protect Lloyd George from a false accusation. Moreover he contends that 'exactly like Law, Asquith, "good easy man" in Beaverbrook's unpublished phrase, did not want a fight'.[13] What actually transpired during Bonar Law's encounter with Asquith will probably never be known in full, but the central question of whether he ever transmitted the resolution and made a frank avowal of the position of the Unionist leadership is almost certainly irrelevant. In all likelihood Bonar Law was not sufficiently aware of the ultimate intentions of his colleagues to be able to explain them adequately to Asquith. This is the only intelligent and logical explanation which can account for the behaviour of all the participants in the crisis.

In one sense Beaverbrook was right. Asquith did react with considerable alarm to the idea of resignation. He did so, however, not because he was too fatuous to interpret Bonar Law's verbal message rightly, but because he was confused over the meaning of a resolution which was obviously directed at Lloyd George, yet called for his own resignation. It was for this reason that Asquith chose to ignore the press campaign which was being waged against him and to seek an accommodation with his rebellious colleague later on Sunday. In a meeting at 10 Downing Street the two Liberal leaders agreed on a scheme which would ensure supreme control for the Prime Minister over the war council, although Lloyd George would serve as its chairman. Their only remaining disagreement now appeared to be over personnel, on which no one expected any insurmountable difficulties. But there remained the latent critical issue of emphasis of responsibility and the extent to which Asquith would tolerate a merely nominal authority over the projected war council. Bonar Law, when informed of this apparent attempt at reconciliation, reported the news to a meeting of Conservative leaders at the end of the day and they agreed to withhold their resignations pending further developments. Concurrently Asquith reported to Pamela McKenna, the wife of the Chancellor of the Exchequer, that he had been forced back to London 'to grapple with a "Crisis"—this time with a very big C'. But he felt confident that this one would follow its many predecessors 'to an early and unhonoured grave. But there were many Wigs very nearly on the green.'[14]

During the next twenty-four hours, however, Asquith received some important new information which led him to repudiate his compromise with Lloyd George and to lay his leadership on the line. His ostensible reason for this change in stance was an article which appeared in *The Times* on Monday 4 December, criticizing the conduct of the war and advocating a small war council with Lloyd George, Bonar Law, and Carson as leading members. 'Unless the impression is at once corrected that I am being relegated to the position of an irresponsible spectator of the war,' wrote Asquith to Lloyd George, 'I cannot possibly go on.'[15] Lloyd George's reply assumed a conciliatory, almost defensive, line. He explained that, although he had not seen *The Times* article, he, unlike Northcliffe, attached 'great importance' to Asquith retaining his present position—'effectively'—and was still willing to stand by their suggested arrangement.[16] In spite of these manifestations of good faith and loyalty Asquith needed more emphatic recognition of his authority in any reconstruction of the Government. He stated that it would now be impossible to accept the war council idea without the Prime Minister as chairman. Though he understood the necessity of delegating the chairmanship from time to time to another minister as *locum tenens*, the Prime Minister, he insisted, must be the 'permanent President'. The only concession he was willing to make to accommodate Lloyd George's views was that the war council should be reduced in size.[17] This bold retort caught Lloyd George by surprise and had to be answered in equally strong terms. After reiterating the concessions which the Prime Minister had originally made to his plan and later retracted, Lloyd George explained that he had no choice but to resign. He did this with the avowed intention of informing the people of 'the real condition of affairs and to give them an opportunity, before it is too late, to save their native land from a disaster which is inevitable if the present methods are longer persisted in'.[18] The only logical course open to Asquith too by the end of the fourth day of the crisis was resignation.

Neither Beaverbrook nor Taylor accept *The Times* leader as 'the real, or the sole, cause of Asquith's action'.[19] Indeed this article was hardly more provocative than other similar productions which had appeared in the press in the preceding weeks. Why then did Asquith choose this particular ground to wage a struggle against Lloyd George? To make more rational Asquith's mode of conduct Beaverbrook cited two factors, which he moulded and magnified to fit the course of his narrative. In the first he related that 'early on Monday' Asquith was visited by McKenna, Harcourt, Runciman, and Grey, who expressed a note of 'surprise, dismay and protest' at Lloyd George's latest proposals. Rather than endure the humiliation of a token premiership they allegedly urged the Prime Minister to 'fight Lloyd George now, to refuse his terms and to crush the rebellion. The Liberal Ministers would swear a pact to stand by Asquith.'[20] Beaverbrook's source for this account was a memorandum prepared by Edwin Montagu, Minister of Munitions, who described his own part in the negotiations.[21] It is corroborated by a record of an interview held with Asquith by Robert Donald of the *Daily Chronicle* immediately following the crisis, but with the important qualification that the Prime Minister did not confer with his Liberal colleagues until 'later in the day' and *after* he had taken preliminary steps to undermine the previous day's agreement with Lloyd George.[22] Unfortunately Beaverbrook overlooked this important statement and chose to rely solely on Montagu's account. But in so doing he misinterpreted Montagu's recapitulation of events which, upon careful reading, is in essential agreement with Donald's

story. Thus while Taylor's insistence that there is 'no independent evidence' of any influence by Liberal ministers on
Asquith's actions must be denied, it is admittedly true that Beaverbrook used these sources in such a casual manner as to jeopardize the validity of his conclusions.[23]

Beaverbrook's other supportive reason for Asquith's conduct
is based on still more tenuous evidence. It is founded on the
premise that 'Lord Robert Cecil had been for some little time
in close contact with the Prime Minister and had kept him
in touch with sentiment in Tory Ministerial circles.' As a result
of this contact Asquith supposedly held a meeting with Curzon,
Chamberlain, and Cecil on 'that [same] Monday morning'
where it was explained to him that their plan of wholesale
resignation was intended not as a threat to the current administration, but 'to make more certain the destruction of the common
enemy'—Lloyd George. This guarantee was bestowed even
greater sanctity by a 'specific assurance' made by Curzon that
'no Tory Minister except Bonar Law would serve under Lloyd
George'. Beaverbrook concluded that out of these contacts
Asquith now perceived his position as one of strength.[24] His
chief source of information for the Conservative meeting was
a memorandum compiled by Lord Crewe several weeks after
the crisis, but no mention is made there of the date or time of
their meeting.[25] Conversely one of the participants, Chamberlain, upon reading Beaverbrook's proofs prior to publication
flatly denied that there was any meeting between Asquith and
the Conservative ministers on Monday. 'Our first and only
meeting with him took place not on Monday the 4th but on
the afternoon of Tuesday the 5th shortly before the meeting
with his Liberal colleagues at which he announced his decision
to resign. As far as I know, none of us saw him on Monday.
Certainly I did not. I am confident that Curzon did not and
I do not think Cecil did.'[26] Chamberlain proceeded to develop
this theme in an extended correspondence with Beaverbrook,
in the columns of the *Daily Telegraph*, and in his subsequent
book, *Down the Years*.

In these accounts he also categorically denied that Curzon
had given Asquith any special assurances. 'We certainly never
gave Curzon authority to make any such a statement on our
behalf,' he assured Beaverbrook, 'and our subsequent action,

no less than his, was inconsistent with it. I do not find the charge in Asquith's book or in Crewe's memorandum, and Crewe himself says that Curzon satisfied him of the propriety of his (Curzon's) conduct.'[27] When asked to supply the source for his information Beaverbrook could reply only vaguely that 'you can get evidence of that fact in any direction', citing McKenna and Crewe as possible examples, though he admittedly had not interrogated them.[28] In actuality Beaverbrook's only evidence of Curzon's involvement was a pencilled note in his own hand stating that 'Harcourt told me Curzon said to Asquith in Cabinet room that Tories would not serve under George— except A. B. L.'.[29] Such second-hand information written by the author himself and unsubstantiated by any further documentation hardly qualifies as evidence of Curzon's culpability. Like his assertion of Asquith's meeting with the aggregate of Conservative ministers, his description of Curzon's conduct has no basis in fact.

Yet the villainous impression of Curzon created by Beaverbrook's account has prejudiced the approaches of all subsequent historians. When an even more damning piece of evidence appeared in Spender and Asquith's joint biography of Asquith shortly after Beaverbrook wrote, it seemed certain that Curzon was indeed guilty of misconduct. They quote Curzon as saying in a letter to Asquith on 4 December that his resignation was 'far from having the sinister purport which I believe you were inclined to attribute to it'.[30] This evidence was employed in tandem with another letter which Curzon had written to Lansdowne the previous day explaining the substance of the Conservative resolution urging Asquith to resign: 'We know that with him [Asquith] as Chairman, either of the Cabinet or War Committee, it is absolutely impossible to win the War ...'[31] This, according to the authors, was irrefutable proof of Curzon's deception, the effect of which was 'to lull the intended victim into a false security'. Yet if Curzon's former letter be read alone, as Asquith most assuredly read it, it contains the same ambiguities that all prior Conservative communications had embodied. Moreover if the remainder of the letter be perused, which Asquith's biographers chose to ignore, Curzon's commitment becomes less assured and his conduct less suspect. Here he divulges to Asquith for the first time in the crisis the true position of the Conservative leaders by recalling the following passages from a Matthew Arnold poem:

> We in some unknown Power's employ
> Move in a rigorous line;
> Can neither when we will enjoy
> Nor when we will resign.

Curzon concluded by requesting Asquith 'to facilitate the process by asking for our seals'.[32] Far from being the culprit who misled Asquith, as nearly all other authors have supposed, Curzon was actually the only Conservative minister who made a frank acknowledgement, albeit disguised in poetic verse, of his party's true intentions. Resignation was simply a means to allow fate to determine who should become the country's next Prime Minister.

Thus Beaverbrook's evidence has been for the most part specious and his conclusions incorrect, yet his hunch about Cecil as the instigator of Asquith's change of heart does provide a substantial clue to the ultimate resolution of the crisis. When he was challenged in his correspondence with Chamberlain for some independent evidence of a Monday meeting of Conservatives, Beaverbrook admitted with some frustration that 'I feel that there was *something* on Monday—possibly a meeting between Asquith and Bob Cecil'.[33] Unknown to Beaverbrook, Chamberlain, or even Taylor, Cecil had been in communication with Asquith either late Sunday night or early Monday morning. There is a document to this effect in the Asquith papers which at once changes the whole complexion of the negotiations and supplies the rational key which Beaverbrook and others were so diligently searching for to explain the Prime Minister's inscrutable behaviour. Sir Eric Drummond, Asquith's former private secretary, had met with Cecil, who expressed dislike for Lloyd George's latest proposals and called them a deliberate attempt to shelve the Prime Minister.

He firmly believes that L.G. means to get out because he thinks we are not going to win and has made such terms as the P.M. cannot accept deliberately. He believes that the best course is to let L.G. go; to resign—neither L.G. or B.L. can form a Govt. and the P.M. comes back & L.G. will have to come back too. He does not think the effect of L.G. getting out would be nearly as serious abroad as if the P.M. or E.G. went.[34]

The importance of this note on Asquith's subsequent behaviour and on the eventual outcome of the crisis cannot be overestimated. It was here that Asquith learned the supposed true purport of the Conservative resolution, which provided him with the essential support and confidence needed to stand up to Lloyd George's pretensions to power.

Given the fact that Asquith was thus so reassured, his conduct later in the day becomes at once rational and easily in accord with the other documentation relevant to the crisis. Upon seeing the critical article in *The Times* Asquith did seize upon it as an opportunity to open a disagreement on the outstanding issue of leadership responsibility, though the two leaders were already in basic agreement on the principle of the war council. Thus when Montagu, at Lloyd George's behest, sought to secure written confirmation of the proposed settlement later on Monday morning 'he found Asquith in a great state of perturbation over the article in the "Times". He felt that everything was up.' Montagu discounted Northcliffe's efforts to create dissension and 'begged Asquith still to write to Lloyd George, putting on record the agreement arrived at. Asquith did so in Montagu's presence, but insisted on prefacing it with some remarks about the "Times" articles.'[35] Lloyd George's conciliatory response was undoubtedly due to his failure to understand fully Asquith's new intent and his genuine belief that an agreement could still be salvaged. Asquith's second note, however, where he seized upon the seemingly uncontroversial issue of personnel, left no doubt that he meant to wage all-out war. In all probability this missive was written after Asquith's additional encounter with the Liberal ministers. This inference is substantiated by Donald's interview with Asquith where it is stated that 'later in the day', after his response from Lloyd George, 'the Prime Minister saw Lord Grey, Mr. McKenna, Mr. Runciman, and some other friends. He gave the subject further mature thought and on Monday night sent a letter to Mr. Lloyd George, closing the negotiations, and leaving the Minister for War no option but to resign.'[36] Montagu's account agreed that 'Things looked like breaking up on Monday night'.[37]

But relinquishing the reins of Government, even if only temporarily, after over eight years of unbroken power was discomforting to Asquith's sense of security and pride. Before resigning therefore he summoned Curzon, Chamberlain, and Cecil on Tuesday the 5th, in order to reinforce the impression made by Cecil's message and to dispel any remaining doubts that resignation was the proper course. But the points of view conveyed by the Conservative ministers did nothing to assure Asquith of the safety of the new position he had assumed. Without eliminating the possibility of ever serving under Asquith again, they made clear their refusal to go on without the services of Bonar Law and Lloyd George. Their 'only object', Chamberlain assured Asquith in typically non-committal fashion, was 'to secure a Government on such lines and with such a prospect of stability that it might reasonably be expected to be capable of carrying on the war; ... This was evidently a great blow to him.' Furthermore when Cecil boldly suggested that 'the finest and biggest thing that he could do would be to offer to serve under Lloyd George', Asquith 'would not allow Cecil to develop this idea, which he rejected with indignation and even with scorn'.[38] No doubt Asquith regarded Cecil's suggestion as well as the position assumed by other Conservatives as a complete inversion of the information contained in Drummond's note which formed the basis for his attack on Lloyd George.

But Asquith had already taken too many provocative steps to permit him to assume once more a conciliatory stance, and there were too many leaders in both parties convinced that immediate resignation was the only way to determine who should ultimately be Prime Minister. Thus later in the day Asquith received a note from Bonar Law who, speaking on behalf of all Unionist ministers, advised him that resignation was the only proper course.[39] Similarly, Balfour, who was ill and not in circulation, asked that his resignation be accepted and that 'a fair trial should be given to the new War Council à la George'.[40] Under these conditions it may seem incredulous that Asquith may still have harboured any notion of the possibility of reforming the Cabinet from within while remaining Prime Minister. But Asquith now feared resignation and at a meeting of coalition Liberals at 5 p.m. he proceeded to explain the many disadvantages inherent in any change of administration in the middle of the war. According to Herbert Samuel, the Postmaster-General, Asquith 'evidently did not like the surrender to a minister in revolt that was involved by resignation. However, we were all strongly of opinion, from which he did not dissent, that there was no alternative. We could not in any case carry on without Ll. G. and without the Unionists, and ought not to give the appearance of wishing to do so.'[41] With only Crewe and Henderson, the Labour leader, showing any reluctance a unanimous decision was reached at 7 p.m. Asquith, undoubtedly bewildered and fully aware of his lack of solid Conservative support, motored to Buckingham Palace to tender his resignation to the King.

According to constitutional practice the King, upon the resignation of a Prime Minister, must not return to that person until all other persons who have been asked to form a ministry have either refused or failed. Although the operation of the party system was much subdued in wartime, the King adhered to tradition by choosing the leader of the former Opposition, who in this instance was Bonar Law. The Conservative leader, however, disappointed him at an interview on the evening of 5 December by saying that he did not have much hope of forming a government; but he thought Lloyd George would be more successful. A major point of disagreement arose on the subject of whether a dissolution could be employed as a justification or a consideration in the creation of any new Government. Indeed Bonar Law told the King that 'he, himself, might succeed in forming a Government if he appealed to the Country'. At any rate, 'he had come to the conclusion that he must decide between following Mr. Asquith or Mr. Lloyd George, and, as he believed the latter would win the War before the former could do so, he had decided to follow Mr. Lloyd George'.[42] For counsel Stamfordham late that night asked Lord Haldane, the ex-Lord Chancellor, whether the King could legally decline a dissolution on any of the grounds made plausible by the war. Haldane compiled for the King a three-point memorandum stating that the Sovereign could at no time act without the advice of a responsible minister, except when he exercised his dismissal prerogative. If, however, the King disapproved of his minister's advice to dissolve, he could either dismiss the minister or receive his resignation. 'This is the only alternative to taking his advice.' Under no circumstances could the Sovereign 'entertain any bargain for a dissolution merely with a possible Prime Minister before the latter is fully installed. The Sovereign cannot before that event properly weigh the situation and the Parliamentary position of the Ministry as formed.'[43] The effect of this pronouncement was to limit the power of the King to determine the conditions under which any new Government was to assume office. Yet the King had raised the question of the propriety of carrying out a dissolution during the war, and any new regime would require some means of justifying itself before the people. Under more normal circumstances the selection process was circumscribed by the possibility of a general election. But even the war could not justify the possession by the King of the dual prerogative of choosing a leader for the Government *and* being able to refuse a dissolution. Britain, after all, could hardly abandon more than two centuries of progress towards responsible government. Therefore some alternative procedure of selection and confirmation was necessary to achieve a modicum of national consensus.

The idea of an interparty conference as a solution was first entertained earlier in the week at a dinner party of secondary figures from both parties at the home of Edwin Montagu. Convinced that this was the best course Sir Eric Drummond, Maurice Hankey, and Robert Young, who were all acting in a secretarial capacity, hastened to inform Balfour, Lord Stamfordham, and Arthur Henderson respectively of their views.[44] It is impossible to determine which of these individuals was most responsible for the calling of a conference, but each of them did play a key role in the train of events leading up to a settlement on Wednesday 6 December. While Stamfordham was not initially impressed with the conference idea, it is almost certain that it was discussed at the meeting (where he was present) on Tuesday night between Bonar Law and the King.[45] Asquith's refusal after this interview to serve under Bonar Law, not to mention Lloyd George, made it even more imperative that some interparty agreement be reached.[46] Then on the following morning Henderson, who had acquired the conference notion from Young, his private secretary, visited Bonar Law at Pembroke Lodge and 'urged that, as the situation was very grave, the King should call a conference at Buckingham Palace of leaders of all the parties'.[47] While Bonar Law's reaction was not encouraging he did decide to invite the opinion of his fellow conspirators, Carson, Lloyd George, and Aitken, to decide what steps should be taken in the formation of a new administration. They agreed that Balfour, though confined to his bed, was a pivotal person and that his views should be elicited. After discussing numerous alternatives Bonar Law, Lloyd George, and Balfour 'agreed that if the Sunday arrangement was to be regarded as finally abandoned, the best thing would be to form a Government in which L. G. would be Chairman of the War Committee, and in which Asquith would be included'. To Balfour this only seemed possible with Bonar Law at the helm, as it was improbable that Asquith would consent to serve under Lloyd George. It was agreed that an all-party conference at Buckingham Palace was by far the best course to follow and this was accordingly summoned by the King for three o'clock on Wednesday afternoon, the 6th.[48]

The Buckingham Palace conference was opened by the King with Asquith, Bonar Law, Lloyd George, Henderson, and Balfour in attendance. The proceedings were utterly dominated by Balfour, who was respected by the King and the others as Britain's senior statesman. He urged an alteration of the structure of the war committee while retaining the coalition form of Government. Balfour believed that no Government would be strong enough to carry on the war without Asquith and he hoped that Asquith could see his way to joining an administration with Bonar Law as premier. Bonar Law and Henderson also made strong appeals to Asquith to join the new Government. Lloyd George repudiated any personal animosity towards Asquith, though they had recently experienced a misunderstanding. He also disclaimed any personal ambition to be Prime Minister. Lloyd George claimed that he was prepared to see Asquith form another Government, and even though he might be excluded he would be willing to give it his full support. Failing that, Lloyd George urged Asquith to join a Government under Bonar Law. But he believed that 'unless a real War Committee, with full and independent powers, was constituted, we should go to ruin and lose the War, which up till now had been mismanaged'. Asquith disagreed. He thought the existing war committee had done creditable work and that it was impossible for the Prime Minister not to be also a member of the war council. He attributed the recent turmoil in the upper echelons of the Government to the insidious machinations of the press. Balfour described their exchange of views as 'very moderate in form, but so far as Asquith and L.G. were concerned, with a subacid flavour'. At the conclusion of the conference Balfour stated his opinion that it would not be possible for Asquith to form an administration and that a Government without Lloyd George would be unthinkable. Bonar Law, he concluded, would be the most likely person to bring the disparate elements together. 'The result of the Meeting', according to Stamford-ham, 'was an agreement that Mr Asquith should consider the proposals made to him, and let Mr Bonar Law know as soon as possible whether he would join the Government under him. If the answer was in the negative, Mr Bonar Law would not form a Government, but Mr Lloyd George would endeavour to do so.'[49]

When the conference adjourned at 4.40 p.m. all indicators were pointing towards Lloyd George as the nation's new leader. While accompanying Balfour home Bonar Law admitted that he was most reluctant to take over the reins of Government because 'by whatever name it might be described, L.G. would undoubtedly be its most powerful member, and he (B.L.) would much prefer that the forms of power and its substance should go together'. Balfour was not successful in convincing him that he might share the leadership, with Bonar Law as Prime Minister and leader of the house and Lloyd George as head of the war council. So utterly convinced was Bonar Law of the necessity of Lloyd George's leadership that he asked Balfour whether 'if A. showed any sort of readiness to serve under him, it was wise to push him to serve under L.G.'. Balfour of course responded negatively.[50] But such tactics proved unnecessary as Asquith unwittingly relinquished the leadership without a struggle. At a meeting of leading Liberals and Henderson at Downing Street it was unanimously agreed that it was not feas-ible to proceed with a Government including no Unionist representation and without Lloyd George. Only Henderson and Montagu showed any sympathy with the idea that Asquith ought to join an administration either under Bonar Law or Lloyd George. The remaining members, including Asquith, believed that any such combination would be 'mistaken and futile'.[51] Asquith's answer to Bonar Law therefore was that he and his followers could not be a part of any ministry under the Conservative leader. At seven o'clock Bonar Law informed the King that he would not be willing to form a Government without Asquith, and Lloyd George was sent for at once.

Lloyd George's eventual success in forming a ministry was largely the work of Bonar Law, Balfour, and other leading Conservatives. On the evening of 6 December Bonar Law and Edmund Talbot, the Conservative whip, offered to Balfour, on behalf of Lloyd George, the Ministry for Foreign Affairs. 'If I consented,' remarked Balfour, 'it would, in the view both of L.G. and himself [Bonar Law], greatly help with the rest of our Unionist colleagues.' In spite of his earlier differences with Lloyd George, Balfour did accept.[52] This act by a former Prime Minister and party leader presumably led to the acceptance by other Conservative leaders of high office under Lloyd George. There is no evidence that this was accomplished, as Beaverbrook suggests, through the singular defection of Curzon, attested only by his acceptance of a seat in the War Cabinet.[53] In an unpublished letter to Crewe over a decade later Beaverbrook elaborated that Bonar Law first saw Cecil, Chamberlain, Curzon, and Walter Long, who stated collectively that they would not accept office until they were certain that Lloyd George could form a ministry. When Long was approached separately by Lloyd George with an offer he declined 'on the ground that he must stand by his friends ... and deal only in group formation'. Then almost as a last resort Bonar Law allegedly sent Edmund Talbot to Curzon 'with an offer of a place in the War Cabinet. That settled it. A meeting was immediately arranged for the four Conservative ex-Ministers with Lloyd George. They found a basis on which they could join the Ministry.'[54] In an effort to substantiate this story Beaverbrook sent a copy of this letter to Lloyd George requesting confirmation of the facts contained in it.[55] But his personal secretary, Frances Stevenson, replied that Lloyd George was 'not quite clear as to what happened on the occasion referred to in your letter and enclosures. He was rather under the impression that Curzon came in with Chamberlain and Cecil, but on the other hand he certainly will not dispute your statement as regards the Edmund Talbot incident. But of the latter he has no clear recollection.'[56] From this evidence it appears more likely that Cecil, Chamberlain, and Curzon joined the Lloyd George coalition in unison after the acceptance of Balfour.

The political crisis of December 1916 can best be understood as a Conservative *coup d'état*. By late 1916 the Conservative leaders were becoming increasingly restive with their situation under Asquith and more amenable to suggestions of an alternative Government under Lloyd George, who appeared to be more sensitive to the dextral swing of the political pendulum during the war. To this end they followed a dual course of appearing content with Asquith while contemplating a change under Lloyd George. This course of action was carried out by Bonar Law, who made the first breach in Asquith's sense of security and pride by requesting, at the behest of his colleagues, his resignation. Perplexed by the meaning of the Conservative message and frightened by the prospect of combating Lloyd George without Conservative support, Asquith first opted for the safer course of reconstruction of the Cabinet from within. He was ultimately led from this course, not by the deception of Curzon, whose communication was no less equivocal than that of Bonar Law, but by Robert Cecil whose message was positive and sure, and led Asquith to believe, that he could safely resign and fight Lloyd George with the full weight of the Tory leaders behind him. That this support was never forthcoming may be attributed to the fact that Lloyd George was given the opportunity to form a Government first and that he offered the Conservatives far more than they had ever had or could ever expect to achieve under Asquith.

In a more general sense this outcome was the result of the interaction of more abstract forces in human nature. If Asquith appeared somewhat tired and overwrought by December 1916 Lloyd George, on the other hand, was fully in possession of the necessary physical and mental strength to undertake the responsibilities of the premiership. Moreover there seemed to be a certain dynamism and inevitability to Lloyd George's accession and that if he was denied the prize there would simply be a return to the old conditions and a continuing struggle for control. F. S. Oliver later described Lloyd George as 'not a man; but rather a natural force—the strongest we have got. . . . He is the most impersonal form of human energy I've met. But I respect him for one thing: he will win the war if he can; and if he can't I don't believe that any man can.'[57] Lloyd George was vaulted into power on the shoulders of three important Conservatives—Carson, Bonar Law, and Balfour respectively. The first mounted an attack on Asquith's record of leadership, the second forced him out of power, and the last replaced him with Lloyd George. Others, notably Beaverbrook and the trio of Cecil, Chamberlain, and Curzon, provided vital assistance by undermining the seemingly solid position of Asquith. Indeed the Conservative hierarchy not only elevated Lloyd George to the premiership, but sustained him through the remaining years of the war and the reconstruction. 'How fruitful this combination was will be amply recorded in history,' wrote Beaverbrook. 'Lloyd George never went wrong until Bonar Law had to leave him.'[58] But Conservative support of the Government also laid a heavy hand on the conduct of the war and the coalition's Irish policy. Lloyd George was the new leader, but he never forgot whom he had to please.

The formation of the Lloyd George coalition in December 1916 had a far greater significance than the mere enactment of a change in Government. It constituted the final and most momentous step towards national unity, to which all previous attempts at interparty conciliation had been directed. As an offshoot of the traditional conference procedure, the Buckingham Palace conference provided a valuable precedent for forming coalitions during times of acute constitutional stress or a national crisis. By elevating the Conservatives to a position of power under Lloyd George it not only produced a more dynamic administration to oversee the war effort, but effectively ended the tortuous decade of constitutional strife which had begun with the election of 1906. Admittedly the party conflict had been lessened by preoccupation with the war and the formation of the 1915 coalition, but it was not until the Conservatives assumed a position of paramountcy, which included control over the Irish issue, that the *casus belli* was removed. Now under the energetic leadership of Lloyd George attention was increasingly focused on encouraging a consensus of opinion which was necessary to win the war and eventually to administer the Government's reconstruction programme. In this era an attempt was made to apply this sense of co-operation to some of the issues which had previously divided the parties and provoked acute controversies in British politics. For this purpose an interparty conference procedure, with a more representative format, was often adopted by the coalition government under Lloyd George. It differed from its pre-war counterparts not so much in its legislative objectives as by the manner in which the negotiations were carried out. The method of these latest conferences was to preserve and utilize, rather than create, any spirit of national unity. That these conditions prevailed by 1916 may be attributed not only to the relaxation of party loyalties, but to the adaptation of Britain's parliamentary system and constitution to the societal pressures for democratic change which had been mounting since the passage of the Second Reform Bill.

The Lloyd George Era

VIII

The Speaker's Conference on
Electoral Reform, 1916–1917

No Government undertakes Reform Bills if they can possibly help it. It is the most ungrateful and difficult task with
which any Government can be confronted.

WALTER LONG[1]

Although most of the history of the electoral reform movement
properly belongs to the pre-war era, its most climactic development coincided with those emergent forces which elevated
Lloyd George to power in 1916 and sustained his coalition
Government for the remainder of the war. Nowhere was the
national trend from division to consensus more striking than
in the change of opinion towards the women's suffrage issue
during the war. Unlike most questions relating to electoral
reform, this topic had never been advocated by either major
party and had never been subjected to interparty controversy.
Yet the women's cause repeatedly excited the passions of the
strongest adherents and the staunchest opponents of both
parties and sexes. For nearly a half century women's suffrage
had been frustrated, despite substantial support within and outside Parliament, by lack of Government facilities and an
adequate procedure to enact a legislative issue which so
thoroughly crossed party lines and national opinion. This
denial eventually gave rise to the most desperate acts of militancy by a small group of women who called themselves 'suffragettes' prior to 1914. The outbreak of the war brought an end
to civil disobedience and the sacrifices of women in the war undoubtedly made women's suffrage more acceptable to members
of Parliament and public opinion. But the question of giving
women the vote or any other electoral matter never would have
arisen if the politicians had not been confronted with the
urgency of granting soldiers and sailors the vote. This issue provided the impetus for the calling of an all-party conference,

chaired by the Speaker of the House of Commons, to consider a broad range of electoral subjects.

The Asquith Government's major attempt to institute electoral reform before the war was its franchise and registration bill of 1912. Unlike previous attempts at piecemeal legislation, the bill intended to shorten the residence qualification for voting, abolish plural voting, and provide for a system of continuous registration, all in a single measure. Furthermore the Prime Minister, though a confirmed antisuffragist, had promised a deputation of women in November 1911 that he would not oppose any amendments which might arise to enfranchise women.[2] This added the most controversial electoral issue to the not-so-tame proposals already in the bill and there was much speculation in the press on whether Asquith would keep his promise to the women.[3] In January of 1913, however, nearly seven months after its second reading, the Speaker, James W. Lowther, abruptly eliminated any possibility of the bill's passage by ruling that the addition of any women's suffrage amendments would so change the character of the bill as to require the introduction of a new one.[4] This ruling, based on a precedent laid down by Speaker Peel in 1889, evinced the mighty influence which the chair could wield over the course of legislation in the house by its ultimate control of procedure. It completely destroyed the chances of the important women's suffrage amendments becoming part of a Government measure and forced the Prime Minister to withdraw the entire bill. In spite of the controversy engendered by the action of the Speaker, whose antisuffragist views were well known, there was no evidence to indicate that the Government had deliberately acted in bad faith or that the Speaker had not acted in accordance with the highest judicial standards of his office. Lowther remarked later, 'I am satisfied that, however unexpected, it was correct.'[5]

The Prime Minister later erred in consoling the suffragists by promising that he would provide facilities for a private member's bill in the following session. 'A Private Member's Bill!' exclaimed Lord Newton. 'The idea that any one could be taken in with an assurance of that kind!'[6] Millicent Garrett Fawcett, the leader of the National Union of Women's Suffrage Societies, wrote, 'It needed not to be a Daniel or a Solomon to see that a private Member's Bill, of which seven had passed Second Reading in the last four years, and four of them in 1908, 1909, 1910, and 1911, was no substitute for a place in a Government Bill.'[7] Even though the Government assured facilities for its passage through the House of Commons and the Parliament Act guaranteed its protection in the House of Lords, suffragists of all persuasions now agreed that only a Government bill stood any chance of success. W. H. Dickinson, who had introduced a private member's bill to enfranchise women in April of 1913, was fully aware of the difficulties it faced even when all obstacles were removed by the Government. 'We have no Junior Lord of the Treasury to stand at the doors into the lobby with an eye like Mars to threaten and command,' he told the house. 'We have no reserves whom we can call up to help us out of a tight place. We have not even the ordinary facility that a Government has of making Members vote against their own opinions. We have only our own powers of persuasion to rely upon, and I assure the House that in my own case I am painfully aware of my shortcomings in this respect.'[8] Although they could not oppose any such legislation, the women's suffrage societies decided to take no part in supporting Dickinson's bill, which was defeated by forty-six votes. A similar fate awaited the Government on 30 April when it introduced its plural voting bill, which had originally been part of its electoral reform programme in the previous session. Bonar Law accused the Government of wasting time on this bill. The real reason for this measure, he argued, was that 'the Government have got into rather troubled waters in connection with woman suffrage. ... In this situation they could not bring in a Bill dealing with the whole question and leave that out.'[9] Although the bill secured a majority of eighty-six in the lower house, it was defeated in the House of Lords as 'a shameless party manœuvre' by 124 votes.[10] Clearly the demand was for a comprehensive treatment of electoral reform, and no such measure was possible unless it recognized the claims of women.

The most obvious frustration over the inability of the Government to secure the passage of women's suffrage was exhibited by the militant suffragist organization, the National Women's Social and Political Union. Mrs Emmeline Pankhurst, its fiery leader, declared, 'Either we must have a Govern-

ment measure, or those men who call themselves Woman Suffragists in the Cabinet must go out, or we take up the sword
again, never to lay it down until the enfranchisement of the
women in this country is won.'[11] Militant outrages, once limited
to mild acts of stone-throwing and general unruliness, now
reached the dimensions of an epidemic. Annie Kenney, one of
the leaders, noted that from the day of the Speaker's ruling 'increased arson was the policy of the Union. Fires everywhere,
long sentences, hunger-strikes, forcible feeding.'[12] For the remainder of 1913 and early 1914 militant suffragists continued
their wanton destruction of public property. Outrages took the
form of bomb explosions, golf-course mutilations, window-
breaking, arson, and personal assaults (both verbal and physical) on the Prime Minister and members of the Government.
In March of 1914 militant lawlessness took a new form when
Miss Mary Richardson attacked the famous *Rokeby Venus* in the
National Gallery with a meat chopper.[13] This act inspired the
suffragettes to new and more spectacular deeds of destruction.
In the next four months they mutilated ten more works of art
and were responsible for nearly a hundred cases of arson and
other serious forms of public outrage, their incidence greatly
exceeding the number of arrests. These activities attracted far
more attention from the public, the press, and Parliament than
the tame proceedings of the constitutional suffragists in trying
to interest the Government in adopting a women's suffrage bill.
But so long as the militant acts of destruction continued there
was little prospect of Parliament enacting any suffragist legislation.

This deadlock was removed by an ironic series of developments over the next several years. At the beginning of the war
all women suffragists, both constitutional and militant, followed the lead of the politicians by calling a truce on domestic
controversies and turning their attention to the prosecution of
the war. From early July 1914 the number of outrages gradually
decreased; by the beginning of August militancy was non-
existent. Mrs Pankhurst and her eldest daughter, Christabel,
now actively supported the Government in its execution of the
war. Christabel wrote, 'As Suffragettes we could not be pacifists
at any price. Mother and I declared support for our country.
We declared an armistice with the Government and suspended

militancy for the duration of the war.'[14] Women's assistance in the war effort was limited at first to work in the traditional areas of medicine and relief where there was no actual replacement of men. But as the demand grew for more men at the front, increased opportunities for employment arose in such fields as railway services, the grocery trade, engineering, architecture, banking, and other occupations formerly dominated by men. By the spring of 1915 women were beginning to be noticed in certain industrial employments. Although these instances provoked much attention, the actual number of women employed in such occupations during the first six or eight months of the war was not significant.[15] Furthermore these activities had little influence as yet on members of the Government or Parliament to change the electoral status of women.

Likewise there was little recognition of the need for any electoral reform until after the voting register, which was compiled in 1914, came into effect in early 1915. Although this register included over eight million voters, it was obsolete because tens of thousands of soldiers and sailors who were serving overseas, though on the register, were incapable of voting.[16] The Government was unwilling to rectify this anomaly for fear of engendering some of those subliminal pre-war electoral controversies such as women's suffrage. After stalling the issue for several months the Government was forced, through an elections and registration bill, to postpone the holding of municipal elections and to abandon the compilation of any new register, pending a thoroughgoing reform of the electoral system. Few recognized this as any more than a temporizing measure. C. P. Scott called the bill 'an abortive attempt to deal with the difficulties of the moment, avoiding all the big issues'.[17] In the fall of 1915 the Government encountered an even more serious dilemma. According to the Parliament Act of 1911, which reduced the life of Parliament from seven to five years, the present body would have to be dissolved in wartime (31 January 1916), unless Parliament enacted legislation to prolong its life. To avoid the divisions and distractions of a general election the Government duly introduced, and Parliament passed, a parliament and registration bill, but not without raising the troublesome questions of soldiers' and sailors' votes and women's services in the war.[18]

During the latter part of 1915 the replacement of men by women in industry progressed much faster than in the first year of the war.[19] By April 1916 Walter Long, Chairman of the Local Government Board, estimated that some 275,000 women were engaged in work in substitution for men in industrial occupations alone, and recognition for these endeavours was soon forthcoming.[20] According to Mrs Fawcett, 'We began to be aware of a new note among the voices that go to make up public opinion when we discovered commercial and financial magnates, managers of railways and other great industrial concerns, and old-fashioned country gentlemen', who hitherto had not favoured women's suffrage, 'joining in the chorus which was now loudly chanting the praises of women's work.'[21] *The Times*, which had administered countless blows to the women's cause before the war, now referred to their work as 'one of the surprises and triumphs of this tremendous upheaval'.[22] Sensing this to be an opportune time to raise the suffrage question, Fawcett and her followers addressed a 'careful letter' to the Prime Minister suggesting that when the Government dealt with the franchise it should consider it along wider lines than simply the removal of the accidental disqualification of soldiers and sailors.[23] But the Government, unable to agree on either a broad or a narrow treatment of electoral reform, proposed that the House of Commons should settle the matter. On 12 July Asquith told the house that the issue went beyond the problem of registration as it raised difficulties with the franchise, for which the Cabinet had been unable to find 'any practical and uncontroversial solution'. Reasoning that the matter concerned the House of Commons more than the Government, he proposed that the lower house set up a 'Select Committee' to settle the matter. While the house was not in actual revolt, it was not very anxious to pursue this task; in addition there arose the problem of who should sit on the committee. Again Asquith abdicated all responsibility. 'The composition of the committee is a matter entirely for the House. The only thing I say about it is that no member of the Government intends to sit upon it.'[24]

This attempt by the Prime Minister to 'wash his hands' of registration and its sister issues did not at first offend the members of the house. A week later, however, when Herbert

Samuel presented substantially the same proposal to the house it encountered considerable hostility and raised a host of questions on what classes should be enfranchised during the war. Sir Edward Carson launched a fierce attack on the Government accusing it of 'humbugging' the house for nearly a year. He declared that the Government had 'no right to leave this country without a register, because at any moment a General Election may be necessary. . . . To carry out a General Election upon a register that is nearly two years old means that you go to the election with the disfranchisement of thousands and tens of thousands who are here in this country, not to talk at all of the men in the trenches.' He urged the house not to confuse the enfranchisement issue with the question of the register by arguing over 'what is a munition worker, what is a woman, and who is a woman, and should a woman have a vote, and all the rest of it'.[25] Although other speakers did not necessarily share Carson's narrow view of the franchise question, they all agreed that this was a matter for the Government to settle. As *The Times* summed up the situation: 'The next move is with the Government, who have already been told, as plainly as any Government ever received instructions from an impatient people, that what is required of them now is action, not excuses.'[26]

Instead of action the Government replied to these demands with more excuses. The first took the form of another parliament and registration bill which amended the previous act and extended the life of Parliament an additional eight months. The other was a special register bill which was a weak proposal to grant the vote to soldiers and sailors without altering the basis of the franchise. This meant that those servicemen who happened to be at home would be able to vote while those serving overseas would still be disfranchised. While Parliament quickly passed the first bill out of necessity, the second one provoked a storm of protest. Carson objected to it because it included only a small portion of servicemen. Sir John Simon, the former Home Secretary, attacked the Government for ignoring the claims of women. But the Prime Minister outdid all of his critics by describing the bill 'not as logical or complete, or anything but a very halting, lop-sided, and temporary make-shift, which may or may not be seaworthy, but which is better than any substitute which exists or has been suggested'.[27] Failing to gain real support from any quarter of the house, Bonar Law, on behalf of the Government, announced that they would not attempt to proceed with the committee stage of the bill before adjournment.

Yet this debate was not entirely devoid of positive results. With no apologies for the bill Walter Long suggested that the house pass it and then try to solve the general problem, not by a committee, but by a 'representative conference'. Envisaging a body that would represent parties and groups of all opinions, Long believed 'such a conference of earnest men— holding strong views and bitterly opposed to each other, but at this particular moment all longing to see a better prospect for the country—would produce an agreed system'.[28] The idea was quickly taken up by the Liberal and Labour benches and by certain quarters outside the house. Sensing a broad basis of support Asquith commented on Long's suggestion of a conference as 'very valuable' and told the House of Commons that he hoped to give effect to it very soon.[29] In the meantime Long had proceeded to outline the nature of the conference he had in mind to Asquith. He hoped it would examine and submit agreed resolutions on all phases of electoral reform, including the franchise, redistribution of seats, voter registration, and the method of elections, and be representative of all shades of opinion in Parliament.[30] As additional stimulation for his plans Long offered to set aside the largest room at the Local Government Board for the sittings of the conference, and to place his staff and papers at its disposal.

According to *The Times* what the conference now needed was 'a distinguished man with an impartial mind such as an ex-Judge, to preside over the proceedings'.[31] Long had originally suggested Robert Romer, a retired Lord Justice of Appeal, for chairman, but he was thought to be too old. Then Lord Buckmaster, the Lord Chancellor, eliminated the possibility of selecting a current judge for the reason that it would take him away from the work of the judicial committee in the House of Lords.[32] Almost as a last resort Asquith secured the consent of the Speaker of the House of Commons to preside over the conference. Lowther remarked that it was 'with some hesitation that I accepted the task. Feeling upon these topics had run very high before the war. ... [But] the war was acting as a strong cementing force, a Coalition Government was in power, and the time was perhaps opportune for an agreement if such a thing were possible.'[33] During the parliamentary recess in September the Speaker attempted to make a balanced selection of interests for the conference from a list of sixty-one names prepared for him by Long. He chose fourteen Unionists, ten Liberals, three Irish Nationalists, two Scottish Liberals, and three Labour members. On the critical women's issue the conference was slightly suffragist, perhaps because this was now the personal position of the Speaker, or more likely because this was his view of the disposition of Parliament on the question. According to the *Nation* the conference was comprised of fifteen suffragists, eleven decided antisuffragists, two so-called 'wobblers', and four Irish members, who from their records were quite incalculable.[34]

On 12 October the Speaker's conference held its first meeting behind closed doors at the Local Government Board. Willoughby Dickinson, a Liberal backbencher and an ardent spokesman for women's suffrage, thought it was a 'very curious meeting and it will be a miracle if we can reconcile such divergent constituents. But it is not impossible if we act circumspectfully.'[35] By this time women's work was having a powerful effect on the formation of public opinion in favour of extending the franchise to women. In 1916–17, to use Mrs Fawcett's expression, 'conversions of important public men and of newspapers came in, not by twos and threes, but by battalions'.[36] On 13 August 1916 the *Observer* completely reversed its position on women's suffrage. 'Time was', wrote J. L. Garvin, 'when I thought that men alone maintained the State. Now I know', he confessed, 'that men alone never could have maintained it, and that henceforth the modern State must be dependent on men and women alike for the progressive strength and vitality of its whole organization.'[37] But the most notable conversion was that of Violet Markham, once head of the antisuffragists, who was converted while performing war work. At the beginning of the war the vast arsenal of Woolwich in London employed only 14,000 workers, without a single woman. By the middle of 1916 there were some 17,000 women out of a work force of 67,000.[38] As the *Spectator* remarked, 'To say "How splendidly women have done!'' has become such a commonplace that it cannot be heard without yawning.'[39]

In the meantime the efforts of the conference to achieve comprehensive reforms in the electoral system were threatened by the more immediate issues of registration and votes for servicemen, which were again before Parliament. It was mainly on the urging of Walter Long, who thought that they would have to wait too long for the Speaker's conference to act on this subject, that the Government decided to proceed with its special register bill.[40] When the bill reached its committee stage on 1 November a number of amendments were presented to ensure servicemen overseas of the right to vote. One such proposal, moved by Colonel Page Croft, intended to enfranchise soldiers and sailors 'apart from any other qualification'. At this juncture the Speaker intervened, as he did in 1913, and stated that this amendment would so widen the bill as to make it inconsistent with the general franchise law. After stating that any change in the law would require an amendment to the franchise acts, the Speaker hatcheted the other amendments in the same manner.[41] The *Daily Telegraph*, pronouncing it a 'complete fiasco', observed that Lowther had slain all the proposals one by one. 'This was not permissible on one ground, that on another. And so on, from the third to the fourth, and fourth to the fifth. There was no health in them. . . . When the Speaker stopped, the paper was bare. It was an artistic performance.'[42] In view of this unexpected ruling from the chair the Government, with considerable loss of dignity, decided to carry its bill no further at present. 'It ought never to have been proceeded with,' said Dickinson. 'I had warned the Whips but Long is stupidly stubborn.'[43] Whether the Speaker acted out of personal motives here to safeguard the conference he was chairing cannot be determined, but his ruling did obstruct the progress of the Government's expedient measure and did contribute mightily to the ultimate success of women's suffrage.

Now the House of Lords attempted to carry out what the Government, owing to the action of the Speaker, had failed to provide—votes for soldiers and sailors on active service. As part of his parliamentary register and elections bill Lord Salisbury proposed that commanding officers of ships and military units and the superintendents of munitions works return to the

Local Government Board the names and addresses of their men over twenty-one. Although this measure passed its second reading, Lord Lansdowne, speaking for the Government, advised against it because Salisbury's bill was to some extent dependent on the Government's proposals in the other house, which did not look very promising.[44] Finally all attempts by Parliament to achieve a limited measure of reform collapsed when the Government on 30 November decided to withdraw permanently its special register bill. 'It would be unwise for the moment', Lansdowne announced, 'to persevere further with this legislation by the knowledge that this and other connected questions have now been for some weeks under examination by the conference presided over by the Speaker of the House of Commons.'[45] By the end of 1916 Lowther and his colleagues had thus assumed complete control, through the elimination of all lesser attempts at reform, over the electoral issue. It was now impossible for women's suffrage to be considered apart from other more politically pertinent topics.

Since its first meeting in October, the Speaker's conference had been meeting two mornings a week. Completely outside of regular parliamentary procedure, its deliberations were conducted in the strictest secrecy, no records were kept, and no special pleading heard. Later the Speaker, in his *Commentaries*, said they devoted the first three months to the intricacies of registration. 'I endeavoured to push off the burning question of women's suffrage as long as I could, and succeeded, for I felt that if we could agree upon other matters, such as owner's vote, the extension of the suffrage, redistribution of seats, and so forth, there might be a greater disposition to come to some satisfactory solution of the women's question.'[46] Such adroit management of affairs characterized the Speaker's leadership throughout the conference. Moreover the war spirit of co-operation had so permeated society and the conference that it simplified the task of reaching a compromise on some of the most stubborn pre-war controversies. At one point the conference was endangered by a shake-up in the Government. In early December Asquith was forced to relinquish the premiership and the conference found itself working under an uncertain mandate. On the heels of these changes three Unionists, Salisbury, Sir Frederick Banbury, and James Craig, resigned ostensibly because 'the Government at whose instance this Conference was appointed no longer exists and it would be impossible therefore to render to it any Report'.[47] This was an effective disguise at least for their inability to agree with some of the conclusions being reached. But the remaining members unanimously agreed that it would be 'a serious misfortune to allow the Conference to break up in view of the progress made and an evident desire to arrive at an agreement'.[48] Furthermore when approached by the Speaker on the subject Lloyd George, the new Prime Minister, urged him to complete his task 'with all dispatch'.[49]

A record of the proceedings would be helpful in understanding the interaction of the various factions in the conference and the role of the Speaker, but no such account is available. A more general summary which the Speaker sent to Lloyd George on 22 December represents the only description (aside from the final report) of the conference's progress. Its accomplishment included an entire remodelling of the machinery for registration, a complete scheme of redistribution, and a reduction of plural voting. There remained the question of enfranchisement, but the conference was already in substantial agreement on a six months' residential qualification and the occupation of business premises of £10 yearly value. In regard to registration and votes for servicemen, which had provided the initial impetus for the conference, Lowther foresaw the possibility of its not being fully worked out until the end of the war, at which time any new system would be useful only for the purposes of demobilization. Nevertheless he was prepared to induce the conference to consider a one month's residence requirement for returning servicemen.[50] Altogether the conference had passed twenty-four resolutions, all but four of which were unanimous. Of these four, three passed with only one dissentient. On the other, which dealt with a form of proportional representation known as the alternative vote, a controversial subject which crossed party lines, the figures were eleven to eight.[51] The extent of agreement on these lesser issues provided valuable momentum for reaching an agreement on the crucial topic of women's suffrage, which was the next topic on the agenda.

By the second week in January of 1917 the conference was back in session and women's participation in the war was reaching its high-water mark. The conference was reinforced by Lord Stuart of Wortley, George Touche, and Edward Archdale who replaced the three Unionists who had resigned. The *Common Cause*, the organ of the constitutional women's movement, regarded the first two as 'staunch Women's Suffragists'.[52] This was important because of those who had resigned Banbury was regarded as one of the bitterest enemies of votes for women and Salisbury, who had voted against women's suffrage in 1914 and would do so again in 1918, was not noted for his enlightened views towards women.[53] This left the Unionists still one member short since there was no one replacing Sir Robert Finlay, who had resigned on becoming Lord Chancellor in December. Of those who remained there was no strong sentiment against women's suffrage and there were a number of members who were strongly in favour of it. On 10 January the conference began its discussion of this important topic. In a division on the expediency of women's suffrage as a whole, according to Dickinson, the conference divided '15 for and 6 against. On the same terms as men was rejected by 12 to 10.'[54] Dickinson then proposed that 'the vote should be accorded to all women who were either "occupiers" themselves or wives of occupiers', which secured a nine to eight majority. 'Thus by one vote', Dickinson asserted, 'we secured for women's suffrage a place in the report that Mr. Speaker brought up to Parliament. Had it not been for this I doubt if there would have been any positive recommendation on Women's Suffrage and the House of Commons would have found itself once again powerless to reconcile the conflicting views of its members.'[55] Although Dickinson may have overstated the importance of this resolution in the final outcome of the reform saga, it did help to ensure the inclusion of women's suffrage in any broad measure of electoral change.

The admission of a majority of the members to the principle of women's suffrage set the stage for a compromise which would achieve a greater degree of unanimity and make the proposal more attractive when it eventually reached Parliament. Sir William Bull, Conservative M.P. for Hammersmith and private secretary to Walter Long, took the lead in bringing the Tories to meet the suffragists halfway. He wrote a year later:

It was clear to us at the Speaker's Conference that the Women's question had to be settled in some shape or way, but their number presented an appalling difficulty. We finally based our scheme on the Local Government Franchise which gave votes for Municipal purposes to widows and spinsters who paid rates. To these we added the wives of men who paid rates.

Even this was found to include too many to satisfy the Conference, so we decided to reduce the number by an age limit which would be fair to all classes.

The ladies in question were willing to accept forty, so I tentatively 'commenced the bidding' with that limit, putting forward as a reason that at that age women had usually finished all the earlier rearing of children, and domestic duties, and had more time to devote to matters political.

This put even the opposition on the Conference in a good humour and the right frame of mind to consider the matter. Forty was felt to be 'derisory', so the majority plumped for thirty-five, which Mr. Walter Long, who had hitherto been an opponent, promptly cut down to thirty when we were drafting the Bill.[56]

In addition to conferring a modicum of suffrage on women the conference made some provision for absentee voting and agreed that the residence qualification for servicemen should be only one month instead of the usual six. At its last meeting on 26 January the conference discussed the report it was to make to the House of Commons for nearly four hours and delegated the Speaker to submit its resolutions in the form of a letter to the Prime Minister. At the conclusion of the meeting T. P. O'Connor, the senior member, presented a silver tray to the Speaker on which were inscribed the names of all the members of the conference, a fitting tribute to the man who had tactfully and expeditiously guided the conference through its twenty-six sittings.[57]

The following day the Speaker submitted the resolutions of the conference to Lloyd George. Those subjects on which there was unanimous agreement included registration, residence, plural voting, absentee voting, redistribution, and the conduct of elections. The issues on which the conference had failed to reach unanimity, but were nevertheless included in the report, were proportional representation and women's suffrage.[58] The response of the public and the press to these resolutions was undeniably favourable and the Speaker was credited for the success of the conference. *The Times* heralded the recommendations as 'accepted almost universally in political circles as marking a great advance on the difficult road of parliamentary reform' and spoke of the majority resolution on women's suffrage as 'a sign of the times that cannot be mistaken'.[59] In support of the proposals Walter Long circulated a memorandum within the Cabinet recommending their adoption and took immediate action to stifle any possible criticism of them within his party. On 3 February he received an ominous note from Sir Arthur Steel-Maitland, Chairman of the Unionist Party Organisation, stating that the Speaker's proposals would be '*absolutely disastrous*' to their party.[60] In reply Long declared that 'our Party will be destroyed if we were to be so mad as to object to these proposals because some people think they would injure our Party' and that he would be compelled to take action within the Cabinet if Steel-Maitland insisted on pressing his views any further.[61] Later, in a letter to the Speaker, Long recognized that 'the results seem to be really splendid. I know how much we owe you; it is entirely thanks to you that the conference has come through so triumphantly.'[62] The Speaker's conference in this instance proved to be an ideal method for consolidating interparty desires, where there was some substantial agreement at large, into a specific legislative proposal.

In spite of the enthusiastic public reception of the Speaker's conference proposals, much depended on how the Government would react to the conference report; and Lloyd George's coalition showed little more eagerness than Asquith's pre-war ministry to deal with electoral reform and to incorporate the conference suggestions into a Government bill. When the War Cabinet met on 6 February it recognized that the franchise and registration issues had been changed by the resolutions of the Speaker's conference, but it was unable to decide on the best method of introducing the question into the House of Commons.[63] This reluctance stemmed partly from Lloyd George's apprehensions that some of the more controversial provisions of the conference report would provoke an active resistance within the Tory Party. These fears were to some extent justified by Carson, who was circulating a petition, which was ultimately signed by over a hundred members of Parliament, denouncing the suggested changes in the electoral system.[64] According to C. P. Scott, the Prime Minister 'sd. he feared he shd. have to fall back on an unambitious scheme for bringing the existing Register up to date, subject to a provision for allowing service with the forces to count as qualifying residence. The difficulty there wd. be with the women who wd. be up in arms.'[65] After nearly two months' delay the Government finally decided to submit the recommendations to the approval of the House of Commons, instead of immediately translating them into a Government bill.[66] It rationalized that such action would preserve the concept of a 'House of Commons bill' as started in the representative conference. But the real reason for such unusual action was that it would free the Government from all responsibility in case some of the more unpopular of the conference recommendations failed. In a further action which disassociated the Government from the proposals, Asquith, whose administration had originally called the conference into being, introduced the resolutions to the house on 28 March. Contrary to the apprehensions of the Government the house was in an extremely good disposition and by a vote of 343 to 64 thanked the Speaker for his services and urged 'that legislation should promptly be introduced on the lines of the Resolutions reported from the Conference'.[67]

Even this clear parliamentary mandate did not assure success for the women's suffrage proposal or its weaker sister, proportional representation. Lloyd George told a deputation of suffragists on 29 March that he had been told by the Speaker that in order to secure a vote on the question it had to be included in the general reform measure, thus avoiding the kind of contretemps associated with previous reform bills which had attempted to alter the basis of the franchise. He was nearly certain that the majority of the Cabinet, though not an overwhelming majority, would vote for its inclusion in the bill. Nor could he make any assurance about the use of Government whips for any part of the reform bill, repeating the fact that the Government still regarded this to be a 'House of Commons measure' and 'not a Government Bill' and that women's suffrage was 'an open question'.[68] When the subject came before the house on 19 June, however, there was little support for Sir Frederick Banbury's motion to exclude women's suffrage from the bill. F. E. Smith exemplified the attitude of many anti-suffragists in the debate when he explained that though he had not been converted, he was prepared to accept the Speaker's conference recommendations in their entirety. 'There was so much that was essential to the vital interests of the country in their recommendations ... that, although I strongly objected to many of these recommendations, it was on the whole worth while and justified to one's conscience to support the whole of them'[69] That the issue was no longer in doubt was indicated by George Thorne, M.P. for West Ham, who contended, 'What is manifest in this Debate is its apparent dullness. . . . It is absolutely clear that the fight is won.'[70] Women's suffrage secured a majority of 330. Proportional representation, however, did not fare nearly so well. It was known that the Prime Minister was not in favour of it, believing it to be a device 'for bringing faddists of all kinds into Parliament and establishing groups and disintegrating parties'.[71] Nor did Parliament eagerly embrace the principle. On 4 July the House of Commons defeated it by 201 to 169.

The other recommendations of the Speaker's conference, which had by now been translated into the Representation of the People Bill, had little difficulty in gaining acceptance. But the work of the Speaker was far from completed. 'My part in the achievement of the success of the Act', he recalled, 'was by no means at an end with the vote of thanks for my services—in fact, the longest though not the most difficult portion of my labours only began in May.'[72] The Speaker was appointed chairman of the boundary commission for England and Wales, which effected the reallotment of seats specified by the redistribution clause of the reform bill. This body held thirty-three sittings throughout the summer and completed its work on 15 September in time for the house to consider its results at the beginning of the autumn session.

While redistribution for England and Wales was under the competent hand of the Speaker and Scotland presented no particular difficulties, political considerations interfered in carrying out the same process in Ireland. John Dillon and other Nationalists complained that redistribution would strengthen the revolutionary Sinn Fein organization at the expense of the Irish parliamentary party. Carson and his associates, on the other hand, recognized that the enactment of the franchise without redistribution would result in the loss of at least three Unionist seats.[73] On 17 October Maurice Healy, a veteran Nationalist, launched a vituperative attack on the Government, accusing it of bad faith and gerrymandering to exclude Nationalists. This bombardment continued for three days, and although the redistribution measure had passed in principle by 217 to 163 votes with the pressure of Government whips, the controversy still raged over the number of seats to be allotted to Tyrone, Fermanagh, and Down, and to the universities. The situation remained critical for several weeks. Finally on 7 December a compromise was reached which enabled the Reform Bill to secure a third reading.[74] It was agreed that a conference should be summoned consisting of two Irish Nationalists, Jeremiah McVeagh and John Clancy, and two Irish Unionists, William Coote and Sir Charles Henry, and chaired by the Speaker. Lowther remarked that 'these gentlemen proved persistent and obstinate in their advocacy, and after five sittings I found myself compelled to give a casting vote'.[75] Being an 'agreed' measure the redistribution of seats (Ireland) bill quickly passed all of its stages and joined the main portion of the Reform Bill for the royal assent in early February of 1918, nearly a year since the Speaker's conference had submitted its report.[76]

The passage of the Reform Bill of 1918 is the story of what happens when a Government is faced with a political issue which is too dangerous to endorse, but too important to ignore. Confronted initially with the necessity of giving soldiers and sailors the vote, the wartime coalition found it could not escape the pleas of women suffragists for equal recognition. After more temporary expedients proved unsatisfactory, the Speaker's conference on electoral reform, contrived by Walter Long and represented by all parties, proved to be the most effective device for dealing with the procedural difficulties occasioned by the abdication of responsibility by the elected leaders in Parliament. An appraisal of the factors leading to the success of the women's suffrage movement, however, must go further than the traditional views of feminist agitation and the work performed by women in the service of their country during the First World War. The chief obstacle encountered by women's suffragists in their fifty-year struggle was procedural as their issue severed the sacred lines of party. This problem was resolved by the Speaker of the House of Commons, who during the war overcame every procedural difficulty which might have hampered women's suffrage by decisive rulings from the chair and resolute action at the conference table. By its integration with other less controversial electoral reforms, women's suffrage gained the equivalent status of a Government measure and was thereby adapted to fit the political realities of the party system in Parliament.

The existence of a coalition Government and a spirit of co-operation engendered by the war undoubtedly contributed to this happy outcome. The Speaker's conference on electoral reform, an adaptation of the interparty conference concept, furnished the necessary institutional framework for this under-taking, and the Speaker played a critical role in personifying the national interest and acting as a focal point for negotiation and compromise. The extent of unanimity was reflected some-what by the greater size and more representative character of this body. Previous conferences had been structured strictly along party lines in Parliament with little consideration for in-dividual or backbench opinion. The Speaker's conference also acted, in a manner not unlike that of the earliest conference endeavours, to corroborate an existing attitude or desire for legislative action. This was not often the case in those pre-war conferences which were contrived simply to satisfy some *pro forma* sentiment for negotiations which would hypothetically eliminate party strife and produce a settlement. In the nine-teenth-century precedents, as in the latest example, interparty negotiations provided a unique channel for enacting into law only those subjects on which there was already a substantial basis for agreement. The great delusion arising from the un-expected success of the Speaker's conference was that such a method could arbitrarily be applied to almost any issue which had provoked party controversy before the war, and that a solu-tion would immediately be forthcoming.

IX

House of Lords Reform, 1917–1918

> Depend upon it, if you ever succeed in so altering the
> character of this House that it consist entirely of deter-
> mined politicians who always attend all the debates and
> attach the same weight and importance that are attached
> to their own opinions by those who sit in the House of
> Commons, you will have pronounced the doom of our
> present system of government.
>
> LORD SALISBURY[1]

One of the direct results of the growth of modern political
parties in the late nineteenth century was the development of
the House of Lords question. The Parliament Act of 1911,
which limited the veto power of the upper chamber to three
sessions and two years, had provided no satisfactory solution.
Indeed this seemingly drastic alteration in the constitution, as
stated in the preamble, was intended as no more than a temporary adjustment until 'a Second Chamber constituted on a
popular instead of hereditary basis' could be brought into
operation.[2] The outbreak of the war had seemed to foreclose
any serious attempt at House of Lords reform until the distant
future. But the spectacular success of the Speaker's conference
on electoral reform raised the serious hope that other oustand-
ing pre-war issues might be settled by a similar process. Like
women's suffrage, upper chamber reform was a topic which
cut across party lines, and a coalition Government was in
power which would help to inspire a sense of unity and co-
operation. But the conditions which had ensured the success
of the electoral reform conference were either not present or
acted in such a way as to devitalize the subsequent second
chamber reform conference. The scope of investigation for the
latter was in no way directly related to the war effort. Hence
the spirit of immediacy and desire inspired by a crisis was
never sufficiently present to make a settlement a national necessity. Furthermore the spirit of co-operation during the war had
so permeated the relationship between political parties in

Parliament that some issues which were hotly contested before 1914 now ceased to provoke any considerable degree of interest. A new, more democratic age was dawning in which the House of Lords had no central place, and where the verdict of the Parliament Act was becoming more tolerable. Consequently the recommendations of the conference for House of Lords reform were relegated to political obscurity.

The idea for a reform of the upper chamber during the war was first inspired by the Lloyd George Government's acceptance of the Speaker's conference electoral reform proposals on 23 March 1917. A week later Walter Long, who had conceived the idea of an all-party conference in 1916, suggested to Lloyd George that it was desirable to 'set up without any delay a Conference to consider and report on the reform of the Second Chamber. It is, I think, a sound argument that if the House of Commons is to be drastically altered [by the franchise act], the same process should be applied to the House of Lords.'[3] Lloyd George agreed, as did Bonar Law, that the existing condition of the House of Lords was quite indefensible and it should be reformed as soon as possible.[4] With a full appreciation of the importance of the Speaker to the success of the preceding conference they began at once to look for an individual who would embody a similar authority and knowledgeability to chair the proposed second chamber conference. In spite of his strong Tory views, Lord Lansdowne was recommended by Bonar Law and Curzon. As a member of the constitutional conference of 1910 and on other occasions during his long parliamentary career he had advocated upper chamber reform. Lansdowne at first declined outright, then accepted the position conditionally.[5] Finally by the end of July he claimed 'no desire whatever to take up the job', and declined even to sit on the conference if it was 'being set up only in order to do lip service to a Parliamentary pledge'.[6] The Speaker of the House of Commons was also consulted, but he refused to oversee yet another conference after his exhausting labours on the previous one, which were still not completed. The Government obtained the services of Viscount Bryce, who was noted chiefly for his popular ambassadorship to the United States and for his writings on that country. It was proposed to Bryce that the conference should include twelve members

from each house and that it should begin its deliberations in
the autumn, following the parliamentary recess.[7] Under the
circumstances Bryce, who was recognized as an authority on
constitutional history and the law, as probably the best possible choice.

By the end of August the chairman had assumed full
authority over the conduct of the conference. The membership
list, which was published in *The Times*, included sixteen Conservatives, twelve Liberals including the chairman, two Irish
Nationalists, one Labourite, and the Archbishop of Canterbury. For secretary Bryce chose G. F. M. Campion, who had
served ably for many years as a clerk in the House of Commons.
The terms of reference called for an investigation of the powers
and composition for a reformed second chamber, and the
adjustment of differences between the two houses.[8] But the
major problem confronting the conference, Bryce admitted to
A. Lawrence Lowell, his American friend, would be that of
composition. 'Some favour election, either by the peers, by Ho.
of C., or by large popular constituencies, or by local bodies like
country and borough Councils. To each of these plans there
are, of course, grave objections.'[9] To formulate proposals for
the conference, thus saving time and regularizing discussions,
Bryce conceived the idea of setting up a small business committee. Lord Crewe, a prospective conference member, later
submitted to Bryce a précis drawn up by the Speaker on the
procedure he had followed in the electoral reform conference.
Part of the secret to the Speaker's success, Crewe noted, was
his ability to dispense with formality in the agenda and the
circulation of papers. Likewise the Speaker's 'avoidance of
divisions, and his system of postponing decisions seem altogether admirable. And his account of the manner in which he
was able to take more charge as the proceedings went on, is
instructive and suggestive.'[10] In a manner similar to that of the
Speaker's conference and the Irish convention, which was also
getting under way, Bryce decided that a preliminary non-
committal discussion would be the best method to get the
conference started.[11]

The first meeting of the second chamber conference was held
on 2 October in a committee room in the House of Lords.
Most of the twenty-one members seemed to desire a greater

co-operation between the two houses, but differed somewhat on the issue of powers, particularly with reference to finance. Lansdowne, drawing on his experience from the 1910 conference, did not think it was possible to devise any statutory definition of 'pure finance'. He suggested a tribunal drawn from both houses to decide whether each individual case falls within the term or not. Sir Thomas Whittaker, a conference radical, injected the idea that the second chamber should be allowed to reject though not to amend a finance bill, which would set the stage for a conference between the two houses or possibly a referendum. His colleague, Sir Charles Hobhouse, expanded on this idea by favouring a strong elected body with substantial financial powers. Conservative Hugh Cecil disagreed, pointing out the impossibility of having two chambers wielding executive powers over the Government. 'You must reserve supreme power to H. of C.', he said. 'The powers of [the] second Chamber must be suspensive—not absolute.'[12] For Selborne this discussion produced 'some great surprises. The one Labour man', he told his wife, 'simply said that he was a single chamber man. But all the Liberal M.P.s expressed frankly their fear of democracy and their wish for an elected House of Lords, elected for a long period of years, automatically renewing itself . . . and with absolutely equal powers with the House of Commons in finance as well as in everything else.'[13] Indeed Selborne and his Unionist colleagues, perhaps from their pre-war experience, feared the non-democratic aspect of the party caucus. What the Conservatives wanted was a second chamber composed on a different basis from the House of Commons. For Conservatives and Liberals alike its powers would ultimately depend on the extent of aristocratic influence in the new chamber.

The importance of this criterion became apparent when the discussion at the fifth meeting of the conference proceeded to the basis for membership of a reconstructed House of Lords. Whittaker spoke at considerable length in favour of an elected chamber, insisting that the destruction of the hereditary character of the house would in no way be detrimental to the monarchy by implication. What he wanted was a strong and effective second chamber which would represent the will of the people, though not exactly a replica of the House of Commons. Crewe, who desired some retention of the hereditary element, expressed nearly the opposite viewpoint. 'The Sec. Ch. shd be strong in capacity of its members but not too strong in its corporate weight,' he said. 'The H. shd. not *at most* be more than 300 or better 225. *One* third having a hereditary character and 2/3 elected freely from the country.' Though an exponent of indirect election, Crewe disapproved of peers being elected by peers or by members of the lower house outright. With the latter he particularly disagreed because any such election would be dominated by the party whips. Instead he favoured a plan whereby the House of Commons would be divided into at least a dozen territorial groups. Elections would be carried out on this basis every three or four years, installing approximately one-third of the House of Commons for a nine- or ten-year term.[14] During the next several sessions as numerous other proposals were discussed the line was clearly drawn between the proponents of direct election and those in favour of an indirect system based on a House of Commons electorate. Much progress appeared to be made, however, when Whittaker and Walter Hudson, the Labour representative, yielded to the inevitability of some form of indirect election. The latter, 'while advocating democratic process and Genl. election recognised the need of *compromise* on the part of members of the Conference and was prepared for such himself. He wd. have the selection made by the H. of Commons.' Others applauded the concession made by the radical members which enabled the conference to proceed to a consideration of the possible modes of indirect election. The most popular notion was that the upper chamber should be elected by the House of Commons, but full agreement was prevented by a group of stalwart Unionists who were concerned over the lack of independent judgement and absence of aristocratic influence in any second chamber chosen solely by the lower house.[15]

With the question of composition still unsettled the conference proceeded at the twelfth session to the subject of settling possible deadlocks between the houses of Parliament. The most important suggestion was that posited by Selborne, who borrowed the ancient concept of conferences and applied it to some of the ideas which had been discussed at the constitutional conference of 1910. He advocated a 'free conference' of 120 individuals (sixty from each house) to settle disputes. This body would have the responsibility of altering disputed sections of a bill for resubmission to Parliament or ultimately to the people by means of a referendum.[16] But Whittaker objected, saying he thought this was tantamount to the creation of a third house of Parliament. As a staunch supporter of representative government Whittaker 'thought there shd. never be any power to pass a measure wh. H. of C. objects to. You might reject a Bill wh. H. of C. wants. But not pass a Bill agst. will of H. of C.' To guard against these dangers he advocated a small conference of ten or fifteen and that referendum should be used only at the request of the Government. Hobhouse agreed, but preferred a conference of about fifty. Other numbers were suggested, but no agreement was reached. In general the Liberals tended to opt for a small body so as to minimize its influence over the House of Commons. When Selborne rose to defend his original proposal he explained that he was not wedded to his figure of 120, but much preferred it to other figures quoted, such as twenty. He was also willing to allow the Government to appeal to a joint sitting or referendum in the event that a free conference rejected the bill *in toto*.[17] At the end of the fourteenth session Bryce attempted to collect the points on which there seemed to be fairly general assent. Either house, it was agreed, should be able to ask for a conference either when a bill passed by one house is rejected by the other, or is returned with damaging amendments. The number in a joint conference should not exceed sixty nor be less than twenty, and its deliberations should be carried out in secret.[18] Although these bases of agreement showed much support for the conference method as the most reliable way of adjusting parliamentary disputes, the public and the press took little notice of these transactions which bore little relation to the progress of the war.

During the latter part of November much time was devoted to the consideration of a referendum as an adjunct to the free conference plan. The most important statement in favour of this alternative was again made by Selborne:

The Government of the United Kingdom is a partnership between the King and the People. The House of Commons is both the representative and the servant of the People. If there was no Second Chamber the House of Commons might usurp the authority of the People. It did so in the time of the Long Parliament and might do so again. The majority of the House of

Commons is more representative of the opinion of the majority of the People than any other body, but it is quite untrue to suggest that the opinion of the majority of the House of Commons is always the opinion of a majority of the People. We want to make sure that the will of the majority of the People shall not be defeated by the sort of influences which are set to work in a highly organised party system. There is always the danger that a minority of the People possessing a temporary majority in the House of Commons may impose its will on the majority of the People. In a matter of second-rate importance this paradox may be tolerated, but in a matter of first-rate importance it would be intolerable and in the long run fatal to democracy. Therefore, there must be a Second Chamber to preserve to the People the right of eventual decision either at a General Election or at a Referendum.

Selborne much preferred the referendum where the electors would be asked to decide one issue, to a general election where many questions would be at stake.[19] While this plan was supported by other Conservatives, such as Lord Balfour of Burleigh and R. A. Sandars, opinion in the conference as a whole was more reticent.[20] The unusual prospect of Conservatives supporting such a highly democratic innovation can best be understood as a tactical move to outflank the Liberal caucus operating in the lower house with Tory democracy appealing directly to the people. But under the circumstances of the wartime coalition this pre-war party alignment was something of an anachronism and never seriously affected the deliberations of the conference.

Several weeks before the Christmas holidays the negotiations appeared to be making definite progress when the leaders of the respective parties in the conference submitted concrete proposals pertaining to the composition of the second chamber. The first was adumbrated by Lansdowne in a paper called 'xyz'. This scheme provided for a second chamber nominated by a small body of fifteen or twenty electors, including x number from the House of Lords, a y number from the House of Commons and a z quantity co-opted by the first two.[21] Assuming that equal weight was assigned to each segment of the electorate the peerage under this plan would still possess considerable authority over the destiny of the upper chamber. Not surprisingly the opinion of the conference, particularly amongst the Liberals, seemed to be against Lansdowne's proposal and more in favour of territorial groups of electors within the House of Commons. These ideas were elaborated in a paper which

Crewe presented to the conference on 14 December. He suggested a second chamber of two hundred, three-quarters chosen by the House of Commons (presumably by territorial groups) and one-quarter by the House of Lords from its own body. Members would serve for a ten-year period with one half retiring every five years. Provision would be made for paying members and election would be carried out by proportional representation.[22] The chief difference between the two plans, aside from the complexity of the latter, was the degree of influence the peerage would possess in the new second chamber. But it was Crewe's scheme, carrying with it the support of the bulk of the Liberal membership in the conference, which formed the basis for a possible compromise.

For the remainder of December Selborne assiduously collected the views of his Conservative colleagues, then composed them into a carefully worded series of amendments to Crewe's original proposals. This document, which also reflected many of Selborne's personal views, expressed throughout a concern for maintaining the dignity of the new second chamber. He did not think this was possible unless the number was increased to over two hundred, at least a quarter of which would be hereditary peers. He suggested 'a House of 240, 80 being elected by the hereditary peers'. A second chamber with any less than two hundred members, Selborne argued, would be overwhelmed by the lower house in any joint sitting. This would be tantamount to single chamber government. As a solution he suggested a referendum or the interjection of a general election, in which case the size of the second chamber would not matter. Furthermore the Conservatives insisted, mainly on the urging of Lansdowne and Rutland, on a twelve-year term of office for members of the second chamber, one-third retiring periodically. In spite of the vociferous objections of Lansdowne, Selborne did not see how the demand for paying members of the upper house could be resisted. Provision would also have to be made for the seating of Archbishops and members of the royal family in the second chamber. But this measure of agreement, as Selborne pointed out, was 'strictly conditional on an agreement as to the powers of the Second Chamber and as to satisfactory arrangements for a Free Conference'.[23] This permitted the Conservatives considerable latitude to condemn any final report which might allocate unlimited dominance to the House of Commons, or failed to make adequate provision for a referendum or other safeguards.

Unfortunately Selborne's amendments were not enthusiastically received by any quarter. Lord Bryce, who believed his task in the conference was 'to discover the path of least resistance and most agreement', was sceptical of referendum. He described it as 'an overbold experiment in the line of direct democracy. It does no harm in the small rural Democracy of Switzerland, but I fear its consequences when applied by Demogogues to the vast masses of such a country as ours. Once introduced, no one can limit the uses to which it may be put.' While Bryce had no personal objection to Selborne's suggestion of a joint sitting after a general election, he did not think the House of Commons would agree to any plan where the second chamber possessed the power of compelling a dissolution. He also doubted the wisdom of recommending to the lower house any scheme where the hereditary peerage made up as much as a third of the upper chamber.[24] As a Liberal and as chairman of the conference Bryce was particularly sensitive to the powers of the House of Commons and was anxious to present a report which that house might find sufficiently attractive to pass. Nor were the Unionists particularly pleased with Selborne's compromise proposals. When the conference resumed its sittings on 15 January Lansdowne again raised the nomination scheme he had introduced before the Christmas holidays. But this plan met with immediate opposition from the more democratic elements in the conference. Whittaker criticized the small body as certain to create a permanent Conservative majority in the upper house, a charge which Lansdowne wholly repudiated. Hudson, the Labourite, also attacked Lansdowne's scheme, favouring a group system of election by the House of Commons. He wanted to make the second chamber 'really *strong*, its powers covering not delay only, but *rejection* in some degree'. By the end of the meeting Lansdowne was resigned to the fact that his scheme was not acceptable to the conference, but he failed to understand what it did want.[25] The time had come for the conference to take some resolute action.

During the next several sessions the chairman brought to a vote many of the issues which had been considered over the previous four months. The biggest surprise was the seventeen to six decision that the new second chamber should contain between 300 and 350 members. That the House of Commons should elect the majority of these delegates was carried by seventeen to four. By seventeen to eight it was decided that the 'group system' of election should be employed. Those dissenting from this plan included Rutland, Lansdowne, Dunraven, Loreburn, Balfour of Burleigh, Lord Sydenham, Hugh Cecil, and Sir George Younger, who favoured a joint committee of selection drawn equally from both houses. By a similar margin the conference voted, in response to a motion by Selborne, that the period of service in the second chamber would be twelve years with renewal of one-third of its membership every four years.[26] At the conclusion of the twenty-eighth meeting Chamberlain declared that 'we have at last ceased talking—very necessary at first but tiresome when prolonged indefinitely. Now we are taking decisions on definite propositions ... and securing a measure of agreement which at times has seemed very unlikely ever to be reached.'[27] The most critical divisions were taken on the subject of the Lords' delegation in the upper house. A plan submitted by Lansdowne for the selection of peers by a joint committee of the two houses was adopted by sixteen to six. A subcommittee of Lansdowne, Crewe, Sandars, and Hobhouse was then enjoined to devise a method for choosing this joint committee. On the contentious topic of the number of peers who should sit in the reformed upper house there was wide divergence of opinion. At the one extreme Sir G. S. Robertson proposed ten, which lacked a second. Lansdowne, on the other side, boldly suggested one hundred, which was ridiculed by Whittaker 'on the contention (strenuously resisted by Lansdowne) that it wd. mean *120* (1/3 of 360) of whom at least 90 wd be conservatives. He wd. have none of it.' While Crewe discounted Whittaker's supposition, he still thought Lansdowne's one-third was too large. Crewe did not think the number of peers sitting as peers should be more than forty or fifty. This led to the suggestion by others that one-quarter of the new house should be taken from the existing House of Lords.[28] At the thirty-first session, on 29 January, there was considerable discussion over fractions and proportions, but the figure one-fourth seemed to be the magic number. Chamberlain's motion to this effect was carried by nineteen to three, while one-third, one-sixth and several other figures lost by considerable margins. A motion by Robertson that peers so chosen should have no vote also lost, by two to twenty.[29] Thus through the exertions of the more moderate members on both sides, a compromise was arranged on the single most important issue facing the conference.

Related to the issue of the hereditary peerage was the question of the eligibility of bishops and law lords in the new second chamber. As the leading spokesman for the church, the Archbishop of Canterbury pointed out that the House of Lords was the oldest constitutional assembly in the world and the bishops were its oldest and most invariable personages. Any departure from this principle, he insisted, would be an unnecessary break with the continuity of the past. Constitutionally he argued that as long as there was an established church the bishops had a place in the House of Lords. Besides they were usually men of great experience and judgement and could add much to the proceedings. He did not suggest that the bishops should be represented in any way like their present number (26 out of 673, 4 per cent), but he thought six out of the three hundred was a reasonable request.[30] Most of the conference members agreed that the church should have some representation, but there was a sharp difference of opinion over how many ecclesiastics should sit and how they should be selected. After a long debate a motion by Hugh Cecil that the two archbishops and the bishops of London and Durham be allowed to sit *ex officio* in the new house was not approved. But Lord Burnham's proposal that five bishops be included among the eighty-two lords in Parliament was carried by sixteen to eight. Then the Archbishop moved that the number be six instead of five, which was lost by a single vote, six to seven. But those who were against any church representation were unhappy even with five. 'Whittaker moved that we at once adjourn and spoke heatedly as to the horribleness of the decision just adopted,' the Archbishop noted. 'The vehemence of his attack evidently did not carry others with him. Chamberlain, Murray Macdonald, Sir Henry Norman and others appealed to him but he was for a time supported by Ellis Davies and Sir C. Hobhouse and wd. not give way tho Selborne and Lansdowne and Hugh Cecil all ptd out how much *they* had given way. Finally Whittaker withdrew the motion.' The discussion on law lords was more tempered and members were inclined to follow the lead of Loreburn, the Lord Chancellor, who favoured their sitting *ex officio* in the new house. This proposition was carried by a sixteen to two vote as was a similar resolution in favour of preserving the Lord Chancellorship.[31] By retaining the law lords, the ecclesiastics, and a segment of the hereditary peerage, though on a somewhat altered basis, the conference had succeeded by the end of February in striking a judicious balance in the proposed chamber between the old and the new elements.

Among those questions on which the conference had not achieved a consensus was the procedure for adjusting differences between the two houses after a free conference had been tried. Opinion in the conference was nearly equally divided between the proponents of referendum and joint sittings. The radicals naturally favoured the former as the most democratic procedure, while their more pragmatic Liberal brethren regarded the joint sitting, with an overwhelming preponderance of members from the lower house, as the best way to deal with an ambitious or unruly second chamber. Conversely, most Conservatives strongly condemned such tactics as likely to allow the Liberals, when in control of the lower house, to implement vast social and political changes. As a means of safeguarding the constitution some Tories vigorously supported the referendum alternative, thus placing them in the unlikely company with the radicals on the opposite end of the political spectrum. So widely divergent was opinion in the conference that Bryce believed the best idea would be 'to agree to differ, and that we should submit the two schemes of Joint Sittings, and of Referendum, to H. M. Govt. in our Report, for them and Parlt. to make the choice between them'.[32] Although there was considerable support for this manner of proceeding, it was thought that some special attempt should be made to adjust a compromise. For this purpose a committee of seven—Loreburn, Cecil, Crewe, Hobhouse, Whittaker, Sandars, and Chamberlain—was set up. This body agreed on an alternative plan which would entail the use of neither the referendum nor the joint sitting. It provided instead that the free conference, with the support of the House of Commons, should have final jurisdiction over disputed legislation. But in order for these two bodies to override the Lords' veto it would be necessary to secure at least a majority of three in the joint conference.[33] The weakness in this plan was that it still allowed the House of Commons, though not without the interposition of the free conference, to impose its will on the upper chamber. As Chamberlain somewhat apologetically explained to Selborne, it was hoped that when a bill did receive the assent of a free conference 'the Second Chamber would feel that in the circumstances they ought not to persist in their opposition and would accept the proposal'. At least Conservatives could derive some consolation from the fact that the second chamber could not be overridden by the House of Commons alone, which had been their major grievance over the Parliament Act of 1911.[34] For Conservatives and Liberals alike the proposal was a compromise.

The remaining sessions of the conference were devoted to the preparation of a final report. According to Bryce, in his remarkably lucid 'letter' to the Prime Minister, the composition of the second chamber was the 'most difficult' of the three major topics confronting the conference. 'It was debated at the greatest length, and it provided the most frequent occasions for reconciling divergent views.' The major recommendations were that the reformed second chamber should consist of 327 members, 246 elected by members of the House of Commons grouped in territorial blocks, and 81 selected by a joint standing committee of both houses. It was further resolved that the members of the second chamber should be elected for twelve years, one-third to retire every four years. The legislative functions (or powers) of the new upper house proved surprisingly to be the least difficult question to resolve, chiefly because no attempt was made to define financial legislation. Instead provision was made for a joint standing committee of seven from each house to determine whether the actual terms and ultimate effects of a bill were strictly financial in character. If not, the upper chamber would be permitted to amend the bill, though subject always to final approval by the House of Commons. If the two houses disagreed over the amendments, their differences would then be adjusted in the same manner provided for settling disputes over ordinary legislation. This procedure, which consumed the final portion of the conference's labours, provided for the creation of yet another joint standing committee—the free conference. Composed of a maximum of sixty representatives from each house, this body was specially designed to arbitrate disputes between the houses and to allow for a modicum of authority to the House of Commons. But this elaborate network of committees would not likely be necessary owing to the agreement reached earlier by the conference on the composition of the upper chamber. Bryce seemed satisfied that the recommendations of the second chamber conference would result in 'a better understanding and closer co-operation between the two Houses of Parliament, than it has in the past been found possible to secure'.[35]

The conference now encountered its most formidable obstacle in getting its plan accepted by the Government and into the parliamentary timetable at an early date. The chairman's report, unlike the Speaker's conference electoral reform proposals, attracted little attention when submitted to the House of Commons on 24 April. As *The Times* noted, 'the Conference have produced a very elaborate and complex scheme on a subject which at the moment has only a secondary claim upon public attention. Reform of the House of Lords is certainly of real moment to the Empire, but it is in no sense an urgent war measure, such as is, for instance, the question of Ireland.'[36] Consequently few M.P.s bothered to read the lengthy document. Nor did the Government show the slightest intention of translating the conference report into legislation. By mid-June, in spite of repeated solicitations by Bryce, it was quite apparent that Parliament would be unable to act on the conference recommendations before the next general election. 'I am afraid we must admit', Chamberlain wrote to Selborne, 'that it had a poor reception in the press and there was nothing to encourage the Government to believe that an attempt to legislate on these lines would receive any general measure of support. Apart from this the Government had pledged themselves to attempt a solution of the Irish policy and it was obviously impossible to take up another large scheme of constitutional reform in the same session.'[37] Eventually the second chamber issue was swept away by the question of Ireland's constitutional status. Furthermore there was much talk about devolution which, if adopted, would alter fundamentally the basis for any reform of the House of Lords. These issues were more relevant to the Government's reconstruction policy, which after November 1918 supplanted the war as Britain's major topic of national interest. Only on the isolated occasion of a general election was House of Lords reform again raised as an issue of any political significance. At all other times it reverted to its pre-war status of an academic question which no Government felt capable of incorporating into its legislative programme.

That the recommendations of the second chamber conference never became law cannot be attributed to any lack of agreement by the members of the conference. Throughout their forty-eight sessions Lord Bryce, a man of considerable parliamentary experience and knowledge, perfected those methods of leadership initiated by the Speaker in the electoral reform conference, to reach a settlement on all of the terms of reference. Of even greater significance was the fact that nearly every recommendation carried a substantial majority and, unlike the Speaker's conference, there were no resignations for reasons of disagreement. According to Bryce, 'every member was not only scrupulously careful to avoid recrimination over past controversies, but also recognised, above and beyond all differences of opinion, the fairness and goodwill of his colleagues, and gave to each and all of them the credit honestly and sincerely of seeking what was best for the country without thought of the special interest of his own class or party.'[38] Why then were the recommendations of the conference never consummated as a permanent part of the British constitution? The answer, it would seem, is that there was no longer any driving need for House of Lords reform. The second chamber conference had begun as a spin-off from the electoral reform conference by those who mistakenly believed that the two issues could be dealt with on the same basis. But by 1918 the House of Lords was no longer a major or even a relevant political issue. Consequently when the initial momentum provided by the Speaker's conference to settle the House of Lords question expired, the second chamber conference had no independent source of public support. In spite of the co-operative spirit engendered by the war which allowed the conference members to reach an agreement, there existed no residual demand in the country to enact these proposals into law. Undoubtedly the second chamber conference, by its very being, did reinforce the concept of the Speaker's conference in British political usage, but its ultimate value as an institution depended more on its successes than its failures.

X

The Irish Convention, 1917–1918

> Home rule, under calm and courteous analysis and with-
> out the accompaniment of superheated rhetoric, will
> probably turn out to be something as different from the
> Home Rule we have dreamed of as the middle-aged
> Columbine over her cup of tea and her bloater is from
> the sprightly sylph in muslin and spangles who danced
> upon the boards.
>
> F. S. OLIVER[1]

The great degree of success attendant upon the Speaker's conference on electoral reform encouraged the prospect in 1917 that
other constitutional ills which Britain had suffered in previous
years might, under the conditions of co-operation inspired by
the war, be settled by the application of a similar procedure.
Such was the object behind the convening of the second
chamber conference under Lord Bryce, which ultimately failed
for the lack of any vital issue at stake. But the most contentious
subject, which had superseded the House of Lords as the paramount issue in British politics, was home rule. This topic had
formed the basis for various discussions between party leaders
before the war, and in 1916 Lloyd George attempted to formulate a compromise between the leaders of the two Irish parties.
Now as Prime Minister and head of a coalition Government he
was again confronted with the Irish question. Lloyd George's
distaste at having to deal with this untimely issue so soon after
his accession to power no doubt made him receptive to ideas
whereby Ireland might be removed from the responsibility of
the Government until the end of the war. The instrument most
closely at hand which might achieve this purpose, even though
the prospects for a settlement might be minimal, was the
Speaker's conference. This concept was expanded into a sort of
constitutional convention of representative Irishmen, resem-
bling the body which had met in South Africa before the war
and which F. S. Oliver had advocated during the negotiations
of 1910.[2] In spite of a general lack of spirit of compromise among

the Irish there was hope that the Irish convention might still gain some degree of success.

The chief hindrance to these designs was that the Irish question had already passed the point beyond which any compromise settlement was likely. The rise of the revolutionary Sinn Fein organization to supplant the power of the Irish parliamentary party in the country seriously endangered the entire venture from the outset. But in the convention itself the intransigence of the Ulster Unionists proved to be the most telling factor militating against a settlement. Even the southern Unionists, who had effectively stifled Lloyd George's negotiation effort in 1916, were prepared to join with the Nationalists in a common effort to thwart the rising Sinn Fein movement. The Ulstermen, however, who did not feel immediately endangered by the rebels in the south, refused to sanction any agreement which included Ulster in a Dublin parliament or sacrificed customs duties to an Irish state. These delegates had no intention of bargaining away their loyalty to the union under any circumstances, a position which would undoubtedly be supported by the Conservatives who controlled the coalition Government. More adroit leadership by the chairman, Horace Plunkett, and closer negotiation by principal figures might have aided the chances for a settlement, but the convention was simply too large and variegated to bring about an agreed course of action. What began as an adaptation of the conference method to settle the Irish issue outside British political circles ended as an exercise in futility. The Irish convention, which consumed the time and energy of many of Ireland's leading citizens for nearly eight months, was an attempt by the Government to extricate itself from the Irish question, from which there was no easy escape.

The idea for an Irish convention first arose amongst proponents of federalism in the Cabinet secretariat in the early months of 1917. In February Leopold Amery, Conservative M.P. and an aide to the Prime Minister, argued that the Irish problem would be solved only if a determined effort was made 'to fit Ireland with a complete working plant of a modern civilization', and if the responsibility of finding a workable form of Irish government within a federalized United Kingdom was placed on the Irishmen themselves. He suggested that a convention of representative Irishmen and devolutionists be summoned.[3] Philip Kerr, another Cabinet secretary, advised caution. He did not think the Government should act until there was a genuine desire amongst Irishmen to come together to settle their internal problems. Pointing to the failures in 1910, 1914, and 1916, he did not believe the time had arrived yet for another conference. 'When it becomes clear that public opinion in Ireland is determined to effect a settlement and that rather than perpetuate disunion it will accept either the South African or the Canadian principle, then we could usefully assist in the summoning of an Irish Convention.'[4] Nor was the idea favourably received by the leaders of the major parties in Ireland. At Cabinet meetings on 2 and 7 March Carson held that there was little possibility of the Irish reaching an agreement among themselves. He did not believe a convention would lead to 'any useful result, as the moment the Convention was started it would be found that the persons nominated were not really able to bind their followers in any way'.[5] Redmond likewise found little favour with the idea of a convention. In a debate on the Irish question on 7 March Redmond declared that after his experiences in the summer of 1916 he would not enter again into negotiations. After stating that nothing less than the implementation of the 1914 home rule bill 'with such additions, amendments and changes as altered circumstances required' would satisfy Ireland, Redmond left the house followed by other members of the Irish party.[6]

The Government nevertheless proceeded to lay the groundwork for an Irish convention as a means of drawing attention from the rising Sinn Fein movement and to appease Irish sentiment in America. The conversion of Carson and his followers to the idea was facilitated on 7 March by Lloyd George's assurance in the House of Commons that no attempt would be made to coerce the population in the north-eastern counties of Ireland to live under a government with which it was not in sympathy.[7] In a memorandum to the Cabinet, Carson suggested that a settlement might be possible if a national consultative assembly of Ireland would meet annually in alternative years in Dublin and Belfast. Composed of Ulster M.P.s at Westminster and a delegation from the Irish parliament, it might frame legislative measures for the whole of Ireland.[8] Alexander McDowell, who conveyed this plan to the Prime Minister, further suggested that any bill conceived on the basis of Carson's memorandum might be devised by a body similar to the Speaker's conference on electoral reform.[9] Later Lloyd George revealed to C. P. Scott that he was much cheered by the fact that 'the atmosphere for settlement which hd. bn very bad in Ulster hd. become much better since he hd. made his speech in the H. of C. repudiating any idea of coercion against Ulster'.[10] On 16 April the War Cabinet met and decided to deal with the Irish question along lines similar to those suggested by Carson's memorandum.[11]

But the Government's plan of formulating a bill on the basis of partition raised a furore amongst the Nationalists. Dillon refused even to talk to the Prime Minister; Devlin would hear of nothing but county option in any attempted division of Ireland and scorned the idea of an Irish council.[12] But Redmond, whose influence was still paramount, though weakening, was eventually won over to the idea of a convention. At a banquet on 16 May honouring General Jan Smuts, Redmond expressed to Crewe an interest in borrowing from the experience of the dominions by submitting the constitutional question to a convention of Irishmen. He believed that no proposal made from Westminster had a chance of being accepted regardless of its merits. On the following morning Crewe saw Lloyd George, who was preparing to submit a letter to Carson and Redmond containing the Government's latest proposals, which he was sure the latter would not accept. Crewe's revelation of Redmond's attitude, however, convinced Lloyd George of the feasibility of proceeding with a convention.[13] What disturbed Redmond was that the Government was apparently planning to employ Carson's memorandum as the basis for discussion in the convention and any eventual legislation. The Nationalists were unwilling to accept any prior conditions for a settlement while the Unionists were insistent on assurances for the protection of Ulster. Furthermore John B. Lonsdale, leader of the Ulster Unionists in the Commons, told the Prime Minister that 'we assume that the Government will consider themselves bound in honour to insist that the Bill shall not be amended in Committee as regards the area to be excluded from Home Rule'.[14] Carson, however, was eventually forced to yield all prior conditions as no other party in Ireland was willing to proceed on the basis of his memorandum.[15]

On 21 May Lloyd George, having received satisfactory replies from all quarters, announced in the House of Commons that an Irish convention would be summoned. In the upper house Lord Curzon made a similar pronouncement where he revealed more fully the intentions of the Government and the precedents for this mode of procedure. In the course of his speech he referred to the convention as being 'as much a war measure as any of the emergency Acts which you have assisted to pass into law'. By this he meant that it was intended to placate Irish public opinion, particularly in America. Curzon then proceeded to explain some of the guidelines that were being used in bringing together this unique body of Irishmen. These bore a close resemblance to ideas propagated for earlier conferences by F. S. Oliver:

> The Convention will doubtless settle its own procedure, following the example set in the Dominions. It will very likely elect to sit at more than one place in succession, though doubtless its first sittings will be in Dublin. Further—here I come to important conditions—if the Convention is to have a reasonable chance of success it must sit with closed doors. There should be no publication of authorized or unauthorized accounts of its proceedings. Here, again, we rest upon sound precedent and example. You may remember that the Philadelphia Convention of 1787 which drew up the American Constitution laid down its essential obligation that the proceedings should be secret, and the same thing happened in the case of the Quebec Conference in 1864. In the case of Australia different circumstances, which I need not enter into, were responsible for publicity of the proceedings, but in the case of South Africa the obligation of secrecy was again imposed.

Most importantly he committed the Government to a policy that 'should substantial agreement' be reached in framing a constitution for Ireland it would 'accept the responsibility of taking all necessary steps to enable the Imperial Parliament to give legislative effect to such conclusions of the conference'.[16] These words eventually rankled in the minds of those moderate members of the convention who assumed the obligations and risks of a compromise only to see the Government cower before the wishes of the convention minority which had no desire to reach a settlement.

In the next several weeks there was much public discussion concerning the size and composition of the convention. The concept was received with mixed feelings in Ulster, but Carson, who was by now deeply committed to the idea of a convention, assured his comrades that Ulster had everything to gain by attending it. The home rule act was already on the statute book and its repeal under current circumstances was regarded as unlikely. Carson told Hugh de Fellenberg Montgomery that 'above all things it must be remembered that under the Home Rule Act, Ulster is "included" *and remains included until some compromise is agreed on and carried through Parliament'.*[17] On 8 June, 350 delegates to the Ulster Unionist Council assembled in Belfast and resolved, with only four dissidents, that since the convention would consider every scheme and since no party would be bound by its decisions, they would send a delegation.[18] The Nationalist extremists, however, were more intransigent. The executive council of Sinn Fein, with Arthur Griffith in the chair, declined to participate unless certain conditions were met. These included elections to the convention by adult suffrage and the bestowal of the power to declare Ireland independent. In addition Sinn Fein demanded that the British government should pledge to the United States and to the European powers that it would ratify the decision reached by a majority of the convention.[19] In all likelihood if representation to the convention had been based on a popular vote Sinn Fein would have been able to control its deliberations. Under the prevailing circumstances, however, which were clearly not in step with Irish opinion, no moderate party was willing to admit such conditions as would be so inimical to its own purposes.

When the War Cabinet met on 31 May to establish guidelines for the convention it likewise ignored the demands of Nationalist extremists. Conversely it adopted provisions which would ensure a moderate majority with an excessive number of Ulster Unionists to give the convention a slightly conservative complexion. Additionally it would contain a small nominated element chosen by the Government, and representatives from the Protestant church and the trades unions. After much deliberation the Cabinet decided to invite the Speaker of the House of Commons to chair the convention. Lowther, however, had a premonition that 'in some quarters of the House my action in getting the Electoral Reform Conference to agree and in putting forward our scheme of reform, is resented as being beyond the province of the Speakership. In the case of Ireland, I think the House would resent my absence if I had to go over to Dublin for the Convention, and it would probably be a prolonged absence.'[20] General Smuts also declined the chairmanship. But Lloyd George was not discouraged about the prospects of the convention. He placed much confidence in the support of Carson. 'So far as I can judge', observed C. P. Scott, 'he cares little about the rest of the members of his Govmt so long as he can carry Carson with him—With Carson he can beat the lot.'[21] Indeed Lloyd George's subservience to the interests of Ulster, which was most clearly apparent in the Government's willingness to submit the membership of the convention to the Ulster Unionist Council for approval, was bitterly resented in Nationalist quarters. 'No other body in Ireland', Dillon regretfully noted, 'has been committed in the same public fashion. If the Ulster Council demand conditions or modifications,—a fresh crisis will arise.' He also attacked the Government's reluctance to release Irish political prisoners as 'stupid beyond words'.[22]

The other faction, besides Sinn Fein, which shared Dillon's disappointment at the proposed composition of the convention was the 'All for Ireland' group under William O'Brien. It was his view that 'the Government scheme, while making a specious appearance of adopting the Conference method, in reality adopts it only to destroy its efficacy—forbids all reasonable hope of any agreement other than one which could only inflame and intensify Irish discontent'. With the likelihood that under such composition there would be a partition of Ireland, O'Brien refused to enter the convention.[23] In spite of the absence of the O'Brienites and the Sinn Fein element R. B. McDowell, the convention's historian, concludes that it 'contained a remarkable number of men of ability and personality'. Politically speaking the ninety-five members who accepted invitations included fifty-two Nationalists, two Liberals, six Labourites, nine southern Unionists, twenty-four Ulster Unionists, plus John Pentland Mahaffey and Horace Plunkett, who defied any labelling attempt. Grouping the members theologically McDowell estimated fifty-three Catholics and forty-two Protestants.[24]

By mid-July delegates began to assemble for the first meeting of the convention, which was scheduled for 25 July in the Regent House at Trinity College, Dublin. The most important question which confronted the convention at the outset was the selection of a chairman. In the final weeks before the convention the Government in desperation secured the consent of H. E. Duke, the Chief Secretary, to serve on an *ad interim* basis until the convention itself elected a chairman and settled on a suitable manner of proceeding.[25] To simplify the process of selection a small committee of ten was created. When this body met Midleton submitted the name of Lord Southborough, who had distinguished himself in various civil service appointments and had some claim to Irish ancestry. Although this secured a six to four majority, George (Æ) Russell, the Irish poet, put forward the name of his close friend, Horace Plunkett. Unless the committee selected Plunkett, he threatened to raise his name on the floor of the convention. In the interests of peace and cooperation Redmond, who had earlier supported Southborough, persuaded Midleton to give way to Plunkett.[26] But the Unionists accepted this nomination only on the condition that Southborough be placed in the position of secretary. This compromise was unanimously approved by the convention.

Of even greater material significance to the outcome of the convention was the rift which was developing between the southern and Ulster Unionists. This schism had begun over the resentment of the southern Unionists to the exclusive aims of Ulster before the war, which seemed to disregard the rest of Ireland. During the abortive negotiations of 1916 these suspicions were fulfilled when the Ulster Unionists expressed their willingness to accede to home rule provided that Ulster was excluded. Consequently in 1917 the southern Unionists, in the belief that the best interests of the north were not identical with those of the south, resisted all attempts of manipulation by the Ulster Unionists. On the evening before the convention began the southern group was told by H. T. Barrie, the leader of the Ulstermen, that his delegates had already decided that no lawyer's name should be considered for chairman. This, Midleton believed, was directed at the Irish Attorney-General, James O'Connor, whom the Ulsterites believed would be antagonistic to their cause. 'Some of our members', Midleton remarked, 'wished to part company with Ulster at once, as it was quite clear that with the Ulster preponderance of numbers, the intention was that we should hew wood and draw water for Ulster, which, in view of the very serious questions affecting the South, we could not do.'[27] Furthermore differences of opinion were emerging between the two conservative Irish groups with regard to an eventual settlement. The Ulster view was expressed privately by Montgomery:

My own view is that the position we should take now must differ in one important point from that which we took last year.

We then virtually undertook not to oppose the setting up of Home Rule in the 26 Counties if 6 Ulster Counties were excluded; in view of what we now know of the state of the Country, it appears to me that to give any kind of consent to the setting up of Home Rule in any part of Ireland would be an act of treason, therefore, our representatives on the Convention should address themselves, after giving the Nationalists plenty of time to show their hand, to affirming that the only possible form of Government for Ireland compatible with the safety of the Realm upon which the safety and prosperity of Ireland depends is the maintenance of a Legislative Union with such modifications as may be thought wise ... being prepared of course to take their stand on the exclusion of the 6 Counties, if it is decided to enact Home Rule for Ireland in spite of our opposition.[28]

Ironically the increasing violence in the south was impelling the southern Unionists in the opposite direction, making it more feasible for them to forge an alliance with the Nationalists in order to protect their lives and property.

When the full convention resumed its sittings on 8 August procedural matters dominated the discussion. Plunkett presented a plan whereby a grand committee representative of all groups would be chosen to exercise from time to time powers delegated to it by the convention. Although the southern Unionists objected, the idea was supported by Redmond, Devlin, and Bishop O'Donnell from the Nationalist side, and Barrie of the Ulster Unionists. The problem of personnel was solved by Redmond's suggestion that the committee of ten which had selected the chairman and secretary should select twenty persons to serve on the grand committee. At the first meeting of this new body, on 14 August, there was a division of opinion between Plunkett, who wanted the convention to engage in a general discussion for the first several weeks, and the southern Unionists, who wanted to get immediately down to business. The latter argued with much force that 'close study of definite concrete issues, which must be determined in the framing of a constitution, was an essential preliminary to practical discussion in the Convention, and was far more businesslike than discursive talk upon general principles'. Midleton's group further desired the appointment of 'sub-committees of the best qualified members of the Convention to deal with such subjects as finance, trade and tariffs, education, the judiciary, police, electoral methods and military affairs'.[29] For reason of simplicity Plunkett's plan was ultimately adopted, but the problem of the convention's great size and the need to allow a free expression of opinion to all delegates remained to plague the deliberations of the convention in the months ahead. Such problems had never existed in the smaller assemblies of party leaders and representatives which had served as pre-cedents for the convention.

The presentation stage was opened on 21 August by the introduction of schemes by W. M. Murphy, proprietor of the *Irish Independent*, and Lord Macdonnell of Swinford, a Govern-ment nominee who had had a long experience in the Indian and Irish civil services. Both plans were strongly nationalist, proposing to grant Ireland full executive, legislative and financial autonomy. Redmond praised them as proposing 'to give to the Irish Parliament far more power than was conceded under the provisions of the Home Rule Act'. The Ulster Unionist position, as stated by Lord Londonderry, was natur-ally much opposed to the schemes. But Lord Oranmore and Browne, a southern Unionist, appeared willing to settle for an amended version of one of the plans. The qualifications he deemed necessary to satisfy his party were adequate representa-tion in the Irish parliament, guarantees of religious liberty, and freedom from oppressive and differential taxation. He also insisted on the ultimate supremacy of the imperial Parliament and that Ireland should bear its share in honouring the war debt.[30] In spite of its reservations, this speech reaffirmed the impression that the southern Unionists were not willing to accept the impossibilist position of their northern brethren. Montgomery wrote to A. V. Dicey, the constitutional historian, that the Ulster delegates 'would have liked to work with the Southern Unionists against any form of Home Rule, but, I am sorry to say, they have found the Southern Unionists not entirely trust-worthy in this matter', and that the Ulster Unionists were 'working independently on their own lines. At present they are proposing nothing, but obstructing everything which would tend to commit the Convention to any form of Home Rule.'[31] In an attempt to heal the breach between the two factions a meeting was held where the southern Unionists expressed to the Ulster Unionist delegates their regret at the action taken by one of their members. The former also promised to establish a subcommittee to maintain a liaison with the Ulster group.[32] Nevertheless a sense of alienation and ill content continued to vitiate the relations between the two parties.

In the early stages of the convention it was decided that the members should visit Belfast and Cork in the course of their sittings in order to improve their knowledge of conditions in other parts of the country. By the time the convention changed its venue to Belfast in early September many delegates were becoming irritated with the slow pace of the deliberations. Midleton, who had disapproved of the chairman's procedure from the beginning, was the most outspoken.[33] But even Mac-donnell, whose plan was still being discussed, told his wife that 'the Convention is getting on well enough but there is too much "orating" and the delay in coming to close quarters is irritating'.[34] On other matters relating to the conduct of the assembly Lord Granard, who was reporting the proceedings to Asquith, remarked that the southern Unionists 'do not see eye to eye with the Ulster party, and I doubt if they would join them in any wrecking motion'. He described Plunkett as 'a poor chairman' as 'an absolute visionary, possessed of a most untidy and disordered mind. If Hopwood [Southborough] were not here, I am afraid that all sorts of trouble would have resulted.' Granard did not believe the convention would reach a unanimous decision. At some point, he believed, the Ulstermen would secede and the remainder of the convention would draft a constitution for Ireland with adequate safeguards for Ulster and the minority in the south and west. Granard's final observation was that there was 'a strong distrust of Lloyd George amongst all parties here. There is a belief that he does not intend to act on the Square with this country.'[35] While in Belfast the accommodations for the convention were, in the words of the chairman, 'ten times as good as in Dublin'.[36] The convention sat only in the mornings, the afternoons being reserved for touring dockyards and other places of interest, showing the industrial strength of the province. This only served to highlight the economic differences between the two regions and to rationalize somewhat Ulster's refusal to sever its ties with the United Kingdom.

When the convention resumed its sittings in Dublin on 11 September the delegates were obviously tired of the long speeches and anxious to come to close quarters. On the second day the convention 'ran out of talk', whereupon both Murphy and Macdonnell made replies to criticisms of their schemes.[37] Seeing the necessity for an alteration in procedure Plunkett drafted an open letter to the members explaining that he had tried without success to stimulate discussion on three further proposals, those of Walter Kavanagh, Captain Gwynn, and the provost of Trinity College. As only two plans remained, those of Lord Dunraven and James Alexander Moles, he hoped that a considerable number of speeches would be forthcoming. Unfortunately the presentation stage, according to the convention's timetable, was not scheduled to end until the delegates returned from Cork in a fortnight. Thus Plunkett was able to offer the convention only more of the same routine from which everyone needed a relief. As an indication of their *ennui* the members of the convention on the following week refused to debate any of the proposals before them. Plunkett thereupon placed seven further topics before the convention, including customs and excise, representation at Westminster, defence, and minority representation. These subjects provoked little more than a general interest in what was otherwise a very dull two weeks.[38] Even the convention's visit to Cork on the week of 24 September provided little more than a repetition of the same arguments presented in earlier sessions. Only the chairman, who believed that 'my Convention procedure has worked better than I could have imagined', seemed oblivious to the dangers inherent in the tremendous amount of time and energy wasted during the presentation stage.[39]

Upon returning to Dublin the plenary sessions of the convention ended and the grand committee set about to create a measure of self-government for Ireland. Again the procedural question arose when Alexander McDowell, an Ulster Unionist, suggested that any further consideration of schemes would be a 'waste of time', and that what was required at this point was 'a confidential exchange of views between the leading spokesmen for the various groups in the Convention', presumably in an even more intimate setting than the grand committee. 'A few vital issues frankly faced, a little give and take, and the rest would be plain sailing.' This line of argument was shared subsequently by most of the other members of the grand committee. Accordingly a subcommittee of nine, consisting of Redmond, Devlin, and the Bishop of Raphoe for the Nationalists; Barrie, Londonderry, and McDowell for the Ulster Unionists; Midleton for the southern Unionists; William Murphy as an independent Nationalist, and George Russell, who allegedly held the confidence of Sinn Fein and labour, was created. After holding its first meeting on the same day it was appointed, the subcommittee decided to adjourn for a fortnight, after which it would meet in London. This infuriated Plunkett, who now realized his mistake of telling the subcommittee that he would not attend its deliberations unless asked. Not only was he not asked, but in his absence the subcommittee, probably at the urging of the Ulster delegates, had adopted a procedure of which he strongly disapproved. By telegraph and post Plunkett summoned the grand committee to a meeting on 15 October where he explained why the decision of the subcommittee was not very wise. Plunkett eventually acquiesced in allowing negotiations on the constitutional issue to take place in London, but only after being consoled by the creation of three additional subcommittees which would sit in Dublin. These included one under the Archbishop of Dublin to consider franchise and electoral systems, another under Lord Macdonnell on land purchase, and a third to consider military and police forces chaired by Lord Desart.[40] In spite of the fact that only eleven members of the grand committee attended this meeting (those from Ulster dissented) Plunkett pronounced it a 'great success'.[41] But his resentment at being excluded from the deliberations of the subcommittee of nine and his desire to dictate procedure to it from the chair further alienated the Ulster Unionist delegates, who became increasingly antagonistic to the whole idea of a convention.

While other subcommittees were meeting in Dublin, the sub-committee of nine met secretly in London on 24 and 25 October to hammer out a plan for an Irish parliament. It devised an upper chamber where elements of the church, the peerage, the privy council, and organized commerce would be represented, and a lower house. It was tentatively agreed that the Unionists would be offered 40 per cent representation in the lower house, while 75 per cent of the upper house would be made up of men with a substantial stake in the country, presumably Unionists also. The numbers were so arranged that in a joint sitting of both houses the parties would be almost evenly balanced. As a further concession to the Ulsterites the upper house would be permitted to bring money bills as well as other legislation to to the attention of a joint sitting.[42] On 31 October, after a short digression on the Sinn Fein menace, the subcommittee tackled the critical issue of finance. While the Nationalists opted strongly for fiscal autonomy, the Unionists clung just as per-sistently to fiscal union with Britain. In an attempt to com-promise, Southborough suggested that Ireland should have complete fiscal autonomy, yet maintain free trade with Great Britain unless she met with unfair competition from British industries. To handle disputes he argued for the establishment of a joint customs board consisting of two members from the British treasury, two from the Irish treasury, and a chairman appointed by the King.[43] When this proved unacceptable to the Ulster delegates Plunkett elicited the assistance of a Cam-bridge economist named Professor Arthur Cecil Pigou to draw up a list of questions for both parties concerning the viability of their stand on fiscal matters. The Nationalists asserted that their chief objection to fiscal union was the fear that divided control of taxation in Ireland would hamper efficient govern-ment and create friction between Irish and imperial authorities. So resentful were the Ulster Unionists of Plunkett's intervention, however, that they refused even to discuss the subject any further. On 14 November Plunkett received a letter from Barrie and Londonderry stating that the deadlocked position of the subcommittee rested on 'points of principle and not of detail. We hold that in matters of fiscal policy and economic life the interests of Ireland are inseparable from those of Great Britain,

and that there can be no customs barrier or differentiation
between the two countries, which are and must continue to be
so intimately associated.'[44] Clearly the Ulsterites had chosen to
take their stand on the continuation of fiscal union, the
elimination of which would be tantamount to the dissolution
of the constitutional ties between Great Britain and Ireland.

When the grand committee reconvened on 22 November
the Ulster delegates were again enjoined either to reply as the
Nationalists had done to the chairman's questions or to join
in a discussion of Southborough's compromise plan. But they
were prepared to do neither. Barrie reiterated that his party
could go no further than the position he had outlined in his
recent letter to the chairman. At this point, however, the
Unionist position was weakened when it appeared that the
southern Unionists did not share the same views as their
northern compatriots. Macdonnell observed that 'there is now
some substantial hope that the Southern Unionists will adhere
to the Moderate Nationalists and that a scheme will be
accepted in Convention which though not all we want, may
be a substantial instrument'.[45] The Ulster delegates were subsequently informed that the southern Unionists were prepared
to accept Southborough's proposals with regard to customs
control by an Irish parliament. This would include acceptance
of the proposition that taxation in both countries should be
similar and that on 1 April each year the Irish government
should ask for the amount they deemed necessary to carry on
Irish services for the year. Notwithstanding these conciliatory
gestures, the southern Unionists were adamant that the Irish
government should have no powers of direct taxation.
Redmond, who was not unreceptive to these ideas, stated that
he would be ready to consider any suggestions for a compromise
if Ulster would make some abatement from her extreme claims.
This induced Barrie to admit, for the first time, that an Irish
parliament should have some taxing power and that there
should be a responsible financial authority in Ireland, presumably an Irish exchequer. But customs and excise, he insisted,
must be left absolutely to the imperial Parliament. Midleton
thereupon proposed that the imperial government reserve the
right to impose and to collect customs duties, and that Ireland's
share of the receipts be determined by a joint commission repre-

senting both Great Britain and Ireland. As a concession to the Nationalists he held out the possibility of full control of all purely Irish affairs, including internal taxation.[46] This it was hoped would provide a basis for agreement between the extremist sections. 'As far as I can see, and hear,' wrote Powell to Midleton, 'you are likely to be the statesman who will have settled the eternal "Irish question".'[47]

All depended, however, on whether the Ulster delegates could be persuaded to accept a compromise on Midleton's terms. For this purpose Bernard and Midleton appealed for Government assistance. In a conference with Lloyd George and Curzon on 5 December in London they explained that it was Ulster which stood in the way of a settlement and that only Government pressure strategically applied could dislodge it. Lloyd George, though he appeared to be pleased with the attitude of the southern Unionists, 'would not say (and did not promise) that she [Ulster] would be forced into a settlement which she did not approve'. The Archbishop, who was much disappointed with this reply, thought it would ultimately mean the break-up of the convention.[48] Plunkett, too, recognized the necessity of forcing the Ulster delegates to succumb to entry into an Irish parliament. To accomplish this he openly encouraged the Nationalists to come to terms with the southern Unionists, thereby setting up a possible four-fifths to one-fifth confrontation within the convention. Under these conditions he reasoned that the Ulstermen would be under considerable pressure to come to an agreement.[49] Shortly before Christmas an attempt was made by Redmond and the southern Unionists to negotiate their outstanding differences. On the crucial fiscal question Redmond expressed his willingness to relinquish customs control. This pleased Midleton, who believed that if the fiscal question was disposed of when the convention met, the others would be easy.[50] But without assurance of Government support these gestures constituted little threat to Ulster's intransigent position.

On 18 December Midleton moved in the full convention that an Irish parliament should be established with control over all purely Irish services, including judicature, police, internal taxation and administration, but that all imperial services, including the levying of customs, should remain under the authority of the imperial Parliament. He also asked the convention to recognize the supremacy of Parliament, Irish representation at Westminster, and the contribution by Ireland to the imperial expenditure. Midleton made it clear that these terms were absolutely irreducible and not made with a view to bargaining. They were well received by all quarters of the convention, though Ulster opinion was reserved. Barrie told the convention that he would first have to submit the proposals to their advisory committee. But he felt bound to say that he and his colleagues much regretted the fiscal provisions, in spite of Redmond's concession, and did not hold out much hope that they would be accepted.[51] Devlin, who was fairly representative of Nationalist opinion in the south as well as the north, agreed with Midleton's proposals, but he did not trust the British government to act on them.

> For the past ten years the Irish Party have been tremendously weakened and almost destroyed by the intense desire shown on their part for peace and reconciliation not only with England but with the Ulster Protestants. Each time we conceded anything our position was imperilled amongst our friends and the problem was not correspondingly brought any nearer solution. I confess I cannot trust the Government, nor do I see that any course we could adopt would force the Government to realise its duty to those who stood by it in the terrible emergencies of the last four years.[52]

The fact which weighed most heavily on the minds of both the Nationalists and the southern Unionists was that Lloyd George would never accept any plan which called for the impressment of Ulster, yet some far-reaching scheme of home rule seemed to be the only way of allaying the Sinn Fein threat.

When the convention reassembled on 2 January Barrie announced that the Ulster advisory committee had rejected Midleton's scheme. He declared that his party had merely come to the convention with the intention of arranging a compromise between the 1914 act and the partition proposals of 1916.[53] Still Midleton remained optimistic that 'such a settlement as we propose, if it commends itself to the whole Convention without Ulster, will be put forward by the Government and passed into law forthwith, and if I were not confident on this point, I should not attach much importance to carrying the proposal'.[54] His success hinged largely on Redmond's intention to move the acceptance of Midleton's compromise on 15 January. If carried, this motion would exert great pressure on the Government to disregard the assurances it had made the previous March not to coerce Ulster. Lloyd George, who was fully aware of this situation, was beginning to feel himself in a bind. 'I take a very serious view of the Irish situation,' he told Bonar Law. 'If the Southern Unionists and the Nationalists agree, as they are likely to, the position of *any* Government that refuses to carry out that compact will be an impossible one. I simply could not face it.' He felt that the Government's refusal to act under such circumstances would incur the censure of the entire world, most notably America, which would insist that the British government was acting simply to please Carson and his small political section. Lloyd George prevailed on his Conservative colleague to 'beg Barrie, who is from all I have seen of him a sensible and broad-minded fellow who is above the mere bigotries of any sect, to lift his Province to the high level of his opportunity'.[55] Lloyd George was relieved of his anxiety of having to force Ulster by a surprise move from the Nationalists. Redmond, who had not been well, discovered on the morning of 15 January that there was rather strong opposition in his party to the modicum of fiscal union implied by Midleton's compromise. He was told that many county councillors opposed his action and that the bishops and Devlin were not inclined to support the compromise.[56] Consequently when the time arrived for the introduction of his motion Redmond declined to move it on the grounds that it might very likely engender a split in the Nationalist Party.

Redmond's capitulation to the dissidents in his party and his temporary abandonment of the Midleton compromise clearly broke the mounting spirit of progress in the convention and a tone of dissension set in. Plunkett, who naïvely believed the convention had been 'stampeded by Sinn Fein', decided that the only way to save the situation was to avert any further decisions and to take the earliest possible opportunity to appeal to the Government in London. Clearly this was a mistake because Redmond's indecision was exactly the kind of weakness Lloyd George was looking for to escape the responsibility of having to force Ulster and thereby incur the wrath of his Conservative colleagues in the Cabinet. Carson in particular was feeling the pressure of his position and signs of his rest-lessness were unmistakable. His wife noted that he was 'on the verge of leaving the Cabinet, as it's impossible for him to remain there while they are trying to settle Ireland, either way! And of course if they tried to coerce Ulster he would come out at once.'[57] Thus when Plunkett appealed to the Prime Minister on 19 January for understanding and advice Lloyd George impressed on him the dismal fact that the Government could take no responsibility for the proceedings of the convention. Adopting a stance similar to that taken towards the labours of the electoral reform conference he explained that 'it was of the essence of their plan that *this* settlement should be Irish in its initiation, sanction and execution'. Besides he felt that the need for Government intervention had not yet arisen. The Prime Minister therefore asked Plunkett to return to Ireland and confer with Redmond about what action would be taken by the Cabinet, if any, in view of its position of non-interference. When Plunkett returned to Ireland he found Redmond still desirous of a compromise, but with 'no hope of further progress without some definite promise of legislation from the Government'.[58] Devlin likewise was under the strong belief that no settlement was possible unless the Government agreed to coerce Ulster.[59] But Carson's resignation from the Cabinet on 21 January served as a warning to Lloyd George that he could advance no further to satisfy Nationalist demands without risk-ing the resignation of other Unionist members.

When the convention returned to its deliberations on the following day the results of Redmond's irresolution and the Government's inaction was evidenced by a split in the Nationalist ranks between those who desired maximum independence within the confines of the empire and those more conservative delegates who were willing to accept a com-promise along Midleton's lines. J. R. Fisher, editor of the *Northern Whig* in Belfast, reported to Montgomery that:

Generally, with regard to the situation in the Convention and in the Government, there is nothing but confusion and uncertainty. The Church, the Murphyite wreckers, the Sinn Feiners of the mild George Russell type, and the Redmondites are all pulling in different directions: not to speak of the Southern 'Unionists' who are selfish and ill guided as usual. Some weeks ago there was a possibility of the Ulstermen finding themselves isolated with all these other elements united against them. That danger is I believe, averted —Midleton and the Bishops are not working together and the question of finance is less near a settlement than ever.[60]

To resolve the deadlock and accompanying confusion Plunkett resorted to a letter which Lloyd George had drafted for him before he left London which was to be read aloud only when the convention had reached an impasse. It suggested that a conference should be held between the Prime Minister and the leaders of the convention. A lengthy debate ensued on this proposal until the Lord Mayor of Dublin posed the following question to Midleton, Barrie, and the Bishop of Raphoe: 'Are you prepared to recede from the position you have taken up over Customs or are you not?' From the three negative answers he received he concluded that 'it is nonsense to say we are not at a standstill. . . . We are in an absolute quagmire.' This placed matters in proper perspective and the grand committee was empowered to select sixteen delegates to go to London.[61]

While the convention remained in adjournment for several weeks Lloyd George carried out interviews with representatives of each delegation of Irishmen. On 6 February he talked with the southern Unionists, who explained to him how adversely Midleton's proposals had been affected by the split which had developed within the Nationalist ranks. Since this eliminated any possibility of forcing Ulster to reach an agreement within the convention, the only remaining alternative was for the Government to apply pressure on Ulster. Lloyd George explained, as he had done earlier with Plunkett, that the Ulster Unionists were 'quite impervious to any public opinion other than that of Ulster, that they were a very narrow and self-centred community, and difficult of persuasion'. Lloyd George denied that the Ulster delegates had entered the convention fortified by any special pledge that no legislation would be enacted which they disapproved. What he had promised was 'immediate legislation if approved by a "substantial majority". If Ulster stood out', he maintained, 'it would be difficult to describe the residual majority as "substantial".'[62] The ultimate result of these conversations was a speech which the Prime Minister delivered to all of the special envoys of the convention on 13 February. It was, as Plunkett noted, 'a long speech with nothing in it but very clever'.[63] It included such platitudes as deploring partition, which was meant to please the Nationalists, disallowing fiscal autonomy for the duration of the war, to please the Unionists, and a proposal for a federal solution, which was calculated to remove the whole issue from any practical basis.[64]

The convention delegates were required to stay in London another several weeks waiting for the Government to make some definite policy statement concerning Ireland. But there was little hope for a settlement in any quarter. Bonar Law admitted to Plunkett 'the immense importance of a settlement but it was impossible because it could only be got by conceding the customs and this would split England (I think he meant the Unionist party) from top to bottom. It was rather hopeless!'[65] Southborough, who was even more privy to Government information, described the atmosphere in the Cabinet to Midleton as one of 'humbug and want of direct intention'. He elaborated:

L. G. described the position of things in the Convention in terms in which its own mother would not have known it! A. J. B. was obviously scoffing at the idea of anything coming out of our deliberations and Walter Long tho' he often expressed his wish for a settlement evidently thought thoughts of years ago. Bonar Law the like. With all this Ulster knows perfectly well that she can take her own line with impunity. The Cabinet will never do anything until it is intimidated. I have no reason to think they would legislate on a 75% basis, on the contrary I am nearly sure they will not.[66]

Finally on the evening of 25 February Lloyd George submitted to Plunkett a summary statement of the Government's position regarding Ireland. The most important point was that the only hope for an agreement lay in the recognition of the essential unity of Ireland (with safeguards for minorities) and the United Kingdom. The Government thought the customs and excise issue should be tabled until the end of the war, at which time a joint exchequer board would be set up to determine the proper sources of Ireland's income. In the meantime all other forms of taxation in Ireland would be handed over to the Irish parliament. Finally the Prime Minister's letter said that the Government, on receiving the report of the convention, would 'give it immediate attention, and will proceed with the least possible delay to submit the legislative proposals to Parliament'.[67] But no one held the slightest hope that the convention would be able to agree on these terms.

After a week's discussion the convention gathered on 5 March to reach a decision on the Prime Minister's letter. The Midleton proposals were passed without a division in order to make way for a set of resolutions by Macdonnell which aimed to implement the designs of the Government. To the first of Macdonnell's resolutions Stephen Gwynn moved an amendment with the object of securing Irish control of customs. Plunkett thought that Gwynn's speech showed 'the extraordinary difficulties in which an Irish Nationalist finds himself when he tries in revolutionary times, to combine the role of the practical politician with that of the popular representative. He knew well that there was not a ghost of a chance of getting the present Parliament to agree to the breaking up of the fiscal system of the United Kingdom, and that the great majority of the Irish people would not listen to reason on the Customs issue.' Unfortunately Gwynn's amendment failed to gain the support of either Murphy or the Bishop of Raphoe, who led important Nationalist groups.[68] Furthermore the position of the Ulster Unionists was beyond retrieval. Barrie assured Carson that the Ulster delegates would 'continue to oppose all proposals threatening fiscal unity even if we are left alone'.[69] Midleton, on hearing of the Government's refusal to act immediately on any plan of fiscal autonomy, declined to associate his party with any Nationalist position. Thus failing to achieve support from any section of the convention Gwynn withdrew his amendment.[70] The Nationalist cause was dealt an even greater blow on the following day by the death of its chief, John Redmond. The Irish leader's health had been deteriorating during the previous year and the decline of his leadership was not an unimportant factor in the failure of the convention thus far to reach an agreement. With Redmond's death, the ever present threat of Sinn Fein, and the lack of Government co-operation, the convention was shrouded by an atmosphere of gloom.

After a week's adjournment the convention met on 12 March and passed Lord Macdonnell's resolution to postpone any decision on customs and excise until after the war by a narrow majority. Later the Ulster Unionists presented their ideas for a settlement in a document entitled 'Outlines of a Scheme of Irish Government based on the Amending Bill, 1914'. They wished to exclude the entire province of Ulster from the authority of an Irish parliament and to place it under a secretary of state who would administer it under direct authority from the Crown. With this pronouncement all hope of any compromise with Ulster vanished, as Barrie's plan was defeated by a vote of fifty-one to nineteen. Macdonnell, in obvious good spirits, reported the outcome to his wife: 'I fancy the Ulster men though defeated will remain on in the Convention, and that there will be no break up. There is now a solid union between the Nationalists, Southern Unionists and the Labour men. Only Ulster is out in the cold.'[71] The convention then proceeded, with the Ulster Unionists dissenting, to agree on five topics—restrictions on the Irish parliament's power; provisions for amending the constitution; executive authority; provisions for summoning, proroguing and dissolving parliament, and royal assent.[72] On 19 March the convention considered the recommendations of its subcommittee on defence. An amendment seeking jurisdiction over the military defence of Ireland by the imperial Parliament was defeated by forty-two to twenty-two while the subcommittee's recommendation for a dual police force, the Royal Irish Constabulary and the Dublin Metropolitan Police, was carried by fifty-seven to eighteen. The convention also adopted the subcommittee's recommendation that conscription could not be imposed on Ireland without the assent and co-operation of the Irish parliament by the same vote.

On 20 March the convention moved to the difficult subject of composition of the Irish parliament. The grand committee's recommendation for a senate was largely upheld with the addition only of representatives from labour and the county councils. For the Irish house of commons proportional representation for constituencies returning three or more members, though negatived by the committee of nine, was finally adopted by the convention. The 40 per cent Unionist representation and the plan for nominating additional members for the southern Unionists were retained, but the Ulster delegates insisted that their advisory council would never approve such a principle, ostensibly on the grounds that it was not democratic. More to the point, such profuse generosity by the Nationalists and other interest groups in Ireland could not be expected to continue and was extended merely to lure the Ulster Unionists into an agreement. Nevertheless in an eleventh-hour attempt to woo Ulster's support the Bishop of Raphoe proposed that twenty additional members should be elected in Ulster to represent commercial, industrial, and agricultural interests. This additional representation, which would give the Unionists a clear majority in any joint sitting in the new legislature, would continue until Ulster no longer desired it. Barrie, however, replied that Ulster had little interest in the question because it could never enter the parliament which was being formed. Instead he proposed that Ulster should donate the twenty proposed nominees to the southern Unionists.

Turning to Irish representation at Westminster the convention concurred with the proposal that the number of Irishmen in the House of Lords should remain unchanged until that institution was reformed. With regard to the lower house the convention adopted a plan whereby forty-two Irish representatives would be elected from five panels of members from the Irish lower house representing the four provinces and the nominated members. On the question of Ireland's contribution to the war Plunkett persuaded the members to accept the principle of a contribution, the amount to be determined at some later date. To the surprise of no one the Ulster Unionists voted against the rest of the convention delegates on the crucial matter of the creation of an Irish exchequer. The convention upheld its decision of 12 March to postpone the question of customs and excise for the duration of the war, thus rendering it impossible for any legislation to be framed on this important subject which lay at the centre of the home rule controversy.[73] The final report, which was drawn up by Plunkett, was carried by a vote of forty-four to twenty-nine with minority reports being submitted by the Ulsterites, the Nationalists, and others.

By the time Plunkett submitted these reports to the Prime Minister on 9 April, nearly a year had passed since the convention had begun its deliberations. Just as the convention was completing its labours the Government undertook to extend conscription to Ireland in spite of the warning of the convention's subcommittee on defence. The dire need for men at the front prevailed over every other consideration. Lloyd George explained to Bonar Law that the subcommittee's report did 'not go beyond stating that when an Irish Parliament is set up, its assent ought to be sought to any proposal for Conscription. ... The Irish Parliament could not possibly come into existence until the new Register is complete. That means it could not meet before October at the very earliest. By that time it is too late. If we could wait until October for this measure, then the case for it goes. It is either an urgent need or not at all.'[74] In any case the Government's adoption of conscription for Ireland clearly indicated how it regarded the deliberations of the convention. In a similar disdainful manner, in spite of its professed intention to enact another home rule bill, the Government proceeded to ignore the other recommendations of the convention. This was at least partially due to the influence of the Conservatives in the Cabinet, who were not only sympathetic to the views of the Ulster Unionists but were encouraging a federal solution as a means of further postponing the Irish question at least until the end of the war. Then presumably the Government would have a free hand to deal with Sinn Fein. However much the Prime Minister might have wished to confer a measure of home rule on Ireland, he was unable to separate himself from the views of the Unionists who controlled his administration.

The failure of the Irish convention to settle the Irish question must be attributed in the first instance to the precipitate desire of the British Government to relieve itself of the burden of coping with Ireland during the war. The Government had shown neither the strength to subdue the violent Sinn Fein Party nor the courage to force home rule on an obstinate Ulster. Its hope that a body of representative Irishmen would be able to overcome these obstacles was purely illusory. The absence of the Sinn Fein or the O'Brien Nationalists produced an endemic weakness in the composition of the convention which was impossible to overcome. Ronald McNeill, one of Carson's comrades, likened the convention in his book to 'a bone thrown to a snarling dog, and the longer there was anything to gnaw the longer would the dog keep quiet'.[75] The convention was also badly conducted. As a contemporary George Bernard

Shaw later told Plunkett's biographer that 'I have, perhaps, more experience of public meetings than most people; and I can testify that he ranked first among the very worst chairmen on earth'.[76] But under the circumstances of nearly one hundred delegates with so many diverse opinions it is hardly surprising that the convention was unmanageable and experienced great difficulty in getting down to serious work. The decisive factor behind the convention's failure, however, was the intransigence of Ulster. In spite of the adherence of the southern Unionists to the Nationalist point of view no resolute attempt was made to bring real pressure to bear on the Ulster Unionist delegation. Instead the anti-Ulster forces attempted to pass this responsibility back to the British Government. This was indicative of the fatal flaw in the convention—that the decision-making machinery had been divorced from the effective centres of political power in Dublin and London. The conference concept was operative in the fullest sense only when its recommendations coincided with the desires of those who were in a position to implement them. Given the unusual size, non-representative composition, and isolation from practical politics of the convention there was little possibility that its results could ever be accepted by those who held power. Hence the Irish question remained in deadlock.

XI

The Federal Panacea, 1919–1920

> The fundamental principle of a Federation is that the States or nations which compose it shall all stand in the same relation to the Central Parliament. ... It would not be a true Federation, and it would be an entirely unworkable arrangement—open to every form of confusion and intrigue—if the Parliament of the Union stood in a different relation to Ireland on the one hand, and to England, Wales, and Scotland on the other.
>
> F. S. OLIVER[1]

Since its popularization by Joseph Chamberlain in the 1880s the idea of devolving the powers of the British Parliament (home rule all-round) had been consistently advocated as the best means of relieving legislative congestion. But its major impetus was derived from its intimate connection with the Irish issue and the question of imperial federation.[2] That federalism might be applied to Ireland and the empire became plausible after its successful application in Canada and Australia, and in the United States of America. This was the viewpoint at least of the small political missionary group transformed from 'Milner's kindergarten', which publicized its philosophy through the *Round Table* magazine. Throughout the first two decades of the twentieth century this aggregation of quasi-intellectuals did more than any other special interest group in British politics to promote a systemic approach to domestic harmony and imperial co-operation. The conference procedure in its many varieties formed a central part of its methodology. But no comprehensive attempt was made by any Government before the war to set up provincial legislatures which might relieve the parliamentary workload, settle the Irish question, or lay the basis for imperial federation. Instead the piecemeal method of setting up a system of grand committees was first adopted in the late nineteenth century to syphon off some of the work of Parliament and to placate regional nationalism.[3] The imperial question of the status of

Britain's dominions and colonies had been handled on a continuing basis by a series of colonial conferences. And Ireland, despite repeated attempts to implement home rule, remained unresolved and unstable.

The prospect of submitting the Irish problem to a possible federal solution during the latter stages of the war was yet another indication of the bankruptcy of the Government's policy towards Ireland. Since 1914 successive attempts had been made to solve the Irish question by party leaders, the British Government, and a large body of Irishmen, through various adaptations of the conference method. Now with a coalition still in power a substantial section of the Unionist Party was proposing federalism as a possible solution or at least as a means whereby the Irish question might be removed from the centre of British politics. Utilizing a procedure very closely akin to the Speaker's conference it was hoped that a federal plan would not only bring peace to Ireland, but lay a basis for the reconciliation of other more nascent forms of nationalism in the Celtic fringe, and further alleviate the parliamentary overload occasioned by the rise of a more democratic society. By the time a conference was set up to consider the matter, however, the military situation had got so far out of hand that Ireland could no longer be retrieved with the palliative of devolution. The decision of the Government to deal with Ireland on a separate basis plunged the federal issue into a state of academic obscurity. Only in the presence of the Speaker, who had presided so successfully over the electoral reform conference, was there any hope that the devolution conference would be able to resolve the remaining question of the congestion of business in Parliament. But the Speaker's insistence on a system of grand councils as a transition stage to pure devolution produced an irreconcilable division of opinion in the conference and removed the issue from any further practical consideration.

Upon presentation of the report of the Irish convention in April 1918 the British Government endeavoured to formulate a new Irish policy. According to Lloyd George this would include the preparation of a new home rule bill, based to whatever extent possible on the convention's recommendations, and the extension of conscription to Ireland as part of the price that country must pay for the war. He justified this latter provision on the grounds that Ireland could no longer be excluded from conscription when it was necessary to put boys of eighteen and men of fifty into uniform from other parts of the United Kingdom to meet the manpower shortage. Lloyd George mistakenly believed the Irish would accept this pill when made more attractive by the grant of local self-government.[4] To assist in the preparation of the new home rule bill Lloyd George asked Austen Chamberlain to join the War Cabinet. Chamberlain, who was aware of the gravity of the situation in Ireland, believed that 'the time has come when the only safe and practicable solution of our difficulty is to be found in a federal organisation of the United Kingdom. I believe this is now required for the satisfactory conduct of business of Great Britain; but I believe also that it is the only scheme which would make Irish Home Rule safe and the union of Ireland possible.'[5] Walter Long, who was Secretary for Colonial Affairs, agreed. 'While very valuable results have followed from the deliberations of the Convention,' he wrote on 14 April, 'it is hopeless to try and bring Nationalists, Southern Unionists and Ulstermen together, and that to provoke a controversy is to lose the Bill. Can we not devise a scheme which could if necessary be adopted as a basis for Federation of United Kingdom and fight it on these lines.'[6] There were also indications that some groups, such as the followers of William O'Brien, which had bolted the Irish convention, might be willing to agree to an Irish bill constructed on federal lines. In the light of these expressions of interest in federalism and the necessity to placate Ireland a Cabinet committee was duly formed on the subject which included Chamberlain and Long, who was to be chairman.

While the Government struggled for an Irish solution there was an outpouring of public interest in federalism. During the next fortnight numerous motions appeared on the order paper of the House of Commons for a discussion of the subject and there was a flurry of excitement in the newspapers in its favour. The foremost advocate of federalism in the press was F. S. Oliver, who authored a series of articles in *The Times* in May designed to educate the public on how devolution could satisfy the demands of Ulster, which was at the heart of the Irish problem. 'The Reform Act, which resulted from the Speaker's Conference' he recognized as 'proof that the very greatest constitutional changes can be effected now, while the spirit of Party is in abeyance, with a speed and good will which would have been inconceivable in pre-war days'.[7] In the Cabinet's Irish committee these optimistic sentiments were promoted by Chamberlain and Long, who were attempting to persuade others to adopt an Irish bill consistent with the federal principle. On 18 April the latter reported to the Prime Minister that the discussions were proceeding very well and that his colleagues seemed to favour 'a commencement towards the establishment of a Federal system for the United Kingdom' as a means of facilitating the passage of any new home rule bill through Parliament.

> Of course it is not to be contemplated that we should proceed now to set up Parliaments in the rest of the United Kingdom, but we can, I think appoint a Commission, or strong Committee—I hope very limited in numbers—and charge them with the duty of preparing schemes for England, Wales and Scotland.
>
> There is no doubt that opinion among members of the Committee has hardened in the direction of a federal system, and the further one goes in the preparation of the Bill, the more evident it is that once you adopt the Federal system, the drafting of the Bill becomes much easier.[8]

But such claims were meaningless in face of the disagreement which emerged among Conservatives at a lengthy Cabinet meeting on 23 April. Although Long and Chamberlain ardently supported a federal settlement, Balfour and Curzon were against it, while Smuts argued for a constitution along the convention model. In the end Long's drafting committee was instructed to continue its work on the Irish bill with the understanding that Ireland simply could not wait for a decision on whether to proceed with the larger question.[9] It was here that the federal alternative was effectively severed from the home rule issue.

With the decision to construct a separate bill for Ireland, Long's committee was immediately confronted with the problem of Ulster, for which there still seemed to be no solution. Carson and his colleagues had taken the view that any attempt to settle the Irish question with the country in its current state of turmoil would be suicidal. Furthermore it was quite evident that opinion in southern Ireland would never tolerate any settlement promulgated on the lines of Lloyd George's home rule *cum* conscription proposal. On 9 May Tom Jones, the Irish committee secretary, noted that differences of opinion were manifest, 'but upon one point every Member of the Committee was agreed, namely, that as a preliminary to proceeding with the Government policy either in respect of conscription or of the grant of self-Government to Ireland it was first necessary that the new Irish Administration should restore respect for government, enforce the law and, above all, put down with a stern hand the Irish–German conspiracy which appears to be widespread in Ireland'.[10] This discussion was indicative of the prevailing mood of the Government. It recognized the need for an immediate restoration of law and order, which became the determining factor behind its Irish policy for the next two years.

An opportunity for the Government to adopt a more constructive approach occurred in mid-June when Lord Brassey, a lifetime crusader for federalism, led a representative deputation from both houses to meet the Prime Minister and the Cabinet. Chamberlain helped to prepare the way by drawing up a memorandum on 'The Irish Question and Federalism'.[11] That the Cabinet might be receptive to such a plan was made more possible by the Government's abandonment in the previous week of its joint home rule–conscription programme.[12] On 26 June Brassey and his colleagues urged the Government to adopt the plan which had worked so well in the dominions and the United States and which he believed 'will in due time be accepted by Irishmen as a reasonable satisfaction of their demand'. Lord Selborne, also speaking for the federal Unionists, pointed out that his party never believed the Irish question was incapable of solution. But since Joseph Chamberlain's opposition to Gladstone's home rule bill in 1886, Unionists believed that the Irish question could not be dealt with apart from the interests and welfare of the United Kingdom and the empire as a whole. Selborne strongly urged the calling of a devolution conference to consider the establishment of provincial legislatures. It was obvious from his reply that the Prime Minister remained unconvinced about the feasibility of federalism.

I am not so clear about the state of opinion in England; that is really what matters. After all, here is a population of 34,000,000 out of 45,000,000 and unless you have got a substantial majority of the English representatives in favour of it, it is idle to attempt it. You cannot attempt a big measure which is highly controverted in the middle of a great war, because national unity is one of the weapons of victory. So you must therefore have unity upon that subject. I have not altogether been quite satisfied and, if I may suggest to those who are in favour of this solution, that is what they have got to address themselves to. It is really a question for the English constituency, and that they have got to make up their minds about.

Lloyd George was also concerned about the likelihood of Ulster accepting any devolution proposal. 'Prophecy is never very safe in the realm of politics,' he cautioned, 'and it is certainly never very safe to indulge in prophecy when you come to talk about Ireland, because there have been so many prophecies and they have always ended in dispute.'[13] But the deputation had obviously made an impression on Lloyd George, who was obliged to place the idea of a devolution conference before the Cabinet which met three days later. Lord Curzon, however, was determined to wreck the proposal. 'The setting up of such a Committee', he said, 'would give the impression that the Government was inclined to accept a Federal solution, and, for his part, he was not prepared to pull up the British Constitution by the roots in order to get Ireland out of her difficulties.' A prolonged altercation was averted by the decision that time, in any case, would most likely not permit any consideration of federalism, before the autumn session or even during the present parliament.[14]

By the time a general election was held, in November of 1918, popular enthusiasm for federalism had largely subsided and the Irish issue still lay in limbo. With Ireland in a state of almost continuous upheaval little likelihood remained that a federal solution would be acceptable to any party in that country. On 29 November Long concurred with A. V. Dicey that

Anybody who thinks that the adoption of the federal system or any other plan of devolution would settle our difficulties in Ireland must be wholly ignorant of the true condition of things there. So far from settling things, we are going to have I believe even greater troubles and anxieties hitherto and I do not look at the Federal plan at all from the Irish point of view. My own belief is that until you federalise the United Kingdom, have local Parliaments for domestic affairs, reserving her central Parliament for great

Imperial questions, you will not be able to deal with more than a fraction of the problems which present themselves for solution.[15]

Therefore as the Government applied more severe measures in Ireland, federalists shifted their emphasis from Ireland to the relief of the congestion in Parliament. This was the intent of Lord Brassey's motion in the upper chamber on 5 March 1919. Selborne, who made the seconding speech, dwelt on the imperial advantages which might accrue from federalism, but little was said about Ireland. Without this contentious issue as a *raison d'être*, devolution was vulnerable to its detractors. The most devastating attack came from Lord Chancellor Birkenhead, who insisted that there was no electoral mandate for setting up provincial legislatures. 'It is now actually proposed that an immense revolution of the Constitution of these Islands is to be carried through after a General Election at which it is not possible to pretend even that one constituency voted with this question before them. To attempt to do so would, in my humble judgement, be a national scandal.' Furthermore he argued that if Ireland was excluded from the proposal 'it is obvious that this gives away the whole case. If it be really true that Devolution cannot at this moment be applied to Ireland, but is to be a Devolution which will be limited in its scope to England, Scotland and Wales, the matter is doomed to failure even before it starts.'[16] These forceful remarks effectively killed Brassey's motion and caused the federalists to alter their strategy.

During the next several months the key to federalists' hopes lay in their ability to recouple the Irish issue with their other aims. This was the intent of Major Evelyn Wood's motion in the House of Commons on 3 June—that the Government should set up a parliamentary body to consider a measure of devolution applicable to England, Scotland, Ireland, and possibly Wales, but 'without prejudice to any proposals it may have to make with regard to Ireland'. It was this saving clause which weakened the proposal and thereby accounted for the reticent support given to it by many ardent supporters of federalism. Long, however, asserted that he would not support any federalist motion which did not include Ireland in its terms of reference. Additionally, as he had done with regard to the electoral question and House of Lords reform, Long suggested that the house should set up a Speaker's conference to consider federalism in all its aspects. Sir Edward Carson, who expressed astonishment at the Irish tone of the debate, was not sympathetic with Wood's motion mainly because it failed to draw any distinction between Ulster and the rest of Ireland.[17] Sir Courtenay Ilbert, a House of Commons clerk, described the two days' debate as 'academic. There is general agreement that the business of Parliament is congested, and that the new system of grand committees is not working satisfactorily but no kind of assurance as to the remedy which ought to be applied and can be applied.'[18] The motion eventually passed by 187 to 34, but the apathy of the house was made manifest by the miserly attendance for the debates, which twice set the bells ringing for lack of a quorum.

In spite of this indifferent response federalists planned in earnest during the summer recess to set up a devolution conference. On 7 August Brassey handed to Lord Crewe a list of suggested members for such a body. This included eleven Englishmen, five Scotsmen, two Welshmen, and four Irishmen —almost without exception trusted exponents of federalism.[19] But before any members were actually selected the Government obtained the services of Speaker Lowther to preside over the conference. This was of the utmost importance because the Speaker possessed a formidable reputation from chairing the electoral reform conference and it was assumed in many quarters that he would be able to pilot successfully any devolutionary measure into law. The Speaker's appointment disturbed the Ulster faction, who had no faith in devolution as a remedy to the Irish question, but could not afford to decline representation in the conference. Hugh de Fellenberg Montgomery wrote to Carson that 'the FD committee could hitherto be regarded as an academical affair or a convenient apparatus for shelving the Home Rule question. The Speaker, however, would not have accepted the Chairmanship unless he meant business.'[20] Curzon, by whose hand the previous attempt to compose a federal solution was struck down, objected to the idea of the conference on the grounds that it had never been discussed or approved by the Cabinet. He complained to Bonar Law that 'the Speaker is asking that evy member of the Conference should already be a partisan of Devolution—and that the other side should not be represented or heard'. As Conservative leader in the House of Lords, Curzon had been entrusted by Bonar Law with the task of composing the Unionist delegation to the conference. But he refused to supply the Speaker with '15 tame sheep who will promise to nibble the pastures into which he leads them'.[21] As a result the final list which was presented to the Prime Minister contained a number of Conservative members, chiefly Ulsterites, who had no wish to effect a settlement. But the mere presence of the Speaker at the head of the conference encouraged the possibility that federalism might be revived as a live political issue fraught with extensive ramifications for Ireland.

The convening of the Speaker's devolution conference, however, at last impelled the Government to take decisive steps to solve the Irish question. At the urging of Walter Long, the Prime Minister resurrected the Cabinet's committee, which once more assumed the responsibility for drafting a bill for the government of Ireland.[22] It was under these untoward circumstances that the Speaker's conference began its sittings on 23 October with Lowther in the chair and G. F. M. Campion as secretary. *The Times*, labelling the conference an 'undistinguished commission', stated:

It has taken the best part of three months to constitute the Devolution Commission and the result is very disappointing. The only hope of an agreed settlement of outstanding constitutional questions lay in the formation of a strong and representative body which would have the moral authority to impose its recommendations on the two Houses of Parliament. Instead, there has been assembled a Commission which is undistinguished and far from representative. The House of Commons delegation is weaker in authority than that of the House of Lords, which at least includes two former Secretaries of State in Lord Gladstone and Lord Harcourt. There is a considerable representation of Irish Unionists, including the Ulster members, Captain Charles Craig and Mr. Moles, and Lord Oranmore and Browne. But there is no Nationalist on the body, and three-fourths of Ireland is unrepresented directly or indirectly. The one hope of success lies in the personality of the chairman. The Speaker achieved an unexampled success with the similar Conference on Electoral Reform as to give the public more confidence than it would otherwise have had in scanning the list of his colleagues. But it would be idle to pretend that this Commission is the one which would have been designated by public opinion to frame a new Constitution for the United Kingdom.[23]

Brassey also lamented the nondescript composition of the conference and the absence of such individuals as J. W. Wilson
and Sir Thomas Whittaker who shared his keen interest in
federalism. 'I cannot understand how all this has come about',
he told the latter, 'unless the Government wished to make the
proceedings of the Devolution Conference as far as possible
abortive. There being so few of us in the Conference who are
really up in the subject makes our task a difficult one.'[24] Perhaps
more than anything else the conference composition served to
show the disciples of federalism, lest they misinterpret the
electoral reform precedent, that the mere calling of a Speaker's
conference was no assurance that their cause would automatically be carried into law.

In regard to the Irish question Brassey did not believe its
diversion to the Cabinet committee would adversely affect the
outcome of the conference. Long's committee, he believed,
would merely decide whether Ireland was to have one or two
parliaments and what special provisions would be necessary for
Ulster. 'This will be a just relief to us in our task—as the
discussions on the purely Irish side of the subject would probably have been very animated and shown wide differences of
opinion.'[25] What Brassey failed to appreciate was that the
extraction of the Irish issue from the conference agenda had
sapped the vital component necessary to the ultimate success
of federalism in Great Britain.

Very little transpired at the first session aside from a general
discussion of the terms of reference, which vaguely called for a
legislative and administrative devolution of the United Kingdom, and a decision to meet three times per week.[26] At the
second meeting of the conference, on 28 October, the question
of what areas should be devolved and whether they should all
possess the same legislative powers was discussed. Brassey and
Murray Macdonald were strongly in favour of what was called
'straight-out devolution' whereby England would comprise
only one governmental unit. But owing to its preponderant
population and wealth some members of the conference believed England should be divided into several areas.[27] This was
especially the position of the Ulster representatives who, without at first alluding directly to their province, recognized the
relevance of this proposal to the Irish question. If a dual

parliamentary system was constructed in England, Ulster could, in the interests of consistency, demand similar treatment for Ireland. In an effort to steer the conference away from the potentially dangerous topic of Ireland, Lord Gorell on 4 November suggested that they should take up the subject of the classes of legislation which should be submitted to sub-ordinate legislatures. But the Ulstermen objected to the conference proceeding to another topic while the critical issue of areas remained unresolved. Captain Charles Craig, whom Gorell described as an 'irreconcilable Ulsterman', spoke at con-siderable length about the Irish question and about the impossi-bility of devolution meeting Ulster's special needs. Gorell surmised that the Ulstermen had come into the conference 'solely as wreckers. It is the first time I've personally come across the Irish question and it's a revelation. Craig said "of course if you can find a solution no one will be more pleased than I, but it's impossible". Not a trace of desiring to help or construct, merely to oppose any and everything.' Although the conference had veritably decided to defer the question of Ireland to Long's Cabinet committee, the federal idea was so pregnant with possibilities for Ireland that during the initial stages of the conference the Irish issue alternately threatened to disrupt the proceedings or to infuse some life into the discussions.[28]

That the conference did not become stalled over Ireland was due to the Speaker's insistence on 11 November that it should decide what powers should be transferred to subordinate legislatures. During the next five sittings near unanimity was reached on nearly one hundred heads of legislation which would be divided into central and local categories. Matters affecting the Crown and the constitution, the defence establish-ment, treaties, foreign affairs, India and the dominions, cur-rency and the national debt, industrial legislation, and post office jurisdiction would be reserved for the imperial legisla-ture. Among the powers to be devolved would be education, health, housing, agriculture, local government, and the police.[29] It was also provisionally agreed that all unspecified powers should be reserved for the central parliament and that the existing veto of the Crown would not be affected under the new arrangements. Any conflict of jurisdiction would be referred to the judicial committee of the privy council for judgement. Acts

passed by a local body would be submitted directly to the
Crown for royal assent, without the interposition of a high com-
missioner. Although it was not deemed essential that the constitutions of each of the legislative bodies be identical, it was
agreed that these bodies should not be subject to dissolution
and that members should be elected for fixed periods, such as
three years.[30] In the midst of these discussions, however, the
cause of devolution was dealt a harsh blow when Lord Brassey
was accidently killed by a car while crossing a street in London.
Gorell remarked that 'as a not very clever specialist on devolution, he was going to be a bore on the conference, but it is
frightfully cruel luck that after advocating it for nearly 30 years
and getting to this point he should have been killed'.[31] Another
conference member, the Master of Elibank, believed 'from that
moment the opponents of devolution on the Commission became more effective'.[32] To consider that the loss of its leading
advocate dealt the cause of devolution an irreparable blow,
however, is to be over sanguine about the legislative potential
of the conference.

Nevertheless Brassey's death was perhaps a premonition of
some of the problems the conference was to encounter in early
December. A controversy arose between the adherents of
'straight-out' devolution, as proposed by Brassey and Macdonald, and those who were so impressed by the disadvantages
of such a scheme that they were being driven to oppose the
very principle of devolution. This growing schism impelled the
Speaker to adopt an expedient alternative to full-fledged devolution. In his *Commentaries* he wrote: 'The more I considered the
proposal of one supreme and four independent legislatures, the
less I liked it. The confusions which might arise, the multi-
plicity of elections, the novelty of five (possibly even more)
Prime Ministers and Cabinets of probably divergent political
views, the enormous expense of building four new sets of Parliament buildings and Government offices and providing all the
paraphernalia of administration, frightened my economical
soul.' Instead Lowther suggested a system of 'standing committees' whereby representatives of existing constituencies in
England, Scotland, and Wales would carry out local government functions in their respective provincial capitals prior to
the assembling of Parliament.[33] The objects of such a scheme

were economy, simplicity, and the satisfaction of legitimate local sentiment. Its glaring weakness lay in the absence of any relief provision for overworked M.P.s, ostensibly the reason for calling the conference. The Speaker's plan immediately encountered strenuous opposition from a substantial portion of the conferees. Gorell became very discouraged with the proceedings, calling the Speaker's pseudo-devolutionary plan a 'perfectly drivelling suggestion' and concluding that Lowther could only see things 'from the House of Commons point of view and also doesn't want his work on Electoral Reform to need alteration'.[34] The Speaker too, in asking Lord Selborne to fill the vacancy left by Brassey's death, recognized that the conference was in the 'doldrums'. Although substantial agreement had been reached on the subjects to be devolved, the conference appeared unable to agree on the extent of devolution, and the overshadowing difficulty of the status of England, which might entail the consideration of Ireland, still lay menacingly in the background.[35] But by the time the conference adjourned for its Christmas recess on 18 December it had already relinquished all control over the Irish issue to the Government's special committee.[36] Now as a result of the Speaker's conservative plan of devolution the conference was on the verge of abdicating its control over the other vital issue on which the conference was summoned—the relief of Parliament. Under such conditions devolution seemed pointless.

During the Christmas recess opposition to the Speaker's plan began to be expressed in more specific terms. In a letter to the Speaker on 20 December Viscount Gladstone re-emphasized the prolonged strain on officials and members of the House of Commons and the uncertain role of the House of Lords inherent in his scheme. 'But in the new "Executive"', he admitted, 'I am absolutely at sea.' At least six existing administrative departments would have to be reorganized of the English, Scottish, and Welsh councils. This would create much confusion in hiring and firing individuals and acquainting them with their new duties. 'Why not limit the Grand Council plan to *legislation*?' he queried. 'It would be strictly "Devolution" and it gets rid of serious and complicated problems. Legislation and not Administration is the chief clog on the H. of C.'[37] Lowther agreed with Gladstone about the liability of devolved

administrators, particularly when they represented a different
party from that of the majority of the electors in a province.
But he reminded Gladstone that their terms of reference summoned them to prepare a scheme of administrative as well as
legislative devolution. Furthermore he proposed to solve the
House of Lords difficulty by allowing any draft bill passed by
any grand council to be laid on the table of both houses and
to become law after thirty days unless either house requested the
Crown to withhold its assent. He still realized that some provision would have to be made in the event that the two houses
differed.[38] What is obvious from this exchange of correspondence is that those who were opposed to the Speaker's plan were
forced to register their disapproval in the most tactful manner
possible and that the opposition would have been much greater
had it not been proffered by the Speaker.[39] In contrast to the
electoral reform conference the Speaker's influence, in this
instance, was acting as a divisive factor and handicap to any
agreement on devolution.

It is not fully clear what transpired at this stage, but a
number of draft letters and memoranda in the Viscount Gladstone Papers indicate that there was some attempt to rally support for an alternative plan. 'I am afraid we shall be landed
on the rocks,' Gladstone wrote to Lord Chalmers. 'The personnel of the Conference with few exceptions is incompetent. . . .
I have spent days in worrying over the Speaker's proposal. The
more detailed exam. I give it, the more impossible it seems to
me as a workable, or *initial* solution.' Gladstone viewed the
Speaker's proposal as chiefly an abdication of the responsibility
with which the conference was charged of drafting a plan of
devolution. But he realized that the Speaker was a very well-
trained, experienced, and respected individual who was at the
very top of his profession. 'It is because *he* has fathered this
proposal that I am worried.'[40] It is doubtful whether this letter
was ever sent, but its contents are a revelation of some of the
undercurrent of feeling generated in the conference against
the Speaker's plan. A much-corrected draft of another letter
to the Speaker also remains where Gladstone pointed out some
of the other problems of the conference. Beyond the difficulty of
getting thirty individuals to agree there seemed to be no enthusiasm in Parliament or in the public for the subject under

consideration. 'The Franchise Conference,' he wrote, 'was in a happier position because while every one had his own opinions we met for the very purpose of making sacrifices in the common interest on matters wh. had been discussed and debated *ad nauseam*. Devolution is really untrodden ground. It is far more difficult and opinions are only in the making. The field of view widens and with it the difficulty.'[41] The Speaker's plan was, in effect, not merely a recognition of these difficulties, but to all appearances a submission to them under the assumption that only by gradual means could devolution be implemented. But those who sought to challenge this idea were stuck in the quandary of drawing up a plan of pure devolution for which the country was not prepared and which the House of Commons would be unlikely to consider.

By the time the conference resumed its sittings in early February, Murray Macdonald had developed an alternative scheme for a system of fully independent provincial parliaments. It differed from the Speaker's proposal chiefly in its provision for separate election of members of subordinate bodies. As discussion proceeded on the opposing schemes it was obvious that the conference would have to reach some decision on which plan it wished to support. On 17 February by a majority of one vote the conference decided to accept the Speaker's plan, the Speaker abstaining.[42] Additionally it was agreed that the councils constructed by this method should elect their own chief administrative officers, thus removing any possibility of simplifying the plan.[43] During the preparation of the final report members discussed both plans, but more attention was devoted to developing details for the Speaker's scheme, which bore the closest resemblance to the existing system. Indeed the plan for pure devolution presented such formidable structural difficulties that its proponents made no attempt to draft any more than an abstract proposal. Gladstone confided to Lord Emmott that 'it must be realized that separate authorities with separate election is the only solution possible. ... But we are not really competent for this. Instead of 32 average men what in the first instance is wanted is a Committee of 10 or 12 really competent men who could hammer out a scheme for free and full discussion.'[44] While the larger scheme of pure devolution remained the federal ideal, its advocates in the conference were forced to concede the inability of the conference to construct, and the unwillingness of Parliament to accept, any more than a weak makeshift proposal.

The final report of the conference was delivered on 27 April in the form of a letter from the Speaker to the Prime Minister. In the course of its thirty sittings the conference had reached substantial agreement only on the powers of the proposed subordinate lgislatures *vis-à-vis* the imperial Parliament. On the subject of areas to be devolved there was considerable disagreement over whether England should constitute one or several territorial governing units. It was generally recognized that the subdivision of England would present such formidable administrative problems that it should not initially form a part of the devolution scheme. The greatest disagreement occurred, however, on the prospective composition of the new legislative bodies, from which two distinct reports emerged, each with thirteen adherents. The Speaker's plan, which provided for a system of quasi-independent councils of M.P.s who would sit during the autumn recess, was designed as a sort of 'half-way house' between the existing system of standing committees and full devolution. It included a two chamber council for England, Scotland, and Wales (including Monmouthshire). The council of peers would consist of representatives nominated by a committee of selection in the House of Lords, with a membership of half that of the Commons council. The administration of justice was to be entrusted to an executive committee in each grand council. This committee's tenure of office could be terminated by its resignation or by the passing of a vote of no confidence by the lower council. The Home Secretary was to act as a link between the subordinate legislatures and the imperial Parliament and would possess the power to test the validity of grand council legislation. Any doubts he might have about a grand council bill would be submitted to the judicial committee of the Privy Council for final decision. Although the devolved legislatures were to be granted several specified sources of revenue, ultimate authority on all matters would reside in the imperial Parliament. Disputes between the two council chambers were to be handled in a manner similar to that recommended in the Bryce second chamber conference report—by a system of free conferences and joint sittings. After a trial period of three years the devolved bodies could make any alterations deemed necessary in the system or even abandon the experiment altogether and revert back to a single legislature at Westminster.[45]

Murray Macdonald's less detailed scheme provided for the separate election of legislative bodies for England, Scotland, and Wales, consisting of the same number of members as represented those countries in the imperial Parliament. Whether there should be one chamber or two would be decided by the Government when it drafted a federal bill. If a bicameral system was adopted it urged the Government to follow the recommendations of the Bryce conference report about composition and powers. Under this plan members of the House of Commons would not be eligible, but peers could be elected to the local legislative bodies. The head of each ministry would be appointed by the King.[46] The main difference between the Speaker's plan, *The Times* recognized, and that espoused by the opposition party was that 'his scheme is tentative. He wishes the country to take two bites at the cherry, partly, perhaps, that we may have a chance of seeing whether we like the taste of it. Mr. Macdonald is so convinced that it will prove agreeable that he counsels us to bolt it whole.'[47] The Speaker's report also acknowledged the existence of a smaller, less resolute group who approved of the fundamental principles of Macdonald's scheme, but were prepared to affix their signatures to both plans in the event that it was found impracticable to set up a system of national parliaments at an early date. According to *The Times*, 'they hope that by accepting the first scheme now they may eventually arrive at the second, on the principle that in any case two bites are better than none. On the whole, we imagine that most people in Parliament and in the country who are in favour of devolution will find themselves in the same quandary, and therefore inclined to follow the same course as the undecided five.'[48] In the appendices of the final report the Speaker included a copy of his scheme and that of Murray Macdonald as well as several memoranda supporting one or the other of these proposals. Under such circumstances it seemed highly unlikely that the Government would attempt to frame any legislation based on the Speaker's report.

When the conference report was issued as a parliamentary

paper on 12 May it provoked almost no interest in the House of Commons. When the Government did not respond positively to the report, some of the conference members called a meeting in early July of all advocates of federalism to consider what action should be taken to further their cause. In support of this gathering *The Times* published a series of articles written by Murray Macdonald, but admitted that the Speaker's report could 'hardly be said to have aroused in the country that attention which its importance demanded'.[49] At the meeting on 6 July the two main speakers, Long and Murray Macdonald, urged that the House of Commons should be made to bring pressure on the Government to introduce federalist legislation, and both stressed the necessity of dealing with devolution and the House of Lords question simultaneously. It was decided also that a deputation of conference members should carry the opinions of the meeting to the Prime Minister as soon as possible.[50] Not until shortly before Christmas, however, after several postponements, was an appointment arranged. On that occasion Lloyd George pronounced himself to be sympathetic with federalist aims, but he was more impressed by the practical difficulties implicit in implementing any such scheme as those recommended in the Speaker's report. Singling out the lack of unanimity on the part of federalists he stated that 'any scheme proposed was likely to come to grief unless there was something like common agreement amongst all those who believed in Federalism'. Furthermore it was obvious that there was no support for the proposal in the country and Lloyd George hastened to point out that 'the Government ... could not move in advance of public opinion'.[51] Finally in the next parliamentary session Murray Macdonald introduced a private member's bill which provided, in addition to the establishment of subordinate parliaments, a provision for second chambers constituted in accordance with the recommendations of the second chamber conference. While this measure attracted the support of the usual advocates of federalism, it died at the outset for lack of Government facilities.

The failure of federalism to solve any of Britain's post-war ills may be attributed to its radical nature and the timidity of politicians to sanction any large-scale restructuring of the basic institutions of government. A long-established convention in

British constitutional history dictated that institutions should be carefully moulded by the process of time and in response to the empirical demands of the political and social environment. While the conference method was designed to facilitate periodic adjustments in the constitutional order, the existence of some semblance of public or partisan agreement and desire for the change was absolutely necessary. In 1919 when the Speaker's conference was convened none of these conciliatory factors was present. It was actuated seemingly for the sake of appearances —to allay the bleatings of persistent federalism advocates and to defer still further any immediate settlement of the Irish question. The presence of any earnest intention to enact a federal system, regardless of any other consideration, among those who held responsible positions of power appears questionable. The uncertain jurisdiction over the Irish issue threatened at several times to provide a greater sense of immediately and urgency to the transactions, but the resumption of control over Ireland by the Cabinet Irish committee, which eventually devised the Government of Ireland Act of 1920, removed any such possibility.

In this weakened state the Speaker attempted to draw up a transitional scheme which might pass the House of Commons and still provide a modicum of devolution until the country recognized the need for a more thoroughgoing plan. But his action, however well intentioned, produced an irreconcilable split between those who advocated straight-out devolution and those who favoured a more cautious approach. The parliamentary overload was relieved eventually, not by devolution, but by the increased use of standing committees and advisory bodies which enabled Parliament handle a host of technical subjects arising from the war. There was simply too little enthusiasm for federalism in the country to expect a successful outcome of the conference proceedings. As the Speaker noted, 'the discussions had been of great interest, as they often raised recondite and sometimes difficult questions of Constitutional lore and law, but all along I felt that the driving force of necessity, which had been so active a factor in the Electoral Reform Conference, was absent'.[52] But the underlying reason for the failure of the devolution conference is inextricably associated with the larger questions of imperial federation and the greatness of Britain in the twentieth century. When the latter ceased to be a reality, some time during the course of the war, there was no longer a necessity or a desire for federation, imperial or otherwise. Similarly when the possibility of reconciling Irish nationalism with the unitary structure of the United Kingdom ceased to be a realistic goal Westminster ceased to presume so much the ideal of an 'imperial' parliament and was better able to perform the functions of a domestic governing body.

XII

The Anglo-Irish Treaty of 1921

Lord Morley once told me that Home Rule would be introduced by the Conservatives.

KING GEORGE V[1]

Since the extension of the franchise in 1867 and the subsequent
growth of mass political parties the Conservative Party had successfully resisted all attempts by the proponents of Irish
nationalism to set up a separate parliament in Dublin. W. E.
Gladstone's 1886 bill fell victim to strong Unionist opposition
in the House of Commons and his 1893 bill was defeated by
the Conservative-dominated House of Lords. In 1910 any
reordering of the relations between the Houses of Parliament
was rendered impossible by that party's refusal to sanction any
settlement, including a coalition, which might lead to the passage of home rule. This legislative occlusion was partially removed by the Parliament Act of 1911, which effectively limited
the veto power of the upper house. But Unionists became so vin-
dictive over this Liberal violation of the rules of constitutional
propriety that they increasingly turned to unconstitutional tactics to resist home rule. All subsequent Liberal attempts to settle
the Irish question by conciliatory means were thwarted by the
Unionist opposition. In 1914 the Buckingham Palace conference, sponsored by the King, broke down owing to ostensible
Unionist refusal to recognize Catholic majorities in Tyrone and
Fermanagh. Likewise the negotiations carried out by Lloyd
George in 1916 after the Easter rebellion were torpedoed by
a revolt of leading Tories in the coalition Cabinet. Even a convention of representative Irishmen in 1917–18 could not break
the intransigence of the Ulster Unionists, supported as they had
always been by the main body of the Conservative Party. By
the end of the war Unionist obstruction over Ulster had so
thoroughly conditioned the British approach to the Irish ques-

tion that nothing short of a Unionist-directed programme had the slightest chance of success.

A constitutional settlement finally came to Ireland under the peculiar formula of a Conservative ministry acting under the direction of a radical Prime Minister—an arrangement effected by the Buckingham Palace conference of 1916. It had taken two generations for Liberal statesmen to realize that Conservative–Unionist intransigence was the principal force to be reckoned with in any resolution of the Irish question. While Pakenham, Macardle, and other writers devote much attention to the growth of Irish nationalism and the negotiations of Lloyd George with the Sinn Fein Party, they give scant recognition to the curious circumstances in British politics which permitted a settlement. There has been little to suggest why the Irish political question, after frustrating all attempts at a solution for thirty-five years, suddenly ceased to menace the British constitution. To a great extent the settlement was a result of important internal changes within the Conservative Party. Without this basis no settlement was possible. But the factor which clinched the success of the negotiations was the lingering fear of a die-hard Unionist revolt over Ulster. It was the genius of Lloyd George to turn this, his greatest political liability, into his foremost asset at the bargaining table. He successfully interpreted and implemented the Conservative position at the Anglo-Irish conference in 1921. Unlike previous interparty gatherings on the Irish question, this conference also included representatives of the heretofore outlawed Sinn Fein Party, which constituted a significant departure in procedure. Such recognition of the effective bases of political power, and the subsequent ability of Lloyd George to formulate a compromise between them, were the determining factors in the outcome of the Anglo-Irish Treaty.

In the three years following the war the Conservative Party exerted its influence toward a settlement through three channels of conciliation. The most immediate was the coalition Government created by Lloyd George to meet the exigencies of war and reconstruction. The coalition was so dominated by Conservatives, that any action in Ireland was essentially that of the Unionist Party; such was the Government of Ireland Bill of 1920. Necessitated by the rapid growth of the independence-minded Sinn Fein Party and a corresponding increase in the level of violence, this bill provided for separate home rule parliaments in Ulster and the south. It also allowed continued Irish representation at Westminster and provided for the creation of an all-Ireland council. Introduced by one staunch Unionist, Walter Long, defended by another, Bonar Law, and acquiesced in by Sir Edward Carson and the Ulsterites, the bill became law on 23 December. It provided the necessary safeguards against Ulster falling under Dublin rule. In his *World Crisis* Winston Churchill describes this measure as 'a decisive turning-point in the history of the two islands. ... From that moment the position of Ulster became unassailable.'[2]

This protection of Ulster by legislative enactment coincided with important changes in the Unionist leadership. On 4 February 1921, a few days before his sixty-seventh birthday, Sir Edward Carson relinquished his direction of the Ulster Unionist Council, leaving the leadership of the new Northern Ireland Parliament to his younger protégé, Sir James Craig. Increasingly involved with his duties at the bar, the fiery die-hard was ennobled on 24 May as Lord Carson of Duncairn and safely removed to the upper house as a member of the nation's highest judicial body. Not until the Irish conference had completed its deliberations in December did Carson fulminate against the Government's position, and then only with a full awareness of the responsibility attached to his high position. More important was the fortuitous retirement of Bonar Law on 17 March occasioned by his sudden illness. Austen Chamberlain, who succeeded him as head of the Unionist Party and leader of the House of Commons, was reported by Lloyd George at first to be 'an awful Tory'.[3] As the son of Joseph Chamberlain, who bolted Gladstone's party in 1886 over home rule, Austen was expected to adhere strongly to Unionist traditions. Unlike his father, however, the new Conservative chief was not an innovator, a strong leader, or a doctrinaire, at least not on issues aside from tariff reform. Unlike Bonar Law, he had no strong ties with Ulster. It was Austen Chamberlain, more than any other Unionist figure, who led his party from the untenable position it had reached before the war. His party's support of the coalition Government's policy of conciliation in Ireland was absolutely essential to any hope of a settlement.

Such a course of action evolved slowly only after months of violence in southern Ireland. Since early 1920 the Government's law enforcement policy in that land had degenerated into a disorderly exchange of reprisals by the 'Black and Tans' and 'Auxiliaries' for outrages perpetrated by the *sub rosa* Irish Republican Army. It became increasingly evident that if Britain would rule south of Ulster, full-scale repression of Ireland by the British army was the only remaining remedy. But it was doubtful whether an army could be raised for that purpose without offending the collective conscience of the British people and ignoring their war-weariness. As early as June 1920, Chamberlain had questioned the practicality of coercion in Ireland. He thought the old Unionist policy was 'not possible, for our people won't give it the time necessary for it to achieve its end'.[4] Nor was Chamberlain alone in this shift of attitude. At a Cabinet meeting in April 1921, Churchill, then Colonial Secretary as a coalition Liberal, suggested a peaceful alternative to 'the unlimited exercise of rough-handed force' in Ireland. 'The Prime Minister', he reported, 'was astonished and indeed startled to find how many Conservatives adhered to this more complicated course.' From this expression of opinions 'Lloyd George reached the conclusion that a policy of unmitigated repression in Ireland would not command whole-hearted support even among the Conservatives'.[5] Since the Government of Ireland Act already was regarded with utter contempt in southern Ireland, the only alternative to coercion was the negotiation of a separate agreement with representatives of the illegal Sinn Fein government.

The proposal for an Anglo-Irish conference, the second channel of conciliation, was fostered mainly by the Conservative Party. Following the change of Conservative leadership, hope for a negotiated settlement was inspired by a number of interviews between important Conservatives and Eamon de Valera, the so-called President of the Irish Republic. In April Lord Derby, a prominent Liverpool Unionist, ventured to Ireland under the pseudonym of 'Mr. Edwards' to encourage negotiations.[6] In May Sir James Craig allowed himself to be escorted along a circuitous route to de Valera's hiding place, where he was treated to a recitation of English oppression of Ireland over the past seven hundred years.[7] It would be difficult to understand why the Ulster leader took such risks if he was not genuinely desirous of a conference. It would be equally difficult to imagine Carson going through such flirtations with the Irish republicans. In the official proceedings which led to a conference, the loyalist allies of the Conservative Party in southern Ireland also played a leading role. On 21 June in a debate in the House of Lords the Government, still clinging feebly to its coercive policy, narrowly escaped defeat by those who were in favour of negotiating a peace with the Irish. Lord Donoughmore, a southern Unionist, moved that the Government expand its 1920 act in the direction of fiscal autonomy and 'propose and authorize negotiations with Ireland'. Two other southern Unionists, Lords Desart and Dunraven, strongly supported this proposal. The latter, who had been instrumental in settling the Irish land question twenty years earlier, sadly told the House that 'he had never seen anything in the least degree to approach the present position. In his opinion deliverance could only come from an immediate amending Act.' Even the calculated eloquence of the Lord Chancellor could not detract from the force of these arguments. To a bitterly disappointed if not hostile house, Birkenhead delivered the dying gasp of the Government's dreary policy of coercion in Ireland.[8] Clearly even among the Conservative Lords a strong countercurrent was at work.

On 22 June the King opened the Northern Ireland Parliament. His speech, drafted along lines originally suggested by Edward Grigg, one of Lloyd George's aides, added impetus to the change in Conservative thinking.[9] He appealed 'to all Irishmen to pause, to stretch out the hand of forbearance and conciliation, to forgive and forget, and to join in making for the land they love a new era of peace, contentment and goodwill'.[10] On the following day Lloyd George and Chamberlain met on the terraces at the rear of their respective residences in Downing Street. Chamberlain argued strongly that 'the spirit of the King's message was incompatible with the whole idea of renewed coercion without one culminating effort for peace'. They were soon joined by Birkenhead, who 'had reached exactly the same conclusion'.[11] On 24 June Lloyd George laid before his Irish subcommittee and later to the whole Cabinet his proposal to invite Craig and de Valera to a conference in London.[12] Churchill wrote that 'No British Government in modern times has ever appeared to make so sudden and complete reversal of policy'.[13] Such a reversal was possible only through the altered attitude of the Unionist leadership towards Irish nationalism.

The negotiations thus set in motion also occasioned the end of hostilities in Ireland. On this occasion it was the southern Unionists who, having the most to lose by continued violence, induced the declaration of a truce. Before replying to Lloyd George's invitation to a conference, de Valera parleyed with this political minority of his country. Lord Midleton, still leader of the southern Unionists, explained the outcome of these intra-Irish talks to the Prime Minister in London. With little difficulty Midleton persuaded Lloyd George to accede to de Valera's wish that Craig be excluded from the projected meeting. But in regard to the truce question the Prime Minister feared that the Sinn Fein would take advantage of any lull in the fighting to improve its position. 'The opinion of the Unionist members of the conference', argued Midleton, 'was especially strong that if Mr. de Valera agrees to go to London there should be a temporary cessation of "operations" on either side. ... Unless I can take with me some written assurances on this point I am afraid it is useless in returning to Dublin tonight as I doubt if any of the Unionist members would attend the Conference tomorrow.'[14] On the force of Midleton's arguments Lloyd George consented to a 'gentleman's agreement' for a truce in Ireland.

In the months that followed the declaration of the truce the Prime Minister engaged in a kind of diplomatic swordplay with de Valera to determine on what terms a conference should meet. Again the action of the Unionist Party was decisive. On 10 August de Valera penned what appeared to be a formal rejection to the Prime Minister's terms for peace. The Cabinet, however, seized upon the ambiguities, hidden from most who read de Valera's response, and professed that far from being an outright rejection it was 'an attempt—even though a clumsy attempt, to keep open the discussion and that the document was intended as merely a step in a prolonged negotiation'. Statements of Sinn Fein representatives in Paris and London supposedly confirmed the notion that the Irish had no desire to break off the negotiations. It was also suggested that the Sinn Fein statement was designed to put de Valera and his colleagues in a safe position *vis-à-vis* the extremist republicans in the Dail Eireann.[15] Such an interpretation, though strained, marked a real advance in Conservative thinking and veritably ensured the eventual meeting of a conference with the Irish leaders.

The principal agent of conciliation through which the Conservative Party exerted its influence was the Prime Minister and ultimate leader of the negotiations, Lloyd George. Throughout the period leading up to the conference the Prime Minister was wavering between a policy of conciliation and repression in Ireland, depending on which he thought would elicit the greater Unionist support. As a member of the 1914 conference he could recall only too well the intransigence of the Unionist Party over Ulster. As recently as 1916 he had been badly burnt by this same unreasonable attitude. It is little wonder that he approached the Irish negotiations in 1921 with extreme reluctance, going no further than the Conservatives who dominated his Government would allow. As late as May 1921 Lloyd George was still relying on the ' "long tradition and unbroken loyalty of [the] Tory party" as the instrument with which he would crush out insurrection in Ireland'.[16] Soon after the King's speech Lloyd George cautiously committed himself to a conciliatory Irish policy. Even then he appeared somewhat incredulous towards the change in the political stance of the Conservative Party. The Prime Minister regarded it as 'The first real justification of [the] Coalition'. On 28 July he told C. P. Scott that he had made great concessions to the Irish, 'and the Cabinet hd. gone further in supporting me than I shd. have thought possible. . . . It wd have bn utterly impossible to carry a settlemt. on such lines as I have proposed in [the] face of a powerful hostile oppositn using the sort of method of attack wh the "Morning Post" uses.'[17] None the less the ever present threat of a Conservative revolt circumscribed Lloyd George's conduct with the Irish in the coming months of negotiation.

Unionist control of the negotiations was reflected also in the composition of the conference. Lloyd George headed the British side, and as leader of the Conservative Party Chamberlain naturally would play a leading role in the negotiations. But Chamberlain did not represent fully that section of the party most insistent on protection of the rights of Ulster. It was of paramount significance, therefore, that Lloyd George obtained the consent of Lord Birkenhead to participate in the conference. Before the war he had acquired the sobriquet of Carson's 'galloper' at a review of the Belfast Volunteers. Now in 1921, with Ulster's standing in the empire secure, Birkenhead's attitude towards self-government in southern Ireland showed considerable advance.[18] Churchill, though by no means predictable on the Irish issue, also consented to serve, as did Sir Laming Worthington-Evans, the Secretary of State for War, and Sir Hamar Greenwood, the Chief Secretary for Ireland. Sir Gordon Hewart, the Attorney-General, was to be a member when constitutional questions arose. On the Irish side the more extremist members of the Dail Cabinet, including de Valera, Cathal Brugha, and Austin Stack, refused to leave Ireland. Presentation of the Irish point of view was left in the hands of the more moderate Arthur Griffith and Michael Collins as leaders, with Robert Barton, George Gavan Duffy, and Eamonn Duggan making up the rest. Both delegations were dominated by moderate elements, but the British, in terms of political experience, had by far the more formidable team.

When the conference met for the first time on 11 October the 'Proposals of the British Government for an Irish Settlement', prepared in July by Lloyd George, Chamberlain, and Balfour, furnished the basis for discussion.[19] As in all previous negotiation attempts Ulster became the chief point of contention. Griffith and his colleagues claimed that the division of Ireland was unnatural and the ill-feeling between north and south had been 'manufactured by Belfast politicians'. The Prime Minister declared that his Government would gladly see Ulster unite with the rest of Ireland, but only by its own free will. He also urged the Irish to face facts:

> Mr Gladstone had attempted to settle the question on the basis of autonomy. The late Mr Chamberlain had made proposals which if accepted by Mr Gladstone might have settled the question at that time. Later, from 1911 to 1913, the Liberal Government had again tried to settle the question. Ulster, declared the Prime Minister, defeated Mr Gladstone and would have defeated us. We could not do it. We must accept facts.

Collins incisively insisted, however, that 'It was not Ulster which had prevented settlement, but the division of English

parties which in turn desired to use Ireland for their own political ends. Now there was a union of parties and the conditions
were different.' Chamberlain and Lloyd George warned Collins to be under no misapprehensions as to the difficulties confronting the British Government. Claiming that the atmosphere
was not growing more favourable to peace, they ominously
asserted that 'the representatives of both the Coalition Parties
in the Conference were taking great risks in endeavouring to
make a settlement on the lines which the Government had suggested'.[20] From this point until the end of the negotiations Lloyd
George used the threat of a Conservative revolt as a device to
wheedle concessions from the Irish representatives.

But his concern at the moment was to keep the Conservative
extremists in check. On 24 October there appeared on the order
paper of the House of Commons a motion signed by thirty or
forty Unionists condemning the negotiations. Typically Lloyd
George took the bold approach by challenging the dissentients
to a debate and division on the Irish negotiations the following
Monday. Chamberlain thought this put 'A cold douche on the
hot heads of some of our friends!'[21] But the Prime Minister was
by no means confident of his position. He told C. P. Scott 'his
present life was not a bed of roses. ... It was a dog's life.' He
faced the dismal prospect of having to fight Sinn Fein on one
side or the die-hard Tories on the other. A conceivable danger
he foresaw was the possibility of a Tory attack led by Bonar
Law, who had recently returned to England fully recovered and
in great vigour. At a recent breakfast he had found the ex-Con-
servative leader 'reasonable and moderate up to a point. Then
suddenly you touched something and he blazed up. At heart
he was an Orangeman and the Orange fanaticism was there.
He had brought it with him from Canada. He mt. at any time,
in defence and what he regarded as an attack on Ulster, lead
a Tory revolt.' Scott also talked with Michael Collins, whom
he found to be a 'straight forward and quite agreeable savage'.
Scott warned him that the Prime Minister 'was fighting their
battle hard under great difficulties and hd done wonders in
bringing over the Tories'. He alone of all the great Liberal
statesmen—Gladstone, Campbell-Bannerman, and Asquith—
was in a position to deliver the goods. Collins replied rather
unsympathetically that 'I know nothing about your politics. I

have only to think of Ireland.' But before leaving Scott exhorted his Irish friend that he must consider British politics if he expected to accomplish anything in the conference.[22]

During the next three weeks Lloyd George, with the spirited co-operation of the Unionist leadership, held his ground with the Conservative Party. But his position was never so strong as to allow him to deviate in the slightest way from current Unionist dogma towards Ireland. This forced him to use all his powers of blandishment and persuasion to extract vital concessions from Griffith, the head of the Irish delegation. An opening appeared on 29 October when the Irish submitted a roughly worded memorandum which more closely approximated the British position on the key issues of Crown, empire, and defence.[23] Thereupon Tom Jones, the Prime Minister's Welsh private secretary, persuaded Griffith, who was later joined by Collins, to meet with Lloyd George and Birkenhead on Sunday 30 October, at Churchill's house. The Prime Minister told Griffith that the Irish response was so worded that he hardly knew where he stood. Lloyd George was in the process of preparing his speech against the die-hard vote of censure on Monday and he sought definite assurances on the main issues in order to defend his position. To clarify the Irish position the two leaders drafted a letter of personal assurance which Griffith ultimately signed.[24] In it he affirmed his willingness to recommend free partnership for Ireland within the Commonwealth, and coastal facilities for the British navy. But this statement, he asserted, 'was conditional on the recognition of the essential unity of Ireland'.[25] According to Griffith, in his letter to de Valera, he had granted these personal assurances so that Lloyd George 'would go down to smite the Die-Hards, and would fight on the Ulster matter to secure "essential unity" '.[26] When the Prime Minister encountered the hostile motion the following day he demanded that the House 'must either trust its negotiators or replace them'.[27] Chamberlain likewise made an appeal to his party to trust its leaders in the negotiations. The result was an overwhelming 439–43 vote of confidence in the coalition Government.

The next crucial test for the Government was the Unionist Party conference scheduled in a fortnight at Liverpool. With this in mind and encouraged by his success thus far, Lloyd

George communicated the principal terms of a settlement, as pledged by Griffith, to Craig. These admitted a retention of all of Ulster's powers conferred by the 1920 act, but also the obligation to establish an all-Ireland Parliament. Contrary to the hopes of Chamberlain and Birkenhead, on 11 November Craig categorically rejected any possibility of political unity in Ireland.[28] This placed Lloyd George in the toughest possible negotiating position. He could do nothing to force the hand of Ulster, particularly in light of the upcoming Unionist conference. Somehow all the concessions on Irish unity had to be wrested from the Sinn Fein side. This impasse was removed by Lloyd George's using his greatest handicap, the threat of the Ulster crowd, to his utmost advantage. Tom Jones laid the groundwork by convincing Arthur Griffith that the Prime Minister was Ireland's best friend and greatest hope for peace. Should he resign, as seemed almost certain in the face of Ulster's obstinacy, the only alternative would be a militarist regime under Bonar Law, who was becoming daily a more serious threat. The only way to avert this, Jones suggested, would be to offer Ulster two alternatives—the choice of an all-Ireland Parliament, or acceptance of her existing powers subject to a delimitation of her area by a boundary commission. The latter, Griffith became convinced, was tantamount to essential unity since Ulster could not function under a further limitation of her boundaries. Rejection of both, on the other hand, would place Ulster in an indefensible position and would prevent Lloyd George from resigning.[29] On 12 November, at the home of Unionist M.P. Philip Sassoon, on Park Lane, the Prime Minister formally confronted Griffith with this tactical manœuvre. Lloyd George argued that unless Chamberlain and Birkenhead could meet their die-hards at Liverpool without the danger that Sinn Fein would later reject this proposal, all would be lost. Griffith thereupon agreed that he would not help the Ulsterites by repudiating the boundary commission alternative. The following day Jones placed the agreement in writing and Griffith approved it.[30]

The importance of this assurance lay not so much in its effect on the forthcoming Liverpool conference as its ultimate effect on the outcome of the negotiations. Contrived under the necessity of safeguarding the Government from its extremists and couched at first in negative terms, the agreement was regarded by Griffith as binding only until the Government had beaten its die-hards at Liverpool. Lloyd George, Chamberlain, and Birkenhead, however, at once interpreted the provisions to mean that the Irish would continue to support the boundary commission proposal after the Liverpool meeting and thereby afford the Government protection from its die-hard elements.[31] These subtle nuances escaped the scrutiny of the Irish and were allowed to pass until the fate of the Irish delegation in the conference was sealed. Griffith's assurance became, in the final stages of the conference, a guarantee that Sinn Fein would not break on Ulster. Viewed with hindsight this manœuvre may appear as a prime example of the wizardry of Lloyd George. There is equally strong reason to believe, however, that the agreement, whatever its ultimate effects, emerged out of a genuine concern on both sides over an Ulsterite revolt at Liverpool. Bonar Law was behaving as if he wanted his leadership back and was willing to lead a die-hard movement against the negotiations to get it. At least these were Chamberlain's impressions. He told his wife that 'Bonar is seeing red on the subject of Ulster'.[32] Although Bonar Law's effect upon members of the Unionist Party was uncertain, Chamberlain observed all the characteristics he had shown in 1911 after Balfour retired and Chamberlain was edged out of the party leadership. Chamberlain resolved that if he carried the party with him on this issue he would never yield to Bonar Law again.[33] But in resisting the advances of the former Conservative chief Chamberlain allied his own fortunes more closely to those of Lloyd George and the coalition and committed himself more deeply to the settlement of the Irish question.

Bonar Law's utterances, however, make it appear that any desire for the leadership was incidental to his avowed concern over Ulster. Clearly he had been undergoing a severe inner struggle. But on 12 November Bonar Law displayed a curious bravado in a letter to J. P. Croal, editor of the *Scotsman*. He admitted that he had been 'a good deal worried', but if Lloyd George continued in his present course he intended to oppose it. 'I shall try to get the Conservative party to follow me,' he said. 'If I succeed we will simply be back on the old lines. If I fail to get the majority which means of course the control of

the organisation, I will simply drop out.' The chief hindrance
to these ambitions, he recognized, was the moral apathy in the
party. But his instincts told him that once the issue was raised
and clearly stated 'the feeling of the Unionist party will be
almost unanimous against the Government'. From the outset
of his career there were only two things he ever regarded as
matters of conviction—one was tariff reform and the other was
fair play to Ulster, 'and I feel as strongly about it as I did then'.[34]
Even without publicly committing himself Bonar Law represented the most likely alternative in the event that the Government made a wrong move in the Irish negotiations.

Much was at stake therefore when the National Union of
Conservative and Unionist Associations held its annual meeting
on 17 and 18 November at Liverpool. As a stronghold of
Orange Toryism, Liverpool did not afford the most favourable
ground for Chamberlain's campaign against the die-hards. But
the conversion of Archibald Salvidge, the head of the local
organization, gave invaluable support to the cause of conciliation. In speaking to the gathering Salvidge expressed the hope
that the conference would succeed in bringing peace to Ireland.
But 'the real issue', he declared, 'is whether you condemn or
support your own elected leader'. He appealed to Unionists to
trust their leadership not to force Ulster.[35] Sir Laming Worthington-Evans, a member of the conference, promised not to
compromise the supremacy of the Crown or Ireland's membership in the empire. He also assured the delegates that he would
not agree to 'any settlement that requires the coercion of Ulster
to assent to it'.[36] In the subsequent division of opinion the die-
hard element mustered fewer than seventy votes out of the 1,800
delegates attending the meeting. That evening Austen
Chamberlain turned the defeat into a rout by delivering the
finest speech of his life. 'I am not afraid of the Die-hards,' he
declared. 'All I ask of them is that they shall wait until they
have the material upon which to judge. ... Give us a little time
longer and the whole story shall be told and you shall judge
whether we have kept the faith or whether we have betrayed
our trust.'[37] He later told his wife that he was 'in complete control of myself and them, and all that had preceded gave me
the fire that I usually lack. ... I suppose that the majority of
the M.P.s had never heard me at a public meeting and I guess

they did not think that I could do it. Today for them and for all there I *am* the leader, instead of merely bearing the title.' Though not wishing to appear too boastful, he confessed that the Prime Minister was very pleased and that Bonar Law was in 'a much softer and chastened mood'.[38] The outcome of the Liverpool conference assured the Government that the Unionist Party would not take a radical stand behind Ulster.

In spite of the fact that the Conservatives were safely dislodged from their old intransigent position, Lloyd George continued to capitalize on its effect to maintain his hold on the Irish. The Prime Minister now pressed definite terms of settlement on the Irish delegation. The formal Irish response to this draft treaty represented 'a complete going-back' on the understanding Lloyd George had reached with Griffith. The Prime Minister told the Irish that his Government had dealt with Conservative dissidents at Liverpool and in the House of Commons on the basis of these assurances. But the latest Irish memorandum created a new situation. 'On the basis of this document', he said, 'instead of having as we had in the House of Commons only forty against us, we should not have had forty Members of our whole party in support of us.' Turning to the details in the Sinn Fein response Lloyd George complained that it made no mention of Ulster's option to vote itself out of a common Parliament. Griffith replied that 'if Ulster accepts your proposal, we will accept it. It is not our proposal, but we would accept it.' Then there was the Sinn Fein insistence on legislative and executive authority in Ireland apart from the Crown. The Irish recommended association with the British Commonwealth merely for 'matters of common concern'. Lloyd George, however, demanded that all acts of the executive should be taken in the name of the Crown. This was fundamental. 'To say that the King was not king for everything was to say that he was not king.'[39] In the next several days the original draft treaty was revised whereby the constitutional status of Ireland in the Commonwealth would be the same as that of the Dominion of Canada.[40]

On 3 December the Irish delegates laid these and other proposals before the Dail Cabinet. This nearly destroyed the tactical advantage Lloyd George had assumed over Sinn Fein. While Griffith spoke strongly in favour of acceptance there was considerable opposition in the Irish Cabinet to the terms. De Valera said 'he personally could not "subscribe to the Oath of Allegiance nor could he sign any document which would give North-East Ulster power to vote itself out of the Irish State." He might understand Griffith giving up independence for National unity, but "you have got neither this nor that".' Ultimately Griffith saw the force in many of his colleagues' arguments and he consented to try to manipulate the negotiations so as to appear that the break in the conference came on Ulster.[41] But to slip his neck from the British noose and thereby make the treaty more palatable to the Dail Cabinet was no simple matter. When Griffith returned to London on 4 December he arranged a midnight conversation with Tom Jones. In recounting how much the Sinn Fein delegation had conceded he pleaded with Jones to obtain from Craig 'a conditional recognition, however shadowy, of Irish national unity' in return for Sinn Fein's acceptance of the empire. 'Will Craig do nothing at all to help? Will he not write you a personal letter as A. G. did saying Ulster will recognize unity if the South accepts the Commonwealth?'[42] On the following morning, at Griffith's instigation, Collins continued the discussion about Irish unity with Lloyd George. But the Prime Minister charmed Collins into believing that the north would ultimately be forced economically to join with the south, particularly after the boundary commission had done its work. At the same time he managed to parry Collins' difficult insistence on a definite reply of acceptance or rejection of Irish unity from Craig before the conference ended. Collins left the interview under the impression that the cause of a united Ireland would triumph in either case.[43]

At the afternoon session of the conference Lloyd George tightened the screw on the Irish delegation. He used two means—the strategem of having to face his own die-hards with the treaty in its present form (though the issue was no longer in doubt from that quarter), and the assurances extracted earlier from Griffith. When Griffith proposed that he would 'accept inclusion in the Empire if Ulster comes in' the Prime Minister once again reminded him of their meeting at Sassoon's house. The Irish leader had accepted the British proposals whether Ulster opted to stay in or drop out of the Irish Free State.

Admitting that this was the case, Griffith replied, 'if you stand by the Boundary Commission, I stand by you'. Turning immediately to Collins, Lloyd George confronted him with the urgency of fulfilling a promise he had made to inform Craig that night whether there was to be war or peace. 'I want to know', said the Prime Minister, 'whether you are prepared to face your Die-Hards as we are prepared to face ours?' Collins argued that it would be just as easy to get Craig's conditional agreement to Irish unity as their own. But Lloyd George insisted that this was not the arrangement to which Griffith had agreed at Sassoon's. 'You agreed to our proposal,' he said, 'and you now put a totally different one to us. If you say now that you are not going to accept the preliminary conditions which to us are fundamental, we are not going to put the rest to Ulster.' At this point Lloyd George produced the document and showed it to the Irish. 'I said I would not let you down on that,' replied Griffith, 'and I won't.'[44] Indeed the risk involved in facing the extremist Tories with the treaty now proved to be as great an asset in holding Griffith to his assurances as it was in getting him to make them several weeks earlier.

But at this stage of the negotiations Griffith's pledge alone was not sufficient. It was necessary for Lloyd George to obtain the consent of all the members of the Irish delegation. Otherwise he could not hope to capture adequate support in the House of Commons for the treaty. 'We asked for a united obligation from the Irish delegation,' he said, 'just as we gave a united obligation ourselves. If we got that we would use all our power to carry the Agreement through, even to the point of the defeat of the Government and of the dissolution of Parliament. The Irish delegation must decide whether they would give their united undertaking or not. On their answer depended whether it was to be peace or war.' The conference adjourned for three hours while the Irish discussed the Prime Minister's ultimatum. What followed was a step-by-step conversion of the Irish delegates to Griffith's position—first Collins, then Duggan, and finally Barton and Duffy. At 2.10 a.m. on 6 December the delegates affixed their signatures to the Anglo-Irish Treaty.[45]

The Prime Minister had good reason to be jubilant over the outcome of the Irish conference. By his consummate skill of persuasion, Lloyd George had steered the negotiations out of dangerous waters. But the real story of the success of the Irish negotiations lay in the transformation of the Conservative Party over the previous year. This began with the Irish Act of 1920. By guaranteeing the permanent tie of Ulster with the United Kingdom it obviated the need for watchdog practices by the British Conservative Party. Then at the beginning of the year the old die-hard leadership, which had safeguarded this connection for so long, yielded to new elements within the party. Bonar Law was replaced by Chamberlain, who showed considerable more flexibility in regard to Ireland than his predecessor. Lord Birkenhead remained a central figure in Ireland's destiny, but with a more conciliatory attitude towards Irish nationalism than at any other point in his career. Sir James Craig was probably no less a guardian of Orange liberties than Sir Edward Carson. But unlike previous attempts to settle the Irish question, the interparty conference in 1921 never included an Ulsterman. Moreover, dissatisfaction with the Government's previous policy of coercion had permeated the Conservative Party from top to bottom. These powerful elements, acting in concert through the coalition, and subsequently the Irish conference and Lloyd George, served to sever, at least temporarily, the alliance between British Conservatism and Ulster Unionism which had prevented a settlement of the Irish question for over three decades. But the conversion of the Unionist Party was never so complete as to allow a reckless acquiescence to Sinn Fein demands. Lloyd George's actions were guarded throughout by an awareness of the heavy hand of the Unionist Party on his administration and the forces it could muster at a moment's notice against any attempt to apply home rule to Ulster. Indeed the threat of a die-hard revolt with the ultimate possibility of a repressive Unionist regime under Bonar Law was so convincing that Lloyd George was able to persuade the Irish to make concessions that would have been impossible under different circumstances. Ulster, which had killed every other attempt at an Irish settlement, in this instance proved to be an invaluable ally of the British delegation. Whether genuine or a pretext (and one is inclined to think it was both), the threat of Unionist intransigence provided the necessary touch required to pry the Irish delegates from their stand on republicanism and Irish unity, and paved the way for dominion status and partition. Such a course of action was the only way Lloyd George could reconcile his Unionist supporters to peace.

The Anglo-Irish Treaty of 1921 marked the end of a great political struggle over Ireland which had begun in the previous century. It was also a climactic event in the utilization of the conference method and constituted one of its greatest individual successes. As a gathering of party leaders it was a resurrection of the original concept of the interparty conference which had been formulated before the war; yet it was a departure from that format inasmuch as the Anglo-Irish conference admitted an illegal party to its proceedings. During the war the Irish independence movement had overtaken the parliamentary party and a partisanship emerged along national lines, exceeding that which had prevailed in British politics a decade earlier. But by 1921 both countries were war-weary and more apt to accept any settlement which might ultimately fulfil their respective national aims. In contrast to all previous encounters with the Irish question, the English party leaders, under the imaginative leadership of Britain's first radical Prime Minister, displayed an unusual degree of unanimity in their negotiations with the Sinn Fein representatives. Obviously the war had effected strong national bonds on both sides. Ironically this reconciliation of conflicting nationalisms by interparty means ultimately resulted in the disintegration of the coalition, a resumption of normal party relations in England, and a civil war in Ireland.

Epilogue and Conclusion

Party is a body of men united for promoting by their joint endeavours the national interest upon some particular principle in which they are all agreed. For my part, I find it impossible to conceive that anyone believes in his own politics, or thinks them to be of any weight, who refuses to adopt the means of having them reduced into practice.

All government, indeed every human benefit and enjoyment, every virtue, and every prudent act, is founded on compromise and barter.

EDMUND BURKE[1]

Political stability is a characteristic which writers and statesmen have often attributed to modern Britain. But the transfer of government from the singular province of the Crown in the Middle Ages to the broad will of the electorate in the twentieth century has occasioned frequent controversies and disorders in the body of state. The acquisition of power by the aristocracy during the first stage of this process in the seventeenth century, exacerbated by the religious issue, necessitated a civil war and a revolution. In the modern period the demands for democratic government, accompanied by the twin ideals of nationalism and socialism, have been met by more enlightened attitudes and more rational methods of change. Undoubtedly the fact that Britain had already engaged in a partial modernization of its constitution several centuries earlier contributed to its receptiveness of further substantive alterations. But the most important aspect of this development, as perceived by Bagehot, was that significant changes in the social bases of government and in the active agencies of power were carried out within existing constitutional structures. The Cabinet served as the critical link in this process. Herein lay the major difference between the development of the modern British state and those of France, Russia, or even America, where drastic methods resulting in an abrupt change of institutions were necessary to induce greater recognition of the democratic principle. Great

Britain was unique inasmuch as it was able to assimilate the prevailing spirit of the times into its ancient forms of government.

In the late nineteenth century, however, this system was challenged by the growth of modern political parties which had arisen in the wake of successive extensions of the franchise. These developments posed peculiar problems owing to their extra-parliamentary character and potential for dividing the country into two hostile camps. Consequently the House of Commons was no longer an assembly where gentlemen gathered to exercise their independent prerogative and reason upon each other, but an arena where members displayed their loyalty and obedience to their respective parties. One of the earliest commentators on this phenomenon was Ostrogorskii, who recognized that

> The election over, the Member returned, once more it is party orthodoxy, according to the daily market quotation certified by the Caucus, which is set up as the criterion of the parliamentary conduct of the Member. If the M.P. is bound to his electors by personal feelings of devotion and affection, which come before party conformity, the Caucus, should a conflict break out, deliberately tries ... to stifle these feelings, to destroy the confidence based on the character of the man, in order to ensure the triumph of conformity of which it is the self-appointed guardian. ... The result is that the English Parliament sustains injury in the 'two conditions which', according to Bagehot, 'are essential to the bare possibility of parliamentary government', and which are 'the extrinsic independence' of the representatives and 'the inherent moderation' which should prevail in the House.[2]

These lines were written almost as a plea to save the British polity from eventual self-destruction. But Ostrogorskii was not aware, any more than Bagehot, of any conciliatory mechanism which might arrest this dehumanizing process or control the excesses of the party system.

Likewise modern scholars have devoted far more attention to the more noticeable and exciting conflicts which were so endemic to this era and have tended to ignore the opportunities which were contrived for conciliation which also abounded. Some of the more important of these diverse proceedings may be categorized as interparty conferences. Although precedents for such endeavours can be cited in the formal conferences which had convened occasionally for centuries to settle disputes between the houses, parliamentary tradition is utterly devoid of any instance of informal talks between party leaders over legislation until quite recent times. Any earlier form of inter-party compromise was obviated by the general lack of any party machinery or spirit in preceding periods. In his study of the topic, H. J. Hanham observes that 'the chief characteristic of party organisation in the nineteenth century, was its impotence. Shorn of the patronage of the eighteenth century, and not yet fortified by the financial strength and undeviating party vote of the twentieth, the Whips and party managers found their influence drastically circumscribed.'[3] It was only after the passage of the Reform Bill of 1867 and the formation of mass political parties that the need arose for some means to promote concern for the national interest. The resultant method was not so much an institutional structure or even a regular system, but a state of mind which emerged at certain times when immoderation threatened to disrupt the legislative or constitutional process. The interparty conference was an ill-defined and unplanned antidote to factious political behaviour which was invoked for many reasons and with varying degrees of success. To the extent that these gatherings evinced any common characteristic it was to promote a greater degree of conciliation and integration. Like so many practices in British government, the interparty conference unobtrusively took root and evolved to fit the peculiar needs of a changing political system.

The two earliest instances of interparty negotiations in 1869 and 1884 over Irish disestablishment and electoral reform respectively set important procedural precedents for the treatment of future political crises. Both conferences revealed that some prior conciliatory disposition was an essential prerequisite to any agreement. Whether the communications gap between the parties could be bridged depended on the extent to which party spirit had crystallized and the degree of pressure exerted upon party leaders by their extensive followings. Acting as an effective counterweight to party orthodoxy was the monarch, a traditional bastion of central authority, who assumed the role of mediator to political conflicts which could not be resolved within Parliament. These two initial successes for the cause of conciliation, however, must be separated from its later history, which was characterized by many near misses and dismal failures.

By the turn of the century party lines had hardened to the extent that any compromise of principles was highly unlikely. Following the ascendancy of the Liberals to a position of power and confidence in 1906 any conference of party leaders was bound to fail. Nevertheless this procedure continued to be invoked as a means of forestalling legislative conflict or moderating party feeling. As such meetings occurred with increasing frequency ideas began to solidify concerning their procedure, thereby imparting a greater sense of permanence to the conference notion as a valuable supplement to the parliamentary system. Following the failure of the education bill conference in 1906 Lord Lansdowne commented on its procedure by contrasting it with those conferences in previous centuries where the Lords appeared formally in their hats and the Commons without a covering. 'The advantage of a discussion such as that which has taken place in the last few days is that it is of a wholly informal character, that proposals or suggestions can be made in the most confidential manner and entirely without prejudice to those who make them.'[4] F. S. Oliver, who more than any other man formalized the concept of the conference and shaped its image in the public mind, stipulated in 1910 that conferences must be small, intimate, dominated by leaders, and open-minded.[5] Although these guidelines were usually followed, interparty conferences were only partially successful in allaying the party strife which was so prevalent in pre-war Britain.

The caucus had by this time become such a potent influence that parliamentary behaviour was growing increasingly regimented and restrictive. Not only did it provide the party in power (in this case the Liberals) with an obedient majority, but it induced a situation where the Government was assuming an almost dictatorial control over the business and time of the House of Commons. The Conservatives were thereby forced to rely on their permanent majority in the upper chamber to stem the tide of radical legislation. In both parties whips played an important role in this highly competitive environment. Lord Marchamley, a retired whip from the Commons, spoke critically of this system in 1910: 'Any Chief Whip worth his salt has no political conscience whatsoever, nor does he hold the conscience of his Party in his hands. . . . He is a very valuable piece of party mechanism. He does what he is told—When he is instructed to go he goeth; when he is instructed to come he cometh; and when he is told that he must Whip for any self-evident proposition, such as that black is white, he does so with the same alacrity and eagerness as if he believed it.'[6] No doubt these deferential attitudes prevailed as well amongst ordinary M.P.s to the extent that the application of independent or rational judgement to any serious political issue became a secondary consideration. In these circumstances, to which was added the vexatious Irish question in 1910, any appeal to reason or compromise was out of the question; interparty conferences served only as respectable alternatives to political violence for the release of party tensions. So intense had the situation become by 1914 that there was a curious resemblance of futility and finality between the King's pleas for domestic peace and Edward Grey's proposal for international conciliation on the eve of the First World War.

After the outbreak of war the conference concept was utilized extensively for the purpose of drawing the parties closer together on issues which might divide the nation if not brought under control. This policy was only slowly developed as the parties increasingly manifested a sense of national purpose which eventually resulted in the formation of a coalition Government. Dissension, on the other hand, was regarded as tantamount to encouraging a German victory. Conferences were now used as a means to forestall problems which might interfere with the war effort, and to promote a national con-sensus. This was apparent in the talks which the King held with coalition leaders at Buckingham Palace in 1915 on the delicate subject of compulsory military service. Asquith perceived that the King's main concern was 'not the abstract merits of the question, but the growing division of opinion and the prospect of a possible political row'.[7] But recourse to a conference was prompted most frequently by the continued prevalence of the Irish question as a disruptive feature in British politics during the war. It was for this reason that immediate steps were taken after the Easter rebellion to establish some semblance of national accord over Ireland. When the method of treatment in this instance proved more potentially divisive than a continued state of unrest in Ireland, the negotiations had to be abandoned. Eventually all grounds for possible party misunderstandings, which were so evident during most of the decade of Liberal domination, were removed by the formation of the Lloyd George coalition by the appropriate means of a Buckingham Palace conference of party leaders.

The ensuing era of total war and readjustment was conducted by Lloyd George in concert with leading Conservatives. So thoroughly did the spirit of national unity permeate British society and government during this period that one political commentator nostalgically questioned in 1918 whether parties were ever going to resume their pre-war footing:

> No one, indeed, who visits the constituencies can doubt that both the great parties are deep in coma; and that the outside public recks little whether that coma passes into death. There is everywhere a friendliness between party leaders fatal to party warfare or to the renewal of it. We have seen at the Front how fatal is fraternisation to the fury necessary for real warfare. Well, there has been a fraternisation between the great political parties throughout Great Britain for nearly four years. Is this fraternisation going to count for nothing? The party swords have been beaten into ploughshares. Is it going to be easy to beat them back into swords?
>
> Then look at the situation at Westminster and Whitehall. There have been two Coalitions, in both of which the lion has lain down with the lamb. It was the claimant prophecy of the outraged Party Press on both sides at first that the Coalition idea would prove short-lived. The lion would awake and the lamb would be found inside him. But though governments have changed the coalition idea has survived. In fact, the second is a more daring combination than the first—more scandalous to the pure partisan, more outrageous to the established priesthoods of the party establishments. That priesthood has lashed itself with knives, and called to its gods. But the party Baal is still on a journey; and the Coalition goes on. The British nation is greater and wiser than either of its great parties.[8]

Throughout this period of national cohesion the conference method was used to deal with issues which might incite controversy or for which a broad basis of support was required. Hence a more representative system of Speaker's conferences arose to consider such topics as electoral reform, the House of Lords, devolution, and Ireland. With the latter in particular conferences were necessary to remove it from the centre of political attention lest the Irish issue should become as contentious as it had been before the war. In this respect the Irish convention was an eminent success, though it never reached an agreement. So extensively was a sense of British nationalism evoked for the sake of winning the war that eventually a common approach emerged even towards Ireland in the form of military suppression. With the corresponding maturation of Irish nationalism under the label of 'Sinn Fein', however, the Irish issue was effectively removed from the British political system and began to resemble an international question. The Anglo-Irish conference between representatives of the British government and the self-proclaimed government of Ireland was indicative of this altered perspective. Nevertheless the concessions made here resulted in a disintegration of both national unities and an eventual end of the era dominated by the politics of Lloyd George.

Had interparty conferences been more outwardly and obviously successful during this prolonged period of crisis they might have become institutionalized. Still they did not disappear from the political scene. Conferences have been utilized repeatedly over the last half century as an extra-parliamentary procedure for the deliberation and occasionally resolution of party disputes. Subsequent conferences pursued the lines set up by those which met before and during the course of the First World War with only modest alterations. So far as can be discerned, there have developed two distinct styles of conferences to which Britain's political disorders have been referred. The most successful format has been the Speaker's conference which has continued to specialize in electoral reform. In his study of the subject J. F. S. Ross has identified three factors which he considers vital to its success:

1. There must be a national crisis of such a kind and of such a magnitude as to still party dissension, and, in particular, to produce a genuinely national all-party coalition government with the full support of the country behind it.

2. The conference must complete its task well before the end of the crisis is in sight.

3. The agreed conclusions of the conference must be given substantial legislative effect without delay, and certainly before the end of the crisis or the dissolution of the all-party coalition government.[9]

These guidelines were established to a great degree on the basis of the striking success of the first Speaker's conference which produced an agreement on women's suffrage. Succeeding conferences in this period were unable to capitalize on the same combination of favourable circumstances.

The next two Speaker's conferences in the twentieth century also occurred during crises. In 1929 James W. Lowther (Lord Ullswater since 1921), who had played such an important role in laying the foundations for the conference method, returned from retirement to preside over another electoral reform conference. It was summoned by Ramsay MacDonald's Labour Government at the behest of the Liberal minority in the House of Commons on whom the Government relied to bolster its slim majority after the recent election. Its purpose was to discuss the feasibility of proportional representation, a democratic device which might assist the Liberals in gaining additional seats in a general election. But the Conservatives, who were content with existing electoral arrangements, refused to permit such an innovation. Besides the crisis over the economy bore no direct relation to the electoral system, and there was no great demand for this reform except from the Liberal Party, which was fast becoming a negligible factor in British politics. By the time the conference finished its labours opinion was divided, as it had been in the devolution conference, and the Labour Party was no longer interested in legislating on the subject. The conference had served simply as a convenient means for tabling the proposal.[10] In the Speaker's conference of 1944 there was a national crisis, a coalition Government, and a spirit of co-operation. Following much the same format as earlier conferences this body produced agreed resolutions on the subjects of redistribution, parliamentary and local government franchises, university and business representation, candidates' expenses and other topics.[11] But the report was not submitted until the final stages of the war and on issues not immediately relevant to it. The recommendations of the conference ultimately were acted on, but not until several years later; and even then some of the provisions, notably those on business and university voting qualifications, were altered to suit the wishes of the Labour Government which had by that time assumed power.[12]

The most recent example of the Speaker's conference is somewhat baffling in light of Ross's maxims. It met from 1965 to 1968 at the request of Harold Wilson's Labour Government for the purpose of ironing out inconsistencies in the electoral law and bringing the work of the two previous reform bills of the twentieth century up to date.[13] To the extent that there was a crisis there may have existed what has been termed the 'youth crisis' of the late sixties, but this was certainly not so apparent at the outset of the conference. Nevertheless the conference took a small step towards meeting this exigency by the time it completed its deliberations by recommending that the voting age be lowered to twenty. Its report was timely and fell at the height of the crisis. But the conditions in which the latest Speaker's conference was conducted, were less than ideal in several other respects. By consuming nearly three years before completing its labours it was the longest-lived of any conference, and this might have been detrimental. This delay was caused by the death of the Speaker, Sir Harry Hylton Foster, in 1966 and the resumption of conference and house duties by his successor, Horace King. But this interruption does not appear to have adversely affected the outcome of the conference, which completed the latest stage in the fulfilment of the democratic ethos. Finally, acting on the partial precedent set in 1948, the Government altered the provisions of the conference's agreed report by lowering the voting age to eighteen. The ministry then acted swiftly in translating the report into legislation, which invoked little party altercation. It may be concluded that the Speaker's conference has become the most institutionalized of the conference forms, to the extent that electoral reform proposals are usually accompanied with the suggestion that they be referred to this type of body.[14] It has come to occupy a place similar to that of *ad hoc* advisory bodies which have also grown up as an adjunct to Parliament since the First World War.[15] The peculiar advantage of the Speaker's conference is that it is able to treat issues which are likely to engender an undue amount of partisan behaviour more dispassionately and in such a way that the interests of the nation are best served.

The most important type of remedy applied to the political ills of Great Britain between 1869 and 1921 was the interparty conference of party leaders. Conceived at the outset of the democratic age, it differed in several important respects from the Speaker's conference—it was less formally conducted, smaller in size, and generally convoked to deal with more urgent matters. Since 1921 there have been relatively few inter-party conferences of party leaders chiefly because there have been too few questions serious enough to provoke acute party controversy. For much of the twentieth century Britain has been governed by coalition Governments—hence there was little need for a means to promote further interparty cohesion. From 1914 until the end of the Second World War, a period of nearly thirty-one years, there were no less than five coalition Governments, lasting a total of nearly twenty-three years, or three-quarters of this period of almost continuous crises. The gradual realization of a more democratic society, accompanied by a general lack of party altercation over substantive issues, obviated the need for any conference arrangement of this kind. In recent years, however, in the absence of any coalition Governments, there have been two examples of interparty conferences, both concerning the House of Lords and neither productive of a settlement. After the Second World War, Clement Attlee's Labour Government decided to trim further the powers of the upper house, specifically for the purpose of gaining adoption of its controversial steel nationalization bill before the adjournment of Parliament in 1951. At the request of the Conservative Party, however, the Government agreed to hold a conference of party leaders to try to reach a compromise. This meeting, the first of its kind since the Anglo-Irish conference of 1921, met for three months and agreed on nine principles relating to the structure of the House of Lords, but on the critical question of powers the leaders could not concur.[16] The Government then proceeded with its parliament bill, which reduced the delaying powers of the upper house to two sessions and one year when it passed into law in 1949. As Conservative Prime Minister in 1953 Winston Churchill attempted to revise this judgement by suggesting another conference on the reform of the House of Lords, but the Opposition did not react favourably to this suggestion.[17]

In the mid-sixties another conference of party leaders met to discuss the Labour Party's intention to reduce further the powers of the upper chamber to only a single session. This gathering broke up in June of 1968 owing to the outrage of the Labour Government over the House of Lords' rejection of resolutions proposing sanctions against Rhodesia.[18] This question was merely a convenient excuse to call off discussions which the Government had called into being merely to convey the impression that the opinions of the Opposition were being taken into consideration on a subject which the Government had no intention of carrying into fruition. The House of Lords was by this time no more than a negligible factor in British politics and not regarded as a serious hindrance to Labour legislation or the will of the people. In early March of 1977 there occurred the latest version of an interparty conference just after the Labour Government's guillotine motion on the devolution bill for Scotland and Wales was defeated. In response to a proposal by the shadow Cabinet, supported by the Liberals, talks were carried out between James Callaghan, the Prime Minister, David Steel, the Liberal leader, and Margaret Thatcher, the Conservative head. Aside from their inconclusiveness, the chief importance attached to these consultations is that they were carried out on an individual basis.[19] There has thus emerged a tradition that it is preferable to hold interparty consultations before proceeding with controversial legislation, especially when it has foreseeable constitutional consequences. Had these conferences been held on a more regular and formal basis they could conceivably have fulfilled the same role as conventions in other countries which create or amend constitutions.

Finally there has been in the twentieth century a continuation of the use of the conference as a means of constructing coalition Governments. This method of conciliation was merely an adaptation of the older interparty conference of party leaders when a transfer of political power was necessary. It was designed for crises when a general election would be unfeasible and a simple designation by the monarch improper. In 1931, in the midst of the great depression, Labour Prime Minister Macdonald found that it was no longer possible to run the Government without making drastic cuts in the national welfare programmes; but rigorous opposition from within his own party to this policy prevented him from taking any decisive action. Acting on assurances, however, that Macdonald could expect adequate support from other parties George V called the party leaders, Stanley Baldwin, Herbert Samuel, and Macdonald, together at Buckingham Palace and a national Government was formed. The King, the parties, and eventually the nation, had acted together in a national crisis to avert a possible financial collapse of the Government.[20] That the same format was employed in the formation of the wartime coalition in 1940 following the resignation of Neville Chamberlain cannot be upheld. While it is true that George VI did consult the party leaders about restructuring the Government, he did so not on a collective but on an individual basis similar to the way Lloyd George approached the Irish negotiations in 1916. In this case there was little doubt about whom the King should or ultimately would select, hence the lack of any need for an actual conference.[21] That there have not been more coalition conferences is not surprising. Party warfare has assumed a more orderly course in recent years and there have been no great crises necessitating the formation of a coalition.

In the future there will doubtless continue to be a demand for conferences of all kinds. The Speaker's conference has found a permanent place in British politics as the most dependable way of bringing electoral laws up to date without engendering party controversy. In light of its reduced participation in political affairs there seems little likelihood that the services of the monarchy will again be needed to assist in forming a coalition Government as they were in 1916 and 1931. But if a prolonged crisis of sufficient magnitude ever develops a Buckingham Palace conference may well be the most useful device in bringing the parties together into a national Government. Indeed the interparty conference of leaders is probably the most valuable form of conciliation and it appears likely that it will be used again to settle legislative deadlocks between the houses and parties. In the absence of any conference committee system, as exists in the American Congress, such an informal process would appear to be a necessity. In the face of an unreformed and unrepentant House of Lords some future Labour Government may find it necessary to instigate further interparty conversations on the status of the upper chamber. But the most serious outstanding British political question remains the Irish issue. The formation of the Irish republic and the passage of over fifty years has solved neither the problem of partition nor the grievances of the Catholic minority in Ulster. In the future it may be advantageous to call a conference on the same lines as the Anglo-Irish conference of 1921. There have already been short talks between the Irish Taoiseach and the British Prime Minister, some interparty conversations on a lower level, and even a constitutional convention in the north reminiscent of the Irish convention, but thus far no changes have been agreed upon which can be practically implemented.[22]

What is now regarded as an acceptable method for dealing with political controversies actually developed in a quiet and unplanned manner to meet the peculiar demands of mass society and party government in the late nineteenth century. Throughout much of its early existence the monarchy played a key role in laying the foundation for the success of conferences (as did the Archbishop of Canterbury and later the Speaker of the House of Commons) by employing its symbolic powers to encourage a compromise. In its role of mediator the monarchy assumed a new and important responsibility in the affairs of the nation. But it would be a mistake to assume that the sovereign exerted any extraordinary influence in bringing the parties to a settlement. Even George V, who pressed his ministers and the Opposition for nearly a full year to settle the Irish question, could not compel the politicians to agree on a matter in which they violently differed. It was in those instances where the party leaders were predisposed to conciliation and not stifled by their massive followings that conferences were most effective. The great weakness of this manner of proceeding was that, even though it provided the necessary channels for communication, it could not create the necessary desire for a settlement. Where the spirit of compromise was absent, as was particularly notable in 1906 and 1914, no amount of special pleas, elaborate plans, or sublime hopes could make the party representatives concur. Where such a spirit prevailed, as was the case in 1884, 1916–17, and to some extent in 1921, the conference stood a reasonable chance of success. In any case the wide variety of such undertakings does show that politicians have had ample opportunities for conciliatory conduct which has added a certain degree of flexibility to the British political system and constitution.

The major function of the interparty conference from 1867 to 1921 was to stabilize the operation of parliamentary government. An exchange of differing, often contrary, opinions in a free society and recognition of a spirit of fair competition has always been regarded as one of the foremost strengths of the English way of life. This pluralistic system was based on an ultimate appeal to reason and a respect for that vague amalgam of precedents, customs, and laws which make up the British constitution. In his 1927 introduction to Bagehot's *English Constitution*, Lord Balfour identified the basis for this national consensus:

Our alternating Cabinets, though belonging to different parties, have never differed about the foundations of society. And it is evident that our whole political machinery pre-supposes a people so fundamentally at one that they can safely afford to bicker; and so sure of their own moderation that they are not dangerously disturbed by the never-ending din of political conflict. May it always be so.[23]

In the nineteenth century, owing to an expansion and organization of the electorate, political power was increasingly wielded by parties outside the traditional parliamentary structure. The most serious aspect of the ensuing struggle was that momentous changes in the British condition of life and style of government could be carried out under the guise of Parliament's sovereignty by a simple majority, after only a limited period of consideration and superficial discussion. The conference method was appropriately derived as a sort of self-regulating mechanism whereby such serious questions were removed from the parliamentary and public eye, and subjected to the deliberation and negotiation of party representatives. This device was clearly contradictory to the prevailing democratic principle of mass participation as well as the traditional authority of Parliament, but it proved to be a valuable expedient for the preservation of both these institutions. At least a dozen times in this period the conference was employed as a haven from political strife and as a means for reaching a solution agreeable to all parties. That such a safety-valve was utilized instead of violence is a tribute to the British politician for his patience and sense of responsibility to his country. It is indicative also of the courage of those who held responsible positions to act independently to preserve Britain's tradition of gradual change and not yield to the fickle desires of the crowd. Indeed it was when the participants could rise above the petty demands of party and personal ambition for the sake of the entire nation and posterity that a conference was most successful.

The principal value of any study of interparty conferences as a procedure of conciliation stems from their revelation of some of the noblest virtues of mankind. Although the life of modern man has been characterized chiefly by divergent behaviour in the form of wars and other lesser forms of conflict, the convergent notion of universal peace is held to be the greatest and ultimate hope for civilization. Interparty conferences reinforced this latter tendency as political idealism (cynics would call it *naïveté*) in the highest degree. Such practices are by no means peculiar to the British system of government, but the Anglo-Saxon tradition has produced some notable examples of conciliatory institutions. Concurrent with the development of conferences on important domestic matters was the growth of colonial conferences to discuss changing imperial relationships. These more formal and regular gatherings lent strength to the concept of consultation and co-operation and ultimately contributed to the orderly dismantlement of the British empire.[24] At present the British Commonwealth of Nations is the principal heir to that tradition. Internationally the idea of acting on the basis of consensus is at least as old as the Congress of Vienna and manifested in the twentieth century by the League of Nations and the United Nations. The common failing of most such conciliatory organizations, however, has been their relative impotence in the face of more pragmatic and partisan forces. A general exception to this rule has been the institution of Parliament which, as an interaction of King, Lords, and Commons, has served as an effective composite for the national will over the centuries. When the authority and structure of this revered body was challenged in the late nineteenth century by the growth of modern political parties, the interparty conference emerged as a protective device to induce an element of normalization into political relationships. This ability to sustain within a single framework a precarious balance between conflict and co-operation serves as a major source of Britain's stability in the twentieth century.

APPENDIX I

MEMBERSHIP OF THE CONFERENCES
(ON THE BASIS OF PARTY)

The Irish Disestablishment Conference

Liberal	Conservative
Lord Granville	Lord Cairns

The 1884 Reform Bill Conference

Liberal	Conservative
Lord Hartington	Lord Salisbury
W. E. Gladstone	Sir Stafford Northcote
Sir Charles Dilke	

The Education Bill Conference of 1906

Liberal	Conservative
Lord Crewe	Lord Cawdor
Augustine Birrell	Lord Lansdowne
Herbert H. Asquith	Arthur J. Balfour

Randall Davidson

The Constitutional Conference of 1910

Liberal	Conservative
Lord Crewe	Lord Cawdor
Herbert H. Asquith	Lord Lansdowne
Augustine Birrell	Arthur J. Balfour
David Lloyd George	Austen Chamberlain

The Buckingham Palace Conference of 1914

Liberal	Conservative
Herbert H. Asquith	Andrew Bonar Law
David Lloyd George	Lord Lansdowne

Irish Nationalist	Ulster Unionist
John Redmond	Sir Edward Carson
John Dillon	Captain James Craig

Chairman: James W. Lowther

The Irish Negotiations of 1916

Irish Nationalist	Ulster Unionist
John Redmond	Sir Edward Carson

Liberal
David Lloyd George

The Buckingham Palace Conference of 1916

Liberal	Conservative
Herbert H. Asquith	Arthur J. Balfour
David Lloyd George	Andrew Bonar Law

Labour
Arthur Henderson

The Speaker's Conference on Electoral Reform, 1916–1917

Liberal	Conservative
Lord Gladstone	Lord Grey
Lord Southwark	Lord Burnham
Sir Ryland Adkins	Sir William Bull
Sir John Bethell	Colonel Page Croft
Ellis Davies	Sir James Larmor
W. H. Dickinson	Donald Macmaster
George Lambert	Basil Peto
T. P. O'Connor	Sir Harry Samuel
Sir John Simon	Edmund Turton
Aneurin Williams	Sir Robert Williams
	Charles Stuart-Wortley
Scottish Liberal	George Touche
W. M. R. Pringle	Edward Archdale
A. MacCallum Scott	
Labour	*Irish Nationalist*
Frank Goldstone	Patrick Brady
Stephen Walsh	Thomas Scanlan
George Wardle	Maurice Healy

Chairman: James W. Lowther
Secretary: W. T. Jerred

The Second Chamber Conference, 1917–1918

Liberal	Conservative
Lord Beauchamp	Lord Balfour of Burleigh
Lord Crewe	Lord Burnham
Lord Denman	Lord Donoughmore
Lord Durham	Lord Dunraven
Lord Loreburn	Lord Lansdowne
Ellis Davies	The Duke of Rutland
Sir Charles Hobhouse	Lord Selborne
J. A. Murray MacDonald	Lord Stuart of Wortley
Sir Henry Norman	Lord Sydenham
J. M. Robertson	Evelyn Cecil
Sir Thomas Whittaker	Lord Hugh Cecil

Irish Nationalist
T. P. O'Connor
Thomas Scanlan

Labour
Walter Hudson

Conservative
Austen Chamberlain
J. A. R. Marriott
A. Clavell Salter
R. A. Sanders
Sir George Younger

Randall Davidson

Chairman: Lord Bryce

The Irish Convention, *1917–1918*

1. Abercorn, Duke of—Tyrone County Council
2. Anderson, R. N.—Mayor of Londonderry
3. Andrews, E. H.—Dublin Chamber of Commerce
4. Armstrong, H. B.—Armagh County Council
5. Barrie, H. T.—Ulster Party
6. Barry, M. K.—Cork County Council
7. Bernard, Dr. J. H.—Archbishop of Dublin
8. Blake, Sir Henry—Southern Unionist
9. Bolger, J.—Wexford County Council
10. Broderick, W.—Youghal Urban District Council
11. Butler, J.—Kilkenny County Council
12. Butterfield, T. C.—Lord Mayor of Cork
13. Byrne, J.—Queen's County Council
14. Clancy, J. J.—Irish Party
15. Clark, Sir G. S.—Ulster Party
16. Clark, Col. J. J.—Londonderry County Council
17. Coen, J. J.—West Meath County Council
18. Condren, D.—Wicklow County Council
19. Crawford, Col. R. G. S.—Down County Council
20. Crozier, Dr.—Primate of Ireland
21. Dempsey, Councillor—Government Nominee
22. Desart, Earl of—Government Nominee
23. Devlin, J.—Irish Party
24. Dooly, J.—King's County Council
25. Doran, Capt. W. A.—Louth County Council
26. Duggan, T.—Tipperary (North Riding) County Council
27. Dunleavy, J.—Donegal County Council
28. Dunraven and Mount, Earl of—Government Nominee
29. Fallon, T.—Leitrim County Council
30. Fitzgibbon, John—Roscommon County Council
31. Flanagan, J.—Ballina Urban District Council
32. Garahan, H.—Longford County Council
33. Goulding, Sir William—Government Nominee
34. Governey, M.—Carlow Urban District Council
35. Granard, Earl of—Government Nominee

36. Gubbins, William—Limerick County Council
37. Gwynn, Capt. S.—Irish Party
38. Halligan, T.—Meath County Council
39. Hanna, J.—Labour (Shipyards)
40. Harbison, T. J.—Irish Party
41. Harty, Dr.—Archbishop of Cashel
42. Irwin, Rt. Rev. John—Moderator, Presbyterian Church of Ireland
43. Jameson, A.—Southern Unionist
44. Johnston, J.—Lord Mayor of Belfast
45. Kavanagh, W.—Carlow County Council
46. Kelly, Dr.—Bishop of Ross
47. Kett, J. K.—Clare County Council
48. Knight, M. E.—Ulster Party
49. Londonderry, Marquis of—Ulster Party
50. Lundon, T.—Labour (Land and Labour Association)
51. Lysaght, E. E.—Government Nominee
52. McCance, J. Stouppe F.—Antrim County Council
53. McCarron, Alderman J.—Labour
54. McCullagh, Sir Crawford—Government Nominee
55. McDonagh, M.—Galway Urban District Council
56. McDowell, A.—Government Nominee
57. McDonnell, J.—Galway County Council
58. Macdonnell of Swinford, Lord—Government Nominee
59. McGarry, J.—Mayo County Council
60. McGeagh, H. G.—Lurgan Urban District Council
61. McHugh, J.—Fermanagh County Council
62. McKay, C.—Labour (Shipbuilding and Engineering Trades Fed.)
63. McKenna, J.—Kerry County Council
64. McMeekan, J.—Bangor Urban District County Council
65. McMullen, H. R.—Cork Chamber of Commerce
66. McRory, Dr.—Bishop of Down and Connor
67. Mahaffy, Rev.—Government Nominee
68. Mayo, Earl of—Irish Peer
69. Midleton, Viscount—Southern Unionist
70. Minch, M. J.—Kildare County Council
71. Murphy, J.—Labour (National Union of Railwaymen)
72. Murphy, William—Government Nominee
73. O'Donnell, Dr.—Bishop of Raphoe
74. O'Dowd, J.—Sligo County Council
75. O'Neill, C. P.—Pembroke Urban District Council
76. O'Neill, L.—Lord Mayor of Dublin
77. O'Neill, P. J.—Dublin County Council
78. Oranmore and Browne, Lord—Irish Peer
79. O'Sullivan, Dr.—Mayor of Waterford
80. Peters, P.—Mayor of Clonmel (Urban District Council)
81. Pollock, H. M.—Belfast Chamber of Commerce
82. Powell, J. B.—Southern Unionist
83. Power, T.—Waterford County Council

84. Quinn, Stephen—Mayor of Limerick
85. Redmond, John—Irish Party
86. Reilly, D.—Cavan County Council
87. Russell, George—Government Nominee
88. Slattery, M.—Tipperary (South Riding) County Council
89. Stewart, George—Southern Unionist
90. Toal, T.—Monaghan County Council
91. Wallace, Col. R. H.—Ulster Party
92. Waugh, R.—Labour (Belfast and Dist. Bldg. Trades' Federation)
93. Whitley, H. T.—Belfast and Dist. Trades Council
94. Whitla, Sir W.—Government Nominee
95. Windle, Sir B.—Government Nominee

Chairman: Sir Horace Plunkett
Secretary: Lord Southborough

The Speaker's Devolution Conference, 1919–1920

Liberal
Lord Aberdare
Lord Brassey
Lord Denman
Lord Emmott
Lord Gladstone
Lord Gorell
Lord Harcourt
Lord Inchcape
Lord Southborough
Sir W. Ryland Adkins
Sir Henry Cowan
J. Hugh Edwards
James M. Hogge
J. A. Murray MacDonald

Conservative
The Duke of Buccleuch
Lord Dufferin and Ava
Lord Faringdon
Lord Hambleden
Lord Oranmore and Browne
Lord Stuart of Wortley
Capt. Charles Craig
Charles Forestier-Walker
Sir Edward Goulding
Donald Macmaster
Ronald McNeill
Thomas Moles
Gideon Murray
Sir Frederick W. Young

Labour
Charles Edwards
William Graham
Tyson Wilson

Chairman: James W. Lowther
Secretary: G. F. M. Campion
Asst. Secretary: C. R. P. Diver

The Anglo-Irish Conference of 1921

British
David Lloyd George
Austen Chamberlain

Irish
Arthur Griffith
Michael Collins

Lord Birkenhead
Sir Laming Worthington-Evans
Hamar Greenwood
Sir Gordon Hewart

Robert Barton
George Gavan Duffy
Eamonn Duggan

APPENDIX II

Lord Granville presents his humble duty to Your Majesty, and ventures to make a few remarks on the answer which Your Majesty proposes to send to Mr. Gladstone as to new Peers. The present circumstances are different from any in which Your Majesty has hitherto judiciously declined adding greatly to the numbers of the House of Lords.

Lord Derby in opposition had a majority not only against Lord Russell, but against Lord Palmerston, than whom no Liberal Prime Minister could be more popular in the Lords.

During his last short tenure of office, notwithstanding his assured majority, and his exclusive command of the Scotch and Irish Peerage, Lord Derby recommended 14 new Peers to Your Majesty, many of them of the most Tory Class of country gentlemen. In the face of a liberal majority in the House of Commons, he increased the Conservative majority in the Lords. Mr. Disraeli added a few. Circumstances obliged them to pass a Reform Bill which has created a greatly increased liberal majority in The Commons, and which makes it idle to suppose that politics will run in precisely the same groove as before.

The position of Your Majesty's Govt. in the Lords is almost intolerable. The majority were wise enough at the last moment to pass the Irish Church Bill, supported as it was by the Commons and the Country, but it is absolute in all ordinary matters of Legislation, on which the credit and utility of a Govt. so much depend. It does not scruple to exercise that power, a course ultimately sure to create great dissatisfaction.

Lord Bessborough has lost from his list of 1850, of those whom he used to summon, 45 Peers whose Peerages have become extinct, who are incapacitated, or who in their own persons or in that of their sons have become Conservatives.

The majority is between 60 and 70 without counting Bishops or Liberals who vote oftener for the Opposition than for the Govt. No one would pretend that a dozen Peers could swamp

* Granville to the Queen, 23 Aug. 1869, Gladstone MSS, Add. MS 44166.

such a majority; but H.M.'s Govt. requires moral support in the House. They are not cordially supported by even the small minority, of whom the most eminent are ex place men, who many of them are not friends of Mr. Gladstone, and prefer the failure to the success of his colleagues. If only 3 or 4 Peers are created, they get awed by the atmosphere in which they find themselves.

The Prince was averse to numerous creations, but it was at a time when there was no such hurtful anomaly as a majority of 100 in the Commons, and an immense majority on the opposite side in the Lords. But even then His Royal Highness constantly told Lord Granville that the House was wanting in Peers representing different classes, and different types of ideas. Lord Salisbury the other day urged this deficiency upon the House as one of the reasons why it was losing ground in public opinion.

Mr Gladstone has taken great pains in selecting the list for Your Majesty. He has endeavoured to avoid taking too many good and moderate men out of the House of Commons. Three of the persons named are possessors of enormous landed property (probably in the aggregate nearer £200,000 than £100,000 a year.) The rest represent various classes, interests, and ideas, and are all men of property.

The notion of a Jew Peer is startling. 'Rothschild a premier Baron Chretieu' does not sound as well as 'Montmorency, a premier Baron Chretieu', but he represents a class whose influence is great by their wealth, their intelligence, their literary connections, and their numerous seats in the House of Commons. It may be wise to attach them to the Aristocracy, rather than to drive them into the Democratic camp. The Carlton Club sent a Jew to be their candidate at Sandwich. Lord Shaftesbury wrote to Mr Gladstone to press Sir M. Montefiore's claims to a Peerage. The Policy of Your Majesty's Govt. is to treat R. Catholics for the future with equality in proportion to their number. Lord Granville does not remember the Creation of a Catholic Peer notwithstanding their wealth and birth. The old Cath. Peers cannot speak. They cannot think for themselves and are under the direction of their Bishops. Sir John Acton would be excluded if Dr. Manning had the power to do so. He and Lord Edward are proposed as greatly superior to any Irish Catholic who could be recommended to Your Majesty

for the honour. Lord Redesdale the strongest of Protestant Conservatives stated in the House that he saw no objection even
to Dr. Manning having a seat in the Lords.

Mr Gladstone has hitherto refrained from troubling Y. M.
Mr. G. and Lord Granville were of opinion that it was better
to avoid making any till after the Irish Church bill had been
dealt with by the H. of Lords.

Lord G. is sure that anything which can give a more liberal
tinge to the H. of Lords and put it more in harmony with the
House of Commons is useful.

It is disadvantageous to the Lords that it should be difficult
to initiate measures in it. It is not good for the Crown that its
servants should be helpless in either branch of the Legislature.

Lord G. humbly apologizes for troubling Your Majesty at
such length. Even if he was not deeply interested in the matter
he should submit to Your M. the same observations, all of which
are not likely to have occurred to you.

APPENDIX III

It has been agreed on the part of Mr. Gladstone with the other Ministers deputed by the Cabinet on the one side, and by Lord Salisbury and Sir S. Northcote on the other as follows:—

1. The Government to propose to obtain the necessary increase of members for Scotland by an increase of the House, but in the event of the House declining to make an addition to its numbers, the necessary increase for Scotland shall be provided partly by a reduction of three in the number returned by Irish Counties and Boroughs, thus reducing the Irish Representation to the number of 100 fixed by the Act of Union and partly from the six vacant seats, and a reduction of the numbers allotted to Counties and Boroughs in the rest of Great Britain.

2. Minorities not to be directly represented, but to be indirectly represented as proposed in 7.

3. Boundaries to be settled by a Commission consisting of Sir John Lambert R.C.B., Sir Francis Sandford R.C.B., W. Henley one of the Inspectors of the Local Government Board, Hon. J. Pelham, Owen Jones R.E., Head of the Boundary Department of the Ordnance Survey, and Major Hector Tullock R.E.

The Commissioners to have regard in dividing Boroughs to the pursuits of the population, and in dividing Counties to the following considerations:—The population of the several divisions to be equalized as far as practicable; care to be taken in all those cases where there are populous localities of an urban character, to include them in one and the same division, unless this cannot be done without producing grave inconvenience, and involving boundaries of a very irregular and objectionable character. Subject to this important rule, each division to be as compact as possible with respect to geographical position, and to be based on well known existing areas, such as Petty Sessional Divisions. No alteration to be made during the passage of the

* 29 Nov. 1884, Iddesleigh MSS, Add. MS 50042.

Bill in the settled Boundaries without Sir Stafford Northcote's consent.

4. Grouping as such to be abandoned as impracticable in England and Ireland (the case of the Monmouth Boroughs excepted), but this principle not to prevent the uniting of contiguous localities.

5. Boroughs and Groups below 15,000 population to be generally merged in County Divisions, except in one or two possible cases which have been named where they are to be brought above the 15,000 line. (This exception may disappear on reconsideration.) Boroughs and Groups between 15,000 and 50,000 having more than one member to lose one. Similar counties to lose one. The City of London to have two members. No diminution to take place in the number of members now allotted to existing constituencies other than those diminutions here mentioned.

6. No diminution to take place in the total number of members allotted to counties in the Government scheme.

7. All counties in the United Kingdom to be in single member districts. All boroughs to be in single member districts, except the City of London, and those Boroughs (with a population of between 50,000 and 150,000) which having two members at the present moment are not to receive more than two. This proposal is subject to the reservation that no one is to be precluded from supporting a proposal for creating a two member nucleus in the large cities.

8. The Government will resist as a vital question (unless by common consent) the insertion in the Bill of any provisions inconsistent with those recited above. With regard to any other new and [?] matter proposed for insertion, they will consult with the leaders of the opposition, and will be prepared to deal with it in the same spirit by which they have been animated in the recent communication. Regarding this Bill as a Bill for the determination of Electoral Areas, they will use their best exertions to prevent the introduction into it of irrelevant and extraneous matter.

9. The Franchise Bill to pass forthwith without any material change, that is to say without the introduction of new contentious matter.

APPENDIX IV

PRIVATE MEMORANDUM BY F. S. OLIVER*

It will be a great imperial as well as a great national misfortune if the Conference does not succeed, directly or indirectly, in settling the question it undertook to consider.

If the Conference fails it will leave a very dangerous issue (the House of Lords) to be fought out sooner or later between the two political parties. The ordinary methods of general elections and parliamentary debates are unsuited for dealing with such constitutional problems. If the coalition be beaten at the next election, I don't think the matter will drop as on former occasions; but, on the contrary, I think it will become a plank in the liberal platform and at no remote date they will be returned to power on it. Don't underrate the force of the feeling against the House of Lords among serious people. And what reason is there for feeling any certainty that the Unionists will win next election—say in January? If they were beaten at the next election on this issue, the British Constitution would be in a very dangerous predicament.

It is of very great importance to give credit to this particular method of settling certain questions—the method of settlement by consent and mutual compromise, after confidential discussion between leading representatives of the various parties. This method appears to be the natural safety valve of popular government in the circumstances in which popular government now finds itself. If you are ever going to make an attempt at Imperial Union this is the only possible method. And also in national affairs; for how is such a matter as the Poor Laws, for example, to be dealt with satisfactorily by party tactics and parliamentary debates? It will take as many years by the latter process as it might take weeks by the former to settle it, and meanwhile men, women and children are dying quite unnecessarily and becoming more and more degraded, while interminable speeches are being made about their sad plight.

The method of conference or convention stands in excellent credit at present (i) owing to the South African Settlement and

* 28 Sept. 1910, Balfour MSS, Add. MS 49861.

(ii) owing to the present Conference having been undertaken. It will be a political disaster of the first magnitude if the breakdown of the Conference should destroy so hopeful an institution in its infancy.

2. There seem to me to be three possibilities: *First*—The Conference may succeed in coming to an agreement on the question submitted to it; or *Second*: it may break down without coming to any agreement upon the question submitted to it; or *Third*: although it may have come, as it were, in sight of a possible agreement upon the particular question submitted to it, it may still break down owing to the existence of other questions which demand to be settled at the same time, and which if they are not so settled have enough force behind them to prevent the settlement of the House of Lords' question on lines which otherwise might be generally approved.

The *first* would clearly be the best issue, but it is very difficult to see how it can be arrived at, owing to the pressure on and by the Irish Party.

The *second* would be the worst issue for the reasons which have already been given.

The *third* would leave the door still open.

3. There are historical analogies which encourage the hope that the *third* course may be adopted should the *first* prove impossible.

The Convention of Annapolis met to consider inter-communication between the thirteen un-united States of America, and other difficult matters about which disagreement was so keen that some of the said States were on the verge of civil war. The Convention of Annapolis came to the conclusion that it was quite unable to settle these pressing matters unless the wider question of Union were also settled, and this it had no warrant to undertake. Accordingly it broke up with a recommendation that a Convention of a more representative character and with a wider warrant should meet in the following year at Philadelphia. The Convention of Philadelphia met accordingly and made the union of the American States.

In like manner the first step towards South African Union was a Conference to consider the burning and very bitter discontent arising out of the working of the Railways by the various States. The same conclusion was reached on this occasion as at Annapolis, viz., that the special matters under discussion could not be settled unless the wider question of closer union were settled at the same time. Accordingly the representative Convention of the African States came into existence shortly afterwards and made the Union of South Africa.

I put forward the suggestion that the present Conference might take a similar course, that it might say in effect 'we do not despair of the possibility of coming to an agreement upon the question submitted to us, but to arrive at such an agreement it is necessary that the question of the domestic government of the country be settled simultaneously, more especially the relations between the United Kingdom and Ireland. We therefore recommend that a Convention of a more representative character should shortly be held with power to consider the constitutional question as a whole'.

4. It is foolish to disregard dramatic force in political affairs. The chance of getting the Irish question as well as the House of Lords' question settled (amicably even!) in the year of the Coronation—possibly *before* the Coronation—would appeal to the popular imagination as few other things would. And to the popular imagination not only at home, but in our Dominions.

5. The Unionist Party cannot offer Home Rule. The *morale* of Politics generally is not particularly robust at the present time. From a national, as well as from a party point of view, it would be disastrous to set on foot the discreditable policy of 'dishing the Whigs'. That would mean complete demoralisation all round.

Even if the Unionist Party were honestly converted to Home Rule they ought not to offer it or to make it a plank in their platform, or seek votes and power by the aid of it. And it is quite impossible that there could be any honest conversion among the rank and file, in a few days time—after reading a few newspaper articles and listening to a few eloquent speeches.

To attempt anything of the kind would be to repeat the offence of Peel in '47 and Gladstone in '86....

But what a party may not make political capital out of, may not adopt for the sake—real or apparent—of votes and power it may accept without dishonour or demoralisation for patriotic reasons. The Unionists cannot champion Home Rule, but it is a question, if they might not submit to it, if a representative

Convention, after careful examination, were able to come to an agreement upon a set of proposals to this end. We could honourably surrender something considerable for the sake of something of even greater imperial importance: as, for instance, for the sake of ending a long and dangerous controversy, and also for the sake of bringing the hope of Imperial Union a stage nearer.

6. But before accepting any invitation to a Convention which would have under its consideration the question of Home Rule, the leaders of both parties would have to agree to approach the matter, not as a thing already judged and done with, but with open minds. Unionists, Liberals and Irish Home Rulers would all have to be prepared to let their cherished ideas run the formidable gauntlet of private and confidential discussion.

Have the circumstances changed to any extent since '86 and '93? Fenianism, Mr. Butt's Home Rule, Mr. Parnell's Home Rule, Home Rule of the Land League, Mr. Gladstone's two Home Rules, devolution, Local Government, Sir Henry Campbell-Bannerman's Home Rule, Mr. Redmond's Home Rule, Home Rule all round, or Federalism—there would be a very wide field of enquiry. For there are differences between each of them. The Fenianist idea was a separate and hostile notion. Mr. Butt's idea was national government in an Imperial Union. Mr. Gladstone's primary and main idea was to get the Irishmen out of Westminster. Sir Henry Campbell Bannerman's idea was a State as independent as Canada. The Federalist's idea is an Ireland as dependent as Quebec. What Mr. Parnell's idea was or what Mr. Redmond's idea is I have no notion, and am probably in the same predicament as these distinguished Statesmen themselves. But clearly there is much room for investigation and not impossibly room also for some workable agreement....

If the suggested confidential Convention for discussing Home Rule were representative of all the important sections in Politics at present, I cannot imagine any experience more interesting for those with the privilege of Membership. Behind closed doors, under the seal of privacy, would Mr. Redmond be found in complete agreement with the schemes of Mr. Dillon?—Mr. Redmond, the Tory, conscious of the need for power if you are to govern anything or anybody, would he be found in agreement with Mr. Dillon and Mr. T. P. O'Connor, the Gladstonians, who believe that by the constant repetition of orthodox and eloquent phrases all things are made possible? and will the rank and file, who ought to be represented too,—will they consider the chances of superior salaries upon the future Irish establishment preferable to the quiet enjoyment of £3 a week at Westminster? Then there is Mr. O'Brien who is also the leader of an important party. And the church—does the church want Home Rule at all, and, if it does, does it want it on such democratic lines as would warm the hearts of Mr. Byles and Mr. Wedgwood? And do the gentlemen who were once landless, but are now (thanks to the Purchase Acts) of the landed class—do they still cherish any very keen interest in these high constitutional problems? And the Unionists—the country gentlemen (such of them as are still alive and out of the bankruptcy courts)—the protestants (South as well as North) do these still regard Home Rule as an altogether unmixed evil? Do they perhaps foresee a not very remote future—American donations having dried up in the meanwhile—when the speechless publican at £3 a week, fond of his whack, which is no great harm, but averse from prison life, which destroys most of his utility to his party, will be dispensed with and persons of capacity and character come into their own again in Irish affairs? And is there not talk already of a clerical and an anticlerical party which will by no means be a clean cleavage between Catholic and Protestant. And what is the real opinion of Ulster?—of the working-men of Ulster, of the industrial capitalists, of the landowners and Presbyterian Ministers of Ulster? Is it so certain that in the candour of their bosoms Home Rule appears still to be necessarily in opposition to the idea of 'to Hell with the Pope'? Does the Vatican stand to win by Home Rule?

The general conclusion which I have drawn from Irish speeches of late is that Home Rule is recognised to be a very difficult thing to work; so difficult in fact that if won by a purely party victory it will prove to be an utter impossibility. Its only hope is a settlement by consent, as in South Africa,—the goodwill of both parties, the active opposition of none during the early years of the experiment, being conditions without which it doesn't stand a dog's chance of anything but fiasco.

Behind closed doors, under the seal of confidence, may not the Members of the Convention expect to hear a good deal of frank and divergent discussion between the representatives of Irish opinion? What conclusions may suggest themselves to the sound and reasonable intelligence of (say) Mr. Shackleton, if he happens to be a Member of the Convention, or to the Prime Minister, or Mr. Lloyd-George, or Mr. Churchill, or the leaders of the Unionist Party, or the high and dry Radical or the high and dry Tory under the conditions imposed by privacy and closed doors, I cannot venture to foreshadow. But Home Rule, under calm and courteous analysis and without the accompaniment of superheated rhetoric, will probably turn out to be something as different from the Home Rule we have dreamed of as the middle-aged Columbine over her cup of tea and her bloater is from the sprightly sylph in muslin and spangles who danced upon the boards.

APPENDIX V

ASQUITH'S MEMORANDA ON IRELAND, 1916*

(Parts II and III)

Ireland

II.—THE FUTURE

For reasons, good or bad, with which my colleagues are familiar, and which it would serve no good purpose now to review, the British Government has allowed in recent years the formation and development in Ireland of a number of independent and irresponsible armed forces—the Ulster Volunteers, the National Volunteers, the Irish Volunteers, and the Citizen Army.

I endeavoured while I was in Ireland to ascertain with as much precision as was possible the strength in men and in equipment of these various bodies. I will submit the approximate figures at the next meeting of the Cabinet. They will, of course, represent what was left of men and arms in Ireland after the despatch to the front of the Ulster division and of the various units which have been wholly or mainly recruited from Nationalist sources.

The Lord Mayor of Belfast, a level-headed and public spirited man, who has taken an active part in recruiting in Ulster, informed me that during the early autumn of last year (1915), when he was trying to secure the necessary draft-supplying reserve for the Ulster Division, he found his energies brought suddenly to a standstill. A sort of atmospheric wave overspread Protestant Ulster. 'We have sent' (such was or became the prevailing opinion) 'the best of our manhood to the front: the Catholics of the South and West have contributed substantially less; if we now allow what remains of our available men to recruit, we shall be left defenceless against a possible, and even probable, Nationalist invasion of our province; and our wives, our children, our homes, our industry, our religion, will be at the mercy of our hereditary foes.' From that day to this recruiting in Protestant Ulster has practically ceased; and

---

* Memorandum on 'Ireland', 19 and 21 May 1916, Selborne Papers, 128/7 and 128/23.

so long as this belief, and the temper which it engenders, persists, not only will there be no effective recruiting for the Army, but there will be a determined resistance to any attempt on the part of the State to disarm those who remain at home.

I asked the representative Ulster leaders, for the most part large employers of labour and prominent citizens, and all ardent Carsonites, whom I met, at the initiation of the Lord Mayor; first, whether they agreed with his representation of the facts, to which question they returned a unanimous affirmative; and *next* whether they themselves shared the apprehensions (which of course seemed to me in the highest degree extravagant) of their co-religionists. They replied—fairly enough—that whether individually they shared them or not, they were satisfied that this was the view of the vast majority of the Protestant population in Belfast and industrial Ulster, and that nothing could dislodge it from their minds.

Disarmament (which they all agreed was ideally desirable) was, therefore, in their opinion, wholly impracticable in Ulster, except at a costly and indeed impossible sacrifice, both material and moral, on the part of the State.

I put to them the alternative (which I know to be favoured in the Cabinet) of the enrollment of all loyal volunteers, both in Ulster and elsewhere, in the Army, with the stacking or warehousing of arms under Government inspection and control, to be accompanied by a prohibition, or of the possession or use of arms, except under licence by bodies or individuals (not so enrolled) throughout Ireland.

To this proposal they made no exception in principle, but they were unanimous that in practice it would not get near the root of the difficulty.

To understand their point of view, and the inference from it which they pressed upon me, it is necessary to realise another side of the Ulster problem. I was told by the Lord Mayor, and his statement was confirmed by all my fellow guests, that in the two or three months which preceded the war (May to August 1914) the imminent possibility of civil strife in Ulster had already checked, and in many directions paralysed, the economic life of Belfast and the adjacent industrial area. Building development (much needed) had been completely arrested; the English and Scottish Banks and Insurance Companies had begun to call in their advances, and refused any fresh commitments; and the mercantile credit of the community was in serious jeopardy. The war came to them (from this point of view) almost as a godsend. To my suggestion that when the war came to an end, with its incalculable toll of material loss and a crushing burden of new taxation, the experiences, of which they had had a brief foretaste, might, and would in all probability, become immeasurably more exacting, and perhaps altogether intolerable, they one and all agreed. That the two armies of the North and the South—both composed of Irishmen, who in the meantime were jointly shedding their blood in the various theatres of war for the common cause— should be held in leash for a final spring at one another's throats, when peace was declared, they thought, quite as strongly as I, would be a disaster and a scandal.

One or two of them repeated the old formulae as to stable and resolute government, but the large majority were clearly of opinion that the only way of escape was by prompt settlement of the whole problem. We did not attempt to discuss details, but what they said clearly pointed to such an amendment of the Home Rule Act as would adequately safeguard the future of the co-religionists.

Mr. Campbell, the Attorney-General, who represents a somewhat different type of Unionism, spoke to me very insistently in the same sense. He thinks it is a case of now or never.

Such representative Nationalists as I saw, e.g., the Roman Catholic Bishop of Cork, seemed to be inclining in the same direction. A deputation of O'Brienites (of the 'All for Ireland' League), headed by Captain Sheehan, M.P., who came to me at Cork, protested warmly against anything in the nature of 'partition.'

My own conclusion is that the arms question cannot be satisfactorily or effectively handled except as part of a general settlement. The last attempt at such a settlement, two years ago, broke down through difficulties arising from the geographical distribution of the adherents of the two creeds in certain parts of Ulster. I am by no means sure that the Nationalists (except the O'Brienites) would not now be disposed to prefer the total exclusion (for the time at any rate) of Ulster.

It appears to me to be the immediate duty of the Government

to do everything in their power to force a general settlement.

III.—TRANSITIONAL

It is clear that the Home Rule Act, however amended, cannot come into operation until the end of the war. Provision has, therefore, to be made for the Executive Government of Ireland in the meanwhile. All the chief officers of the Executive have resigned, and the only post which has yet been filled up is that of the Under-Secretary.

I have come very clearly to the opinion that no successor ought to be appointed to the Lord-Lieutenant. The Viceroyalty in Ireland has become a costly and futile anachronism. Its inutility has never been more clearly demonstrated than during the last few months. No fault, so far as I can discover, is to be attributed to the last holder of the office. I found a complete consensus among Irishmen of all creeds and parties that Lord and Lady Wimborne had done everything that their position and powers allowed to attract the confidence and affection of the people. The Lord-Lieutenant is the nominal and ostensible head of the Irish Executive; he is believed, both in Ireland and elsewhere, to have an effective voice in the government of the country; in fact, he has been reduced to a cipher, to the role of a *vice-roi faineant*, clothed with apparent power and responsibility, but obliged in practice to content himself day by day with the crumbs that may fall from the Under-Secretary's table. It is not, under actual conditions, an office that any self-respecting man of parts and ability can be asked to undertake.

It is true that the Irish are susceptible to what may be called the ceremonial side of government, and this has been the only function of any value which of late years the Lord-Lieutenant has been expected to discharge. It is obvious that the need, such as it is, of ritual and spectacular display could be far more effectually met by periodical and systematic visits of the Sovereign. I believe that during a reign of over sixty years Queen Victoria only went to Ireland twice; King Edward in nine years, and our present King in six years, each only once. For nearly eighty years these have been the only occasions, none of them, I think, lasting more than a few days, when Irishmen have had the opportunity of seeing their Sovereign on Irish soil. There has been during that time a long procession of viceroys, some of them men of eminence, all creatures of the party system, and subject to the vicissitudes of British politics, and with the best intentions incapable, by the conditions of their tenure, of evoking and stimulating the latent sense of personal loyalty and devotion which is inherent in the Irish temper and character.

I am glad to be able to say that His Majesty whole-heartedly accepts the necessity of the change, and is prepared and anxious to arrange for an annual residence of himself, the Queen, and the Court in Ireland.

With the disappearance of the viceroyalty would disappear also the fiction of a Chief Secretary. There must be a single Minister controlling and responsible for Irish administration.

It has been suggested that during the transitional time with which I am now dealing, the Minister might be assisted by an Advisory Council, small in number, and drawn from the leading members of the various Irish parties. The Attorney-General for Ireland strongly pressed upon me the advisability as a temporary measure of this expedient. It has an attractive look, and I do not wish, until I know the views of my colleagues, to rule it out. I have, however, grave doubts as to its practical expediency. What would be the functions of such a Council? The Minister would either be bound, or not bound, to follow its advice. If bound, *he* ceases to be responsible; if he is not bound, they are reduced to the position of a Greek chorus, or of a debating society.

There are a number of matters of detail, of minor but still of considerable importance, which in any event will require careful examination and adjustment. I have confined myself in this memorandum to the larger issues which call for immediate decision.

APPENDIX VI

WOMEN'S SUFFRAGE VOTING RECORDS OF SPEAKER'S CONFERENCE MEMBERS

Members & Party	Votes on Women's Suffrage Bills before Parliament									Probable Vote in Conference
	'08	'09	'10	'11	'12	'13	'14	'17	'18	Jan. 1917
Earl Grey (Con)							o	+		Aye
Lord Burnham (Con)							o	+		Aye
Vsc. Gladstone (Lib)							o	+		Aye
Lord Southwark (Lib)							o	+		Aye
William Bull (Con)	+	o	+	o	o	o		+		Aye
Page Croft (Con)	o	o	−	−	−	−		+		No
James Larmor (Con)	o	o	o	o	−	−		+		No
J. Macmaster (Con)	o	o	−	−	−	−		+		No
Basil Peto (Con)	o	o	+	+	o	−		−		No
Harry Samuel (Con)	o	o	−	o	−	−		+		No
Edmund Turton (Con)	o	o	o	o	o	o		+		Aye
R. Williams (Con)	o	−	−	−	−	o		−		No
Ryland Adkins (Lib)	o	o	o	o	o	o		+		Aye
John Bethell (Lib)	+	+	+	+	o	+		+		Aye
Ellis Davies (Lib)	o	o	+	o	o	+		+		Aye
W. H. Dickinson (Lib)	+	+	+	+	+	+		+		Aye
George Lambert (Lib)	o	o	−	o	o	o		o		No?
T. P. O'Connor (Lib)*	o	+	o	o	o	−		o		Aye?
Sir John Simon (Lib)	o	o	+	+	+	+		+		Aye
A. Williams (Lib)	o	o	o	o	o	o		+		Aye
W. Pringle (Sc. Lib)	o	o	−	−	o	−		+		No
MacCallum Scott (S Lib)	o	o	o	−	o	o		−		No
Patrick Brady (I. Nat)	o	o	o	o	−	−		+		No
Thos. Scanlan (I. Nat)	o	o	+	+	o	−		+		Aye
Maurice Healy (I. Nat)	o	o	o	o	o	+		+		Aye
F. Goldstone (Lab)	o	o	o	+	+	+		+		Aye
Stephen Walsh (Lab)	+	o	+	+	o	+		o		Aye
George Wardle (Lab)	+	+	+	+	+	o		+		Aye
Stuart-Wortley (Con)	o	−	+	+	+	+		o		Aye
George Touche (Con)	o	o	o	+	+	+		+		Aye
Edw. Archdale (Con)	o	o	o	o	o	o		+		Aye

+ = Voted for Women's Suffrage.   − = Voted against Women's Suffrage.
o = Did not vote.

Probable disposition of the Conference on women's suffrage: Ayes—21 Noes—10
Actual vote of the conference on the women's suffrage proposal: Ayes—15 Noes—6

* O'Connor, the only Nationalist M.P. representing an English constituency, is not usually regarded as a Liberal, but the Speaker in his initial selection of the conference designated him as such.

APPENDIX VII

16 August 1916	Walter Long's suggestion of a representative conference on electoral reform.
12 October 1916	First meeting of the Speaker's conference.
27 January 1917	Speaker's conference submitted its report to the Prime Minister.
28 March 1917	House of Commons agreed to accept the proposals of the Speaker's conference.
15 May 1917	First reading of the Representation of the People Bill in the House of Commons.
23 May 1917	Second reading of the reform bill carried.
6 June 1917	Committee stage begun.
19 June 1917	Women's suffrage principle passed by the House of Commons.
8 November 1917	Completion of the committee stage.
29 November 1917	Completion of the report stage.
7 December 1917	Third reading carried. Reform bill sent to the House of Lords.
11 December 1917	First reading in the House of Lords.
19 December 1917	Second reading in the House of Lords.
10 January 1918	Women's suffrage principle passed.
23 January 1918	Completion of the committee stage.
29 January 1918	Completion of the report stage.
1 February 1918	House of Commons completed consideration of Lords' amendments.
6 February 1918	Differences between the two houses finally adjusted.
6 February 1918	Royal assent and Representation of the People Bill placed on the Statute Book.

APPENDIX VIII

ARTICLES OF AGREEMENT FOR A TREATY BETWEEN
GREAT BRITAIN AND IRELAND
(6 December 1921)*

1. Ireland shall have the same Constitutional status in the community of Nations known as the British Empire as the Dominion of Canada, the Commonwealth of Australia, the Dominion of New Zealand, and the Union of South Africa, with parliament having powers to make laws for the peace and good government of Ireland, and an executive responsible to that parliament, and shall be styled and known as the Irish Free State.

2. Subject to the provisions hereinafter set out the position of the Irish Free State in relation to the imperial parliament and government and otherwise shall be that of the Dominion of Canada, and the law, practice, and constitutional usage governing the relationship of the crown or the representative of the crown and of the imperial parliament to the Dominion of Canada shall govern their relationship to the Irish Free State.

3. The representative of the crown in Ireland shall be appointed in like manner as the governor-general of Canada, and in accordance with the practice observed in the making of such appointments.

4. The oath to be taken by members of the parliament of the Irish Free State shall be in the following form: I do solemnly swear true faith and allegiance to the constitution of the Irish Free State as by law established and that I will be faithful to H.M. King George V, his heirs and successors by law in virtue of the common citizenship of Ireland with Great Britain and her adherence to and membership of the group of nations forming the British Commonwealth of nations.

5. The Irish Free State shall assume liability for the service of the public debt of the United Kingdom as existing at the date hereof and towards the payment of war pensions as existing at that date in such proportion as may be fair and equitable, having regard to any just claims on the part of Ireland by way

* Edmund Curtis and R. B. McDowell, eds., *Irish Historical Documents, 1172–1922* (London, 1943), pp. 322–6.

of set off or counter-claim, the amount of such sums being determined in default of agreement by the arbitration of one or more independent persons being citizens of the British empire.

6. Until an arrangement has been made between the British and Irish governments whereby the Irish Free State undertakes her own coastal defence, the defence by sea of Great Britain and Ireland shall be undertaken by his majesty's imperial forces, but this shall not prevent the construction or maintenance by the government of the Irish Free State of such vessels as are necessary for the protection of the revenue or the fisheries. The foregoing provisions of this Article shall be reviewed at a conference of representatives of the British and Irish governments to be held at the expiration of five years from the date hereof with a view to the undertaking by Ireland of a share in her own coastal defence.

7. The Government of the Irish Free State shall afford to his majesty's imperial forces

(a) In time of peace such harbour and other facilities as are indicated in the annex hereto, or such other facilities as may from time to time be agreed between the British government and the government of the Irish Free State; and

(b) In time of war or of strained relations with a foreign power such harbour and other facilities as the British government may require for the purposes of such defence as aforesaid.

8. With a view to securing the observance of the principle of international limitation of armaments, if the government of the Irish Free State establishes and maintains a military defence force, the establishments thereof shall not exceed in size such proportion of the military establishments maintained in Great Britain as that which the population of Ireland bears to the population of Great Britain.

9. The ports of Great Britain and the Irish Free State shall be freely open to the ships of the other country on payment of the customary port and other dues.

10. The government of the Irish Free State agrees to pay fair compensation on terms not less favourable than those accorded by the act of 1920 to judges, officials, members of police forces, and other public servants who are discharged by

it or who retire in consequence of the change of government effected in pursuance hereof.

Provided that this agreement shall not apply to members of the Auxiliary Police Force or to persons recruited in Great Britain for the Royal Irish Constabulary during the two years next preceding the date hereof. The British Government will assume responsibility for such compensation or pensions as may be payable to any of these excepted persons.

11. Until the expiration of one month from the passing of the act of parliament for the ratification of this instrument, the powers of the parliament and the government of the Irish Free State shall not be exercisable as respects Northern Ireland, and the provisions of the *Government of Ireland Act, 1920*, shall, so far as they relate to Northern Ireland, remain of full force and effect, and no election shall be held for the return of members to serve in the parliament of the Irish Free State for constituencies in Northern Ireland, unless a resolution is passed by both houses of the parliament of Northern Ireland in favour of holding of such elections before the end of the said month.

12. If, before the expiration of the said month, an address is presented to his majesty by both houses of the parliament of Northern Ireland to that effect, the powers of the parliament and government of the Irish Free State shall no longer extend to Northern Ireland, and the provisions of the *Government of Ireland Act, 1920* (including those relating to the council of Ireland), shall so far as they relate to Northern Ireland continue to be of full force and effect, and this instrument shall have effect subject to the necessary modifications.

Provided that if such an address is so presented a commission consisting of three persons, one to be appointed by the government of the Irish Free State, one to be appointed by the government of Northern Ireland, and one who shall be chairman to be appointed by the British government shall determine in accordance with the wishes of the inhabitants, so far as may be compatible with economic and geographic conditions the boundaries between Northern Ireland and the rest of Ireland, and for the purposes of the *Government of Ireland Act, 1920*, and of this instrument, the boundary of Northern Ireland shall be such as may be determined by such commission.

13. For the purpose of the last foregoing article, the powers

of the parliament of Southern Ireland under the *Government of Ireland Act, 1920*, to elect members of the council of Ireland shall after the parliament of the Irish Free State is constituted be exercised by that Parliament.

14. After the expiration of the said month, if no such address as is mentioned in Article 12 hereof is presented, the parliament and government of Northern Ireland shall continue to exercise as respects Northern Ireland the powers conferred on them by the *Government of Ireland Act, 1920*, but the parliament and government of the Irish Free State shall in Northern Ireland have in relation to matters in respect of which the parliament of Northern Ireland has not power to make laws under that act (including matters which under the said act are within the jurisdiction of the council of Ireland) the same powers as in the rest of Ireland, subject to such other provisions as may be agreed in manner hereinafter appearing.

15. At any time after the date hereof the government of Northern Ireland and the provisional government of Southern Ireland hereinafter constituted may meet for the purpose of discussing the provisions subject to which the last foregoing article is to operate in the event, of no such address as is therein mentioned being presented, and those provisions may include;—

(a) Safeguards with regard to patronage in Northern Ireland;

(b) Safeguards with regard to the collection of revenue in Northern Ireland;

(c) Safeguards with regard to import and export duties affecting the trade or industry of Northern Ireland;

(d) Safeguards for minorities in Northern Ireland;

(e) The settlement of the financial relations between Northern Ireland and the Irish Free State;

(f) The establishment and powers of a local militia in Northern Ireland and the relation of the defence forces of the Irish Free State and of Northern Ireland respectively,

and if at any such meeting provisions are agreed to, the same shall have effect as if they were included amongst the provisions subject to which the powers of the parliament and government of the Irish Free State are to be exercisable in Northern Ireland under Article 14 hereof.

16. Neither the parliament of the Irish Free State nor the parliament of Northern Ireland shall make any law so as either directly or indirectly to endow any religion or prohibit or restrict the free exercise thereof or given any preference or impose any disability on account of the religious belief or religious status or affect prejudicially the right of any child to attend a school receiving public money without attending the religious instruction at the school or make any discrimination as respects state aid between schools under the management of different religious denominations or divert from any religious denomination or any educational institution any of its property except for public utilities purposes and on payment of compensation.

17. By way of provisional arrangement for the administration of Southern Ireland during the interval which must elapse between the date hereof and the constitution of a parliament and government in accordance therewith, steps shall be taken forthwith for summoning a meeting of members of parliament elected for constituencies in Southern Ireland since the passing of the *Government of Ireland Act, 1920,* and for constituting a provisional government, and the British government shall take the steps necessary to transfer to such provisional government the powers and machinery requisite for the discharge of its duties provided that every member of such provisional government shall have signified in writing his or her acceptance of this instrument. But this arrangement shall not continue in force beyond the expiration of twelve months from the date hereof.

18. This instrument shall be submitted forthwith by his majesty's government for the approval of parliament and by the Irish signatories to a meeting summoned for the purpose of the members elected to sit in the house of commons of Southern Ireland and if approved shall be ratified by the necessary legislation.

Notes

INTRODUCTION

[1] Sir Ivor Jennings, *The British Constitution* (Cambridge, 1966), p. 29.

[2] Walter Bagehot, *The English Constitution* (London, 1958), pp. 3–14, first published in 1867.

[3] Moisei Ostrogorskii, *Democracy and the Organization of Political Parties* (2 vols., New York, 1902), i.

[4] A. Lawrence Lowell, 'Influence of Party upon Legislation in England and America' in the *Annual Report of the American Historical Association*, i (1901), 321–542. Also see the chapter entitled 'The Strength of Party Ties' in Lowell's *Government of England* (2 vols., New York, 1912).

[5] Robert Michels, *Political Parties* (New York, 1915).

[6] George Dangerfield, *The Strange Death of Liberal England, 1910–1914* (New York, 1935).

[7] William D. Muller, ed., *British Politics Group Research Register* (Ames, Iowa, 1977).

[8] See C. P. Ilbert, 'Conferences Between the Two Houses of Parliament', *Contemporary Review*, xcviii (10 Aug. 1910), 129–39.

[9] Sir Thomas Erskine May, *A Treatise on the Law, Privileges, Proceedings and Usage of Parliament* (London, 1917), p. 535.

[10] A. V. Dicey, *England's Case Against Home Rule* (London, 1886), pp. 142–51.

[11] L. P. Curtis, *Anglo-Saxons and Celts, A Study of Anti-Irish Prejudice in Victorian England* (Bridgeport, Conn., 1968).

[12] Samuel H. Beer, *Modern Political Development* (New York, 1958), pp. 39–43.

[13] *Cabinet Memo.*, 22 June 1910, CAB 37/102/23.

[14] See explanation in Bibliography.

CHAPTER I

[1] A. L. Rowse, *The Question of the House of Lords* (London, 1934), p. 17.

[2] *3 Parl. Debs.*, cxci, Commons (23 Mar. 1868), 32–3.

[3] The report of the census commissioners of 1861 placed the population of Ireland at 5,788,415, while members of the established church numbered only 693,357. Roman Catholics numbered 4,505,365, or about ten out of every thirteen people in Ireland. See Hugh Shearman, *How the Church of Ireland was Disestablished* (Belfast, 1970), p. 10.

[4] John Morley, *The Life of William Ewart Gladstone* (3 vols., London, 1903), ii, 240.

[5] Disraeli to the Queen, 23 Mar. 1868, George Earle Buckle, *The Letters of Queen Victoria* (3 vols., 2nd ser., London, 1932), i, 516–18.

[6] Grey to the Queen, 24 Mar. 1868, RA D23/59.

[7] The Queen to Disraeli, 24 Mar. 1868, Buckle, *Letters ... Queen*, i, 518–19.

[8] *3 Parl. Debs.*, cxcii, Lords (25 June 1868), 2067.

[9] For the complete text of these papers see J. C. Beckett, 'Gladstone, Queen Victoria, and the Disestablishment of the Irish Church, 1868–9', *Irish Historical Studies*, xiii (Mar. 1962), 38–47.

[10] P. T. Marsh, *The Victorian Church in Decline, Archbishop Tait and the Church of England, 1868–1882* (Pittsburgh, 1969), pp. 31–2.

[11] The Queen to Gladstone, 31 Jan. 1869, Buckle, *Letters ... Queen*, i, 578–9.

[12] Gladstone to the Queen, 1 Feb. 1869, ibid., 580–3.

[13] RA Queen Victoria's Journal, 3 Feb. 1869.

[14] Memo by Grey, 11 Feb. 1869, RA D25/31.

[15] The Queen to Gladstone, 12 Feb. 1869, ibid., D25/34.

[16] Gladstone to the Queen, 14 Feb. 1869, ibid., D25/40.

[17] The Queen to Tait, 15 Feb. 1869, Randall Davidson, *The Life of Archibald Campbell Tait, Archbishop of Canterbury* (2 vols., London, 1891), ii, 8–10.

[18] Tait to the Queen, 22 Feb. 1869, ibid., 12–14.

[19] *3 Parl. Debs.*, cxciv, Commons (1 Mar. 1869), 412–66.

[20] Diary, 14 Mar. 1869, Davidson, *Life of Tait*, ii, 17–18.

[21] Disraeli to Tait, 24 Mar. 1869, ibid., 18–19.

[22] Diary, 10 Apr. 1869, Tait MSS, 75/268.

[23] Derby to Cairns, 4 May 1869, Cairns MSS, PRO 30/51/8.

[24] Memo by Tait, 8 May 1869, Tait MSS, letters, 75.

[25] Tait to Disraeli, 8 May 1869, Disraeli MSS, B/XXI/T/8.

[26] Stanley to Grey, 2 June 1869, RA D26/14 and D26/15.

[27] Tait to Gladstone, 3 June 1869, Davidson, *Life of Tait*, ii, 20.

[28] Gladstone to Tait, 3 June 1869, ibid., 21.

[29] General Grey, like many other observers, was surprised by Cairns's change of attitude. Grey told the Queen he had always believed that 'the Lds. wd. surely pass the 2nd Reading.—He had always been assured that such was the determination of the Leaders of the Opposition.—It is only within the last few days that a contrary belief has gained ground—caused by the pressure put upon Ld Cairns by the more violent members of the Party—and, it is said, by Ld. *Derby* himself!' Grey to the Queen, 7 June 1869, RA D26/23.

[30] Ellicott to Tait, 5 June 1869, Tait MSS, personal letters, 87/129.

[31] The Queen to Derby, 7 June 1869, Buckle, *Letters ... Queen*, i, 603–4.

[32] Derby to the Queen, 9 June 1869, ibid., 606–8.

[33] Tait to the Queen, 7 June 1869, Davidson, *Life of Tait*, ii, 26–7.

[34] The Queen to Granville, 9 June 1869, Buckle, *Letters ... Queen*, i, 605.

[35] *3 Parl. Debs.*, cxcvi, Lords (14 June 1869), 1662.

[36] *The Times*, 15 June 1869, p. 11.

[37] Bright to Granville, 17 June 1869, Granville MSS, PRO 30/29/31.

[38] *3 Parl. Debs.*, cxcvii, Lords (17 June 1869), 10–14.

[39] Grey to the Queen, 20 June 1869, RA D26/43.

[40] Gladstone to Granville, 21 June 1869, Granville MSS, PRO 30/29/57/62.

[41] Granville to Salisbury, 23 June 1869, Salisbury MSS, Granville/1869/6.

[42] Granville to Salisbury, 4 July 1869, ibid., Granville/1869/7.

[43] Granville to Gladstone, 6 July 1869, Gladstone MSS, Add. MS 44166.

[44] Gladstone to the Queen, 4 July 1869, Buckle, *Letters ... Queen*, i, 612–15.

[45] Wellesley to the Queen, 7 July 1869, RA D26/57.

[46] Granville to Gladstone, 11 July 1869, Gladstone MSS, Add. MS 44166.

[47] Diary, 8 July 1869, Tait MSS, p. 46.

[48] Gladstone to the Queen, 10 July 1869, RA D26/10.

[49] *3 Parl. Debs.*, cxcvii, Commons (15 July 1869), 1902–5.

[50] Queen's Journal, 17 July 1869, Buckle, *Letters ... Queen*, i, 618.

[51] Memo. by Gladstone, 17 July 1869, Gladstone MSS, Add. MS 44758.

[52] Cairns to Disraeli, 16 July 1869, Disraeli MSS, B/XX/Ca/77.

[53] Memo. by Gladstone, 19 July 1869, Gladstone MSS, Add. MS 44758.

[54] Ibid.

[55] Ibid.

[56] Ibid.

[57] Gladstone to the Queen, 21 July 1869, RA D26/98.

[58] Granville to Gladstone, 21 July 1869, Gladstone MSS, Add. MS 44166.

[59] Cairns to Granville, 22 July 1869, Memo. by Gladstone, ibid., Add. MS 44758.
[60] Granville to Gladstone, 4 Aug. 1869, ibid., Add. MS 44166.
[61] Memo by Gladstone, 22 July 1869, Add. MS 44758.
[62] Granville to Gladstone, 4 Aug. 1869, ibid., Add. MS 44166.
[63] Granville to the Queen, 22 July 1869, RA D26/105.
[64] *3 Parl. Debs.*, cxcviii, Lords (22 July 1869), 408–9.
[65] The Queen to Granville, 27 July 1869, Granville MSS, PRO 30/29/31. The Queen, however, believed that 'the Archbishop had not been very dexterous' in arranging a settlement. RA Queen Victoria's Journal, 24 July 1869.
[66] Granville to the Queen, 23 Aug. 1869, Gladstone MSS, Add. MS 44166. See Appendix II.

CHAPTER II

[1] Tennyson to Gladstone, 14 Nov. 1884, Sir Wemyss Reid, *The Life of William Ewart Gladstone* (2 vols., London, 1899), ii, 676.
[2] Arthur James Balfour, *Retrospect: An Unfinished Autobiography, 1848–1886* (London, 1930), p. 178.
[3] See Bibliography.
[4] Corinne Comstock Weston, 'The Royal Mediation in 1884', *English Historical Review*, lxxxii (Apr. 1967), 296–322. See my rebuttal to Weston's argument in 'Royal Mediation in 1884: A Reassessment', ibid., lxxxviii (Jan. 1973), 100–13, from which this chapter was substantially taken.
[5] Mary E. J. Chadwick, 'The Role of Redistribution in the Making of the Third Reform Act', *The Historical Journal*, xix (Sept. 1976), 665–83.
[6] *3 Parl. Debs.*, ccxc, Lords (8 July 1884), 112.
[7] Richmond to Lord Grey, 10 July 1884, Goodwood MSS, 872.
[8] Gladstone to Granville, 9 July 1884, RA C49/18. Granville to the Queen, 9 July 1884, ibid., C49/11.
[9] Cairns to Salisbury, 11 July 1884, Salisbury MSS, E/Cairns/77.
[10] Granville to the Queen, 9 July 1884, RA C49/11. Ponsonby to the Queen, 10 July 1884, ibid., C49/21.
[11] Ponsonby to the Queen, 9 July 1884, ibid., C49/19.
[12] The Queen to Gladstone, 10 July 1884, Philip Guedalla, *The Queen and Mr. Gladstone* (2 vols., London, 1933), ii, 610.
[13] Northcote to Salisbury, 10 July 1884, Salisbury MSS., E/Northcote, iii, 660.
[14] Salisbury to MacColl, 11 July 1884, Lady Gwendolyn Cecil, *Life of Robert, Marquis of Salisbury* (4 vols., London, 1931), iii, 110.
[15] Morley, *Life of Gladstone*, iii, 126.
[16] *Manchester Guardian*, 10 July 1884, p. 5.
[17] Northcote to Cairns, 12 July 1884, Cairns MSS, PRO 30/51/5.
[18] Diary, 12 July 1884, Dudley W. R. Bahlman, *The Diary of Sir Edward Walter Hamilton* (2 vols., Oxford, 1972), ii, 652.
[19] Salisbury to Raikes, 15 July 1884, Henry St. John Raikes, *The Life and Letters of Henry Cecil Raikes* (London, 1898), p. 218.
[20] The Queen to Argyll, 17 July 1884, Buckle, *Letters ... Queen*, iii, 520–1.
[21] Argyll to the Queen, 18 July 1884, ibid., 521–2.
[22] The Queen to Gladstone, 11 July 1884, Guedalla, *Queen ... Gladstone*, ii, 611.
[23] Memoirs, 23 July–4 Aug. 1884, Chamberlain MSS, JC 8/1/1.
[24] The Queen to Gladstone, 25 July 1884, Guedalla, *Queen ... Gladstone*, ii, 616.
[25] Memoirs, Gladstone MSS, Add. MS 44791. The memo, in its abridged form of 25 Aug. 1884, is in the Gladstone MSS, Add. MS 44768.
[26] Granville to Gladstone, 28 Aug. 1884, Agatha Ramm, *The Political Correspondence of Mr. Gladstone and Lord Granville, 1876–1886* (2 vols., Oxford, 1962), ii, 238.

[27] Diary, 29 Aug. 1884, Bahlman, *Diary of Edward Hamilton*, ii, 677.

[28] Richmond to Cairns, 16 Sept. 1884, Cairns MSS, PRO 30/51/4.

[29] Cairns to Richmond, 19 Sept. 1884, ibid., PRO 30/51/22.

[30] Richmond to Cairns, 1 Oct. 1884, ibid., PRO 30/51/4.

[31] *The Times*, 18 Aug. 1884, p. 8.

[32] Gladstone to Granville, 18 Aug. 1884, Granville MSS, PRO 30/29/128. Hartington to Gladstone, 21 Aug. 1884, Bernard Holland, *The Life of Spencer Compton, Eighth Duke of Devonshire* (London, 1911), ii, 52–3.

[33] Stephen Gwynn and Gertrude M. Tuckwell, *The Life of the Rt. Hon. Sir Charles W. Dilke* (2 vols., London, 1917), ii, 65.

[34] Cecil, *Life of Salisbury*, iii, 112–13.

[35] *The Times*, 2 Oct. 1884, p. 7.

[36] Ibid., 6 Oct. 1884, p. 4.

[37] Morley to Chamberlain, 1 Oct. 1884, Chamberlain MSS, JC 5/24/575.

[38] Gladstone to Chamberlain, 6 Oct. 1884, Gladstone MSS, Add. MS 44547.

[39] The Queen to Argyll, 7 Oct. 1884, Buckle, *Letters ... Queen*, iii, 547.

[40] Salisbury to Northcote, 11 Oct. 1884, Iddesleigh MSS, Add. MS 50020. Salisbury to Winn, 13 Oct. 1884, Salisbury MSS, D/85, XVII/189. Richmond to the Queen, ibid., F/Queen.

[41] The Queen to Hartington, 11 Oct. 1884, Devonshire MSS, 340.1549.

[42] Hartington to Ponsonby, 11 Oct. 1884, ibid., 340.1553. Hartington to Gladstone, 11 Oct. 1884, Gladstone MSS, Add. MS 44147.

[43] Salisbury to Ponsonby, 20 Oct. 1884, Buckle, *Letters ... Queen*, iii, 552. Ponsonby to Hartington, 21 Oct. 1884, Devonshire MSS, 340.1559.

[44] This speech was only partially printed in *The Times*, 22 Oct. 1884, p. 7, leaving out the vital portion. See Carnarvon to Salisbury, 27 Oct. 1884, Salisbury MSS, E/Carnarvon, 11/480. Chadwick apparently is mistaken in suggesting that the notion of an interparty conference 'occurred to both Gladstone and Salisbury by late September'. 'Redistribution in the Third Reform Act', 672. Hartington's letter to Gladstone, 29 Sept. 1884, Gladstone MSS, Add. MS 44147, which she cites as evidence, contains no such recognition.

[45] Diary, 22 Oct. 1884, Bahlman, *Diary of Edward Hamilton*, ii, 714. Gladstone to Argyll, 24 Oct. 1884, Gladstone MSS, Add. MS 44547. Gladstone to Norton, 24 Oct. 1884, ibid.

[46] Memo by Northcote, 24 Oct. 1884, Iddesleigh MSS, Add. MS 50043.

[47] 'Notes of Conversation with Sir Michael Hicks Beach', 29 Oct. 1884, Holland, *Life of Devonshire*, ii, 54–8.

[48] Hartington to Gladstone, 3 Nov. 1884, Devonshire MSS, 340.1565. Memo by Hartington, ibid., 340.1566.

[49] The Queen to Salisbury, 31 Oct. 1884, Buckle, *Letters ... Queen*, iii, 563.

[50] Salisbury to the Queen, 3 Nov. 1884, ibid., 566.

[51] Gladstone to the Queen, 31 Oct. 1884, ibid., 565.

[52] Gladstone to the Queen, 12 Nov. 1884, ibid., 569.

[53] Memoirs, 13 Nov. 1884, Andrew Lang, *Life, Letters and Diaries of Sir Stafford Northcote, First Earl of Iddesleigh* (2 vols., London, 1890), ii, 206–7. Sir Algernon West, *Recollections, 1832 to 1886* (London, 1900), p. 365.

[54] Northcote to Salisbury, 13 Nov. 1884, Iddesleigh MSS, Add. MS 50020. Gladstone to Granville and Hartington, 14 Nov. 1884, Gladstone MSS, Add. MS 44768.

[55] Salisbury to Northcote, 14 Nov. 1884, Salisbury MSS, E/Gladstone/16. Northcote to Gladstone, 14 Nov. 1884, Gladstone MSS, Add. MS 44217.

[56] Gladstone to the Queen, 15 Nov. 1884, *Cab. Mins.*, CAB 41/18/51.

[57] Gladstone to Granville, 15 Nov. 1884, Ramm, *Pol. Corres. of Gladstone and Granville*, ii, 284.

[58] The Queen to Richmond, 14 Nov. 1884, RA B65. Ponsonby to the Queen, 15 Nov. 1884, ibid., Addl. MSS A/12/1092.

[59] Ponsonby to Peel, 16 Nov. 1884, ibid., C50/112.

[60] Peel to Ponsonby, 17 Nov. 1884, ibid., Addl. MSS A/12/1102.

[61] Richmond to the Queen, 17 Nov. 1884, Buckle, *Letters ... Queen*, iii, 575.

[62] Granville to Gladstone, 17 Nov. 1884, Ramm, *Pol. Corres. of Gladstone and Granville*, ii, 284–5. Granville to Gladstone, 'Confidential', 17 Nov. 1884, ibid., ii, 285.

[63] *3 Parl. Debs.*, ccxciii, Lords (17 Nov. 1884), 1806–9.

[64] Salisbury to Northcote, 17 Nov. 1884, Iddesleigh MSS, Add. MS 50020.

[65] *3 Parl. Debs.*, ccxciii, Commons (17 Nov. 1884), 1820–4.

[66] 'Query sent by Balfour to the Govt. A', 17 Nov. 1884, Iddesleigh MSS, Add. MS 50020.

[67] 'Gladstone's answer taken down by Hartington', ibid.

[68] Brett to Hartington, 17 Nov. 1884, Devonshire MSS, 340.1573.

[69] Salisbury to Northcote, 17 Nov. 1884, Iddesleigh MSS, Add. MS 50020.

[70] Richmond to the Queen (with enclosed memo by Lord Cairns), 18 Nov. 1884, Goodwood MSS, 872/89.

[71] *3 Parl. Debs.*, ccxciv, Lords (18 Nov. 1884), 1–10. Mention should be made that Salisbury did afterwards raise the irritating point about the Government making the passing of redistribution 'a Vital Question'. Granville refused to commit anyone but himself, but he told Salisbury he had 'not the slightest doubt that we mean to make a vital question of the passing of the Bill with regard to all its general principles and characteristics which may be settled upon'. When Salisbury still insisted on an absolute answer Granville replied, 'I think mistrust sometimes has its limits. I really think we ought not to be suspected, after giving these solemn declarations involving our personal and political honour, of not wishing to do everything in our power to give effect to them.' With this reproof Salisbury pressed his point no further.

[72] Memoirs, 19 Nov. 1884, Dilke MSS, Add. MS 43938.

[73] 'Notes of Conferences, First Meeting', 19 Nov. 1884, Gladstone MSS, Add. MS 44768. Gladstone to the Queen, 19 Nov. 1884, *Queen ... Gladstone*, ii, 630.

[74] Gladstone to the Queen, 20 Nov. 1884, *Cab. Mins.*, CAB 41/18/54.

[75] Memoirs, 1884–5, Gladstone MSS, Add. MS 44791.

[76] Dilke to Chamberlain, 22 Nov. 1884, Chamberlain MSS, JC 5/24/77. Dilke uses exclamation points because the counties were traditionally regarded as Tory strongholds.

[77] Chamberlain to Dilke, 23 Nov. 1884, Dilke MSS, Add. MS 43886.

[78] Diary, 24 Nov. 1884, Hamilton MSS, Add. MS 48638. This idea never went beyond the preliminary stages owing to the possibility that Gladstone might refuse and thereby create an awkward situation or feel obliged to accept the honour against his convictions.

[79] Gladstone to Bright, 25 Nov. 1884, Gladstone MSS, Add. MS 44547.

[80] Memoirs, 25 Nov. 1884, Dilke MSS, Add. MS 43938.

[81] Dilke to Chamberlain, 26 Nov. 1884, ibid., Add. MS 43886.

[82] Gwynn and Tuckwell, *Life of Dilke*, ii, 76.

[83] Memoirs, 27 Nov. 1884, Dilke MSS, Add. MS 43938.

[84] I could find only the covering letter to the original memorandum (Gladstone to Salisbury, 27 Nov. 1884, Salisbury MSS, E/Gladstone/18), but the points made were essentially the same as those concluded in the final agreement. See Appendix III.

[85] Gladstone to the Queen, 27 Nov. 1884, Guedalla, *Queen ... Gladstone*, ii, 632.

[86] Salisbury to Gladstone, 27 Nov. 1884, Gladstone MSS, Add. MS 44488.

[87] Gladstone to Dilke, 27 Nov. 1884, ibid., Add. MS 44547, and Dilke to Salisbury, 28 Nov. 1884, Salisbury MSS, E/Dilke/15. There is no supportive evidence for Lady Gwendolyn Cecil's contention that Lady Salisbury was instrumental in bringing about

an accommodation on the university seats question. Cecil, *Life of Salisbury*, iii, 123–124.

[88] 'Memorandum on the Conferences', 28 Nov. 1884, Gladstone MSS, Add. MS 44768. Memoirs, 28 Nov. 1884, Dilke MSS, Add. MS 43938.

[89] Salisbury to Gladstone, 29 Nov. 1884, Gladstone MSS, Add. MS 44488.

[90] Northcote to Salisbury, 30 Nov. 1884, Salisbury MSS, E/Northcote, III/767.

CHAPTER III

[1] Oliver to Kerr, Good Friday, 1918, Lloyd George MSS, F/91/7/3.

[2] See Lord Salisbury's correspondence with the Queen on this subject in the spring of 1888 in the *Cabinet Minutes* and the Royal Archives, the information contained in *Lord Rosebery* (2 vols., London, 1931), i, 318, by the Marquess of Crewe, and J. A. Spender's *The Life of the Right Hon. Sir Henry Campbell-Bannerman, G.C.B.* (2 vols., London, 1923), i, 170–1.

[3] The Queen to Rosebery, 17 Mar. 1894, Buckle, *Letters ... Queen*, 3rd ser., ii, 383–384.

[4] Memo by Rosebery, 7 Dec. 1894, Rosebery MSS, Box 108.

[5] For details concerning the 1902 act see John William Adamson, *English Education, 1789–1902* (Cambridge, 1930), and Craven Allen Burris, 'Political Aspects of the Passage of the English Education Act, 1902', unpublished M.A. thesis, Duke University, 1959.

[6] For a concise précis of this bill see G. K. A. Bell's biography of *Randall Davidson, Archbishop of Canterbury* (2 vols., London, 1952), i, 517–18.

[7] Augustine Birrell, *Things Past Redress* (London, 1937), p. 188.

[8] *The Times*, 16 Jan. 1906, p. 6.

[9] Balfour to Lansdowne, 13 Apr. 1906, Lord Newton, *Lord Lansdowne, A Biography* (London, 1929), p. 354.

[10] *4 Parl. Debs.*, clxii, Commons (3 Aug. 1906), 1551.

[11] Davidson to Knollys, 13 Apr. 1906, RA W64/100.

[12] Davidson and Campbell-Bannerman, 28 Sept. 1906, Davidson MSS, Birrell 6.

[13] *South Wales Press*, 4 Oct. 1906. At the Buckingham Palace conference in 1914 Lloyd George reputedly told Balfour 'when you get up to speak you know what you're going to say and you say it; when I get up to speak I don't know what I have said till I see it in the paper the next morning'. Lord Gorell, *One Man ... Many Parts* (London, 1956), pp. 220–1.

[14] Tweedmouth to Campbell-Bannerman, 4 Oct. 1906, Campbell-Bannerman MSS, Add. MS 41213. Tweedmouth to Campbell-Bannerman, 15 Oct. 1906, ibid.

[15] Lord Selborne later described Crewe as a good party man: 'I think he had only one political conviction and that he believed with all his heart, that the party labelled Liberal was necessary to salvation.' June 1916, Selborne MSS, 285–90.

[16] Davidson, Birrell, Crewe, and Campbell-Bannerman, 28 Oct. 1906, Davidson MSS, Birrell 6.

[17] Campbell-Bannerman to the King, 7 Nov. 1906, *Cab. Mins.*, CAB 41/30/74.

[18] Davidson and Morley, 16 Nov. 1906, Davidson MSS, Birrell 6.

[19] Davidson and the King, 17 Nov. 1906, ibid.

[20] Davidson and Campbell-Bannerman, 18 Nov. 1906, ibid.

[21] Esher to Brett, 17 Nov. 1906, Maurice V. Brett, *Journals and Letters of Reginald Viscount Esher* (4 vols., London, 1934), ii, 202. Interestingly Esher (formerly R. B. Brett), who acted as a go-between for Gladstone and Salisbury in 1884, later (in 1909) attributed that settlement to the Queen, who supposedly 'arranged the compromise which was agreed to by both parties'. Ibid., 413. I am indebted to C. C. Weston for bringing this passage to my attention.

[22] Knollys to Campbell-Bannerman, 23 Nov. 1906, Spender, *Life of Campbell-Bannerman*, ii, 301–2.

[23] The King to Campbell-Bannerman, 25 Nov. 1906, ibid., 302. Reference to the biography of Archbishop Tait appears to have been the suggestion of Esher. Esher to the King, 22 Nov. 1906, Brett, *Journals and Letters of Esher*, ii, 203–204.

[24] Davidson and Campbell-Bannerman, 25 Nov. 1906, Davidson MSS, Birrell 6. Campbell-Bannerman to the King, 27 Nov. 1906, Spender, *Life of Campbell-Bannerman*, ii, 303–4.

[25] Campbell-Bannerman, not aware of the purpose of Thring's mission, wrote to Birrell: 'What is it I hear of Thring having been one of a nice little party—A. J. B., Hartington, Black Michael etc—telling them exactly what we would and what we would not?' Campbell-Bannerman to Birrell, 25 Nov. 1906, Birrell MSS, MS 10/2, p. 8.

[26] Devonshire to Davidson, 24 Nov. 1906, Davidson MSS, Birrell 6.

[27] A. Chamberlain to M. Chamberlain, 27 Nov. 1906, Chamberlain MSS, AC 4/1/121.

[28] Lansdowne House Conferences, 23, 26, and 27 Nov. 1906, Davidson MSS, Birrell 6.

[29] *Oxford Chronicle*, 7 Dec. 1906.

[30] Knollys to Campbell-Bannerman, 5 Dec. 1906, Spender, *Life of Campbell-Bannerman*, ii, 316–17.

[31] Campbell-Bannerman to the King, 8 Dec. 1906, *Cab. Mins.*, CAB 41/30/79.

[32] The King to Campbell-Bannerman, 9 Dec. 1906, RA R27/120.

[33] Devonshire to Balfour, 9 Dec. 1906, Balfour MSS, Add. MS 49770.

[34] Lansdowne to Crewe, 6 Dec. 1906, Crewe MSS. Crewe to Lansdowne, 7 Dec. 1906, Ripon MSS, Add. MS 43518.

[35] Lansdowne and Davidson, 11 Dec. 1906, Davidson MSS, Birrell 6.

[36] Campbell-Bannerman to the King, 10 Dec. 1906, RA R27/121.

[37] 5 *Parl. Debs.*, clxvi, Commons (10 Dec. 1906), 1581.

[38] Davidson to Campbell-Bannerman, 11 Dec. 1906, Campbell-Bannerman MSS, Add. MS 41239.

[39] 5 *Parl. Debs.*, clxvii, Commons (11 Dec. 1906), 154–9.

[40] Lansdowne House Conference, 12 Dec. 1906, Davidson MSS, Birrell 6.

[41] Campbell-Bannerman to the King, 12 Dec. 1906, *Cab. Mins.*, CAB 41/30/8.

[42] Davidson, Crewe, and Birrell, 14 Dec. 1906, Davidson MSS, Birrell 6. Davidson, Lansdowne, and Balfour, ibid.

[43] Crewe to Devonshire, 14 Dec. 1906, Devonshire MSS, 340.3248A.

[44] 5 *Parl. Debs.*, clxvii, Lords (17 Dec. 1906), 915–39. John Redmond, the Irish Nationalist leader, was disturbed by Crewe's use of the phrase, 'consultative voice', instead of giving his firm assurance of the parents' committees' absolute consent which Birrell, Asquith, and Crewe had originally promised. Redmond to Birrell, 17 Dec. 1906, Redmond MSS, MS 15169(1).

[45] Campbell-Bannerman to the King, 18 Dec. 1906, *Cab. Mins.*, CAB 41/30/8.

[46] Memo by Balfour, 18 Dec. 1906, Balfour MSS, Add. MS 49729.

[47] Memo by Lansdowne, 18 Dec. 1906, Newton, *Lord Lansdowne*, pp. 356–7.

[48] Memoir by Chamberlain, 18 Dec. 1906, Sir Charles Petrie, *The Life and Letters of The Right Hon. Sir Austen Chamberlain* (2 vols., London, 1940), i, 195.

[49] Conference proceedings, 18 Dec. 1906, Davidson MSS, Birrell 6. Unfortunately no Liberal account of this meeting is available.

[50] Conference proceedings, 19 Dec. 1906, ibid.

[51] Davidson to Knollys, 19 Dec. 1906, ibid.

[52] 5 *Parl. Debs.*, clxvii, Lords (19 Dec. 1906), 1375–6. For an excellent survey of political and press opinion on the failure of the conference see the *Manchester Guardian*, 20 Dec. 1906.

[53] *5 Parl. Deb.*, clxvii, Commons (20 Dec. 1906), 1740.

[54] Ibid., Lords (19 Dec. 1906), 1409.

[55] Landowne to Knollys, 20 Dec. 1906, RA W65/47.

CHAPTER IV

[1] 'John Bull on the Conference', *Punch*, cxxxviii (29 June 1910), 482.

[2] Blanche E. C. Dugdale, *Arthur James Balfour* (2 vols., London, 1936), ii, 32. The standard account of this conflict is Roy Jenkins's *Mr. Balfour's Poodle: An Account of the Struggle between the House of Lords and the Government of Mr. Asquith* (London, 1954).

[3] There is evidence to suggest that the conference method was employed to a limited extent to reach an accord on Liberal legislation blocked by the House of Lords. In August 1907 Crewe and Birrell met with Lansdowne and Walter Long to discuss the Government's evicted tenants bill. Birrell to Redmond, 22 Aug. 1907, Redmond MSS, MS 15,169(1). In November of 1909 several conferences were held with leading Lords over the housing and town planning bill which subsequently passed. Birrell to Redmond, 10 Nov. 1909, ibid., MS 15,169(2). Burns to Asquith, 11 Nov. 1909, Burns MSS, Add. MS 46282.

[4] Memo by Campbell-Bannerman, 31 May 1907, Spender, *Life of Campbell-Bannerman*, ii, 351.

[5] For a discussion of the alternative plans for dealing with the House of Lords through the 1910 crisis see Corinne Comstock Weston, 'The Liberal Leadership and the Lords' Veto, 1907–1910', *The Historical Journal*, xi (1968), 508–37.

[6] *5 Parl. Debs.*, xiii, Commons (2 Dec. 1909), 546.

[7] O'Connor to Lloyd George, 9 Feb. 1910, Lloyd George MSS, C/6/10/3.

[8] *5 Parl. Debs.*, xiv, Commons (21 Feb. 1910), 68–74. See also his speech in Dublin on 10 February in *The Times*, 11 Feb. 1910, p. 10.

[9] *5 Parl. Debs.*, xiv, Commons (21 Feb. 1910), 52–63.

[10] The King apparently made his appeal against the wishes of Asquith who expressed serious doubts whether any such step 'however informal in character and tactful in method—would at this stage be productive of useful results. . . .' Asquith to the King, 14 Feb. 1910, RA R30/98.

[11] Memo for the King by Balfour, 15 Feb. 1910, Newton, *Lord Lansdowne*, p. 389.

[12] J. L. Garvin, *The Life of Joseph Chamberlain* (3 vols., London, 1933), ii, 9.

[13] *5 Parl. Debs.*, xiv, Commons (3 Mar. 1910), 972.

[14] See F. S. L. Lyons, *John Dillon, A Biography* (London, 1968), pp. 313–17, for the most thorough account of these proceedings.

[15] Memo by the Master of Elibank, 14 Apr. 1910, Arthur C. Murray, *Master and Brother, Murrays of Elibank* (London, 1945), p. 48.

[16] Asquith to the King, 13 Apr. 1910, Roy Jenkins, *Asquith, Portrait of a Man and an Era* (London, 1964), p. 209.

[17] *5 Parl. Debs.*, xvi, Commons (14 Apr. 1910), 1548.

[18] An expression used by Ian Colvin, *The Life of Lord Carson* (3 vols., London, 1932–6), ii, 42.

[19] T. M. Healy, *Letters and Leaders of My Day* (2 vols., New York, 1929), ii, 498.

[20] Jenkins, *Mr. Balfour's Poodle*, pp. 121–2.

[21] In particular see Lucy Masterman, *C. F. G. Masterman, A Biography* (London, 1939), pp. 159–61, and Wilfred Scawen Blunt, *My Diaries, Being a Personal Narrative of Events, 1888–1914* (2 vols., New York, 1922), ii, pp. 288–300.

[22] Memo by Elibank, 14 Apr. 1910, Murray, *Master and Brother*, p. 46.

[23] Ibid. Throughout the crisis, according to Blunt, Irish trust lay with Lloyd George. Dillon, Blunt wrote on 27 April, 'has no great confidence in Asquith's keeping his promise of resigning at once when the King refuses to give the assurances', whereas Lloyd

George 'was a Celt, entirely in sympathy with Ireland and all the causes Irishmen care for'. Blunt, *My Diaries*, p. 300.

[24] A record of the proceedings of Rosebery's committee is available in the Davidson MSS, under 'House of Lords'.

[25] Balfour to 'Clan' [Lansdowne], 29 Dec. 1909, Balfour MSS, Add. MS 49835. Lansdowne to Balfour, 3 Jan. 1910, ibid., Add. MS 49730. Sandars to Balfour, 28 Jan. 1910, ibid., Add. MS 49766.

[26] Nash to Asquith, 15 Dec. 1909, Asquith MSS, 28/58, Cabinet Minute.

[27] There were doubtless some who blamed the Government for the King's death. The dowager Queen allegedly told Austen Chamberlain that 'the policy of the Govt.', which she linked with Asquith's statement in the Commons on 14 April, 'had killed the King'. A. Chamberlain to Mary Chamberlain, 17 May 1910, Chamberlain MSS, AC 4/1/563.

[28] Harold Nicolson, *King George the Fifth, His Life and Reign* (London, 1953), pp. 61–63.

[29] Memo by the Master of Elibank for his private lunch with the Prince of Wales at Thurloe Sq., 29 Mar. 1910, Elibank MSS, MS 8802.

[30] Lansdowne to Lord Roberts, 18 May 1910, Balfour MSS, Add. MS 49730.

[31] *The Times*, 6 May 1910, p. 10.

[32] Alfred M. Gollin, *The Observer and J. L. Garvin 1908–1914, A Study of Great Editorship* (London, 1960), p. 185.

[33] Balfour later described Oliver as 'an Edinburgh man by birth, "Trinity" Cambridge by education, and is Manager-Partner of Debenham and Freebody,—a great College friend of Austen's, a strong imperialist, but one who thinks for himself, and stands outside the minutiae of party politics'. Balfour to 'Reggie', 22 Oct. 1910, Balfour MSS, Add. MS 49836.

[34] *The Times*, 23 May 1910, p. 36.

[35] Ibid., 8 June 1910, p. 10.

[36] Cabinet memo by L., 29 May 1910, *Cabinet Memorandum*, CAB 37/102/21. An earlier memo submitted by Crewe along the same lines is mentioned in a letter by John Burns to Asquith, 20 May 1910, Asquith MSS, 28/112.

[37] Cabinet memo by Asquith, 1 June 1910, *Cabinet Memorandum*, CAB 37/102/20.

[38] O'Connor to Redmond, 6 June 1910, Denis Gwynn, *The Life of John Redmond* (London, 1932), pp. 179–80. Redmond to O'Connor, 7 June 1910, ibid.

[39] Samuel to Gladstone, 25 June 1910, Viscount Gladstone MSS, Add. MS 45992.

[40] A. Chamberlain to I. Chamberlain, 15 June 1910, Chamberlain MSS, AC 4/1/583.

[41] This is the view of Alfred Gollin in *Balfour's Burden* (London, 1965), p. 53.

[42] For Lansdowne's views on Ireland see 'Lord Lansdowne and Ireland', in Newton, *Lord Lansdowne*, pp. 497–505.

[43] Memo by Balfour, 22 June 1910, *Cabinet Memoranda*, CAB 37/102/23.

[44] First and second meetings, 17 and 23 June 1910, Chamberlain MSS, AC 10/2/35, 10/2/36 and 10/2/65. Chamberlain's account, later supplemented by Lansdowne's notes, constitutes the most complete extant record of the negotiations. See his *Politics From Inside: An Epistolary Chronicle, 1906–1914* (London, 1936), pp. 289–90.

[45] Lord Ripon, Lord Privy Seal, first raised the possibility of joint sittings in the Liberal Cabinet committee in 1907–8, and his name continued to be associated with the proposal.

[46] Third, seventh and eighth meetings, 27 June, 13 July, and 15 July 1910, Chamberlain MSS, AC 10/2/37, 10/2/40, 10/2/41, and 10/2/65. The fourth through sixth meetings were devoted to presentation of evidence of American and colonial methods of dealing with legislative deadlocks.

[47] Ibid.

[48] Tenth meeting, 25 July 1910, ibid., AC 10/2/65.

⁴⁹ Ibid., AC 10/2/44. Also see Lansdowne to Balfour, 25 July 1910, Balfour MSS, Add. MS 49730.

⁵⁰ 'A Suggested Scheme for Dealing with Deadlocks' by Asquith, 19 July 1910, *Cabinet Memorandum*, CAB 37/103/34, and ninth meeting, 19 July 1910, Chamberlain MSS, AC 10/2/43.

⁵¹ Eleventh meeting, 26 July 1910, ibid., AC 10/2/45 and 10/2/65.

⁵² Ibid. and twelfth meeting, 27 July 1910, ibid., AC 10/2/46.

⁵³ Thirteenth meeting, 28 July 1910, ibid., AC 10/2/47. Before the conference adjourned Crewe had suggested that they should meet at Crewe Hall when they resumed their sittings. Lansdowne, however, was 'convinced that the public would not understand our meeting under Crewe's roof. It would be said that the whole affair was a picnic, and that business of such importance ought not to be transacted in an environment of such a kind. Supposing, on the other hand, that *per impossibile* we were to arrive at an agreement, it is bound to contain a number of points which will meet with severe criticism at the hands of our friends. Will not that criticism be much more severe if it can be said that we had been "softened" by the excellence of Crewe's champagne, and the other attractions of a hospitable and luxurious country house?' Lansdowne to Balfour, 2 Aug. 1910, Balfour Papers, Add. MS 49730.

⁵⁴ Tom Jones, *Lloyd George* (London, 1951), pp. 13–14.

⁵⁵ Esher correspondence, Garvin Papers, Humanities Research Center, University of Texas at Austin.

⁵⁶ Bentley B. Gilbert, *The Evolution of National Insurance in Great Britain, The Origins of the Welfare State* (London, 1966), p. 327.

⁵⁷ Memo by Chamberlain [*sic*], 29 Jan. 1915, Lloyd George MSS, C/3/14/8.

⁵⁸ Churchill to Lloyd George, 6 Oct. 1910, ibid., C/3/15/1.

⁵⁹ Chamberlain to Cawdor, 21 Oct. 1910, Sir Austen Chamberlain, *Politics From Inside*, p. 286.

⁶⁰ Oliver to Balfour, 28 Sept. 1910, Balfour MSS, Add. MS 49860. See Appendix IV. Oliver apparently understood the Utopian nature of his arguments. 'Austen says they are rather wild,' he told Balfour, '—I'm not sure that he did not say "*very* wild".' Oliver to Balfour, 11 Oct. 1910, ibid., Add. MS 49861.

⁶¹ P. Kerr to L. Curtis, 31 Aug. 1910, cited in J. E. Kendle, 'The Round Table Movement and "Home Rule all Round"', *The Historical Journal*, xi (1968), 338.

⁶² Kerr to Curtis, 10 Aug. 1910, Lothian MSS, GD 40.17.2.

⁶³ Lansdowne to Balfour, 10 Sept. 1910, Newton, *Lord Lansdowne*, p. 397.

⁶⁴ Balfour to Lansdowne, 20 Sept. 1910, Balfour MSS, Add. MS 49836.

⁶⁵ Lansdowne to Balfour, 24 Sept. 1910, ibid., Add. MS 49730.

⁶⁶ Salisbury to Lansdowne, 6 Sept. 1910, ibid.

⁶⁷ Fourteenth meeting, 11 Oct. 1910, Chamberlain MSS, AC 10/2/48. For the creation of this body on 27 July see twelfth meeting, AC 10/2/46.

⁶⁸ Fifteenth meeting, 12 Oct. 1910, ibid., AC 10/2/49.

⁶⁹ Sixteenth meeting, 13 Oct. 1910, ibid., AC 10/2/50 and AC 10/2/65.

⁷⁰ Seventeenth meeting, 14 Oct. 1910, ibid., AC 10/2/51.

⁷¹ Asquith to Haldane, 14 Oct. 1910, Haldane MSS, MS 5909.

⁷² Memo by Lloyd George, 29 Oct. 1910, Lloyd George MSS, C/16/4/3.

⁷³ Lansdowne to Balfour, 24 Oct. 1910, Balfour MSS, Add. MS 49730.

⁷⁴ Balfour to Chamberlain, 24 Oct. 1910, ibid., Add. MS 49736.

⁷⁵ Balfour to Garvin, 22 Oct. 1910, partially transcribed in Gollin, *The Observer and J. L. Garvin*, pp. 216–18. The original is in the Garvin MSS.

⁷⁶ David Lloyd George, *War Memoirs of David Lloyd George* (6 vols., London, 1933), i, 37–8. See Eric Alexander Akers-Douglas Chilston, *Chief Whip: The Political Life and Times of Aretas Akers-Douglas, 1st Viscount Chilston* (London, 1961), pp. 345–6, for an explanation of Akers-Douglas's position.

[77] Kenneth Young, *Arthur James Balfour, The Happy Life of the Politician, Prime Minister, Statesman and Philosopher* (London, 1963), pp. 298–9.

[78] Blanche E. C. Dugdale, *Arthur James Balfour*, ii, 76. Similarly J. R. Fanning shows that Balfour's experience with Unionist intransigence over Ireland from 1906 onwards had effectively conditioned his approach to the question in 1910. 'The defence of the union', he contends, 'was the one great principle about which some sort of party unity seemed assured.' J. R. Fanning, 'The Unionist Party and Ireland, 1906–10', *Irish Historical Studies*, xv (1966), 169.

[79] Eighteenth meeting, 1 Nov. 1910, Chamberlain MSS, AC 10/5/52 and AC 10/2/65.

[80] A. Chamberlain to Ivy Chamberlain, 1 Nov. 1910, ibid., AC 6/1/81.

[81] Nineteenth meeting, 2 Nov. 1910, ibid., AC 10/2/53.

[82] A. Chamberlain to I. Chamberlain, 2 Nov. 1910, ibid., AC 6/1/81.

[83] Twentieth meeting, 3 Nov. 1910, ibid., AC 10/2/54 and AC 10/2/65.

[84] Asquith to Balfour, 3 Nov. 1910, J. A. Spender and Cyril Asquith, *Life of Herbert Henry Asquith, Lord Oxford and Asquith* (2 vols., London, 1932), i, 289.

[85] Balfour to Asquith, 3 Nov. 1910, Balfour MSS, Add. MS 49692.

[86] Asquith to Balfour, 3 Nov. 1910, ibid.

[87] Twenty-first meeting, 4 Nov. 1910, Chamberlain MSS, AC 10/2/61.

[88] Smith to Balfour, 9 Nov. 1910, Balfour MSS, Add. MS 49861.

[89] Masterman, *C. F. G. Masterman*, p. 175.

[90] 'Copy of Sir R. Finlay's Notes of the Meeting of the Unionist Leaders to hear Balfour's Report of the Proceedings at the Constitutional Conference', 18 Dec. 1910, Chamberlain, *Politics From Inside*, pp. 295–7.

[91] Masterman, *C. F. G. Masterman*, p. 175. The figures quoted here are probably correct, but Lloyd George and Balfour were not, as is stated, dealing with 'the question of the numbers by which the Conservative majority in the House of Lords could outrule a Liberal majority in the Commons'. If such were the case Lloyd George would certainly not have opted for '40' and Balfour for '60'.

[92] See Nicolson, *King George V*, pp. 133–8.

[93] Spender and Asquith, *Life of Asquith*, i, 291.

[94] The relationship between the American constitutional experience as interpreted by Oliver in his *Life of Alexander Hamilton* on the establishment of the Union of South Africa and other imperial developments is described by D. G. Boyce and J. O. Stubbs in 'F. S. Oliver, Lord Selborne and Federalism', *The Journal of Imperial and Commonwealth History*, v (Oct. 1976), 53–81.

CHAPTER V

[1] Walter Bagehot, *English Constitution*, p. 40.

[2] *The Times*, 27 July 1912, p. 8. For additional extracts of speeches by prominent Conservatives see John Joseph Horgan, *The Complete Grammar of Anarchy* (London, 1919), or Stephen McKenna, *While I Remember* (London, 1921), pp. 112–15.

[3] 'Notes made by F. E.', Carson to Bonar Law, 20 Sept. 1913, Bonar Law MSS, 30/2/15.

[4] One commentator on royalty suggests that the King was influenced to intervene personally by his 1910 experience where he 'had been treated as of very little importance, and he had found himself reduced to peddling good advice which nobody wanted, and to which nobody paid any particular attention.' Sir Charles Petrie, *The Modern British Monarchy* (London, 1961), p. 125.

[5] Memo by Birrell, 24 July 1913, Asquith MSS, 38/109.

[6] Lansdowne to Stamfordham, 31 July 1913, Bonar Law MSS, 29/6/32.

[7] Nicolson, *King George V*, pp. 223–4.

[8] Memo by Asquith, Sept. 1913, Asquith MSS, 38/8.   [9] Ibid., 38/9.

[10] Nicolson, *King George V*, pp. 225–9. For the Prime Minister's final rebuttal see Asquith to the King, 1 Oct. 1913, Asquith MSS, 38/2/6.

[11] Crewe to Asquith, 8 Sept. 1913, ibid., 39/126. The King's arguments, Crewe thought, had been inspired by an article entitled 'The King and the Constitution', in the *Spectator*, cxi (9 Aug. 1913), 200–1.

[12] See Nicolson, *King George V*, p. 231, for the impressions which the King recorded in his diary.

[13] *The Times*, 11 Sept. 1913, p. 7. The idea for this letter originated in a discussion between Loreburn and Lord George Hamilton, former India Office Secretary under Balfour's Government. See memo by G. Hamilton, 24 Sept. 1913, Bonar Law MSS, 30/2/27.

[14] Bonar Law to Balfour, 16 Sept. 1913, Balfour MSS, Add. MS 49693.

[15] Churchill to Asquith, 17 Sept. 1913, Asquith MSS, 38/193. Bonar Law's account of this conversation is quite different from Churchill's but does not contradict it. He seems quite concerned with making the point that it was Asquith who had written to Churchill suggesting their meeting. Bonar Law also barely mentions the fact that an interparty conference was discussed. Bonar Law to Lansdowne, 18 Sept. 1913, Robert Blake, *The Unknown Prime Minister, The Life and Times of Andrew Bonar Law, 1858–1923* (London, 1955), pp. 155–6.

[16] Churchill to Bonar Law, 21 Sept. 1913, Bonar Law MSS, 30/2/18. In a memorandum prepared for the Prime Minister, T. P. O'Connor summarized the Nationalist position, pointing out 'the absolute impossibility of our supporting the exclusion of Ulster: and I went the length of saying that I thought it would compel us to oppose the Government if they assented to it'. O'Connor to Dillon and Devlin, 1 Oct. 1913, Denis Gwynn, *The History of Partition (1912–1925)* (Dublin, 1950), pp. 60–1.

[17] Stamfordham to Bonar Law, 26 Sept. 1913, Bonar Law MSS, 30/2/28.

[18] Stamfordham to Bonar Law, 1 Oct. 1913, ibid., 30/3/1.

[19] Lansdowne to Bonar Law, 6 Oct. 1913, ibid., 30/3/8.

[20] Bonar Law to Stamfordham, 4 Oct. 1913, Balfour MSS, Add. MS 49693.

[21] Nicolson, *King George V*, p. 232.

[22] Asquith had acted on the assumption that it was Bonar Law who suggested their meeting to Churchill. Bonar Law claimed that Churchill had made the original suggestion at Balmoral and he assumed that he was acting under the direction of the Prime Minister.

[23] Gwynn, *History of Partition*, p. 64.

[24] 'Conversation with B. L.', 14 Oct. 1913, Asquith MSS, 38/231. 'Notes on Conversation with P.M.', 15 Oct. 1913, Blake, *Unknown Prime Minister*, pp. 161–3.

[25] 'Memo. on Conversation with Asquith', 7 Nov. 1913, Balfour MSS, Add. MS 49693. Asquith's notes, 6 Nov. 1913, Jenkins, *Asquith*, pp. 290–2.

[26] Conversation with Redmond, 17 Nov. 1913, Asquith MSS, 39/23. Interview with Dillon, 17 Nov. 1913, Lloyd George MSS, C/20/2/4. Gwynn, *History of Partition*, pp. 66–8.

[27] The King to Asquith, 30 Nov. 1913, Asquith MSS, 39/38.

[28] Discussion with Bonar Law, 10 Dec. 1913, ibid., 39/42. 'Notes on meeting with Asquith', 10 Dec. 1913, Balfour MSS, Add. MS 49693.

[29] Meeting with Carson, 16 Dec. 1913, Asquith MSS, 39/44.

[30] Asquith to Carson, 23 Dec. 1913, Balfour MSS, Add. MS 49693.

[31] Carson to Asquith, 10 Jan. 1914, Gwynn, *History of Partition*, p. 76.

[32] Nicolson, *King George V*, p. 233.

[33] Bonar Law to Stamfordham, 26 Jan. 1914, Blake, *Unknown Prime Minister*, pp. 169–70.

[34] Nicolson, *King George V*, pp. 233–4.

[35] Stamfordham to Asquith, 28 Feb. 1914, Asquith MSS, 39/132.

[36] Asquith to the King, 5 Mar. 1914, *Cab. Mins.*, CAB 41/35/6. For Redmond's memo indicating the limits of concession to which his party was prepared to go see Gwynn, *History of Partition*, pp. 93–6.

[37] The King to Bonar Law, 7 Mar. 1914, Bonar Law MSS, 31/4/11.

[38] *5 Parl. Debs.*, Commons, lix (9 Mar. 1914), 934. Redmond's memo, however, had stipulated that this period should be for three years only. At Asquith's insistence Redmond was obliged to concede to six. Gwynn, *History of Partition*, pp. 236–7.

[39] Nicolson, *King George V*, pp. 236–7.

[40] One of these was the so-called 'round-table proposal' which was drawn up by Churchill and several contributors to the *Round Table* magazine, who had been associated with 'Milner's Kindergarten' a decade earlier. This plan envisaged the passage of home rule and the exclusion of Ulster with the creation of a complicated system of conventions which would ultimately enact a federal scheme. Memorandum, 6 Apr. 1914, Lloyd George MSS, C/19/3/21.

[41] Asquith to the King, 7 Apr. 1914, Asquith MSS, 39/157.

[42] Lowther to Asquith, 3 May 1914, ibid., 39/165.

[43] Asquith to the King, 2 May 1914, *Cab. Mins.*, CAB 41/35/12. The King to Asquith, 3 May 1914, Asquith MSS, 39/161.

[44] Bonar Law to Balfour, 6 May 1914, Balfour MSS, Add. MS 49693. Also see Asquith to Redmond, 6 May 1914, Redmond MSS, MS 15,165(4).

[45] The King to Asquith, 12 May 1914, Asquith MSS, 39/176.

[46] Rothermere to Bonar Law, 29 June 1914, Bonar Law MSS, 32/4/32.

[47] For more details on these negotiations see Gwynn, *Life of Redmond*, pp. 328–30, and *History of Partition*, pp. 105–14.

[48] Message from B. L. to Asquith, 16 July 1914, Murray of Elibank MSS, MS 8803.

[49] Notes by the King, 17 July 1914, Asquith MSS, 3/235. Note in the King's handwriting, no date, ibid., 39/229. Also see Maurice Bonham Carter to Lloyd George, 17 July 1914, Lloyd George MSS, C/6/11/18.

[50] *5 Parl. Debs.*, Commons, lxv (20 July 1914), 69–70.

[51] Ibid., Lords, xvii (20 July 1914), 22–4.

[52] *The Times*, 20 July 1914, p. 20.

[53] *Manchester Guardian*, 21 July 1914, p. 8.

[54] Gwynn, *Life of Redmond*, p. 337.

[55] Memo by Redmond, 21 July 1914, Gwynn, *History of Partition*, pp. 120–3.

[56] Ibid., pp. 337–40. Memo by Bonar Law, 21 July 1914, Bonar Law MSS, 39/4/44. Gwynn, *History of Partition*, pp. 117–23.

[57] *Daily News & Leader*, 21 July 1914, p. 8.

[58] *Morning Post*, 22 July 1914, p. 8.

[59] E. H. Mair to Scott, 22 July 1914, C. P. Scott MSS, Add. MS 50908.

[60] Stamfordham to Asquith, 20 July 1914, Asquith MSS, 3/239. Diary, 27 July 1914, C. P. Scott MSS, Add. MS 50901.

[61] Gwynn, *History of Partition*, pp. 123–5. Memo by Bonar Law, 22 July 1914, Bonar Law MSS, 39/4/44. Gwynn, *Life of Redmond*, p. 340.

[62] Gwynn, *History of Partition*, p. 128.

[63] Memo by Bonar Law, 23 July 1914, Bonar Law MSS, 39/4/44. For the Speaker's account see Viscount Ullswater, *A Speaker's Commentaries* (2 vols., London, 1925), ii, 162. Gwynn, *History of Partition*, pp. 125–30.

[64] 'Interview with the King', 24 July 1914, Gwynn, *History of Partition*, pp. 130–1.

[65] Winston S. Churchill, *The World Crisis* (5 vols., New York, 1927), i, 205.

CHAPTER VI

[1] Diary, 27 June 1918, C. P. Scott MSS, Add. MS 50905.

[2] Nicolson, *King George V*, p. 270. Frank Hardie, in *The Political Influence of the British Monarchy, 1868–1952* (London, 1970), p. 160, likens this meeting with others held at Buckingham Palace in 1914, 1916, and 1931, citing the Balmoral Castle talks between the King and various party leaders in the autumn of 1913 as a precedent.

[3] The Government of Ireland Act was signed into law on 18 Sept. 1914, but was accompanied by a Suspensory Act which withheld its operation until the end of the war.

[4] *5 Parl. Debs.*, lxxxi, Commons (27 Apr. 1916), 2511–12.

[5] Ibid., lxxxii, Commons (9 May 1916), 502.

[6] Diary, 9–10 May 1916, Trevor Wilson, *The Political Diaries of C. P. Scott, 1911–1928* (London, 1970), pp. 204–5.

[7] Memo on 'Ireland', 19 and 21 May 1916, Selborne MSS, 128/7 and 128/23. For the second and third portions of this memorandum see Appendix V.

[8] Memo on Irish Negotiations by Maurice Bonham Carter, 1916, Asquith MSS, 41/151.

[9] *The Times*, 26 May 1916, p. 9.

[10] Long to Lloyd George, 23 May 1916, Lloyd George MSS, D/14/1/9.

[11] Midleton to Lloyd George, 27 May 1916, ibid., D/14/1/26.

[12] Memo of interview with Lloyd George, 29 May 1916, Midleton MSS, PRO 30/67/31. For a detailed analysis of the critical role of the southern Unionists throughout the negotiations see Patrick Buckland, *Irish Unionism: The Anglo-Irish and the New Ireland, 1885–1922* (2 vols., Dublin, 1972), i, 51–82. Also see George Dangerfield's examination of the Lloyd George negotiations in *The Damnable Question, A Study in Anglo-Irish Relations* (Boston, 1976).

[13] Diary, 22–6 May 1916, Wilson, *Diaries of Scott*, pp. 206–7.

[14] This account was conveyed to Lansdowne by Asquith at a later stage in the negotiations. Lansdowne to Chamberlain, 24 June 1916, Chamberlain MSS, AC 14/5/6.

[15] Hugh de Fellenberg Montgomery to Charles Hubert Montgomery, 9 June 1916, Montgomery MSS, D.627/429/26.

[16] Colvin, *Life of Carson*, iii, 165–6.

[17] The proposals were: '(1) To bring the Home Rule Act into immediate operation. (2) To introduce at once an Amending Bill as a strictly War Emergency Act, to cover only the period of the war and a short specified interval after it. (3) During that period the Irish Members to remain at Westminster in their full numbers. (4) During the war emergency period six Ulster counties to be left as at present under the Imperial Parliament. (5) Immediately after the war an Imperial Conference of representatives of all the Dominions of the Empire to be held to consider the future government of the Empire, including the question of the government of Ireland. (6) Immediately after the Conference, and during the interval provided for by the War Emergency Act, the permanent settlement of all the great outstanding problems, such as the permanent position of the six exempted counties, the question of finance, and other problems which cannot be dealt with during the war, would be proceeded with.' Gwynn, *History of Partition*, pp. 151–2.

[18] Long to Lloyd George, 29 May 1916, Lloyd George MSS, D/14/1/37.

[19] Stewart to Long, 31 May 1916, ibid, D/14/1/45. Also see 'The Irish Scheme', a memo compiled by Long on 13 June. Selborne MSS, 87/178–84.

[20] Lansdowne's memo on Lloyd George's proposals, 2 June 1916, Lloyd George MSS, D/15/1/10.

[21] Resolutions of 2 June 1916, Midleton MSS, PRO 30/67/31.

[22] Lloyd George to Carson, 3 June 1916, Colvin, *Life of Carson*, iii, 167–8, and Carson MSS, 1507/1/1916/25.

[23] Colvin, *Life of Carson*, iii, 170–2.

[24] Resolution passed at a meeting of both houses, 6 June 1916, Midleton MSS, PRO 30/67/31.

[25] O'Connor to Lloyd George, 9 June 1916, Lloyd George MSS, D/14/2/23.

[26] Dillon to Lloyd George, 11 June 1916, ibid., D/14/2/23.

[27] June and July 1916, Bonar Law MSS, 53/3/8.

[28] *The Times*, 12 June 1916, p. 7.

[29] Walter Long, 'The Irish Scheme', 13 June 1916, Selborne MSS, 87/178–84.

[30] Long to Lloyd George, 11 June 1916, Lloyd George MSS, D/14/2/29.

[31] Lloyd George to Long, 12 June 1916, ibid., D/14/2/32.

[32] Long to Lloyd George, 12 June 1916, ibid., D/14/2/33.

[33] Lloyd George to Asquith, 12 June 1916, ibid., D/14/2/29.

[34] Lloyd George to Asquith, 12 June 1916, ibid., D/14/2/30.

[35] Lloyd George to Dillon, 12 June 1916, ibid., D/14/2/31.

[36] Montgomery to Willis, 10 June 1916, Montgomery MSS, D.627/429/28.

[37] Carson to Bonar Law, 14 June 1916, Colvin, *Life of Carson*, iii, 171–2.

[38] Owen to Lloyd George, 14 June 1916, Lloyd George MSS, D/14/2/37.

[39] *The Times*, 15 June 1916, p. 10.

[40] Selborne to Asquith, 16 June 1916, Lloyd George MSS, D/14/3/9.

[41] Montgomery to Willis, 17 June 1916, Montgomery MSS, D.627/429/28.

[42] Interview with P.M., 17 June 1916, Chamberlain MSS, AC 14/5/20.

[43] Lloyd George to Dillon, 17 June 1916, Lloyd George MSS, D/14/3/11.

[44] R. Montagu Smith (correspondent for the *Daily Mail*) to Lloyd George, 20 June 1916, ibid., D/14/3/21.

[45] Lady Carson's Diary, 14 June 1916, Carson MSS, D.1507/6/2.

[46] Lloyd George to Asquith, 20 June 1916, Lloyd George MSS, D/14/3/21.

[47] Notes of meeting at 1 Carlton House Terrace, 20 June 1916, Chamberlain MSS, AC 14/5/2.

[48] A. Chamberlain to I. Chamberlain, July [June?] 1916, ibid., AC 6/1/208.

[49] Selborne to Asquith, 24 June 1916, Asquith MSS, 18/213.

[50] Asquith to the King, 27 June 1916, *Cab. Mins.*, CAB 37/150/23.

[51] Chamberlain to Lansdowne, 30 June 1916, Chamberlain MSS, AC 15/5/9.

[52] Chamberlain to Asquith, 1 July 1916, Asquith MSS, 37/79.

[53] Asquith to the King, 5 July 1916, *Cab. Mins.*, CAB 41/37/25.

[54] 5 *Parl. Debs.*, lxxxiv, Commons (10 July 1916), 57–62.

[55] Ibid., xxii, Lords (11 July 1916), 645–52.

[56] *The Times*, 13 July 1916, p. 9.

[57] O'Connor to Lloyd George, 12 July 1916, Lloyd George MSS, E/2/22/2.

[58] *The Times*, 14 July 1916, p. 9.

[59] Ibid., 15 July 1916, p. 9. Lansdowne was encouraged in this course by Long, in whose papers can be found a list of members comprising this organization. Long to Lansdowne, 15 July 1916, Long MSS, 947/268.

[60] 5 *Parl. Debs.*, lxxxiv, Commons (24 July 1916), 1432–44.

[61] Diary, 27 July 1916, Wilson, *Diaries of Scott*, p. 223.

[62] Asquith later told Redmond, in a sort of postscript to their negotiations, that he was 'inclined at one time to suggest ... a reopening of the Buckingham Palace Conference, but this would be premature at present'. Gwynn, *History of Partition*, p. 158.

CHAPTER VII

[1] 3 *Parl. Debs.*, cxxiii, Commons (16 Dec. 1852), 1653.

[2] Lord Beaverbrook, *Politicians and the War, 1914–1916* (London, 1960), p. 288. The original two-volume edition was published by Butterworth in 1928 and 1932.

[3] At the time of his resignation from the Cabinet in June 1916 Selborne described Asquith as 'quite hopeless' as a wartime premier. 'He had no vision, no power or desire of prevision, no ounce of drive in his composition, not a spark of initiative, no power of leadership of any sort or kind. He gave the Cabinet no lead; he never bound our work together; Cabinets were mere wastes of time; he was the worst chairman I ever sat under at any committee; he kept no sort of order at Cabinet councils nor even attempted to bring us to a decision; he hardly ever expressed any opinion himself. The desire on all occasions to avoid a decision was an absolute disease with him. That the Cabinet was always too late in everything it did, the supply of munitions, the reconstitution of the General Staff, the supply of men, the supply of food, was his fault.' Lloyd George, on the other hand, he saw as 'very clever, with vision, prevision, desiring power and courage in wonderful combination. His performance at the Ministry of Munitions was a wonderful one, for it was done notwithstanding the fact that his office there was, as always, a perfect welter of disorganization and intrigue.' Selborne MSS, 285–90.

[4] Beaverbrook, *Politicians and the War*, pp. 347–8.

[5] Asquith to Lloyd George, 1 Dec. 1916, Lloyd George, *War Memoirs*, ii, 983–5.

[6] Lloyd George to Asquith, 2 Dec. 1916, Lloyd George MSS, E/2/23/11.

[7] Lloyd George to Bonar Law, 2 Dec. 1916, Frank Owen, *Tempestuous Journey, Lloyd George, His Life and Times* (London, 1954), p. 337.

[8] Beaverbrook, *Politicians and the War*, pp. 410–11, 422–3.

[9] Jenkins, *Asquith*, p. 435.

[10] Curzon to Lansdowne, 3 Dec. 1916, Newton, *Lord Lansdowne*, pp. 452–3.

[11] Chamberlain to Chelmsford, 8 Dec. 1916, Sir Austen Chamberlain, *Down the Years* (London, 1935), p. 118.

[12] Beaverbrook, *Politicians and the War*, pp. 426, 480–1, and 487–8. According to accounts by Maurice Bonham Carter and Lord Errington (later Cromer), Asquith did not actually see the Conservative resolution until Cecil showed it to him on 5 December. Note by B.C. and memo by Lord Errington, RA GV K.1048A/10 and K.1048A/2.

[13] A. J. P. Taylor, *Beaverbrook* (New York, 1972), p. 117.

[14] Asquith to P. McKenna, 3 Dec. 1916, Beaverbrook MSS, 4/VIII.

[15] Asquith to Lloyd George, 4 Dec. 1916, Lloyd George, *War Memoirs*, ii, 987–8.

[16] Lloyd George to Asquith, 4 Dec. 1916, Spender and Asquith, *Life of Asquith*, ii, 265–6.

[17] Asquith to Lloyd George, 4 Dec. 1916, Lloyd George, *War Memoirs*, ii, 990–2.

[18] Lloyd George to Asquith, 5 Dec. 1916, Spender and Asquith, *Life of Asquith*, ii, 266–7.

[19] Taylor, *Beaverbrook*, p. 118.

[20] Beaverbrook, *Politicians and the War*, p. 439.

[21] 'Montagu's account of the part he played in, and his knowledge of the political crisis of December, 1916', Beaverbrook MSS, Box V.

[22] Donald's interview with Asquith, 7 Dec. 1916, ibid., Box 4/XXII.

[23] Taylor, *Beaverbrook*, p. 118.

[24] Beaverbrook, *Politicians and the War*, pp. 440–2.

[25] 'Lord Crewe's Memorandum on the Break-up of the Coalition Government, December, 1916', James Pope-Hennessy, *Lord Crewe, 1858–1945, The Likeness of a Liberal* (London, 1955), pp. 181–90.

[26] Chamberlain to Beaverbrook, 29 June 1931, Beaverbrook MSS, Box 4/II.

[27] Chamberlain to Beaverbrook, 24 May 1932, ibid., Box 4/II. It was Chamberlain's private view that there was 'a tendency' in Beaverbrook's account 'to suspect Curzon of ulterior motives—which I think is quite unfounded'. It was also intended 'to show that Beaverbrook himself played an important part' and 'to exalt Bonar for whom

he had a sincere affection and profound admiration'. Chamberlain to Cecil, 10 July 1931, Cecil MSS, Add. MS 51079.

[28] Beaverbrook to Chamberlain, 16 June 1932, Beaverbrook MSS, Box 4/II.

[29] Note by Beaverbrook (undated), ibid., Box XXIII.

[30] Curzon to Asquith, 4 Dec. 1916, Spender and Asquith, *Life of Asquith*, ii, 260.

[31] Curzon to Lansdowne, 3 Dec. 1916, Newton, *Lord Lansdowne*, pp. 452–3.

[32] Curzon to Asquith, 4 Dec. 1916, Spender and Asquith, *Life of Asquith*, ii, 260. These lines were transmitted correctly, though without commas, from Matthew Arnold's 'Stanzas in Memory of the Author of "Obermann" '. If the poem be read in entirety it can be seen that Curzon did not extract them out of context. A. Dwight Culler, ed., *Poetry and Criticism of Matthew Arnold* (Boston, 1961), pp. 115–20.

[33] Beaverbrook to Chamberlain, 30 June 1931, Beaverbrook MSS, Box 4/II. When pressed by Chamberlain on this point, however, Cecil denied recollection of 'any special personal relations with Asquith at that time'. See Chamberlain to Cecil, 30 June 1931, Cecil MSS, Add. MS 51079, and Cecil to Chamberlain, 9 July 1931, ibid.

[34] Drummond to Asquith, 2 or 3 Dec. 1916, Asquith MSS, 31/13.

[35] 'Montagu's account', Dec. 1916, Beaverbrook MSS, Box 4/V.

[36] 'Donald's interview with Asquith', 7 Dec. 1916, ibid., Box 4/XXII.

[37] 'Montagu's account', Dec. 1916, ibid., Box 4/V.

[38] Chamberlain to Chelmsford, 8 Dec. 1916, Chamberlain, *Down the Years*, p. 124.

[39] Bonar Law to Asquith, 5 Dec. 1916, Blake, *Unknown Prime Minister*, p. 334.

[40] Balfour to Asquith, 5 Dec. 1916, Blanche E. C. Dugdale, *Arthur James Balfour*, ii, 174–5.

[41] Notes by Samuel, Herbert Samuel, *Memoirs* (London, 1945), pp. 120–2. See also Samuel's memo on 'Resignation of Asquith Government—5 December 1916', Samuel MSS, A/56.

[42] Stamfordham's memo, 5 Dec. 1916, RA GV K.1048A/1.

[43] Memo by Haldane, 6 Dec. 1916, Haldane MSS, MS 5913. Harold Nicolson is misleading in his application of this document in *King George V*, pp. 289–90. He states that Stamfordham had consulted Haldane 'during the course of that evening', and that the King, 'fortified by such expert judgement', told Bonar Law that 'he would refuse, if asked, to accord him a Dissolution'. The copy of Stamfordham's request in the Haldane papers, however, indicates that it was not sent until '10.30 p.m.' (the King met Bonar Law at 9.30) and that the ex-Lord Chancellor's reply was not expected until the following morning (the 6th). Stamfordham to Haldane, 5 Dec. 1916, Haldane MSS, MS 5913. Furthermore it would seem that Nicolson misapplied Haldane's message in light of its true context. Contrary to giving the King the power to refuse a dissolution, that reply outlined a strict constitutional course for the monarch to follow whereby his powers were strictly limited. This hardly seems consistent with the King's earlier statement to Bonar Law.

[44] 'Montagu's account', Dec. 1916, Beaverbrook MSS, Box 4/V.

[45] Memo by Balfour, 7 Dec. 1916, Balfour MSS, Add. MS 49692.

[46] Stamfordham's memo, 6 Dec. 1916, RA GV K.1048A/1.

[47] Copy of short statement by Arthur Henderson, taken down by Robert Donald for Beaverbrook, 17 Apr. 1917, Beaverbrook MSS, Box 4/II.

[48] Memo by Balfour, 7 Dec. 1916, Balfour MSS, Add. MS 49692.

[49] Ibid., and Stamfordham's memo in Nicolson, *King George V*, pp. 289–90.

[50] Memo by Balfour, 7 Dec. 1916, Balfour MSS, Add. MS 49692.

[51] Earl of Oxford and Asquith, *Memories and Reflections, 1852–1927* (2 vols., Boston, 1928), ii, 134–6.

[52] Balfour's memo for 7 Dec., Dugdale, *Arthur James Balfour*, ii, 180–1.

[53] Beaverbrook, *Politicians and the War*, p. 516. It would appear that Curzon, Cecil, Chamberlain, and Long were invited to join the Government by Bonar Law, on behalf

of Lloyd George, on the afternoon of 7 December. 'Memorandum of Conversation between Mr. Lloyd George and certain Unionist ex-Ministers, 7 December 1916' by Curzon 11/12/16, Long MSS, 947/502.

54 Beaverbrook to Crewe (undated—October 1928?), Beaverbrook MSS, Box 4/II.
55 Beaverbrook to Stevenson, 11 Oct. 1928, ibid., Box 4/II.
56 Stevenson to Beaverbrook, 15 Oct. 1928, ibid., Box 4/II.
57 Oliver to Carson, 7 May 1918, Colvin, *Life of Carson*, iii, 353.
58 Beaverbrook, *Politicians and the War*, p. 485.

CHAPTER VIII

1 Sir Charles Petrie, *Walter Long and His Times* (London, 1936), p. 211.
2 Agnes E. Metcalf, *Woman's Effort* (Oxford, 1917), p. 183.
3 See J. L. Hammond, *C. P. Scott of the* Manchester Guardian (London, 1934), p. 114, and the *Daily Telegraph*, 22 Jan. 1913, p. 11.
4 *5 Parl. Debs.*, Commons, xlvii (27 Jan. 1913), 1020–1.
5 Ullswater, *Speaker's Commentaries*, ii, 137.
6 *5 Parl. Debs.*, Lords, xvi (5 May 1914), 39.
7 Millicent Garrett Fawcett, *The Women's Victory and After* (London, 1920), p. 51.
8 *5 Parl. Debs.*, Commons, lii (1 May 1913), 1705.
9 Ibid., 1519.
10 Ibid., Lords, xiv (24 July 1913), 1382.
11 Metcalfe, *Woman's Effort*, p. 241.
12 Annie Kenney, *Memories of a Militant* (London, 1924), p. 220.
13 *The Times*, 11 Mar. 1914, p. 9. Sylvia Pankhurst, the second daughter of Emmeline, estimated that militant destruction in the first seven months of 1914 exceeded that for the entire previous year. The damage done to the *Rokeby Venus* alone was £45,000. E. Sylvia Pankhurst, *The Suffragette Movement* (London, 1931), p. 544.
14 Christabel Pankhurst, *Unshackled: The Story of How We Won the Vote* (London, 1959), p. 269.
15 Irene Osgood Andrews and Margaret A. Hobbs, *Economic Effects of the World War Upon Women and Children in Great Britain* (New York, 1921), p. 30.
16 The actual number on this register was 8,357,648. *The Times*, 22 Feb. 1915, p. 5.
17 Scott to Sharp, 28 July 1915, Evelyn Sharp, *Unfinished Adventure* (London, 1933), p. 168.
18 *5 Parl. Debs.*, Commons, lxxvi (14 Dec. 1915), 1983.
19 Andrews & Hobbs, *Economic Effects of the War*, p. 35.
20 *5 Parl. Debs.*, Commons, lxxxi (4 Apr. 1916), 1032.
21 Fawcett, *Women's Victory & After*, p. 113.
22 *The Times*, 8 Mar. 1916, p. 7.
23 Fawcett, *Women's Victory & After*, p. 127.
24 *5 Parl. Debs.*, Commons, lxxxiv (12 July 1916), 344–5. The 'Select Committee' was the suggestion of Balfour in a memorandum entitled 'Proposed Registration Bill', 2 June 1916, *Cabinet Memo*, CAB 37/149.
25 *5 Parl. Debs.*, Commons, lxxxiv (19 July 1916), 1046–7.
26 *The Times*, 8 Aug. 1916, p. 7.
27 *5 Parl. Debs.*, Commons, lxxxv (15 Aug. 1916), 1910.
28 Ibid., 1949.
29 Ibid., lxxxvi (21 Aug. 1916), 2266.
30 Long to Asquith, 18 Aug. 1916, Asquith MSS, 17/48.
31 *The Times*, 22 Aug. 1916, p. 7.
32 D. D. to Asquith, 18 Sept. 1916, Asquith MSS, 17/87.
33 Ullswater, *Commentaries*, i, 198.

[34] *Nation*, xx (14 Oct. 1916), 66–7. In his article on 'Politicians and the Woman's Vote 1914–1918' Martin Pugh estimates that the conference was comprised of '17 suffragists against 10 anti-suffragists, plus 5 who were doubtful or changing their minds'. *History*, lix (Oct. 1974), 363.

[35] Diary, 12 Oct. 1916, Hope C. White, *Willoughby Hyett Dickinson, 1859–1943* (Gloucester, 1956), p. 142.

[36] Fawcett, *Women's Victory & After*, p. 117.

[37] Ibid., p. 132.

[38] Hall Caine, 'Britain's Daughters at Dangerous Tasks', *Current History Magazine*, v (Dec. 1916), 423.

[39] 'Pride and Prejudice', *Spectator*, cxvii (5 Aug. 1916), 152.

[40] W. H. Long, 'Special Register Bill', 5 Oct. 1916, Lloyd George MSS, E/9/1/15. This apparent inconsistency was recognized by Selborne as a trait of Long's, whose 'opinion did vary from day to day quite incomprehensibly and one never knew where he would be. I think his opinion must have depended on what he had for breakfast.' June 1916, Selborne MSS, 285–90.

[41] 5 *Parl. Debs.*, Commons, lxxxvi (1 Nov. 1916), 1750–2.

[42] *Daily Telegraph*, 2 Nov. 1916, p. 9.

[43] Diary, 1 Nov. 1916, White, *Willoughby Hyett Dickinson*, p. 142.

[44] 5 *Parl. Debs.*, Lords, xxiii (7 Nov. 1916), 400–1.

[45] Ibid., 780.

[46] Ullswater, *Commentaries*, ii, 197–8.

[47] Salisbury, Banbury, and Craig to Lowther, 13 Dec. 1916, Lloyd George MSS, F/46/12/1.

[48] Lowther to Lloyd George, 14 Dec. 1916, ibid., F/46/12/1.

[49] Lloyd George, *War Memoirs*, iv, 207.

[50] Lowther to Lloyd George, 22 Dec. 1916, Lloyd George MSS, F/46/12/2. The best general account of the Speaker's conference was written by W. H. Dickinson for J. Renwick Seager's *Reform Act of 1918* (London, 1918), pp. 7–23. Also see Dickinson's account in the *Contemporary Review*, cxiii (Mar. 1918), 241–9, or that by Aneurin Williams, another conference member, in the same journal cxii (July 1917), 14–19.

[51] Lowther to Lloyd George, 14 Dec. 1916, Lloyd George MSS, F/46/12/1. The inclusion of this innovation was largely the doing of the Speaker, a recent convert on the subject. Though it was destined to fail, its adoption by the conference illustrates the powerful influence of the Speaker on the decisions which were reached. Ullswater, *Commentaries*, ii, 205.

[52] *Common Cause*, 5 Jan. 1917, p. 509.

[53] Craig, however, was a suffragist. His youngest son, Dennis, wrote to me, 'as regards the Speaker's Conference on Electoral Reform, my father was one of the few Tory MPs who was pro votes for women, hence his inclusion among the "Blest" and not the "Blast" by Wyndham Lewis in the 1st number of "Blast"'. Craig to Fair, 14 Feb. 1969.

[54] Diary, 10 Jan. 1917, White, *Willoughby Hyett Dickinson*, p. 143. For the probable vote of members of the Speaker's conference on women's suffrage see Appendix VI.

[55] Dickinson to Miss Barry, 20/1/43, based on notes written at the time. Dickinson MSS. Cited in Pugh, 'Politicians and the Woman's Vote 1914–1918', *History*, lix (Oct. 1974), 363–4.

[56] I found this amidst some press cuttings of Sir William Bull which were deposited by his son, George, in the Hammersmith Public Library. The disclosure of the compromise in the *Englishwoman*, Mar. 1918, 184–90, is remarkable because the proceedings of the conference, especially at this time, were regarded as absolutely confidential.

[57] Ullswater, *Commentaries*, ii, 203.

[58] Letter from Mr Speaker to the Prime Minister, Conference on Electoral Reform, *Parl. Paps.*, 1917–18, xxv.
[59] *The Times*, 1 Feb. 1917, p. 8.
[60] Steel-Maitland to Long, 3 Feb. 1917, Long MSS, 947/675.
[61] Long to Steel-Maitland, 4 Feb., 1917, ibid., 947/675.
[62] Ullswater, *Commentaries*, ii, 204.
[63] *War Cab. Mins.*, 6 Feb. 1917, CAB 23/1/56/7. See Appendix VII for a chronological 'Progress of the Reform Bill of 1918'.
[64] Carson to Lloyd George, 8 Mar. 1917, Lloyd George MSS, F/6/2/19.
[65] Diary, 26 Feb.–1 Mar. 1917, C. P. Scott MSS, Add. MS 50903.
[66] *War Cab. Mins.*, 26 Mar. 1917, CAB 23/2/105.
[67] 5 *Parl. Debs.*, Commons, xcii (28 Mar. 1917), 465. On the following day Long confided to Sir George Younger, Unionist whip, that 'after last night's division it really is important that the machinery of the Unionist Party should not be used to stimulate, much less to organize opposition to a policy which, as it seems to me, has now become definitely that of the Government'. Long to Younger, 29 Mar. 1917, Long MSS, 947/675.
[68] *The Times*, 30 Mar. 1917, p. 3.
[69] 5 *Parl. Debs.*, Commons, xciv (19 June 1917), 1673.
[70] Ibid., 1718.
[71] Diary, 3 Apr. 1917, Wilson, *Diaries of Scott*, p. 274. It is interesting to contrast Lloyd George's position on proportional representation here with that which he later assumed as head of a truncated Liberal Party trying to regain power. *The Times*, 14 June 1929, p. 9.
[72] Ullswater, *Commentaries*, ii, 206.
[73] Diary, 20–1 Oct. 1917, C. P. Scott MSS, Add. MS 50904.
[74] Guest to Lloyd George, 7 Dec. 1917, Lloyd George MSS, F/21/2/9.
[75] Ullswater, *Commentaries*, ii, 222.
[76] Letter from Mr Speaker to the Prime Minister, Conference on Redistribution of Seats in Ireland, *Parl. Paps.*, 1917–18, xxv.

CHAPTER IX

[1] 3 *Parl. Debs.*, cccxxiii (19 Mar. 1888), 1598.
[2] *Parl. Paps.*, 1911, Cmd. 206, iv, 547.
[3] Long to Lloyd George, 30 Mar. 1917, Sir Charles Petrie, *Walter Long*, p. 211. Long's idea appears to have been inspired by a communication from Sir George Younger following the division on the Speaker's conference proposals on the night of 28 March. It was Younger's opinion that their party should concentrate on 'a demand that, concurrently with a great extension of the franchise, we should insist upon the reform and strengthening of the Second Chamber'. Younger to Long, 30 Mar. 1917, Long MSS, 947/675.
[4] Lloyd George to Long, 30 Mar. 1917, Lloyd George MSS, F/32/4/59.
[5] Lansdowne to Chamberlain, 22 July 1917, Chamberlain MSS, AC 12/116.
[6] Lansdowne to Chamberlain, 30 July 1917, ibid., AC 12/118.
[7] Lloyd George to Bryce, 10 Aug. 1917, Lloyd George MSS, F/5/7/3.
[8] *The Times*, 27 Aug. 1917, p. 6.
[9] Bryce to Lowell, 13 Sept. 1917, Bryce MSS, U.S.A. 23/85.
[10] Crewe to Bryce, 19 Sept. 1917, Crewe MSS, 1917.
[11] Bryce to Crewe, 23 Sept. 1917, ibid.
[12] Second, third, and fourth meetings, 5, 9, and 10 Oct. 1917, Davidson MSS, H. of L., 1917–18. The Archbishop's record of the proceedings, though not without gaps, is the best surviving account of what transpired in the conference. It is corroborated

for the most part by Bryce's final report which describes the work of the conference on a more general level. See 'Conference on the Reform of the Second Chamber', *Parl. Paps.*, 1918, Cmd. 9038, x, 569.

13 Selborne to Lady Selborne, 9 Oct. 1917, Selborne MSS, 103/33.

14 Fifth and sixth meetings, Davidson MSS, H. of L., 1917–18.

15 Seventh meeting, ibid., H. of L., 1917–18.

16 'Adjustment of Differences between the two Houses and the Removal of Dead-locks', Oct. 1917, Selborne MSS, 85/10a.

17 Twelfth and thirteenth meetings, Davidson MSS. H. of L., 1917–18.

18 Fourteenth meeting, ibid., H. of L., 1917–18.

19 Memo by Selborne, Dec. 1917, Selborne MSS, 85/31.

20 Fifteenth to eighteenth meetings, Davidson MSS, H. of L., 1917–18.

21 Twenty-first meeting, ibid., H. of L., 1917–18.

22 'Second Chamber Conference', memo by Crewe, 12 Dec. 1917.

23 Selborne to Crewe, 31 Dec. 1917, ibid., 85/61. There are letters in the Selborne MSS from Lansdowne, Rutland, Balfour of Burleigh, Chamberlain, and Hugh Cecil, which he used to draw up his amendments.

24 Bryce to Selborne, 2 Jan. 1918, ibid., 85/70b.

25 Twenty-seventh meeting, 15 Jan. 1918, Davidson MSS, H. of L., 1917–18.

26 Twenty-eighth meeting, ibid., H. of L., 1917–18.

27 A. Chamberlain to H. Chamberlain, 18 Jan. 1918, Chamberlain MSS, AC 5/1/56.

28 Thirtieth meeting, 24 Jan. 1918, Davidson MSS, H. of L., 1917–18.

29 Thirty-first meeting, 29 Jan. 1918, ibid., H. of L., 1917–18.

30 The Archbishop's speech on bishops, 29 Jan. 1918, ibid., H. of L. 1917–18.

31 Thirty-second meeting, 31 Jan. 1918, ibid., H. of L., 1917–18.

32 Bryce to Crewe, 27 Feb. 1918, Crewe MSS, 1918.

33 'Conference on Reform of the Second Chamber', *Parl. Paps.*, 1918, Cmd. 9038, x, 569.

34 Chamberlain to Selborne, 15 Mar. 1918, Chamberlain MSS, AC 15/6/13.

35 'Conference on the Reform of the Second Chamber', *Parl. Paps.*, 1918, Cmd. 9038, x, 569.

36 *The Times*, 25 Apr. 1918, p. 7.

37 Chamberlain to Selborne, 13 June 1918, Selborne MSS, 85/80.

38 'Conference on the Reform of the Second Chamber', *Parl. Paps.*, 1918, Cmd. 9038, x, 569. David Close, who cites neither the chairman's report nor the Archbishop's record of the proceedings, mistakenly refers to the 'extent of disagreement' in the conference and the 'illusory' hope of an agreed settlement in 'The Collapse of Resistance to Democracy: Conservatives, Adult Suffrage, and Second Chamber Reform, 1911–1928', *The Historical Journal*, xx (Dec. 1977), 910.

CHAPTER X

1 Oliver to Balfour, 28 Sept. 1910, Balfour MSS, MS 49860.

2 See Oliver's memo in Appendix IV.

3 Memo by F. S. A., 18 Feb. 1917, Lloyd George MSS, F/66/3/1.

4 Kerr to Lloyd George, 3 Mar. 1917, ibid., F/89/1/3.

5 Carson to Lloyd George, 3 Mar. 1917, ibid., F/6/2/18.

6 5 *Parl. Debs.*, xcl, Commons (7 Mar. 1917), 480.

7 Ibid., 459.

8 Colvin, *Life of Carson*, iii, 224–6.

9 McDowell to Carson, 2 Apr. 1917, Carson MSS, D1507/1/8/3.

10 Diary, 2 Apr. 1917, C. P. Scott MSS, Add. MS 50903.

11 *War Cab. Mins.*, 16 Apr. 1917, CAB 23/2.

12 Diary, 1 May 1917, C. P. Scott MSS, Add. MS 50904.

[13] Crewe to Asquith, 16 May 1917, Asquith MSS, 37/140.
[14] Lonsdale to Lloyd George, 17 May 1917, Lloyd George MSS, F/2/4/1.
[15] Montgomery to Carson, 18 May 1917, Montgomery MSS, D.627/430/14.
[16] *5 Parl. Debs.*, xxv, Lords (21 May 1917), 198–9.
[17] Carson to Montgomery, 28 May 1917, Montgomery MSS, D.627/430.
[18] *The Times*, 9 June 1917, p. 6.
[19] Dorothy Macardle, *The Irish Republic* (London, 1968), pp. 204–5.
[20] Lowther to Bonar Law, 6 June 1917, Lloyd George MSS, F/30/2/17.
[21] Diary, 8 June 1917, C. P. Scott MSS, Add. MS 50904.
[22] Dillon to Scott, 8 June 1917, ibid., Add. MS 50909.
[23] O'Brien to Lloyd George, 18 June 1917, Lloyd George MSS, F/41/9/3.
[24] R. B. McDowell, *The Irish Convention, 1917–18* (London, 1970), pp. 99–100. See Appendix I for a complete list of convention members.
[25] Duke to Bernard, 13 July 1917, J. H. Bernard MSS, Add. MS 52782.
[26] Earl of Midleton, *Records & Reactions, 1856–1939* (London, 1939), pp. 237–8.
[27] Ibid., pp. 236–7.
[28] Montgomery to Coote, 24 July 1917, Montgomery MSS, D.627/430/74.
[29] *Confidential Report*, pp. 7–8.
[30] Ibid., pp. 11–12.
[31] Montgomery to Dicey, 23 Aug. 1917, Montgomery MSS, D.627/430/80.
[32] Ulster Unionist Delegates' Minutes, 22 Aug. 1917, D.1327/3/10.
[33] Diaries, 29 Aug. 1917, Plunkett MSS.
[34] Macdonnell to Lady Macdonnell, 30 Aug. 1917, Macdonnell of Swinford MSS, MS Eng. Hist. e218.
[35] Granard to Asquith, 31 Aug. 1917, Asquith MSS, 37/142.
[36] Diaries, 4 Sept. 1917, Plunkett MSS.
[37] Diaries, 12 Sept. 1917, ibid.
[38] *Confidential Report*, pp. 25–7.
[39] Diaries, 27 Sept. 1917, Plunkett MSS.
[40] *Confidential Report*, pp. 38–40.
[41] Diaries, 15 Oct. 1917, Plunkett MSS.
[42] *Confidential Report*, p. 42.
[43] Ibid., pp. 42–3.
[44] Ibid., pp. 44–8.
[45] Macdonnell to Lady Macdonnell, 23 Nov. 1917, Macdonnell of Swinford MSS, MS Eng. Hist. e218.
[46] *Confidential Report*, p. 55.
[47] Powell to Midleton, 1 Dec. 1917, Midleton MSS, PRO 30/67/33.
[48] Memo by the Archbishop, 5 Dec. 1917, Bernard MSS, Add. MS 5278.
[49] Diaries, 11 Dec. 1917, Plunkett MSS.
[50] Interview with Redmond, 12 Dec. 1917, Bernard MSS, Add. MS 52782.
[51] *Confidential Report*, pp. 57–8.
[52] Devlin to Plunkett, 26 Dec. 1917, Plunkett MSS.
[53] *Confidential Report*, p. 61.
[54] Midleton to Raphoe, 7 Jan. 1918, Midleton MSS, PRO 30/67/36.
[55] Lloyd George to Bonar Law, 12 Jan. 1918, Bonar Law MSS, 82/8/4.
[56] Southborough to Adams, 15 Jan. 1918, and Plunkett to Adams, 15 Jan. 1918, Lloyd George MSS, F/64/6/10, F/65/1/35.
[57] Lady Carson's Diary, 18 Jan. 1918, Carson MSS, D.1507/6/4.
[58] *Confidential Report*, p. 73.
[59] Diaries, 21 Jan. 1918, Plunkett MSS.
[60] Fisher to Montgomery, 25 Jan. 1918, Montgomery MSS, D.627/433/14.
[61] *Confidential Report*, p. 77.

[62] Memo of Interview with the War Cabinet, 6 Feb. 1918, Bernard MSS, Add. MS 52781.

[63] Diaries, 13 Feb. 1918, Plunkett MSS.

[64] Memo of interview at 10 Downing St, 13 Feb. 1918, Bernard MSS, Add. MS 52781.

[65] Diaries, 15 Feb. 1918, Plunkett MSS.

[66] Southborough to Midleton, 19 Feb. 1918, Midleton MSS, PRO 30/67/36.

[67] *Confidential Report*, pp. 85–7.

[68] Ibid., pp. 92–3.

[69] Barrie to Carson, 5 Mar. 1918, Plunkett MSS.

[70] *Confidential Report*, pp. 92–3.

[71] Macdonnell to Lady Macdonnell, 15 Mar. 1918, Macdonnell of Swinford MSS, MS Eng. Hist. e218.

[72] *Confidential Report*, pp. 102–6.

[73] Ibid., pp. 111–15.

[74] Lloyd George to Bonar Law, 10 Apr. 1918, Lloyd George MSS, F/30/2/31.

[75] Ronald McNeill, *Ulster's Stand for Union* (London, 1922), p. 258.

[76] Bernard Shaw to Digby, 16 June 1948, Plunkett MSS.

CHAPTER XI

[1] *The Times*, 6 May 1918, p. 6.

[2] The federal idea, at least so far as Ireland was concerned, was formulated by Isaac Butt as part of his original home rule proposal. See Lawrence J. McCaffrey, *Irish Federalism in the 1870's: A Study in Conservative Nationalism* (Philadelphia, 1962).

[3] A Scottish grand committee, consisting of all the Scottish M.P.'s and fifteen others to ensure a proper balance in the House, was first created in 1894 and has exercised a varying degree of control over the passage of Scottish legislation. In 1960 a similar arrangement was made for Wales, though a more informal decentralized treatment of Welsh legislation had been used for many years. Northern Ireland and the Isle of Man of course have constituted special cases. Sir Gilbert Campion, *An Introduction to the Procedure of the House of Commons* (London, 1947), p. 40, and James G. Kellas, *Modern Scotland, The Nation Since 1870* (London, 1968), pp. 174–7.

[4] 5 *Parl. Debs.*, Commons, civ (9 Apr. 1918), 1357–64.

[5] Chamberlain to Lloyd George, 10 Apr. 1918, Petrie, *Life & Letters of Chamberlain*, ii, 114–15.

[6] Memo by Long, 14 Apr. 1918, Balfour MSS, Add. MS 49777.

[7] *The Times*, 6 May 1918, p. 6.

[8] Long to Lloyd George, 18 Apr. 1918, Lloyd George MSS, F/32/5/23.

[9] Diaries, 23 Apr. 1918, Fisher MSS, Box 8.

[10] Diary, 9 May 1918, Tom Jones, *Whitehall Diary*, ed. Keith Middlemas (3 vols., London, 1969), iii, 9.

[11] 'The Irish Question and Federalism', June 1918, Selborne MSS, 85/82.

[12] *War Cab. Mins.*, 19 June 1918, CAB 23/6/433.

[13] Report of a Joint Deputation from the Houses of Parliament to the Prime Minister on Federal Devolution, 26 June 1918, Lloyd George MSS, F/74/26/3.

[14] *War Cab. Mins.*, 29 July 1918, CAB 23/7/453.

[15] Long to Dicey, 29 Nov. 1918, Long MSS, 947/207, in response to a letter from Dicey, 22 Nov. 1918, ibid.

[16] 5 *Parl. Debs.*, Lords, xxxiii (5 Mar. 1919), 526.

[17] Ibid., Commons, cxvi (4 June 1919), 2126–7.

[18] Diary, 4 June 1919, Sir Courtenay Ilbert MSS.

[19] Brassey to Crewe, 6 Aug. 1919, Crewe MSS, 1919.

20 Montgomery to Carson, 11 Aug. 1919, Montgomery MSS, D.627 434/52.
21 Curzon to Bonar Law, 7 Aug. 1919, Bonar Law MSS, 98/1/5.
22 Long to Lloyd George, 24 Sept. 1919, Lloyd George MSS, F/33/2/73.
23 *The Times*, 17 Oct. 1919, p. 13.
24 Brassey to Whittaker, 25 Oct. 1919, Frank Partridge, *T.A.B., A Memoir of Thomas Allnutt Second Earl Brassey* (London, 1921), pp. 223–4.
25 Brassey to Gladstone, 25 Oct. 1919, Viscount Gladstone MSS, Add. MS 46084.
26 Notes on conference, 23 Oct. 1919, ibid., Add. MS 46104.
27 Ibid., 28 Oct. 1919, Add. MS 46104.
28 Diaries, 6 Nov. 1919, Gorell MSS.
29 'Conference on Devolution, Letter from Mr. Speaker to the Prime Minister', 27 Apr. 1920, *Parl. Paps.*, 1920, Cmd. 692, Appendix III.
30 Lowther to Bonar Law, 18 Dec. 1919, Bonar Law MSS, 98/5/15.
31 Diaries, 13 Nov. 1919, Gorell MSS.
32 Gideon Murray, *Viscount Elibank, A Man's Life* (London, 1934), p. 242.
33 Ullswater, *Commentaries*, ii, 269–70.
34 Diaries, 9 and 15 Dec. 1919, Gorell MSS.
35 Lowther to Selborne, Dec. 1919, Selborne MSS, 87/60.
36 Lowther to Bonar Law, 18 Dec. 1919, Bonar Law MSS, 98/5/15.
37 Gladstone to Lowther, 20 Dec. 1919, Viscount Gladstone MSS, Add. MS 46084.
38 Lowther to Gladstone, 23 Dec. 1919, ibid.
39 One of the most lucid criticisms of the Speaker's plan and an expression of support for subordinate national legislatures, from an imperial perspective, was contained in a memorandum on the 'Devolution Conference' circulated by Sir Edward Goulding, Wargrave MSS, A 3/6/1.
40 Gladstone to Chalmers, early Feb. 1920, Viscount Gladstone MSS.
41 Gladstone to Lowther, 22 Feb. 1920, ibid.
42 Ullswater, *Commentaries*, ii, 270. Murray Macdonald to Gladstone, 5 May 1920, Viscount Gladstone MSS, Add. MS 46084.
43 Notes on conference, 25 Feb. 1920, ibid., Add. MS 46104.
44 Gladstone to Emmott, 3 Mar. 1920, Emmott MSS, MS Emmott 6/288.
45 'Conference on Devolution', *Parl. Paps.*, Cmd. 692, Appendix I.
46 Ibid., Appendix II.
47 *The Times*, 13 May 1920, p. 17.
48 Ibid.
49 Ibid., 6 July 1920, p. 15.
50 Ibid., 7 July 1920, p. 14.
51 Ibid., 20 Dec. 1920, p. 14.
52 Ullswater, *Commentaries*, ii, 271.

CHAPTER XII

1 Diary, 7 Dec. 1921, Fisher MSS, Box 8.
2 Churchill, *World Crisis*, v, 299.
3 Petrie, *Life and Letters of Chamberlain*, ii, 159. On 1 April Sir Robert Horne replaced Chamberlain as Chancellor of the Exchequer. Other major appointments included Sir Alfred Mond to the Ministry of Health, Lord Fitzalan as Lord Lieutenant of Ireland, and Stanley Baldwin to the Board of Trade.
4 Ibid., pp. 150–1.
5 Churchill, *World Crisis*, v, 305–6.
6 Randolph S. Churchill, *Lord Derby, 'King of Lancashire'* (London, 1959), pp. 409–410.

[7] 'JC's visit to De Valera' by Lady Craigavon, 5 May 1921, Craigavon MSS, D.1415/B/32.

[8] The Second Earl of Birkenhead, *The Life of F. E. Smith, First Earl of Birkenhead* (London, 1959), pp. 369–70.

[9] Grigg to Lloyd George, 15 June 1921, Lloyd George MSS, F/86/1/8.

[10] Macardle, *Irish Republic*, p. 427.

[11] Frank Pakenham, *Peace by Ordeal* (London, 1935), pp. 77–8.

[12] PRO, Conference of Ministers at 10 Downing Street, 24 June 1921, *Cab. Mins.*, CAB 23/39/104. Cabinet meeting, 24 June 1921, ibid., CAB 23/26/53.

[13] Churchill, *World Crisis*, v, 308.

[14] Midleton to Lloyd George, 7 July 1921, Lloyd George MSS, F/38/1/19.

[15] Cabinet meeting, 13 Aug. 1921, *Cab. Mins.*, CAB 23/26/66.

[16] Beaverbrook to Bonar Law, 13 May 1921, Lord Beaverbrook, *The Decline and Fall of Lloyd George* (New York, 1963), pp. 262–3.

[17] Diary, 28 July 1921, C. P. Scott MSS, Add. MS 50906.

[18] Birkenhead to Lloyd George, 10 Aug. 1921, Lloyd George MSS, F/4/7/30.

[19] *Correspondence relating to the Proposals of His Majesty's Government for an Irish Settlement*, 20 July 1921, in *Parl. Paps.*, 1921, Cmd. 1502.

[20] Chamberlain's record of the negotiations, 14 Oct. 1921, Chamberlain MSS, AC 31/4/5.

[21] A. Chamberlain to I. Chamberlain, 27 Oct. 1921, ibid., AC 6/1/436.

[22] Diary, 28 Oct. 1921, Wilson, *Diaries of Scott*, pp. 402–4.

[23] Second Irish Note, 29 Oct. 1921, *Irish Conference, 1921*, CAB 43/4 (S.F.C. 21A).

[24] Pakenham, *Peace By Ordeal*, p. 194.

[25] Griffith to Lloyd George, 2 Nov. 1921, *Irish Conference, 1921*, CAB 43/4.

[26] Pakenham, *Peace By Ordeal*, p. 194.

[27] 5 *Parl. Debs.*, cxlvii, Commons (31 Oct. 1921), 1419–20.

[28] *Correspondence Between His Majesty's Government and the Prime Minister of Northern Ireland Relating to the Proposals for an Irish Settlement*, 10 and 11 Nov. 1921, in *Parl. Paps.*, 1921 Cmd. 1561.

[29] Pakenham, *Peace By Ordeal*, pp. 204–9.

[30] Ibid. See also Meeting with the Irish Representatives on 5 Dec. 1921, *Irish Conference, 1921*, CAB 43/4.

[31] Pakenham, *Peace By Ordeal*, pp. 216–20.

[32] A. Chamberlain to I. Chamberlain, 8 Nov. 1921, Chamberlain MSS, AC 6/1/458.

[33] A. Chamberlain to I. Chamberlain, 9 Nov. 1921, ibid., AC 6/1/457.

[34] Bonar Law to Croal, 12 Nov. 1921, Bonar Law MSS, 107/1/83.

[35] Stanley Salvidge, *Salvidge of Liverpool* (London, 1935), p. 209.

[36] *The Times*, 18 Nov. 1921.

[37] Salvidge, *Salvidge of Liverpool*, p. 214.

[38] A. Chamberlain to I. Chamberlain, 19 Nov. 1921, Chamberlain MSS, AC 6/1/466.

[39] Chamberlain's record of the negotiations, Chamberlain MSS, AC 31/4/9.

[40] Draft of the Articles of Agreement, *Irish Conference, 1921*, CAB 43/4 (S.F.C. 29A). For the final text of the treaty see Appendix VIII.

[41] Pakenham, *Peace By Ordeal*, pp. 258–62.

[42] Tom Jones to Lloyd George, 4 Dec. 1921, Lloyd George MSS, F/25/2/51.

[43] Pakenham, *Peace By Ordeal*, pp. 274–5.

[44] Meeting with the Irish Representatives, 5 Dec. 1921, *Irish Conference, 1921*, CAB 43/4.

[45] Ibid.

EPILOGUE AND CONCLUSION

¹ Ross J. S. Hoffman and Paul Levack, *Burke's Politics, Selected Writings and Speeches of Edmund Burke on Reform, Revolution and War* (New York, 1967), pp. 41–89.

² Ostrogorskii, *Democracy and the Organization of Political Parties*, i, 314.

³ H. J. Hanham, *Elections and Party Management, Politics in the Time of Disraeli and Gladstone* (London, 1969), p. 347.

⁴ *4 Parl. Debs.*, clxvii, Lords (19 Dec. 1906), 1375–6.

⁵ *The Times*, 8 June 1910, p. 10.

⁶ *5 Parl. Debs.*, v, Lords (16 Mar. 1910), 343.

⁷ Oxford and Asquith, *Memories and Reflections*, ii, 109.

⁸ Harold Spender, 'The War and the Parties', *Contemporary Review*, cxiii (June 1918), 135–43.

⁹ J. F. S. Ross, *Elections and Electors, Studies in Democratic Representation* (London, 1955), p. 365. This is one of the few scholarly attempts to reckon with the nature of the Speaker's conference.

¹⁰ Good primary sources begin thinning out about this period and speculative newspaper accounts are often the only form of evidence. There are some relevant letters on this conference, however, in the Viscount Samuel MSS and the Viscount Templewood MSS. Also see *Parl. Paps.*, 1929–30, Cmd. 3636, xiii, 347.

¹¹ Ibid., 1943–4, Cmd. 6534, iii, 213, and Cmd. 6543, iii, 221.

¹² Ross devotes considerable attention to the nature of the Speaker's conference agreement and whether it was binding on a later Government in *Elections and Electors*, pp. 355–7, as does D. E. Butler in *The Electoral System in Britain since 1918* (Oxford, 1963), pp. 111–17. The former also concludes that 'a gentleman's agreement' based on 'mutual trust and good faith between the parties' had been reached, which was not a legally binding contract. Also see Lord Salter, *Memoirs of a Public Servant* (London, 1961), pp. 327–33, for a discussion of the Conservative position.

¹³ See Tom Driberg, 'Speaker's Conference on British Electoral Law', *The Parliamentarian: Journal of the Parliaments of the Commonwealth*, xlviii (Oct. 1967), 213–16.

¹⁴ See *The Times*, 24 Feb. 1977, p. 7, and 27 July 1977, p. 1, for Speaker's conference suggestions.

¹⁵ Speaker's conferences in the First World War acted as forerunners to the present system of advisory bodies which play an important role in expediting modern parliamentary business on technical matters. See R. V. Vernon and N. Mansergh, *Advisory Bodies, A Study of Their Uses in Relation to Central Government, 1919–1939* (London, 1940), or K. C. Wheare's important study of *Government by Committee: An Essay on the British Constitution* (Oxford, 1955).

¹⁶ *Parl. Paps.*, 1947–8, Cmd. 7380, xxii, 1001.

¹⁷ Herbert Morrison, *Government and Parliament, A Survey from The Inside* (London, 1959), pp. 190–1.

¹⁸ Although discussion on second chamber reform was intended to resume and there was to be a 'constitutional commission' created to investigate the possibilities for devolution for the United Kingdom, the election of Edward Heath's Conservative Government in 1970 effectively ended these efforts. See the Queen's speech in *The Times*, 31 Oct. 1968, p. 8.

¹⁹ *The Times*, 24 Feb. 1977, p. 1, 25 Feb., p. 1, 2 Mar., p. 1, and 3 Mar., p. 3.

²⁰ See Reginald Bassett, *Nineteen Thirty-One Political Crisis* (London, 1958), G. C. Moodie, 'The Monarch and the Selection of a Prime Minister: A Re-examination of the Crisis of 1931', *Political Studies*, v (Feb. 1957), 1–20, and Lord Samuel, 'The Constitutional Crisis of 1931: A Memorandum', *Western Political Quarterly*, xii (Mar. 1959), 5–8. By far the most sensible account to appear on this subject has been written by H. Hearder on 'King George V, the General Strike, and the 1931 Crisis' in H. Hearder

and H. R. Loyn, eds., *British Government and Administration, Studies Presented to S. B. Chrimes* (Cardiff, 1974), pp. 234–47.

[21] See John W. Wheeler-Bennett, *King George VI, His Life and Reign* (London, 1958), pp. 439–44.

[22] See *The Times*, 28 Sept. 1972, p. 1, for a summary of the outcome of the Darlington conference between representatives of several parties in Northern Ireland. For a commentary on the Sunningdale agreement between the British and Irish governments see 'After Sunningdale', *Hibernia* (14 Dec. 1973). One of the best recent surveys of the unsuccessful attempts to reach a negotiated settlement in Northern Ireland is Paul F. Power, 'The Sunningdale Strategy and the Northern Majority Consent Doctrine in Anglo-Irish Relations', in *Eire–Ireland*, xii (Spr. 1977), 35–67.

[23] The First Earl of Balfour, in 'Introduction' of Bagehot, *English Constitution*, xxiv.

[24] See John Edward Kendle, *The Colonial and Imperial Conferences, 1887–1911: A Study of Imperial Organization* (London, 1969), or Heather J. Harvey, *Consultation and Cooperation in the Commonwealth Conferences from 1887–1932* (3 vols., London, 1952).

Bibliography of Works Cited

Research on British interparty conferences has posed some peculiar problems. Owing to the secretive and informal nature of these proceedings no official minutes or records were usually kept. Therefore this study has necessarily depended mainly on manuscript materials. The most valuable sources on conferences were those in which one or more members kept a detailed personal record of their discussions. This was done in a surprising number of cases. The Gladstone Papers, for instance, contain much information essential to understanding the two nineteenth-century precedents, while Archbishop Davidson prepared a valuable account of the negotiations on the education bill and later on the House of Lords reform conference. The most meticulous conference records, however, were the diaries made by Austen Chamberlain (in a way typical of his family) in 1910 and 1921. Likewise the report prepared by Sir Horace Plunkett and the correspondence of Viscount Gladstone were very useful in understanding the Irish convention and the Speaker's devolution conference respectively. These and other records were probably kept by members so that their movements would not be lost to posterity or possibly as a written defence for their particular positions. For this reason these important documents have had to be used with caution or balanced whenever possible with rival accounts in order to avoid bias. When available, diaries were a very valuable source since members often confided to them knowledge, insights, or opinions which they could not divulge elsewhere. The bulk of information for this study, however, was derived from correspondence. Much of this concerns ideas which never materialized into action, but those portions which describe the movements, positions, or beliefs of the members of the conferences were very useful. Letters exchanged between members of opposite sides or reports of conversations carried on between conference meetings were particularly useful. Memoirs, where available, were also good sources, but it was necessary to make some allowance for the author's tendency to forget or confuse details. Whatever success this study has achieved in revealing the pertinent facts about these secretive and obscure gatherings must be attributed to the deep respect held for the written word by members of Britain's ruling classes.

MANUSCRIPT SOURCES

Asquith Papers—Bodleian Library
Balfour Papers—British Library
Beaverbrook Papers—House of Lords Record Office
Bernard Papers—British Library
Birrell Papers—Liverpool University Library
Bonar Law Papers—House of Lords Record Office
Bryce Papers—Bodleian Library
Bull Papers—Hammersmith Public Library
Burns Papers—British Library
Cairns Papers—Public Record Office
Campbell-Bannerman Papers—British Library
Carson Papers—Public Record Office of Northern Ireland
Cecil Papers—British Library
Chamberlain (Austen) Papers—Birmingham University Library
Chamberlain (Joseph) Papers—Birmingham University Library
Courtney of Penwith Papers—London School of Economics
Craigavon Papers—Public·Record Office of Northern Ireland
Crewe Papers—Cambridge University Library
Davidson Papers—Lambeth Palace Library
Devonshire Papers—Chatsworth House
Dilke Papers—British Library
Disraeli Papers—Hughenden Manor
Edward VII Papers—Royal Archives
Elibank Papers—National Library of Scotland
Emmott Papers—Nuffield College Library
Fisher Papers—Bodleian Library
Garvin Papers—University of Texas at Austin
George V Papers—Royal Archives
Gladstone (Herbert) Papers—British Library
Gladstone (William) Papers—British Library
Goodwood Papers—West Sussex County Record Office
Gorell Papers—Bodleian Library
Granville Papers—Public Record Office
Haldane Papers—National Library of Scotland
Hamilton Papers—British Library
Iddesleigh Papers—British Library
Ilbert Papers—House of Lords Record Office
Lloyd George Papers—House of Lords Record Office
Long Papers—Wiltshire County Record Office

Lothian Papers—Scottish Record Office
MacDonnell of Swinford Papers—Bodleian Library
McNeill Papers—Public Record Office of Northern Ireland
Midleton Papers—Public Record Office
Montgomery Papers—Public Record Office of Northern Ireland
Plunkett Papers—Plunkett Foundation for Cooperative Studies
Redmond Papers—National Library of Ireland
Ripon Papers—British Library
Rosebery Papers—National Library of Scotland
St Aldwyn Papers—Shire Hall, Gloucester
Salisbury Papers—Hatfield House
Samuel Papers—House of Lords Record Office
Scott Papers—British Library
Selborne Papers—Bodleian Library
Tait Papers—Lambeth Palace Library
Templewood Papers—Cambridge University Library
Ulster Unionist Delegates' Minutes—Public Record Office of Northern Ireland
Queen Victoria Papers—Royal Archives
Wargrave Papers—House of Lords Record Office

PRINTED SOURCES

ADAMSON, JOHN WILLIAM, *English Education, 1789–1902*, Cambridge University Press, Cambridge, 1930.

ANDREWS, IRENE OSGOOD, and HOBBS, MARGARET A., *Economic Effects of the World War Upon Women and Children in Great Britain*, Oxford University Press, New York, 1921.

ARNOLD, MATTHEW, *Poetry and Criticism of Matthew Arnold*, ed. by A. Dwight Culler, Houghton Mifflin Co., Boston, 1961.

BAGEHOT, WALTER, *The English Constitution*, Oxford University Press, London, 1958.

BAHLMAN, DUDLEY W. R., *see under* HAMILTON.

BALFOUR, ARTHUR JAMES, *Retrospect: An Unfinished Autobiography, 1848–1886*, Cassell & Co., London, 1930.

BASSETT, REGINALD, *Nineteen Thirty-One Political Crisis*, Macmillan, London, 1958.

BEAVERBROOK, LORD, *Politicians and the War, 1914–1916*, Collins, London, 1960.

—— *The Decline and Fall of Lloyd George*, Duell, Sloan & Pearce, New York, 1963.

BECKETT, J. C. 'Gladstone, Queen Victoria, and the Disestablishment of the Irish Church, 1868–9', *Irish Historical Studies*, xiii (Mar. 1962), 38–47.

BEER, SAMUEL H., *Modern Political Development*, Random House, New York, 1958.

BELL, GEORGE KENNEDY ALLEN, *Randall Davidson, Archbishop of Canterbury*, Oxford University Press, London, 1952.

BIRKENHEAD, SECOND EARL OF, *The Life of F. E. Smith, First Earl of Birkenhead*, Eyre & Spottiswoode, London, 1959.

BIRRELL, AUGUSTINE, *Things Past Redress*, Faber and Faber, London, 1937.

BLAKE, ROBERT, *The Unknown Prime Minister: The Life and Times of Andrew Bonar Law, 1858–1923*, Eyre & Spottiswoode, London, 1955.

BLUNT, WILFRED SCAWEN, *My Diaries, Being a Personal Narrative of Events, 1888–1914*, 2 vols., Martin Secker, New York, 1922.

BOYCE, D. G., and STUBBS, J. O. 'F. S. Oliver, Lord Selborne and Federalism', *The Journal of Imperial and Commonwealth History*, v (Oct. 1976), 53–81.

BRETT, MAURICE V., *see under* ESHER.

BUCKLAND, PATRICK, *Irish Unionism: The Anglo-Irish and the New Ireland, 1885–1922*, 2 vols., Gill and Macmillan, Dublin, 1972.

BUCKLE, GEORGE EARLE, *see under* VICTORIA.

BURKE, EDMUND, *Burke's Politics, Selected Writings and Speeches of Edmund Burke on Reform, Revolution, and War*, ed. by Ross J. S. Hoffman and Paul Levack, Alfred A. Knopf, New York, 1967.

BURRIS, CRAVEN ALLEN, 'Political Aspects of the Passage of the English Education Act, 1902', unpublished M.A. thesis, Duke University, 1959.

BUTLER, D. E., *The Electoral System in Britain since 1918*, Clarendon Press, Oxford, 1963.

CAINE, HALL, 'Britain's Daughters at Dangerous Tasks', *Current History Magazine*, v, (Dec. 1916), 423–25.

CAMPION, SIR GILBERT, *An Introduction to the Procedure of the House of Commons*, Macmillan, London, 1947.

CECIL, GWENDOLYN, *Life of Robert, Marquis of Salisbury*, 4 vols., Hodder & Stoughton, London, 1931.

CHADWICK, MARY E. J., 'The Role of Redistribution in the Making of the Third Reform Act', *The Historical Journal*, xix (Sept. 1976), 665–83.

CHAMBERLAIN, SIR AUSTEN, *Down the Years*, Cassell & Co., London, 1935.

— — *The Life and Letters of the Right Hon. Sir Austen Chamberlain*, ed. by Sir Charles Petrie, 2 vols., Cassell & Co., London, 1940.

— — *Politics From Inside: An Epistolary Chronicle, 1906–1914*, Cassell & Co., London, 1936.

CHILSTON, THIRD VISCOUNT, *Chief Whip: The Political Life and Times of Aretas Aakers-Douglas, 1st Viscount Chilston*, Routledge & Kegan Paul, London, 1961.

CHURCHILL, RANDOLPH S., *Lord Derby, 'King of Lancashire'*, Heinemann, London, 1959.

CHURCHILL, WINSTON SPENCER, *The World Crisis*, 5 vols., Charles Scribner's Sons, New York, 1928.

CLOSE, DAVID H., 'The Collapse of Resistance to Democracy: Conservatives, Adult Suffrage, and Second Chamber Reform, 1911–1928', *The Historical Journal*, xx (Dec. 1977), 893–918.

COLVIN, IAN and MARJORIBANKS, EDWARD, *The Life of Lord Carson*, 3 vols., Macmillan & Co., London, 1932–6.

Common Cause, 1917.

CREWE, MARQUESS OF, *Lord Rosebery*, 2 vols., John Murray, London, 1931.

CULLER, A. DWIGHT, *see under* ARNOLD.

CURTIS, EDMUND, and McDOWELL, R. B., eds., *Irish Historical Documents, 1172–1922*, Barnes & Noble, London, 1943.

CURTIS, L. P., *Anglo-Saxons and Celts, A Study of Anti-Irish Prejudice in Victorian England*, Conference on British Studies, Bridgeport, Conn., 1968.

Daily News & Leader, 1914.

Daily Telegraph, 1913–18.

DANGERFIELD, GEORGE, *The Strange Death of Liberal England, 1910–1914*, H. Smith & R. Haas, New York, 1935.

—— *The Damnable Question, A Study in Anglo-Irish Relations*, Little, Brown & Co., Boston, 1976.

DAVIDSON, RANDALL, *Life of Archibald Campbell Tait, Archbishop of Canterbury*, 2 vols., Macmillan & Co., London, 1891.

DICEY, A. V., *England's Case Against Home Rule*, J. Murray, London, 1886.

DICKINSON, W. H., 'The Greatest Reform Act', *Contemporary Review*, cxiii (Mar. 1918), 241–9.

DRIBERG, TOM, 'Speaker's Conference on British Electoral Law', *The Parliamentarian: Journal of the Parliaments of the Commonwealth*, xlviii (Oct. 1967), 213–16.

DUGDALE, BLANCHE E. C., *Arthur James Balfour*, 2 vols., Hutchinson & Co., London, 1936.

Englishwoman, 1918.

ESHER, REGINALD VISCOUNT, *Journals and Letters of Reginald Viscount Esher*, ed. by Maurice V. Brett, 4 vols., Ivor Nicholson & Watson, London, 1934.

FAIR, JOHN D., 'Royal Mediation in 1884: A Reassessment', *English Historical Review*, lxxxviii (Jan. 1973), 100–13.

FANNING, J. R., 'The Unionist Party and Ireland, 1906–10', *Irish Historical Studies*, xv (1966), 147–71.

FAWCETT, MILLICENT GARRETT, *The Women's Victory and After*, Sidgwick & Jackson, London, 1920.

GARVIN, J. L., *The Life of Joseph Chamberlain*, 3 vols., Macmillan & Co., London, 1933.

GILBERT, BENTLEY B., *The Evolution of National Insurance in Great Britain, The Origins of the Welfare State*, Michael Joseph, London, 1966.

GLADSTONE, W. E., and GRANVILLE, LORD, *The Political Correspondence of Mr. Gladstone and Lord Granville. 1876–1886*, ed. by Agatha Ramm, 2 vols., Oxford University Press, Oxford, 1962.

GOLLIN, ALFRED M., *The* Observer *and J. L. Garvin, 1908–1914: A Study of Great Editorship*, Oxford University Press, London, 1960.

—— *Balfour's Burden*, Anthony Blond, London, 1965.

GORELL, LORD, *One Man ... Many Parts*, Odhams Press, London, 1956.

Great Britain, *Cabinet Minutes*, Public Record Office.

—— *Cabinet Memoranda*, Public Record Office.

—— *Irish Conference, 1921*, Public Record Office.

—— *Parliamentary Debates*, 1869–1921.

—— *Parliamentary Papers*, 1906–1967.

GUEDALLA, PHILIP, *The Queen and Mr. Gladstone*, 2 vols., Hodder & Stoughton, London, 1933.

GWYNN, DENIS, *The History of Partition (1912–1925)*, Browne & Nolan, Dublin, 1950.

—— *The Life of John Redmond*, George G. Harrap & Co., London, 1932.

GWYNN, STEPHEN, and TUCKWELL, GERTRUDE M., *The Life of the Rt. Hon. Sir Charles W. Dilke*, 2 vols., J. Murray, London, 1917.

HAMILTON, SIR EDWARD WALTER, *The Diary of Sir Edward Walter Hamilton*, ed. by Dudley W. R. Bahlman, 2 vols., Clarendon Press, Oxford, 1972.

HAMMOND, J. L., *C. P. Scott of the* Manchester Guardian, G. Bell & Sons Ltd, London, 1934.

HANHAM, H. J., *Elections and Party Management, Politics in the Time of Disraeli and Gladstone*, Longmans, London, 1969.

HARDIE, FRANK, *The Political Influence of Queen Victoria, 1861–1901*, Frank Cass & Co., London, 1935.

—— *The Political Influence of the British Monarchy, 1868–1952*, Batsford, London, 1970.

HARVEY, HEATHER J., *Consultation and Cooperation in the Commonwealth Conferences from 1887–1932*, Oxford University Press, London, 1952.

HEALY, T. M., *Letters and Leaders of My Day*, 2 vols., Frederick A. Stokes, New York, 1929.

HEARDER, H., and LOYN, H. R., eds., *British Government and Administration, Studies Presented to S. B. Chrimes*, University of Wales Press, Cardiff, 1974.

Hibernia, 1973.

HICKS BEACH, LADY VICTORIA, *Life of Sir Michael Hicks Beach*, 2 vols., Macmillan & Co., London, 1932.

HOFFMAN, ROSS J. S., and LEVACK, PAUL, *see under* BURKE.

HOLLAND, BERNARD, *The Life of Spencer Compton, Eighth Duke of Devonshire*, 2 vols., Longmans Green & Co., London, 1911.

HORGAN, JOHN JOSEPH, *The Complete Grammar of Anarchy*, Nisbet & Co., London, 1919.

ILBERT, C. P., 'Conferences Between the Two Houses of Parliament', *Contemporary Review*, xcviii (10 Aug. 1910), 129–39.

JENKINS, ROY, *Asquith, Portrait of a Man and an Era*, Chilmark Press, New York, 1964.

—— *Mr. Balfour's Poodle: An Account of the Struggle between the House of Lords and the Government of Mr. Asquith*, Heinemann & Co., London, 1954.

JENNINGS, SIR IVOR, *The British Constitution*, Cambridge University Press, Cambridge, 1966.

JONES, ANDREW, *The Politics of Reform, 1884*, Cambridge University Press, Cambridge, 1972.

JONES, TOM, *Lloyd George*, Oxford University Press, London, 1951.

—— *Whitehall Diary*, ed. by Keith Middlemas, 3 vols., Oxford University Press, London, 1969.

KELLAS, JAMES G., *Modern Scotland, The Nation Since 1870*, Frederick A. Praeger, London, 1968.

KENDLE, JOHN EDWARD, *The Colonial and Imperial Conferences, 1887–1911: A Study of Imperial Organization*, Royal Commonwealth Society, London, 1969.

KENDLE, JOHN EDWARD, 'The Round Table Movement and "Home Rule All Round"', *The Historical Journal*, xi (1968).

KENNEY, ANNIE, *Memories of a Militant*, Edward Arnold & Co., London, 1924.

'The King and the Constitution', *Spectator*, cxi (9 Aug. 1913), 200–1.

LANG, ANDREW, *Life, Letters and Diaries of Sir Stafford Northcote, First Earl of Iddesleigh*, 2 vols., William Blackwood & Sons, London, 1890.

LLOYD GEORGE, DAVID, *War Memoirs of David Lloyd George*, 6 vols., Ivor Nicholson & Watson, London, 1933.

LOWELL, A. LAWRENCE, *The Government of England*, 2 vols., The Macmillan Co., New York, 1912.

—— 'The Influence of Party Upon Legislation', *Annual Report of the American Historical Association*, i (1901), 321–542.

LYONS, F. S. L., *John Dillon, A Biography*, Routledge & Kegan Paul, London, 1968.

MACARDLE, DOROTHY, *The Irish Republic*, Corgi Books, London, 1968.

McCAFFREY, LAWRENCE J., *Irish Federalism in the 1870's: A Study in Conservative Nationalism*, American Philosophical Society, Philadelphia, 1962.

McDOWELL, R. B., *The Irish Convention, 1917–18*, Routledge & Kegan Paul, London, 1970.

McKENNA, STEPHEN, *While I Remember*, Thornton Butterworth Ltd, London, 1921.

McNEILL, RONALD, *Ulster's Stand for Union*, John Murray, London, 1922.

Manchester Guardian, 1884–1918.

MARSH, P. T., *The Victorian Church in Decline, Archbishop Tait and the Church of England, 1868–1882*, University of Pittsburgh Press, Pittsburgh, 1969.

MASTERMAN, LUCY, *C. F. G. Masterman, a Biography*, Frank Cass & Co., London, 1939.

MAY, SIR THOMAS ERSKINE, *A Treatise on the Law, Privileges, Proceedings and Usage of Parliament*, Butterworth & Co., London, 1917.

METCALFE, A. E., *Woman's Effort*, B. H. Blackwell, Oxford, 1917.

MICHELS, ROBERT, *Political Parties*, Hearst's International Library, New York, 1915.

MIDDLEMAS, KEITH, *see under* JONES, TOM.

MIDLETON, THE EARL OF, *Records and Reactions, 1856–1939*, J. Murray, London, 1939.

MOODIE, G. C. 'The Monarch and The Selection of a Prime Minister: A Re-examination of the Crisis of 1931', *Political Studies*, v (Feb. 1957), 1–20.

MORLEY, JOHN, *The Life of William Ewart Gladstone*, 3 vols., The Macmillan Co., New York, 1903.

Morning Post, 1914.

MORRISON, HERBERT, *Government and Parliament: A Survey from the Inside*, Oxford University Press, London, 1959.

MULLER, WILLIAM D., 'British Politics Group Research Register', British Politics Group, Ames, Iowa, 1977.

MURRAY, ARTHUR C., *Master and Brother: Murrays of Elibank*, John Murray, London, 1945.

MURRAY, GIDEON, *Viscount Elibank, A Man's Life*, Hutchinson & Co., London, 1934.

Nation, xx (14 Oct. 1916), 66–7.

NEWTON, LORD, *Lord Lansdowne, A Biography*, Macmillan & Co., London, 1929.

NICOLSON, HAROLD, *King George The Fifth, His Life and Reign*, Constable & Co., London, 1953.

OLIVER, FREDERICK SCOTT, *Alexander Hamilton, An Essay on American Union*, Archibald Constable & Co., London, 1906.

OSTROGORSKII, MOISEI, *Democracy and the Organization of Political Parties*, 2 vols., The Macmillan Co., New York, 1902.

OWEN, FRANK, *Tempestuous Journey: Lloyd George, His Life and Times*, Hutchinson & Co., London, 1954.

OXFORD AND ASQUITH, EARL OF, *Fifty Years of British Parliament*, 2 vols., Little, Brown & Co., Boston, 1926.

—— *Memories and Reflections, 1852–1927*, 2 vols., Little, Brown & Co., Boston, 1928.

Oxford Chronicle, 1906.

PAKENHAM, FRANK, *Peace By Ordeal*, J. Cape, London, 1935.

PANKHURST, CHRISTABEL, *Unshackled: The Story of How We Won the Vote*, Hutchinson & Co., London, 1959.

PANKHURST, E. SYLVIA, *The Suffragette Movement*, Longmans, Green & Co., London, 1931.

PARTRIDGE, FRANK, *T. A. B., A Memoir of Thomas Allnutt Second Earl Brassey*, John Murray, London, 1921.

PETRIE, SIR CHARLES, *The Modern British Monarchy*, Eyre & Spottiswoode, London, 1961.

—— *Walter Long and His Times*, Hutchinson & Co., London, 1936.

—— , ed., *see under* CHAMBERLAIN.

PLUNKETT, SIR HORACE, *The Irish Convention, Confidential Report to His Majesty the King by the Chairman*, 1918.

POPE-HENNESSY, JAMES, *Lord Crewe, 1858–1945: The Likeness of a Liberal*, Constable & Co., Ltd, London, 1955.

POWER, PAUL F., 'The Sunningdale Strategy and the Northern Majority Consent Doctrine in Anglo-Irish Relations', *Eire–Ireland*, xii (Spr. 1977), 35–67.

'Pride and Prejudice', *Spectator*, cxvii (5 Aug. 1916), 152–3.

PUGH, MARTIN, 'Politicians and the Woman's Vote, 1914–1918', *History*, lix (Oct. 1974), 358–74.

Punch, 1910.

RAIKES, HENRY ST JOHN, *The Life and Letters of Henry Cecil Raikes*, Macmillan & Co., London, 1898.

RAMM, AGATHA, *see under* GLADSTONE and GRANVILLE.

REID, SIR WEMYSS, *The Life of William Ewart Gladstone*, 2 vols., Cassell & Co., London, 1899.

ROSS, J. F. S., *Elections and Electors: Studies in Democratic Representation*, Eyre & Spottiswoode, London, 1955.

ROWSE, A. L., *The Question of the House of Lords*, Hogarth Press, London, 1934.

SALTER, LORD, *Memoirs of a Public Servant*, Faber & Faber, London, 1961.

SALVIDGE, STANLEY, *Salvidge of Liverpool*, Hodder & Stoughton, Ltd, London, 1935.

SAMUEL, VISCOUNT, *Memoirs*, The Cresset Press, London, 1945.

—— 'The Constitutional Crisis of 1931 : A Memorandum', *Western Political Quarterly*, xii (Mar. 1959), 5–8.

SCOTT, C. P., *The Political Diaries of C. P. Scott, 1911–1928*, ed. by Trevor Wilson, Collins, London, 1970.

SEAGER, J. RENWICK, *Reform Act of 1918*, The Liberal Publication Dept., London, 1918.

SHARP, EVELYN, *Unfinished Adventure*, Bodley Head Ltd, London, 1933.

SHEARMAN, HUGH, *How the Church of Ireland was Disestablished*, Church of Ireland Disestablishment Centenary Committee, Belfast, 1970.

South Wales Press, 1906.

SPENDER, HAROLD, 'The War and the Parties', *Contemporary Review*, cxiii (June 1918), 135–43.

SPENDER, J. A., *The Life of the Right Hon. Sir Henry Campbell-Bannerman*, 2 vols., Hodder and Stoughton, London, 1923.

—— and ASQUITH, CYRIL, *Life of Herbert Henry Asquith, Lord Oxford and Asquith*, 2 vols., Hutchinson & Co., London, 1932.

TAYLOR, A. J. P., *Beaverbrook*, Hamilton, London, 1972.

The Times (London), 1869–1921.

ULLSWATER, VISCOUNT, *A Speaker's Commentaries*, 2 vols., Edward Arnold & Co., London, 1925.

VERNON, R. V., and MANSERGH, N., *Advisory Bodies: A Study of their Uses in Relation to Central Government, 1919–1939*, George Allen & Unwin Ltd, London, 1940.

VICTORIA, QUEEN, *The Letters of Queen Victoria*, ed. by George Earle Buckle, 5 vols., 2nd and 3rd series, John Murray, London, 1932.

WEST, SIR ALGERNON, *Recollections, 1832 to 1886*, Harper & Brothers, London, 1900.

WESTON, CORINNE COMSTOCK, 'The Liberal Leadership and the Lords' Veto, 1907–1910', *The Historical Journal*, xi (1968), 508–37.

—— 'The Royal Mediation in 1884', *English Historical Review*, lxxxii (Apr. 1967), 296–322.

WHEARE, K. C., *Government by Committee: An Essay on the British Constitution*, Clarendon Press, Oxford, 1955.

WHEELER-BENNETT, JOHN W., *King George VI, His Life and Reign*, Macmillan & Co., London, 1958.

WHITE, HOPE C., *Willoughby Hyett Dickinson, 1859–1943*, privately printed, Gloucester, 1956.

WILLIAMS, ANEURIN, 'The Reform Bill and the New Era', *Contemporary Review*, cxii (July 1917), 14–19.

WILSON, TREVOR, *see under* SCOTT.

YOUNG, KENNETH, *Arthur James Balfour: The Happy Life of the Politician, Prime Minister, Statesman and Philosopher*, G. Bell & Sons, London, 1963.

Index

Index